Softdesk Solutions

SOFTDESK SOLUTIONS

The Essential Guide to Auto-Architect®

Dennis Neeley, AIA

B. Robert Callori, AIA

John Wiley & Sons, Inc.
New York • Chichester • Brisbane • Toronto • Singapore

Publisher: Peggy Burns

Editor: Janet Feeney

Managing Editor: Diana Cisek

Text Design and Composition: SunCliff Graphic Productions

This text is printed on acid-free paper.

Library of Congress cataloging in Publication Data:
Neeley, Dennis.
    Softdesk solutions: the essential guide to Auto-Architect /
Dennis Neeley, Bob Callori.
        p. cm.
        Based on an earlier version published in 1993 as: CAD and the practice of architecture.
        Includes index.
        ISBN 0-471-15418-0 (alk. paper)
        1. Auto-Architect (Computer file)   2. Softdesk Core (computer file)   3. Architectural drawing—Data processing.   4. Architectural design—Data processing.n.   5. Computer-aided design.   I. Callori, B. Robert.   II. Neeley, Dennis. CAD and the practice of architecture.   III. Softdesk, Inc. IV. Title.
NA2728.N433 1996
720′.284′028553—dc20   96-7187

Printed in the United States of America

10 9 8 7 6 5 4 3 2 1

I want to recognize my two business partners, Terry Lofrano, AIA, who helped me learn about architecture, and Mehdi Khalvati, Ph. D., who is teaching me about software. One's knowledge is a collection of others knowledge, and I could not have wished for better tutors.

I commend everyone who has dedicated themselves to the creation of software; this is a most exciting era and you are the architects of this era's tools. This book is dedicated to you, the readers, who are facing challenges and opportunities that have never existed before. Hopefully this book will be of some help. I wish you the best.

Dennis Neeley

Encouragement, support, and motivation to write a book frequently comes from individuals who are always close to you in mind, body, and/or spirit, that profoundly affect the course and direction of your daily lifestyle—Earl W. Halstead, Jerry Thorne, Josephine Callori, Michael A. Callori, Sr., and Michael T. Callori, Jr.

B. Robert Callori

CONTENTS

CHAPTER THIRTEEN   Wall Settings   217

CHAPTER FOURTEEN   Walls   233

CHAPTER SEVENTEEN   Window Settings   309

PREFACE

"Why does this book contain both a discussion about CAD and a Softdesk Auto-Architect® Tutorial?" That's simple; you need to know about how to use CAD, even if you are not going to draw with CAD, and you need to know all the ways that CAD and digital information can and will be used.

It is important that teachers, students, draftspersons, and architects understand the full significance of CAD and the Softdesk Auto-Architect application. Everyone involved in architecture has been or will be significantly touched by the digital era. For teachers and students, who are teaching and learning architectural theory and design, CAD and digital information will bring tremendous changes. The sooner these changes are understood, the better. For teachers of drawing and drafting, the tutorial section of this book is an excellent step-by-step course that will teach the student how to draw with Auto-Architect. Assigning the text at the front of the book will widen the student's perspective of CAD and digital information.

Every member of the architectural firm—principals, team leaders, spec writers, designers, and draftspersons—is part of the electronic revolution. CAD must be understood, both its purpose, and its operation. Even if you are never going to draw with CAD, look at the tutorial to understand what is involved in CAD use. If all you do is draw with CAD, go through the tutorial to improve your efficiency. Look through the first section of the book and you may come up with additional ideas to expand CAD usage within your office or even new services your office can provide.

The practice of architecture is radically changing; it will be those who command the digital tools that will lead the path into the future.

Dennis Neeley

ABOUT THE TUTORIAL

The tutorial (Part II) is intended to help guide you through the new features offered by the Softdesk 7 Core and Auto-Architect® software modules. You will discover how the new editing tools offered in AutoCAD® Release 13 will significantly affect CAD productivity and procedures. The merging of Softdesk and ASG software products along with AutoCAD® Release 13 for Windows® technology dictate a new learning curve for everyone.

Although I considered myself as a veteran ADG user for many years, this particular software upgrade and merger has in many ways repositioned me back to novice user status. We are facing this new challenge together as we experience anticipation and frustration accompanied by any new software release. To accelerate the journey and ease the pain for both Softdesk and ADG users, I sincerely hope that this prompt-by-prompt tutorial succeeds in helping you understand how to use the product effectively.

Experienced Ascadd users may encounter a slight advantage of procedure over ASG users, although both sides will tend to leap-frog along the edge of the learning curve. Softdesk's strategy to retain Core as the foundation for all modules offers ASG users some familiarity with previous versions of the software. I have taken advantage of *CAD and the Practice of Architecture, ASG Solutions*, a prompt-by-prompt ASG Architectural tutorial, co-authored by Dennis Neeley and myself, by repeating the same exercises for this new tutorial. *Softdesk Solutions: The Essential Guide to Auto-Architect* will serve as both the update version to ASG Architectural Release 6.0a and the first release version of Softdesk 7.5

The 15 chapters of Part II will help to explain the Softdesk environment, introduce Core commands, then present Auto-Architect/ASG Architectural features and applications. This tutorial will demonstrate how Softdesk manages the design process from inception to final presentation for the design of a three-story building. The tutorial commences with an overview of Softdesk's Core startup procedures, then offers a detailed account of the Softdesk settings. Explanations include layer and text-style management as well as controlling settings for walls, doors, windows, and roofs.

The architectural module show the preliminary design process being created with Softdesk commands to arrange rectangular areas as a series of single-line diagrams into a space diagram. Each space is then converted to double-line walls of varying thickness. Proceeding to the design development phase, doors and windows with specification tags are added to the plan. As the building's volume develops, a roof is created to enclose the structure and a draft elevation is extracted to help visualize the design. Later, annotation keynotes and reference tags are inserted to describe or label specific details. The initial placement of 3D plumbing fixtures follows the subsequent visualization of viewing completed work in 3D. ADS-compliant symbols are parametrically drawn using Softdesk commands to draw toilet stalls, urinals, and countertops. Procedures describe creating 3D objects in modelspace for the design of a single-story building that are used to generate a three-story structure. Finally, presentation techniques for creating a paperspace drawing with a titleblock containing plan, isometric, and elevation views completes the tutorial.

B. Robert Callori

ACKNOWLEDGMENTS

This book is the second version of *CAD and the Practice of Architecture, ASG Solutions*. The first version, published in 1993, was based upon ASG Architectural. After the merger of ASG and Softdesk, portions of ASG software and portions of Softdesk software were combined to create Softdesk Core and Softdesk Auto-Architect, thereby creating a new product line and the reason for this new book. I want to thank all the dedicated employees of ASG for the help they provided me with the first book, as well as everyone at Softdesk who has made this book possible.

I thank Bob Callori for taking on the monumental task of creating a new tutorial. This book is scheduled to be released at the same time as the software, which means that the tutorial was being written as the software was being created. This placed an almost impossible burden upon Bob. However, he has mastered the challenge and created an excellent tutorial.

Although I no longer have an ownership position with Neeley/ Lofrano Architects, my friendship for and admiration of Terry Lofrano continue. Many of the illustrations in the book come from Neeley/ Lofrano. Terry practices architecture with a love for the profession and a desire for perfection that I believe is the goal of most architects. I also want to thank Mehdi Khalvati, my partner in my new company, CAD-SPEC, who has allowed me the opportunity to try to multitask in both starting a new company and at the same time pursuing my desires to write as well as influence the educators of our future architects. I thank Carnegie Mellon University for the opportunity to teach there last year. This experience taught me about the university system and allowed me to fine-tune my convictions about the future of architectural education.

I am sitting here writing these pages on January 1, 1996 with the urging and support of my wife, Karen, and my son, Mark. They have supported my various adventures and tolerated my excitement in such things as architecture, CAD, the integration of architectural data, teaching, and now multimedia architectural information. Eleven years ago my son sat in front of a computer in this same room and, using our first product, AutoCAD AEC Architectural, with just five minutes of instruction, set off over the next hour, on his own, and drew a graphically perfect and dimensioned floor plan. (The room sizes and layouts were a bit strange.) He is home for the holidays, from the University of Oregon, and this week both he and my wife tested a multimedia catalog CAD-SPEC that is ready to release. This time with less than one minute of instruction, they were able to navigate the entire electronic catalog finding technical data, drawings, videos, specifications, photographs, and even a local dealer for the product. We are truly entering a new era where all information will be available and easily used.

The personal computer has involved us all in an amazing adventure that will forever change architecture as well as the rest of our lives. Thank you for your interest. Be creative with these tools; they are very powerful when used to enhance our knowledge and our environment.

Dennis Neeley

Every project requires a team of talented individuals to make it successful. Without the assistance of gifted professionals and invaluable expertise of Edward Thorpe (technical editor), Cliffton M. Fischbach (design and composition), Dennis Neeley (co-author), Diana Cisek (managing editor), Donna Singer (copy editor), Janet Feeney (associate editor), and Jonathan Solomon (Softdesk reviewer) this book would not have been written. John Wiley & Sons, Inc. also deserves my personal gratitude for accepting the challenge to publish a technical document about Softdesk software applications. Finally, I wish to express special thanks to Softdesk team members Majorie J. Matty, David S. Pothier, Kelly Malone, and Gail Hambleton.

B. Robert Callori

The Use of Computers, CAD, and Electronic Information in Architecture

Dennis Neeley

PART ONE OVERVIEW

CHAPTER ONE

Using CAD in the Architecture Office

When we first purchased CAD, I thought that it would be nothing more than an electronic drafting board. I am amazed at what CAD is able to do.

This chapter reviews the effects of CAD—computer-aided design (or drafting)—upon the basic architectural design process and office organization. The rest of Part I of the book is organized around this design process and gives detailed examples of how CAD can be used from the preliminary programming and design phases to facilities management. Part I ends with a look into the future.

The Design Process

When CAD was first introduced into the Neeley/Lofrano, Architects, office in 1984, we considered it simply a more efficient way to draw. However, we quickly realized that CAD was much more than an elec-

Figure 1.1 The traditional architectural design process

tronic drafting board. It was the route to a qualitatively new and better way of organizing our time and energy.

The traditional architectural design process consists of the following phases (see Figure 1.1):

Programming

Feasibility study

Preliminary design (schematic design)

Design development

Presentation and approvals

Contract documents and bidding

Construction

Facilities management

The Hand-drawing Design Process

In the traditional hand-drawn process, moving from one phase to the next often requires redrawing. The programming phase determines the scope of the project. The feasibility study is a preliminary stab at a solution to see if the project is feasible. At the start, the programming and design phases are rough and are intended only to sketch out the concept and feasibility of a project. Once the project is determined to be viable, the design development phase refines and modifies the design. In the design development phase changes are expected as the design, materials, and layouts are finalized. The contract document phase adds detail to each drawing and coordinates the drawings with specific selections for all the materials and finishes. Presentation and approval drawings are made throughout the process as necessary to show the design ideas to the client, investors and approval agencies. Changes are part of the design process; changes often leave hand drawings in sad shape or require them to be completely redrawn.

After the contract documents and bidding stages are finalized, the construction documents phase sometimes finds a firm making major modifications to the drawings to reflect the final decisions on the design of the project. In addition, during construction, the contractor often maintains as-built drawings of the constructed project. Finally, the contract documents and the as-built drawings are turned over to the facilities manager. The facility is then maintained and modified over the life of the building.

The CAD Drawing Design Process

Nothing magic happens when you move to CAD. CAD does not change the phases of architectural design nor the goals of each phase; however, it definitely changes the user's approach, time necessary to spend in each phase, and movement within those phases.

For example, as soon as the architectural firm receives a commission for a project, they enter the survey, topography, trees, existing structures, and soils information into the CAD. This base information is then used, without taking time for redrawing, on a multitude of drawings for both architectural and consultant information. The office never needs to draw the site plan again or worry about its accuracy. Better yet, the firm may receive the CAD drawings from surveyors; in which case, they do not need to spend any time drawing the site information. As part of this early phase, information may be entered on this survey drawing for any and all subjects, such as setbacks, easements, and height restrictions. Because of CAD layering capabilities, it is easy and efficient to let the drawing warehouse all important information. The information placed on a layer, such as all the survey points or site electrical information, can be displayed or hidden.

A preliminary architectural design begins with laying out basic shapes, parking, landscaping, and area calculations. CAD is ideal for this phase, as shown in Figure 1.2. The Auto-Architect® software easily creates spaces that may then be moved and placed in the appropriate locations. These space diagrams can be given wall heights for preliminary massing studies. Areas are automatically calculated.

With hand drafting, we often fooled ourselves into believing that we had a viable solution only to find that when we drew the solution accurately, it wouldn't work. With CAD, though, the accurate solution is drawn early in the design process. Although, at times you may find this accuracy confining, you will probably decide that the advantages are well worth the trade-off.

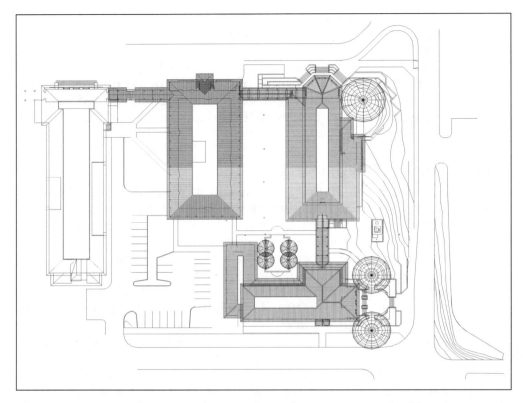

Figure 1.2 Start with a CAD drawing from the surveyor and add architectural elements.

Design development once required completely redrawing the site, parking, buildings, and so on. With CAD, you need only draw the changes. As architects are constantly checking to make sure that nothing has been overlooked, this program can help to make sure that you have not dropped a setback or forgotten a site line. With CAD, entered information is always available and is never lost. CAD drawings are additive; that is, they aren't created from scratch each time, which had always carried the risk of losing crucial information. CAD design studies are therefore easy to make. You can save a drawing, experiment with options for windows and roofs by making several studies, then move ahead with the design you choose. If you later decide to reopen an earlier solution, you can call up the saved original version and begin again from that point.

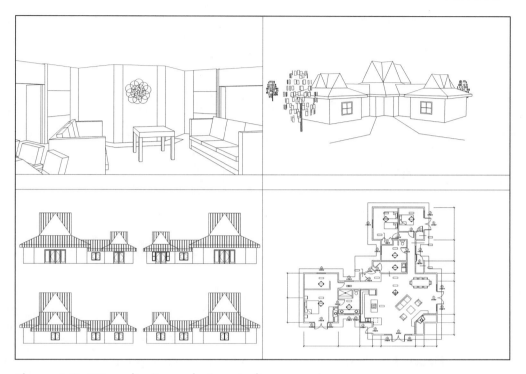

Figure 1.3 3D preliminary design studies.

In many offices, design presentations have been drastically changed by using CAD. Three-dimensional wire frames are used to quickly study massing (see Figure 1.3). Quick shades of the wire frame allow for more detailed massing studies. There are commands in CAD which allow the user to easily and quickly set a view point and a target point and have a perspective drawing automatically generated.

CAD geometry is often used as the background for hand-drawn perspectives, saving hours of boring, repetitive, labor-intensive layout work. CAD-generated perspectives easily and quickly provide ample views so that you can pick the best viewpoint location (see Figure 1.4). Rendering and animation transform the geometry to realistically render and animate your design. Because CAD is more flexible, more dynamic, and more sensitive, clients and public organizations understand CAD designs better than when hand-drawn renderings, colored elevations, and plans were used. CAD can absorb more data faster and do more with the data, thus approximating more closely the fluidity and perceptive-

Figure 1.4 Perspective views from any vantage point are created from the 3D model.

ness of the human eye and feelings. As a consequence, people feel more at ease with the architectural designs presented and accept and interact with the concepts more comfortably.

The contract document phase is based on the design development phase. Here the speed capability of CAD is truly realized. Plans develop quickly, with details added from your CAD detail libraries, manufacturers' CAD detail libraries, or quickly drawn using CAD detailing software. The software also offers many automatic routines that increase drawing speed. Backgrounds drawn for architectural and engineering drawings pop up instantaneously, and repetitive elements that draftspeople used to dread, such as scores of windows on elevations, as shown in Figure 1.5, can now be rapidly reproduced in exactly the correct locations.

The geometry of the CAD drawing can now be automatically fed into analysis software that is interfaced with CAD applications. This interfacing saves time and increases accuracy. In many cases, the results of the analysis are the basis for an automatic drawing of the correct solution.

Figure 1.5 CAD is ideal for designs with repetitive elements.

The drawing data can now serve as the basis for the automatic generation of the specifications, resulting in faster and more accurate specifications.

The bidding phase is likewise eased by CAD applications. Now you can automatically export information from the CAD drawings into estimation software. Estimates that used to take days or even weeks can be calculated in a matter of minutes.

During construction, the architects' and engineers' drawings are used as the basis for as-built drawings, which property owners then use as the foundation for their facilities management program.

Neeley/Lofrano has used 100 percent computer-assisted design since early 1985. In the mid-1980s CAD usage was rare with less than 3 percent of all architectural firms with even one CAD station. Just 11 years later, over 85 percent of all architectural firms have at least one CAD station. Thousands of small firms and hundreds of large firms are 100 percent CAD. Around 50 percent of all architectural drawings are drawn with CAD. In a few years all drawings will be created with CAD. We are in the midst of a revolution. Some have and some do not have CAD; some understand its full potential, but most do not yet understand its full potential.

While CAD doesn't eliminate parts of the process, it does change how work is distributed among the phases. Of course, the upcoming generations of CAD may very well change the phases themselves.

Although the use of CAD continues to grow in uses and importance, many users and managers do not understand the true significance of CAD or the broad scope of the use of digital information. Part I of this book is intended to provide an overview of how CAD and the use of digital information touches each step of the design process.

Chapter 7, on the future of CAD, gives you some previews of the near future, a future that will be substantially different than today. Architects need to be aware of what is coming to ensure their contributions and roles.

How CAD Affects Architectural Practice

"I have a small firm and we do one-of-a-kind projects. I could never use CAD."

"We have a large firm and we have just a few CAD stations."

"We have CAD in the office but only use it on our repetitive projects. Most of our employees are still on the drafting boards."

"We have made the commitment to be 100 percent CAD and it is the best decision we ever made."

CAD has already had a profound impact upon each of the offices described in these quotations, even in the first case, where the designer is not yet using CAD. There the potential effect is actually the greatest. Many architects and engineers who are now using CAD tell me that they wish they had switched to CAD earlier because now they see the time savings that are possible; time, as any good financial planner knows, is money.

CAD lets you seize opportunity without fumbling. It lets the designer envision an idea and transfer it into a real plan without having to plod through intermediate steps. In the hand-drawing process, the designer creates a sketch; the draftsperson draws up the sketch; the designer checks and corrects the sketch; then the draftsperson redraws it, incorporating all the corrections. This process is repeated over and over until the desired result is realized. CAD, however, lets the designer leap from an idea to an elaborated plan directly, without the long and error-ridden hand-drawing phase (see Figure 1.6).

The second quotation, describing an office that has just a few workstations, reveals another case: Often the problem lies in the type of hardware or computer being used to apply CAD. In the past, a mainframe was the only type of computer that was powerful and fast enough to handle CAD. These offices would have scores of employees drawing by

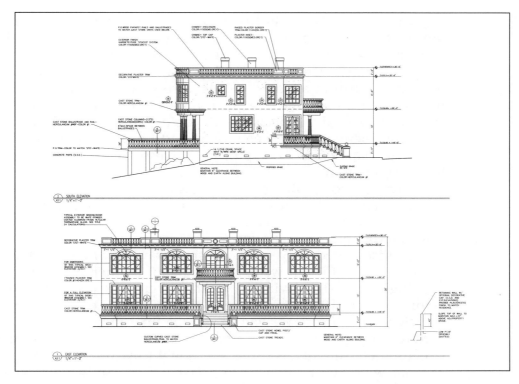

Figure 1.6 CAD lets the designer move quickly from an idea to an elaborated design.

hand with a few on computers. While most have abandoned mainframe computers, they have not yet realized that each draftsperson needs a computer.

The third quotation brings up an important concern: An office that decides to use CAD must also decide (1) how much of the office will move onto CAD and (2) what projects will be drawn with CAD. Certain hard realities will influence these decisions.

First, how much money can you afford to spend? In our case, we quickly realized that if CAD really is a good idea, it should be used on all projects; and, if it is to be used on all projects, then each person in our office would need a PC workstation. In 1986 we calculated that if all of our projects were on an hourly basis, we could cover the cost of installing and using CAD by increasing our hourly rates $5 per hour (2,080 hours times $5 per hour = $10,400). I have not yet talked with any firm where this additional $5 per hour would have negatively impacted their business. Indeed, firms that have properly implemented CAD have decreased errors and increased productivity.

At any rate, even if you decide to switch totally to CAD, the switch itself is not instantaneous; you need to determine which projects, or parts of projects, are the most logical for CAD applications. Surprisingly, this is not a difficult decision. If you're handling projects that have repetitive elements, such as motels and hospitals, put them on CAD first. The plans for all your projects are also logical candidates because, for CAD, plans are used as background drawings for other architectural drawings and for engineering drawings. Likewise, elevations that have many repetitive elements are good candidates. In truth, as application software and hardware have developed muscle power, CAD is worth using all the time on all projects.

We discovered very early on that ways of working that we had thought quite efficient were, in fact, painfully inefficient once we were drawing with CAD. Previously, we started creating background drawings before we were 100 percent sure of the design; we even started blocking out elevations before we had made our final dimension decisions. We used to firm up dimensions before we reached complete agreement with structural consultants, because we thought by jumping the gun in this way we were being efficient and fast. Of course, we also spent time redrawing when the final decisions were made.

With CAD, in contrast, the backgrounds take only minutes to draw. The elevations are partially generated from the plans. Engineers are called in earlier, and the structural information they provide is quickly reflected in the CAD drawings, as shown in Figure 1.7. Now we spend more time planning and investigating before we begin drawing. Once we do start drawing, we become accurate much earlier than before and without difficulty. The rewards are that projects are more efficiently developed and require fewer revisions, which translates into savings of time and money.

The last quotation is from an architect whose office is now committed to CAD. As an architect, you probably want to design and manage. You want to make decisions that help create buildings and interiors. You don't want to spend time proving that you can draw a wall and a window in that wall. You also don't want to spend your evenings checking dimensions, knowing that no matter how carefully the drawings are checked, some error will slip by—a ghost that will come back to haunt you and your firm when someone tries to use your drawing in the field.

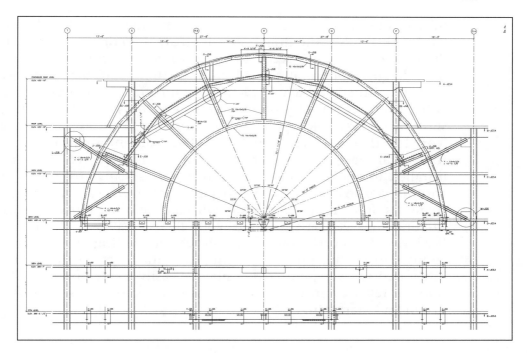

Figure 1.7 Structural CAD drawings may become the basis of architectural details.

With CAD software, the dimensions calculate and are noted automatically. CAD eliminates much of the busywork for the architectural office, leaving you with more freedom and more confidence.

Company Size and CAD

How does the size of your architectural firm affect the decision to use CAD? Such questions are important for chief executive officers who are weighing costs and benefits. Here are some answers.

In the small firm, the user can create directly with CAD, an extremely efficient process because ideas flow directly from your mind into the drawing. New CAD users are amazed at the quantity and quality of drawings that can be created in a single day.

In the medium-size firm, there are two basic methods of using CAD. In one method the designers use it to create preliminary designs and design development drawings while the contract documents are turned over to the draftspeople to be drawn. In other firms, the designers still use hand sketches and drawings, which are then drawn up in CAD by the draftspeople. As CAD becomes faster, more powerful, and easier to use, both designers and drafters will surely be using CAD for all applications.

Large firms that have implemented integrated applications have benefited from improved productivity. Integrated applications, such as the suite of professional applications offered by Softdesk, are designed to work together, to be coordinated, and to share information. Firms taking full advantage of this suite of products most often have networks installed to allow for the easy transfer of drawings from one group to another. For instance, the civil department starts with the site and then shares its drawings electronically with all the other disciplines that need site drawings as a base for their work. Plans created by the architects are the basis of electrical, plumbing, structural, heating, ventilation and air-conditioning, fire safety, and interiors drawings. Through the use of integrated software, employees may be easily trained on several applications. Integrated software is also easier for the CAD administrators to install and maintain.

Manual Drafting/CAD

Some hand drafters object to the impersonal and graphical look of some CAD drawings. While this concern was valid in the early years of CAD, it is no longer a valid observation. CAD drawings can have multiple line weights, hand-lettering fonts, and be as artistically drawn as any hand drawing (see Figure 1.8). The same skills of organization and layout, selecting the proper line weights, and organizing the placement of dimensions and notes will make the difference between a good CAD drawing and a poorly executed CAD drawing, just the same as these skills determined the quality of the hand-created drawing. We find that the urge to hand draw to express individuality and creativity fades quickly when the draftsperson no longer needs to spend the entire day redrawing a repetitive element tens or even hundreds of times. Once CAD itself is seen as the medium for artistic expression, it can easily become as favored and pleasurable a tool as, say, an expensive drafting pen set.

Moreover, CAD allows more drawing comfort than hand drawing. Employees with bad backs no longer need to lean over a drafting table. In addition, people who are not able to draw by hand, such as those with physical disabilities, can use CAD to create perfect drawings.

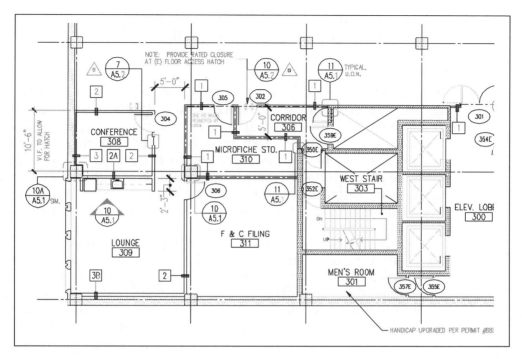

Figure 1.8 Variable line weights and shading are part of CAD drawing.

In the past, pregnant women in our office found it difficult to hand draw the last few weeks before delivery. Today, they can sit in any position and draw with CAD. Many drafters who have been injured and who no longer are able to draw by hand have constructed individualized input devices that allow them to draw once again.

Similar devices for the disabled range from voice commands to special keyboards to unique pointing devices that are operated by hand, by head, or even by eye movement. Drawings by disabled people may take longer to create, but once completed, they are perfect; the lines, dimensions, and text are the same in CAD no matter how the instructions are conveyed to the computer and the CAD software.

Drawing Management

Drawing management deals with the assignment of layer names; with drawing storage, revision procedures, and the mixing of hand drawing with CAD on the same sheet; with plotting; and with networking workstations. The following is a broad overview of drawing management.

Layer Names

If you are ever at a meeting of CAD experts and energy is dragging, just mention layer names and you will instantly provoke a lively discussion. To understand why, note that CAD allows drawing elements, such as lines, walls, doors, notes, fixtures, trees, and so on, to each be placed on unique layers. This feature is powerful because it lets you dissect the drawing at any time to create background drawings, just as surgical texts offer many different drawings of the human body with each showing the elaboration of a full system or layer such as musculature, lymph nodes, skin, and bones.

The problem arises with the need to name the many systems or layers of architectural data in a way that conveys similar meanings to all users. Auto-Architect offers prenamed layers; however, tens of thousands of people who use CAD have added and named their own layers and modified the preassigned layers (see Figure 1.9). These modifications would be fine if all the drawing stayed within the architectural office,

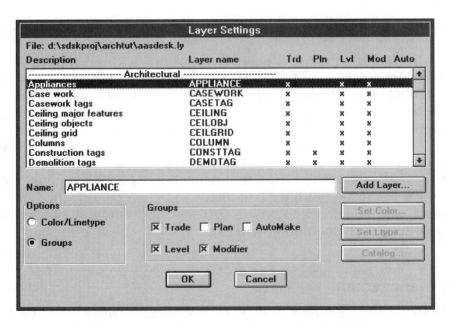

Figure 1.9 The user may determine the names of CAD layers.

but as soon as such a drawing is sent out to consultants or owners, the problem of creative layer naming becomes crucial. If your consultant works for 10 architects, he or she may work with 10 different layering schemes. As a result, the consultant is constantly trying to keep track of each office's in-house standard, an inefficient activity. If the architect works for several owners, it is very likely that they will encounter conflicting owner layer standards.

This is a major problem with no solution in sight. While several organizations and committees have taken a stab at the solution, one has yet to emerge. The American Institute of Architects (AIA) has published a layer-naming guideline, which unfortunately was vastly inadequate in scope. Several CAD consultants have their own systems. Government agencies have layer standards and many major owners have their own systems. It would be wonderful if we could all agree on a consistent set of layer names, but I have little faith that will ever happen.

Realizing that it is unlikely that any standard will exist soon, if at all, Auto-Architect has preassigned default layer names. I recommend that you use these names unless there is an overriding reason to use another set. Softdesk software has powerful layer-naming tools that will allow you to rename existing layers to conform with other layer-naming systems. These tools allow you to convert from one layer-naming system to another automatically; this is one very practical answer to the layer-naming controversy.

In your office, the most important layer-naming decision is selecting which standard you are going to use and remaining consistent thereafter. All Softdesk products have a coordinated layer-naming-scheme; thus, if you adopt the Softdesk system, you are assured of consistency and can avoid layer-naming conflicts.

Drawing Names

The name you give a drawing is a crucial tool for software users, so it must be thought out carefully or you will quickly create a frustrating mess. At first, most CAD users name their drawings to reflect the actual drawing. But, until Windows® 95, you only had eight alphanumeric spaces for the name, so confusing names became the rule, not the exception.

For example, if you are working on a three-story building, you may find it logical to name the first floor plan FLOOR1. If you have several projects under way, though, you must also indicate the individual client: SMITHFL1. Soon you may have a revision and want to keep a copy of the plan as it was before the revision, so now you have to shorten the name Smith and the drawing becomes SMIFL1R1.

We have now created an almost meaningless name, with little relation to the previous drawing name, although it is supposed to function as the foundation of a whole system. Obviously, drawing names are crucial and should follow a logical pattern from the moment you introduce CAD.

Following is a simple system which has proven workable over several years. This system produces a drawing name, such as AB01A201. The AB represents the client. We started with AA, AB, AC, and so on; we have a list that relates the two letters to our clients' names. The first 01 indicates the revision number on the drawing. The note A2 indicates that the drawing is an architectural drawing and that it is a floor plan. We have adopted, with a minor modification, the naming system of the Northern California chapter of the AIA, where the final 01 indicates that this is the first sheet of floor plans. Figure 1.10 is an example AB01A201. With a system such as this, you can be sure that drawing names make sense and are useful.

Client	Revision Number	Type of Drawing		Type of Plan		Sheet Number
AB	01	A		2		01
		A	Arch	0	Title	
		C	Civil	1	Site	
		L	Landscape	2	Floor plans	
		S	Structural	3	Sections - elevations	
		E	Electrical	4	Detail plans	
		M	Mechanical HVAC	5	Interior elevations	
		P	Mechanical Plumbing	6	Reflected ceiling	
				7	Vertical circulation	
				8	Interior details	
				9	Exterior details	

Figure 1.10 An "exploded" drawing name example.

Drawing Storage

One of the first questions I am asked by architects who are considering a switch to CAD is, "How can you entrust your entire livelihood—and that of many others—to some magnetic charges on a plastic disk"? The answer is simple: You need to have a consistent and reliable system of backups. The reality is that it is safer to have disk copies stored in several locations, as well as to have paper plots, than it is to have all your original drawings lying in a drawer in your office. You are only protected if you have taken precautions to be protected, but with CAD, you are better protected from loss than with paper drawings.

In a Non-networked Office

Here is a simple system that we used for years prior to installing a network. Start a drawing and, when finished for that session, save the drawing on the computer hard disk. Immediately save the same drawing on a floppy disk, which is considered the original and is stored in a fireproof file (see Figure 1.11). The next time the drawing is to be worked on, the draftsperson checks out the floppy, loads it into the computer, and con-

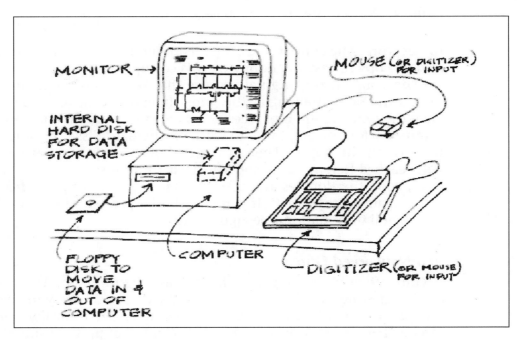

Figure 1.11 Standalone computers.

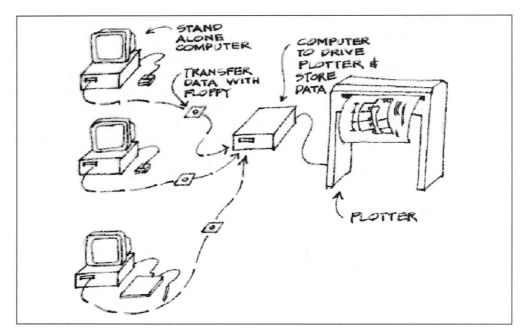

Figure 1.12 Non-networked computers.

tinues work. The copy stored on the computer hard disk is used only as a backup copy in case the floppy copy is corrupted.

The floppy is the original because that keeps two people from working on the same drawing at the same time; if you have the floppy, you have the drawing. If employees are allowed to work off the hard disk, it is too easy for one employee to work off the hard disk copy and another to work off the floppy. Then at the end of the day, you have two originals, each different, and one will need to be tossed out. On a regular basis, copy the floppies and take the safe copy out of the office to protect it against fire or theft. If you take similar precautions, you will never lose digital information (see Figure 1.12).

In a Networked Office

If your office has a network, the process is simplified. The file server computer stores all the drawings. You check out the drawing and work on it at your workstation after the drawing is electronically transferred to you. The network operating system can be set up to ensure that only

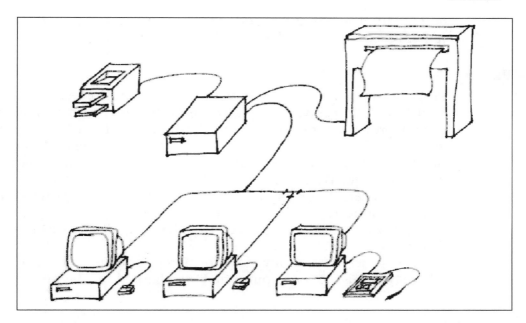

Figure 1.13 Networked computers, printers, and plotters.

one person has the drawing at any one time. Backup copies can be stored on your workstation hard disk; files on the network server hard disk should be saved onto disk, tape, or CD-ROM (compact disk, read-only memory) at regular intervals and taken out of the office for storage (see Figure 1.13).

Hand Drawing Mixed with CAD

Now, let's say that you are almost ready to go to bid. You have 50 sheets in the set. Touchup work is needed on several sheets, but if you make the corrections in CAD, it will take hours to replot the sheets. What should you do? You probably pull out your pencil and add the information to the existing plots, by hand.

The crucial question is what to do next. You can move on to another project and file the mixed CAD/hand drawing in the flat file or you can go back to the computer and make the changes and add the information to the CAD drawing. The second path is by far the most efficient in the long run. The real value of CAD is that it creates an accurate database of information that can be used for years into the future. If the hand-entered information is not added to the CAD drawing, that drawing will remain incomplete and have less long-term value.

Plotting

Plotting can be a weak link in your use of CAD. However, you may also find that it forces you to plan more efficiently and to make better, calmer presentations. With hand drafting, one hour before a meeting you can call out to the drafting room to stop drawing and to copy a set of the drawings; one hour later you will walk into the meeting with copies in hand. While you follow the same process with CAD, you place your call several hours or days earlier. If you are using a pen plotter, plotting a complicated drawing will take 30 to 60 minutes. If you are using an electrostatic or ink jet plotter, the plot will take 5 to 10 minutes (see Figure 1.14).

At first, we were annoyed by this forced change to our normal operating style, but we soon found that we planned for the plotting process

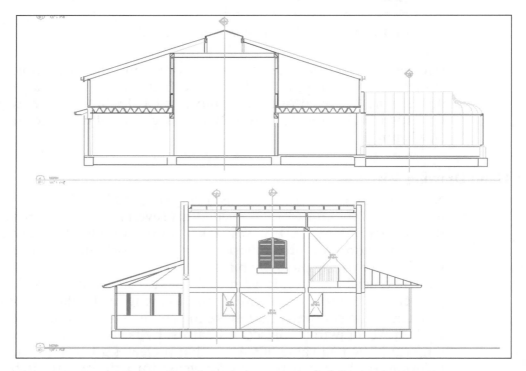

Figure 1.14 Layers may be plotted using several different line types.

and stopped drawing when necessary. The side benefit of stopping the drawing process earlier was that we entered meetings more relaxed and better prepared because we had not been rushing around until three minutes before the meetings making last-minute decisions and changes in the drawings.

Computers and Networking

When I first became involved with CAD in 1984, there were simple distinctions among mainframe, mini, and micro computers. The micro or PC (personal computer) was inexpensive (less than $6,000). It was a standalone machine that could not be networked; it was not very powerful because it had limited storage capacity (20 Mb, or megabytes) and not very fast (0.1 mips, or millions of instructions per second). However, it was managed individually by the user, which allowed the expression of personal style, and it had enough power to draw architectural drawings when combined with AutoCAD and application software (see Figure 1.15).

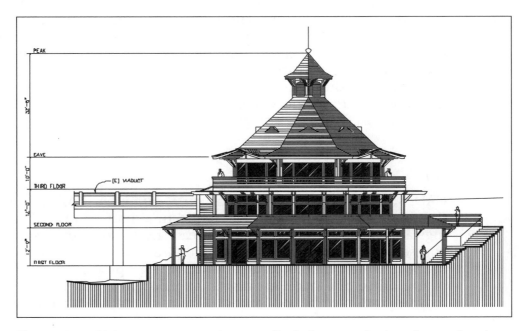

Figure 1.15 Using a computer does not limit the complexity of your drawing.

The mini was more expensive ($30,000 to $60,000), usually networked so that several users could easily communicate and share files, and moderately powerful, with storage capacities of 100 Mb and speeds of 1 to 5 mips. Although some CAD packages were available, the cost discouraged CAD usage, so minis were predominantly used for word and data management.

The mainframe computer was CAD's cradle. Hardware and software were expensive ($150,000). The computer was powerful, with speeds of 1 to 5 mips; storage capacity was limited only by your checkbook ($1,000 per megabyte). The mainframe computer was based on workstations connected to the host.

Today, the situation is very different. The separation between micro and mini has disappeared, with the price of each ranging from $3,000 to $16,000, depending on the exact configuration. The power of these computers exceeds the mainframe power of just a few years ago. A PC today will operate at over 100 mips, will have storage capacities of thousands of megabytes (1,000 Mb = 1 Gigabyte GB. We just purchased a 9GB disk for under $3,000) and are capable of displaying video, animations, and creating sophisticated and complex drawings.

The mainframe computer has taken on the role of a file server or has been replaced completely. The micro and mini can operate either as standalone workstations or as part of a network. Nowadays, a network may be set up so that each computer is still the center of the computing power, with the network simply used to transfer information and to store data and drawings. In addition, the network may be set up with a host micro or mini and satellite terminals that are used only for input, with the host doing the computing.

Conclusion

CAD is much more than drawing on a computer. CAD is the catalyst that brought computing to the architectural professions. With computing came database management, spread sheets, word processing and, of course, CAD. The computer and digital information have already resulted in tremendous changes to the design process, the organization of the office, the need for capital expenditures, and the services that may be performed by the architect. We have just scratched the surface.

CHAPTER TWO

BASIC CAD FEATURES

When I read my first hardware and software brochures, it was as if I was reading a foreign language. Actually, it was worse, because I knew the words but had no idea of what they meant in the context of the brochure.

Users must understand certain fundamental concepts in order to work with the computer, or hardware, and the programs, or software. This chapter gives an overview of what you need to know in order to use and understand CAD. If you are already knowledgeable about hardware, AutoCAD®, and Softdesk software, you should skim through this chapter.

The PC workstation has revolutionized the architectural design profession. Since the earliest days of construction—ever since the labor was divided among planners and builders—the planners have had to make drawings to convey the design to the builders. These were hand drawings that were laborious, slow, and repetitious to do as well as prone to errors. In the last 11 years, the PC and CAD software have together started a revolution that will forever change the method by which drawings, schedules, and specifications are developed. CAD drawings are created efficiently, base information is easily shared without wasteful redrawing, and errors are decreased because of the inherent accuracy of the CAD drawing.

Each year, PC power continues to increase without driving up the cost. Each year, PC software increases in both speed and functionality. Within the next five years, the computer will dominate all the drawing professions, with the PC and CAD able to give you the ability to design, present, and create drawings in a fraction of the time you presently need and with spectacular results.

The PC frees the architectural designer from the constraints of the office. Today, you can take the computer to your client to document the program requirements, then take it on to the site itself to work on preliminary design. You may even find, as I have, that on some days you are more efficient staying at home and working on the computer there, saving hours of commuting time and becoming part of the telecommuting trend that will change our needs for transit and increased highway construction, thus conserving our natural environment and resources. Whether from your home, or from any phone, or almost anyplace if use your cellular phone, you can call up your host computer at work to look at, check, and work on drawings or other files.

Integrated CAD Solutions

Drawings are the medium of expression for the architect's work. They transmit the design first to the client, next to the approval agencies, then to the contractors for construction, and finally to the facilities managers who maintain the building. Hand drawings have no intelligence; they are a static medium. But smart electronic drawings are associated with data; they are dynamic. They can change even as you watch them by flipping, rotating, angling, and showing movement. They can also be transferred from discipline to discipline, from surveyors to architects, and from engineers to city planners.

Softdesk Auto-Architect is one of several AEC application software packages developed by Softdesk, each standardized and integrated to the others, ensuring that what is drawn by one professional can be used and elaborated on by other design consultants. Softdesk products also include interfaces to analysis software. CAD is fast moving toward the day when all the information you need to design and document a project will be available on your computer. Standardization and integration also ensure that once you have learned one application, you will be well on the way to mastering other applications.

We are getting closer to the day when all information necessary to design and document will be available digitally. My current company, CADSPEC, was formed specifically to help bring vast quantities of technical information to the design professions using simple-to-use Multi-Media interfaces. CADSPEC and others are currently working on manufacturers' electronic catalogs. These catalogs will provide information about products, the company, details, and specifications. The information will be easy to access and easily transferable to your drawings and specifications. This information will be available on CD-ROM and over the Internet.

CAD software is moving away from a simple replacement for the parallel bar toward an automatic drawing tool. You are now able to draw a few lines, have that information transferred into analysis software, and have the results fed back into the CAD software for the automatic creation of the drawings. In the future, you'll do less actual drawing; instead, you'll direct the software to develop solutions you will then study and refine.

Drawing Speed

Speed is a constant topic among CAD users. I am continually asked if CAD is faster than hand drawing. The general answer is yes. However, there is no simple answer to this question because there are several variables. First, the draftsperson must know the software. Some employees are faster than others at working with the software, just as some employees are faster than others at hand drawing. One-of-a-kind complex drawings are slower to create than either repetitive drawings or drawings that use other drawings as backgrounds. Next, various computers run at different speeds and calculate differently, thus affecting the time you need to draw and move that drawing around. Various graphics boards process the data differently, producing major speed differences. Various versions of the AutoCAD software run at different speeds. The size of your drawing, too, has a major effect on the speed with which you perform operations. Finally, CAD drawing involves selecting one item after the other in sequence. The coordination and the logical organization of these sequential steps in the software also heavily affect drawing speed.

As a rule, always buy the fastest computer available. The faster the hardware solution, the more work you can complete. First, though, take the time to learn to be efficient. Put your drawing management system in place before you create flurries of drawings. It does no good to produce piles of drawings created quickly if they are wrong or if you don't store them where you can find them.

AutoCAD®

Personal computer CAD, or PC CAD, created in the early 1980s, was at first advertised as having 80 percent of the power of mainframe CAD at 20 percent of mainframe cost. Several vendors brought PC CAD to the market at about the same time, but one company Autodesk®—with its product, AutoCAD—quickly dominated the marketplace (see Figure 2.1).

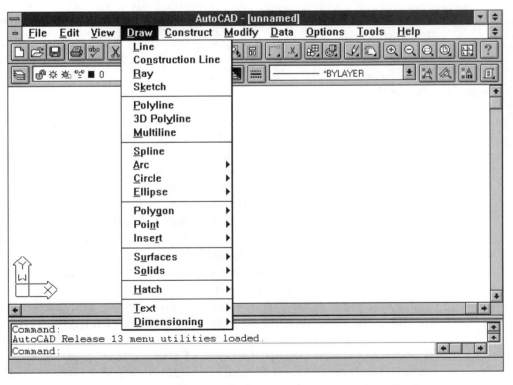

Figure 2.1 Basic AutoCAD® menu before application is installed.

AutoCAD was easily customized, which led to the development of hundreds of add-on specialty programs (third-party applications) that increased the functionality of the basic AutoCAD graphic engine. These add-on programs, such as the line of Softdesk applications, automated the basic AutoCAD commands and features. By customizing AutoCAD, operations that would formerly have taken several minutes and scores of individual steps could be completed in seconds and with only a few steps.

Although application software simplifies the use of AutoCAD and decreases your need to understand its commands, you still must know some basic AutoCAD commands before you start to work with the applications. There are many ways to learn AutoCAD.

1. Simply load the AutoCAD software and start drawing.
2. There are several excellent books designed to teach you AutoCAD.
3. There are video tapes on how to use AutoCAD.
4. Many software dealers provide AutoCAD classes.
5. There are hundreds of authorized AutoCAD Training Centers (ATC) and vocational schools across the country that are devoted to teaching AutoCAD and CAD applications.
6. Many students are learning AutoCAD as early as high school.

Although this book is not intended to teach AutoCAD, the next few pages introduce the basic features, commands, and functions the user will need to understand. Once you add a Softdesk application "on-top" of AutoCAD you will find that many of the commands are automated and simplified, which makes AutoCAD easier to use. Also, because Auto-CAD is a generic graphic engine used by all drawing disciplines, it is not necessary to know all the AutoCAD features to become proficient with applications such as Softdesk Auto-Architect.

Layers

One of CAD's most important features is its ability to assign different categories of objects and lines to different layers within the drawing. All doors can be assigned to one layer, all plumbing fixtures to another, and all notes to yet another. Think of each layer as a clear sheet and the CAD drawing as an unlimited stack of clear sheets or layers. You can draw on any sheet you wish and then look down through the stack to see all the sheets and a final drawing. If you want to create a presentation drawing, you can pull out the sheets that show the notes, dimensions, and section and elevation targets. In the example, just as you can pull out sheets, the CAD user can turn a layer on or off, thus displaying that aspect of the drawing while simultaneously suppressing the rest.

Layers are constantly manipulated during the drawing session (1) to study objects on various levels of the building, (2) to create presentation drawings from contract documents, (3) to show several proposed designs, and (4) to simply turn off or on layers to make it easier and faster to work on the drawing.

AutoCAD can either turn layers ON or OFF, or FREEZE or THAW the layers. While both functions may seem to have the same results, the difference is worth noting. In a large drawing, the speed of the computer falls off as the drawing size grows. If you turn layers off, the layer database continues to be carried with the drawing database, so no drawing speed is gained. However, if you freeze layers, the database for the selected layers is no longer carried with the drawing database, so the computation accelerates. The price you pay for using the FREEZE or THAW commands is that when you thaw a layer, it requires a *regen*, or regenerate, instead of just a redraw phase. The regen process rebuilds the database, which takes several times longer than the redraw process, if you have a large drawing.

As previously noted, layers are automatically created and given the preprogrammed names when you are using Softdesk Auto-Architect (see Figure 2.2). You can rename the layers and also create new layers or move objects and lines from one layer to another. The layer names supplied with the program are single names. However, you can create an elaborate hierarchy and assign several modifiers to each layer name.

Softdesk applications use a unique layer-naming scheme that lets you further identify the layer names. Instead of simply naming a layer Wall, you can identify the wall with any attributes such as (1) First Floor, (2) New, (3) Full Height, and so on. These modifiers can then be used to search for items in the drawing. For example, you can look at all the new walls on the first floor or for all the new full-height walls on the first floor.

Scale and Units

AutoCAD creates all drawings at full size within the AutoCAD database. If you plotted an AutoCAD drawing at a scale of 1:1, it would plot out at full size. To plot out a drawing at an architectural scale of 1/4 inch=1

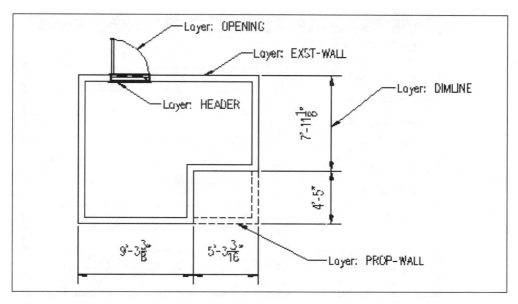

Figure 2.2 Example of layer names.

foot, you plot the drawing at 1:48. While working on a drawing, keep in mind that you are looking at a full-scale drawing, then zooming in and out for closeup or distance views. The size of the image on the monitor has no relation to scale: It is simply how close or how far you have moved from the image. At first, a few users find this "not to any common scale" difficult to comprehend, but this concern quickly becomes unimportant as you use CAD.

AutoCAD works on the basis of a unit of measure. When working on Softdesk Auto-Architect with the imperial setting, unit of measure defaults to 1 inch. If you have chosen the metric setting, your choice of units is millimeters or meters. With the imperial setting, when you are asked to enter a distance, you may enter either 12 or 1' to indicate 12 inches. Because the unit of measure is inches, note that you do not need to enter the inch mark (") after the number 12.

Attributes and Entity Handles

CAD's ability to attach attributes to symbols is one of its most powerful features (see Figure 2.3). When a hand drawing is completed, you have graphite on paper and that's just about all. The CAD drawing, however,

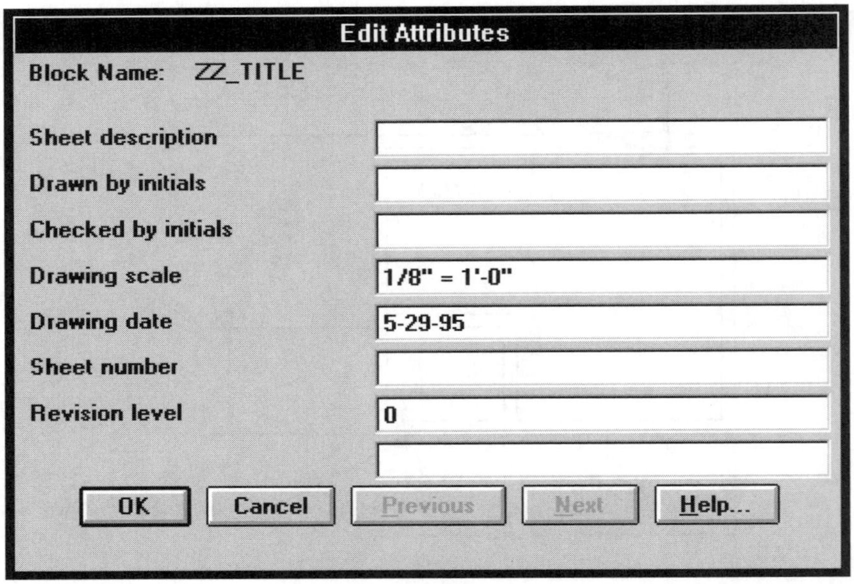

```
┌──────────────────────────────────────────────────────────┐
│                      Edit Attributes                     │
│  Block Name:   ZZ_TITLE                                  │
│                                                          │
│  Sheet description    ┌──────────────────────────────┐   │
│                       └──────────────────────────────┘   │
│  Drawn by initials    ┌──────────────────────────────┐   │
│                       └──────────────────────────────┘   │
│  Checked by initials  ┌──────────────────────────────┐   │
│                       └──────────────────────────────┘   │
│  Drawing scale        ┌──────────────────────────────┐   │
│                       │ 1/8" = 1'-0"                 │   │
│                       └──────────────────────────────┘   │
│  Drawing date         ┌──────────────────────────────┐   │
│                       │ 5-29-95                      │   │
│                       └──────────────────────────────┘   │
│  Sheet number         ┌──────────────────────────────┐   │
│                       └──────────────────────────────┘   │
│  Revision level       ┌──────────────────────────────┐   │
│                       │ 0                            │   │
│                       └──────────────────────────────┘   │
│                       ┌──────────────────────────────┐   │
│                       └──────────────────────────────┘   │
│                                                          │
│   ┌──────┐ ┌────────┐ ┌──────────┐ ┌──────┐ ┌───────┐   │
│   │  OK  │ │ Cancel │ │ Previous │ │ Next │ │ Help… │   │
│   └──────┘ └────────┘ └──────────┘ └──────┘ └───────┘   │
└──────────────────────────────────────────────────────────┘
```

Figure 2.3 Dialog box prior to entering attribute data; the attributes are linked to the drawing element.

is both a drawing and a database. The attributes attached to symbols are used to develop (1) bills of materials, (2) schedules, (3) estimates, and (4) specifications that accurately represent the drawing.

AutoCAD automatically gives each distinct line and/or object in the AutoCAD drawing a unique alphanumeric code. The application developer and the user can use this unique alphanumeric code, or entity handle, to manipulate the objects and populate the database. The combination of attributes and entity handles is the foundation for the database of the drawing, which is used to unleash the power of CAD.

Parametric Design

As you draw with AutoCAD, lines and objects are added to the drawing in three basic ways: by selecting the LINE command, by selecting a predrawn symbol, or by using the parametric process.

At times, you may add lines directly by selecting the LINE command, then indicating the start and end points for the line. It will be drawn.

At other times, you may select a predrawn symbol, such as a bathtub, then pull the symbol into the drawing and specify where the symbol should be inserted. Then you rotate the symbol to the correct orientation and it is added to the drawing.

Finally, there is the parametric symbol. Although this process appears the same as in selecting a predrawn symbol, the internal functioning of the application's software is quite different. The difference is one of precision. Although you may be able to specify a size for a predrawn symbol, the symbol is just a representation. In the parametric process, the symbol is drawn to the exact size you specify from a parametric formula, which describes the object or objects to be drawn. When you indicate that you want to draw an object of a specific size, the software first finds the formula and references a look-up table of sizes for the object; then the software automatically creates the drawing. The door or window you draw is so accurately sized that you can figure wall lengths, frame sizes, and so on.

With parametrically created objects, you can see that by changing or adding to the look-up table, you can easily modify your drawing. Parametrically created symbols are very efficient, as you do not need to store hundreds of predrawn shapes; thus, using parametrics decreases the amount of information that must be stored in your computer. Through the use of look-up tables, it is easy to add, delete, or modify numbers for new models of objects. It is also possible to link one parametric function to another. Without a doubt, parametric design is shaping the future of CAD and the future of architecture.

Blocks and Write Blocks

With AutoCAD, you can identify objects within the drawing to be saved and reused, either in the current drawing or in any drawing. Blocked items are specific to the drawing you are working on, such as all the suites of a motel. Write-blocked items are saved on your hard disk and may be recalled and inserted into any drawing, such as all the master suites of a given franchise motel type. As you use this powerful function while drawing, you will quickly recognize the massive amounts of time and energy that this recycling capacity saves for your office.

Reference Drawings

Reference drawings are an even more sophisticated way to increase your productivity and speed. Reference drawings work similarly to the use of blocks. With blocks you create an object, then save it as a block. You then physically insert the block wherever you want it in the drawing.

With a reference drawing you also create a block, but you do not actually insert the reference drawing into the drawing; you simply indicate where it should be placed for either viewing or printing.

The use of reference drawings is ideal for repetitious projects. For example, if you are working on a motel with similar rooms, you can create the reference drawing of one suite. On the master floor plan you then indicate the insertion point for the reference drawings. You can display the reference drawings on the master floor plan at any time. Prior to reference drawing availability, if you needed to make a revision to the master floor plan, you would need to go to each suite and make the revisions. With the use of reference drawings all you need to do is change the suite reference drawing and all of the suites on the master floor plan are instantly updated.

Drawing Commands

The first step that most people venture to take with CAD is to first draw free-form lines, then lines with increasing accuracy. The free-form line is easy; just start and stop and start and stop. The lines can be drawn at any angle and at any length. If staying on a 90-degree orientation is important, you can switch on the ORTHO toggle, after which all lines are drawn either horizontally or vertically.

If exact lengths are important, you can enter the exact distance and orientation in the following format: @10'3<90. This draws a line 10 feet 3 inches straight up on the monitor. The AutoCAD convention is that zero (0) degrees is to the right on your screen. Angles are defined in a counterclockwise direction, so that 270 degrees is down. Although you can modify this base setting, it is recommended that you not change it because it has become a standard.

AutoCAD has many commands, most of which are easy to understand and use. Commands such as COPY, MOVE, TRIM, and ERASE all do exactly what you would expect. Luckily, you will rarely need to use the most complicated AutoCAD commands, such as the ARC command. When you do need to, though, they have been automated and simplified by Softdesk software.

An excellent example of how the Softdesk software has simplified AutoCAD is the perspective-generating command (D view) which requires several minutes and some skill to create a perspective view. In fact, very few seasoned AutoCAD users could exactly set the target point and height and the view point and height. With the EYE commands found in Softdesk Core it takes only a few seconds to select the perspective target and to start the computer generating the perspective.

One of the most important capabilities of AutoCAD is the OSNAP, or object snap feature, which can be used to accurately lock-on to a desired location of an object. OSNAP commands are provided for endpoints, centers, midpoints, intersections, and so on (see Figure 2.4). Without OSNAP it would be very difficult and time-consuming to accurately locate one object in relation to another.

Settings

AutoCAD has hundreds of thousands of users. Over the years, these users have asked for many changes to AutoCAD, often suggesting additions that are needed by a majority of AutoCAD users; at other times, they ask for additions needed by only a few. Autodesk has added hun-

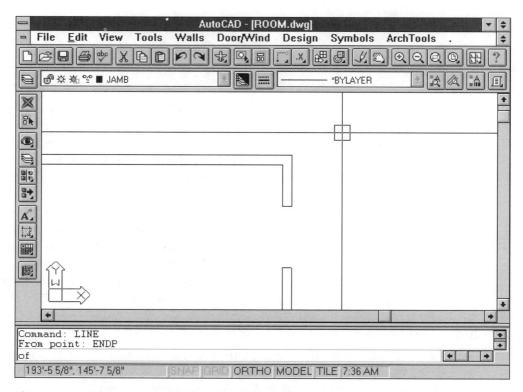

Figure 2.4 Object snap (OSNAP) settings allow precise selections of points.

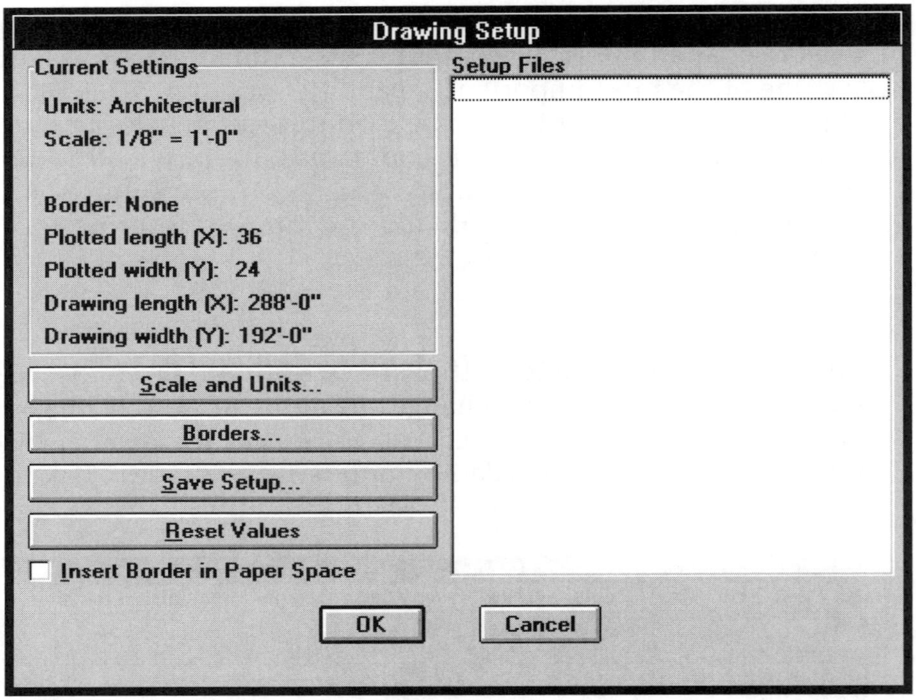

Drawing Setup

Current Settings

Units: Architectural
Scale: 1/8" = 1'-0"

Border: None
Plotted length (X): 36
Plotted width (Y): 24
Drawing length (X): 288'-0"
Drawing width (Y): 192'-0"

[Scale and Units...]
[Borders...]
[Save Setup...]
[Reset Values]
☐ Insert Border in Paper Space

Setup Files

[OK] [Cancel]

Figure 2.5 Dialog boxes allow you to easily set up the drawing environment.

dreds of these features, among them the opportunity to choose how you will set up AutoCAD to best suit your drawing style (see Figure 2.5).

AutoCAD and Softdesk software come out of the box with certain default settings so that you can go straight to work. After you become familiar with the software, you may find that you want to change these settings. For example, it was previously indicated that an angle of zero (0) draws a line to the right on the page. However, if you would rather that a zero angle draw a vertical line up on the page, you can set Auto-CAD to do so. Softdesk has assembled all the settings in one location on the settings menu. This simplifies how you locate and change settings.

Attributes and Toggles

As you draw you may desire to periodically modify attributes and settings (see Figure 2.6). Attributes set the way you will draw objects such as, doors, windows, and walls. For example, through the attribute dialog

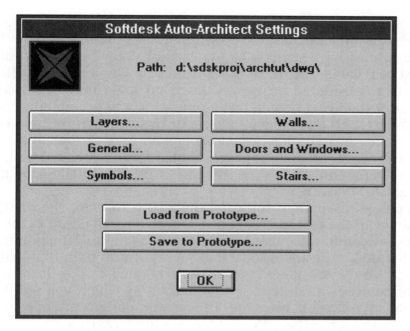

Figure 2.6 The software is customizable by the user with settings and toggles.

box you can set doors to be drawn as a single line, or a double line for the door, you can set to have the door drawn closed, open 45 degrees, 90 degrees or 180 degrees. The door may be indicated in elevation as a slab door or a paneled door. Walls may be drawn at a predetermined height, thickness, as two lines or as multiple lines. The hatch pattern may be determined from a list of available patterns. Toggles are available to turn on and off settings such as drawing in 2D or 3D. Almost every feature may be customized by you to draw the way you want.

Editing

AutoCAD gives you several options that define the characteristics of objects you insert into your drawing, such as layer, line color, object elevation, thickness (extruded height), and others. Or you may want to change the characteristic from the way it was originally inserted into the drawing; for instance, perhaps you put the object on the wrong layer. The CHANGE command lets you make such modifications, thus providing the kind of flexibility for which CAD is justly famous.

The Interface

Application software must have a whole collection of features to be truly useful: It must have symbols to use, it must draw the objects you want, it must be reliable, and, most of all, it must be easy to use. The first CAD software I considered using was based on mainframe hardware. The salesperson said that I could really only expect to become productive as an architect with this program after four to six months of training. I felt this lag time was absolutely unacceptable; in fact, it was also unnecessary. The interface had been poorly thought out; it was not designed for a practicing architect, but for someone who was totally specialized in making CAD drawings.

In designing modern software, the goal is to make the draftsperson productive in the first week. We also aim to have the head of the project feel just as comfortable using the software as the full-time draftsperson does. Softdesk software of today has more features than that mainframe software I once considered, yet it has remained easy to learn and use. The difference is the interface, the method by which you tell the computer what you want to create. In software design, interface design is just as important as the code that triggers the functions.

The primary interfaces that are available include (1) the keyboard, (2) the pull-down menus, (3) the icon menus. Just as you have a favorite color, chair, or automobile, so also will you have a favorite interface with the software. A good interface lets you choose your own preferred method of using the software. Softdesk Auto-Architect lets you choose, from all the possible AutoCAD interfaces, the one that is the most comfortable for you. You can even move between interfaces at any time as you work. You will find that you will start a command on the keyboard, then make the next selection for the particular function from a pull-down or icon menu.

In addition to the interface, you can choose tools to enter information into the drawing. Your choices include (1) mouse, (2) the keyboard, (3) the stylus, (4) the puck, and (5) the track ball, all of which are discussed in the following sections.

Input Devices

The first versions of CAD provided only one interface, the keyboard. On this device, if you wanted to draw a line, you typed in LINE and the starting and ending coordinates, or the relative distance and angle, and the line was drawn. To help simplify the keyboard process, often the software used a key letter instead of requiring that the entire word be typed in. For example, with AutoCAD, you could simply type in D, instead of DYNAMIC when you wanted to give the dynamic ZOOM command.

A few early CAD users still prefer the keyboard; they can enter information quickly because they have memorized not only the keyboard but also the key letters for the commands they use. However, for beginners and most seasoned users, the keyboard is not the most effective way to learn and use CAD. The other interfaces require less memorization, so you are free to devote your energy to learning the software.

Not long ago the input device of choice was the digitizer and template with stylus or puck. The *digitizer* is an electronic pad that senses the location of a *stylus*—a pen-like pointing device—or a *puck*—a mouse-shaped pointing device that works in conjunction with the digitizer tablet. The tablet is subdivided into a drawing area or selection areas.

Over the digitizer, you can lay a *graphic template* that shows the various commands you need. The selection areas, which look like little boxes, can be programmed so that when you point at them, or select them, the computer software performs a function. For instance, if you pick the box for LINE, the software performs the same function as if you had typed in the word LINE.

For both the beginner and the experienced user, the template is a great way to enter information. The commands appear in a graphical format and are printed right on the template so that you don't need to memorize the correct key word or letter to call up a command. Therefore, if you don't use CAD every day, the template lets you easily stay productive because all the commands are easy to find. The one disadvantage is that you must constantly look back and forth between the monitor screen and the digitizer. The digitizer interface does not limit your selections to only the digitizer; you are able to have selections from the pull-down, screen, and onscreen icons.

With the introduction of pull-down interfaces and now the Windows interface, the popularity of the digitizer tablet has decreased. Softdesk no longer provides a plastic template with its software.

The Mouse, Track Ball, and Pointer

The mouse looks like a puck but works on a different principle. The digitizer is an exact-pointing interface while the mouse is a relative-pointing interface. The mouse doesn't need a digitizer pad; instead, it has a small ball that rolls around on the bottom of the device. As you move the mouse around on the table surface, the ball also moves and the crosshairs, or target, on the screen also move, following the mouse. The mouse doesn't work with a template but, like the digitizer pointing device, the mouse lets you select options listed on the screen and draw on the screen.

A track ball is conceptually the same as the mouse; it's sort of an upside-down mouse, except that the ball is on the top and you roll the ball around with your fingers or hand. Both the mouse and track ball have buttons for return and select.

In the last few years the manufacturers of laptop computers have introduced several types of built-in pointing devices that work with the same concept as the mouse. You move the pointing device and depress buttons to make your selections.

Visual Interfaces

Here we discuss the monitor icon interface and the pull-down interface, as well as combined approaches.

The Icon Interface

An AutoCAD or Softdesk icon—a little picture or graphic symbol—interface can be called up on the screen. There are icons available for most of the commands that you will use for your drawing. The software comes with default icons displayed; however, you are able to modify the displays to customize the icon locations to correspond with your desires (see Figure 2.7). Sometimes the icons can be overwhelming, but as you continue to use the software you will quickly learn to recognize the ones that are important to you. If you are just beginning to learn CAD or have forgotten a command and need a graphic image to remind you, the icon interface is excellent.

The Menu Bar

Along the top of the screen is displayed a menu bar, a line of spaces that may be programmed with key words or letters. When you choose one of these key words or letters by first highlighting, then selecting it, another menu is pulled down and displayed below this key word, offering you further selections (see Figure 2.8). If you select one of these words, letters, or short phrases, the software either performs an operation or dis-

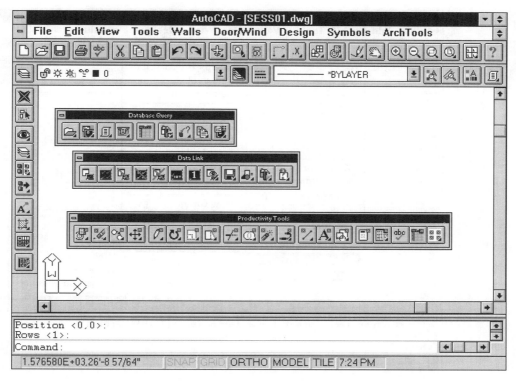

Figure 2.7 Onscreen icons may be picked to run the software.

plays yet another pull-down menu from which you are invited to select an operation

AutoCAD Information, Commands, and Prompts

AutoCAD information about your current drawing is displayed at the top and bottom of the monitor screen. The information displayed includes the current active layer name and layer color; the toggle status for ORTHO, OSNAP, or GRID; and the coordinates of the crosshairs on the drawing (which may be set to be absolute or to be relative to the last drawing point specified).

At the bottom of the monitor is the command prompt area that first tells you that AutoCAD is ready for a command, then shows your response line. Softdesk Auto-Architect uses the area to ask questions and to tell you what is happening. If you follow the requests and informa-

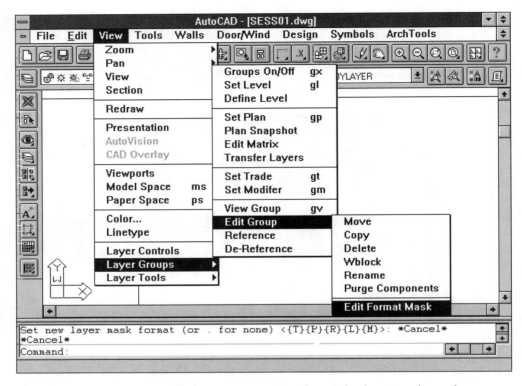

Figure 2.8 On-screen pull-down menus may be picked to run the software.

tion displayed, you will be able to perform most operations without reference to the manual.

The Combination Interface

Most users employ a combination of all the interfaces. I have often observed a draftsperson working with the pull-downs and drawing with one hand and typing in commands and shortcut key letters with the other hand. All of the interfaces are available and you may experiment with them to choose the one or the combination that is the most productive and comfortable for you.

Standardization

All Softdesk interfaces are standardized. All the AutoCAD commands are placed in exactly the same template location for each Softdesk product. The pull-down menus are each laid out the same way. This standardization is critical to the efficient use of CAD. Once you have learned one

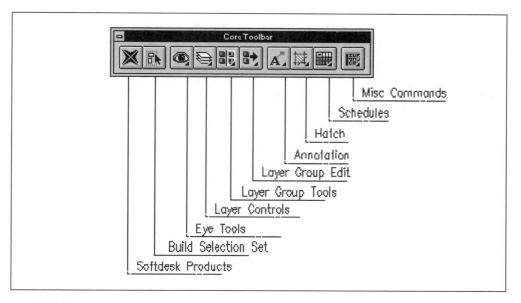

Figure 2.9 Softdesk Core is the foundation for the suite of integrated applications.

Softdesk product, you have learned a large portion of all Softdesk products. Most users do not limit themselves to one application, so the standardization greatly decreases the time needed to learn additional application products.

Softdesk Core

Softdesk applications use Softdesk Core as a foundation for the storage of common commands and operations needed for all the application software. Core is also a tool used to integrate all the software (see Figure 2.9). Once again, after you have learned to use Core, you will be familiar with the foundation of all Softdesk applications. Softdesk application products require Softdesk Core be loaded into the computer. As you add applications, Core will be updated to include the application in the selection menu. Softdesk applications use program routines found in Core in order to operate.

Softdesk Core is also a collection of utilities that will automate the use of AutoCAD. You will find routines for setting up the drawing scale and sheet size. You will be able to control layers through Core, which contains programs for building your own templates, screen menus, and libraries of shapes.

CHAPTER THREE

PROGRAMMING, PRELIMINARY DESIGN, AND DESIGN DEVELOPMENT

With hand drawing, I am convinced that during the design of a building as much time is wasted redrawing and rewriting information as is spent in productive work.

The organization of this chapter follows the phases of the architectural design process and demonstrates how CAD can be used to automate that process. Obviously, each project is unique, with each process modified for its specialized requirements. By following the basic design process, you can develop a good understanding of how to use CAD. In addition, the tutorial in Part II will take you through the steps of creating a drawing.

The Programming Phase

The initial programming of each project begins with gathering information and efficiently entering it into the architectural design, so that it

45

can be useful during the entire designing, building, and managing process. CAD can substantially eliminate the need to redraw graphical information or recopy alphanumeric data, both of which characterize the hand-drawing process. We have found that the sooner the information is transferred into CAD the better.

The Site

All projects start with the site. Information is needed on the boundaries, setbacks, easements, existing buildings, utilities, topography, soil conditions, roads, trees, and other physical aspects. Once this information is entered into the CAD drawing, it never needs to be drawn again; with Softdesk COGO, the electronic field data automatically creates the drawing. By manipulating layers, you can easily use the boundary drawing for the site plans, as well as the utility plans for the mechanical and electrical consultants. CAD reduces the amount of drawing needed for location maps and phase drawings.

Softdesk Core and Softdesk Auto-Architect have several features that simplify the base site drawing for architects. However, if you are doing extensive site work, I recommend the Softdesk civil engineering applications which are specifically designed for surveyors and civil engineers (see Figure 3.1).

Boundaries

Using Softdesk Auto-Architect, the boundary information is best entered in a rather roundabout method. Previously it was noted that AutoCAD creates drawings based on units of linear measurement. The default unit in Auto-Architect is the inch. For example, when you enter 22, the software will interpret this entry as 22 inches. Most surveys give dimensions in a decimal format, such as 225.75' is 225'9" or 225 feet 9 inches.

Naturally, you don't want to spend your day converting tenths and hundredths of a foot into inches and fractions thereof, so instead of converting the surveyor's units to feet and inches, you can simply enter 225.75 and the angle and a line will be drawn. Yes, the line is 225.75 inches long, not 225.75 feet (not yet, anyway). Continue to enter distances and angles until the boundary is completed. You now have a miniature version of the boundary. Now, move to the AutoCAD SCALE command, highlight your boundary drawing, and enlarge the drawing by a factor of 12. You now have a boundary drawing at the correct size (see Figure 3.2).

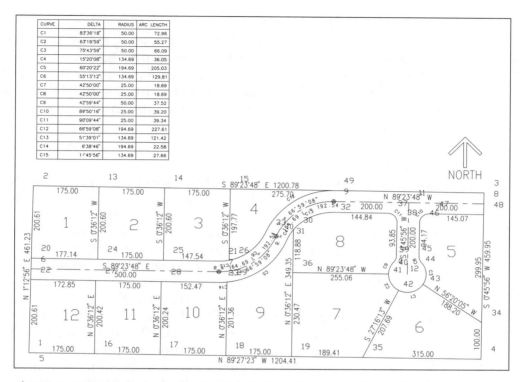

CURVE	DELTA	RADIUS	ARC LENGTH
C1	83°36'18"	50.00	72.96
C2	63°19'59"	50.00	55.27
C3	75°43'59"	50.00	66.09
C4	15°20'08"	134.69	36.05
C5	60°20'22"	194.69	205.03
C6	55°13'12"	134.69	129.81
C7	42°50'00"	25.00	18.69
C8	42°50'00"	25.00	18.69
C9	42°59'44"	50.00	37.52
C10	89°50'16"	25.00	39.20
C11	90°09'44"	25.00	39.34
C12	66°59'08"	194.69	227.61
C13	51°39'01"	134.69	121.42
C14	6°38'46"	194.69	22.58
C15	11°45'56"	134.69	27.66

Figure 3.1 Surveys created with Softdesk civil engineering software forms the basis of an architectural site plan.

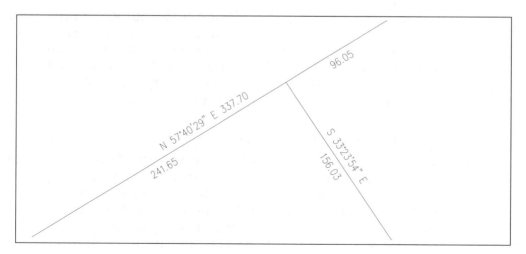

Figure 3.2 CAD boundary lines.

Line Types and Line Labels

Both Softdesk Core and Softdesk Auto-Architect provide you with a comprehensive set of line types that can be used to indicate fences, existing buildings, setbacks, and so on. The process to select and use the line types is simple. You can also label lines with the BREAK MARKS command found in Softdesk Core; this command automatically breaks the line and inserts a label.

Topography

Several types of lines can be used to represent topography. Note that AutoCAD has a command that at first may seem the logical choice, but isn't. The SKETCH command will ask you for the increment at which you wish to locate points, usually several hundred or thousand to the inch. As you sketch, each point must be stored in the database. Clearly, you will quickly fill your drawing database with thousands of coordinates for the points on the sketched line. You could use LINE; however, these lines don't lend themselves to the normal curves found in a topographic drawing; each segment of the line is an independent entity.

The most logical choice is the POLYLINE command, which lets you locate points along a broken line—although the entire line is a single entity within AutoCAD. Polylines can also be modified automatically into curved lines. Furthermore, elevations can often be assigned to the topography polylines so that you can use the drawing for elevation studies later.

The process of assigning elevations to AutoCAD lines is important and can be done in two ways. You can set your drawing level with the SET LEVEL command found in Softdesk Core; all elements that you draw are inserted on the chosen elevation. You can also set the elevation using the AutoCAD CHANGE command, which lets you change an existing line or object to an elevation.

Curbs, Gutters, and Sidewalks

Under the site symbols section, you will find functions that automatically draw curbs and gutters. The software gives you prompts or requests for the size of the curb, the gutter, the landscape strip, and the sidewalk. Then you set starting and ending points and the drawing is created. In addition, you can add driveway cuts and ramps for the disabled automatically with other selections available in this section.

Figure 3.3 Site design is automated with CAD.

Site Symbols

Softdesk Auto-Architect provides a full complement of symbols available for highway markers, trees, playing fields, cars, boats, and parking layouts as shown in Figure 3.3.

Once the site information is complete, the drawing can be used as needed for other architectural drawings or for other consultants by turning on and off (or FREEZE and THAW) layers or by transferring information to other drawings.

Building and Organizational Information

During the programming phase, the architectural office gathers basic information on area requirements, relationships, and goals of the project. As it progresses, the information gathered becomes more specific and complex. Eventually, the program shows exact areas, people, equipment, room layouts, and relationships. CAD is the ideal medium for both storing and manipulating this information.

Organizational Information

CAD is very useful for creating organizational charts for your clients. We leave meetings ladened down with slips of paper and individual department charts and go back to our office, where we put together that company's organizational chart in CAD. Throughout the project, we update this chart as needed. CAD is an excellent graphic tool for the preparation of charts and text.

Area and Spatial Requirements

The client shows you either (1) areas that are needed for the facility or (2) needs that must be accommodated, which you convert into area and space. At the same time, the relationships between the spaces are indicated.

Several functions are available on Softdesk Auto-Architect that help record these program requirements. If you want to create a relationship diagram with equal-size bubbles, use the basic drawing command to create circles or bubbles that may be labeled and then arranged, given the program requirements. We often use the SPACE command to create bubbles, because the software automatically calculates and annotates the areas of bubbles. The use of bubbles for the preliminary design phase (see Figure 3.4) of the project will be discussed in the following section.

Workspace Requirements

During the programming phase on interior projects, it is common to discuss workspace requirements. Typical layouts are determined for secretaries, managers, and top management. Special equipment rooms are discussed and specific requirements determined. We immediately convert this information to CAD, which lets the client review and confirm the basic layout. Drawing accurate spaces gives an accurate calculation of the building's total space requirements. Softdesk Auto-Architect has several predrawn furniture symbols that help with office layouts. These can be inserted either as two- or three-dimensional symbols (see Figure 3.5). Specific attributes, such as manufacturer, model, finish, or cost can be attached to the symbols at any time.

Equipment

We have worked on several biotech laboratories that are dense with complicated technical equipment requiring specific electrical connec-

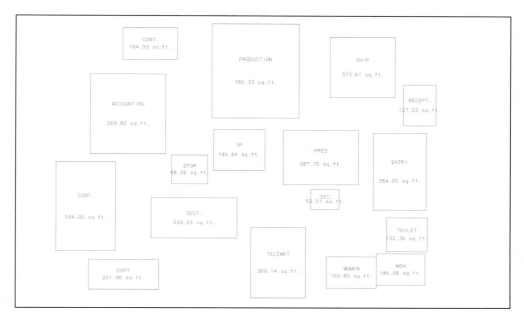

Figure 3.4 The design process begins with a bubble diagram.

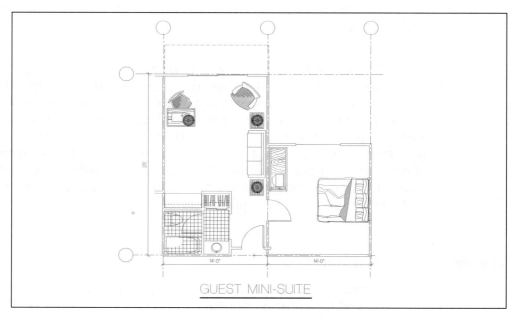

Figure 3.5 Auto-Architect includes 3D symbols to design interiors.

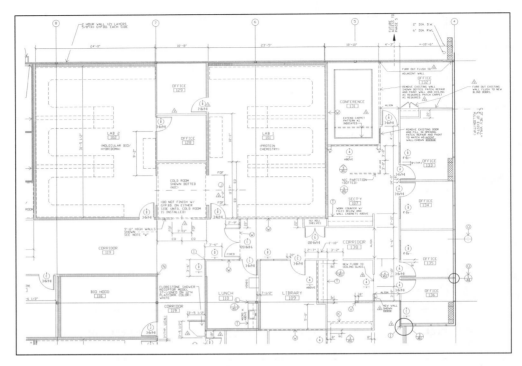

Figure 3.6 Floor plan of biotech laboratory.

tions and special air, gas, and waste connections. Not only are the types of connections crucial, but so are the exact locations. Before CAD, we had to manage pages and pages of fixture cuts and notes on the equipment. Today, we immediately draw up the equipment in CAD and accurately locate all the utility connections, the service sizes, and the connection requirements, as shown in Figure 3.6. All the information we ever need is attached to the CAD drawing. During the layout phase, it is easy to check for clearances and to check that all the proper services have been provided to the equipment.

The Preliminary Design Phase

The preliminary design phase is the experimental phase where you move back and forth from concept to program requirements. This phase may take several forms: It may be a quick study to determine the approximate size of the potential development to help determine if the project is even remotely feasible or it may be the first series of physical massing solutions for the project. The preliminary design can show the basic layouts and the architectural concept. By definition, the preliminary design is whatever information is needed to let the client and the architect move into the next phase.

Some parts of this phase must stay fluid and uninhibited while other segments are frankly tedious and analytical. So far, CAD is not always well suited for the spontaneous needs of the preliminary design phase, although it is excellent for other parts of this phase. In hand drafting, you tend to move from the simple to the complex as you move through the designing process. CAD does not require this progression; although with CAD it is difficult to be loose, it is fast and easy to assemble simple pieces and to study complex relations. Experiment with the space command to create massing studies and layout studies.

The AutoCAD STRETCH command is one of the most useful commands at your fingertips. During the preliminary design phase, it is easy to push and pull a bit on the design, then quickly look at results with the View commands.

Bubble Diagrams

Bubble diagrams were created as part of the programming phase. In the preliminary design phase, the bubbles are moved around to study various solutions. When you are satisfied with a basic layout, you can automatically convert the bubbles to a wall drawing; for this feature to work, all the bubble lines must align. Often we use the bubbles to determine basic location, and we don't worry about overlaps. This initial drawing is saved as a block, then reinserted; new bubbles that align are created on top of the block, then the original block is erased and the new bubble drawing is converted automatically to a drawing with walls.

Mass Studies

During the preliminary design phase, the architect studies the basic massing of the project (see Figure 3.7). With hand drawing, the process begins with the massing ideas, sketches, and thumbnail perspectives. Often foam board study models are made, torn apart, and remade as the designer modifies the design.

Softdesk Auto-Architect has functions that let the designer quickly study the building massing. As you create walls, using either the basic

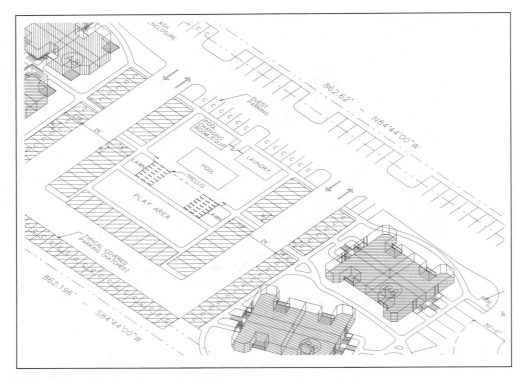

Figure 3.7 Preliminary site and massing study.

WALL command or the SPACE command, you assign wall heights (see Figure 3.8). The visualization commands found in the View area allow you to look at your drawing in isometric and perspective, and even walk through and around the structure (see Figures 3.9 and 3.10).

Site Plans

The site plan information is developed in the programming phase, so you always start with an accurate base drawing. We draw the building masses and move them around on the site drawing. With hand drawings, we used to end up with piles of sketches; now we can save the electronic studies as drawing files for electronic review and only print out those solutions that have merit.

Parking layouts become a crucial factor during the project design. The balance among parking, building coverage, and hard and soft surfaces is crucial to the project's economic viability. In most projects, the number of parking spaces determines the area allowed for the building.

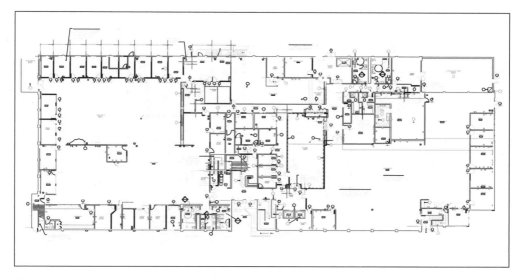

Figure 3.8 CAD is ideal for laying out repetitive interior partitions.

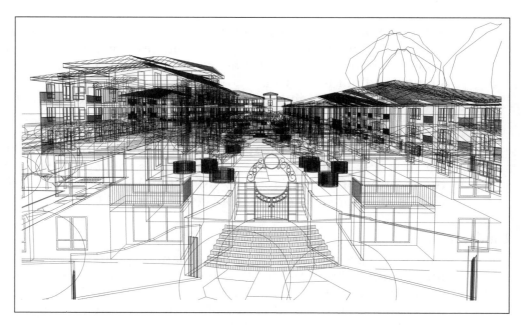

Figure 3.9 Perspective study of a housing complex prior to its hidden line removal.

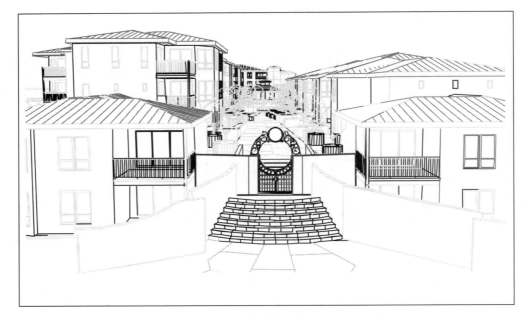

Figure 3.10 Housing complex with hidden lines removed.

Before CAD, we used to spend days on large projects simply laying out parking, trying 90-, 60-, and 45-degree angles along with other combinations to arrive at the most efficient layout. The process was time-consuming and not much fun.

Softdesk Auto-Architect has a parking layout function that can save hours of time on each project. You can preset the size and the angle of the spaces. You then indicate the starting location for the row of spaces, either single or double rows, and then the ending location or the number of spaces in the row; the software draws the layout. You can adjust the location of parking rows by using the AutoCAD MOVE command. CAD is ideal for parking lot layouts (see Figure 3.11).

Landscaping

During the preliminary design phase, landscaping is added to the drawings. Softdesk Auto-Architect's site symbols section offers a full complement of tree and bush shapes. We often use AutoCAD Fill Patterns to indicate the landscaped areas. The AutoCAD MULTIPLE COPY command lets you lay out a forest in seconds.

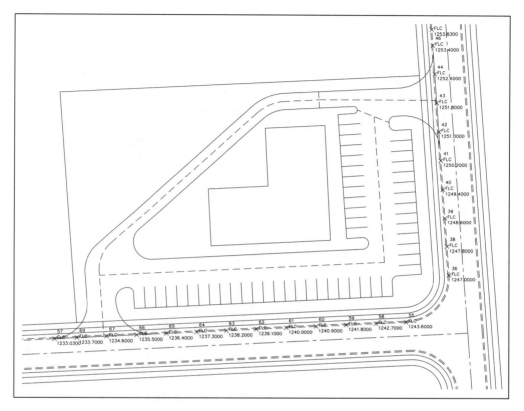

Figure 3.11 Preliminary parking layout study.

Preliminary Design Plots

CAD creates accurate drawings that tend to look like final design solutions. During the preliminary design phase, this finished appearance may not work to your advantage. At this stage, the designer is looking for feedback and wants to encourage change to improve the design. If the drawings look too complete, some people hesitate to suggest modifications.

We have found that with pen plotters you can use an old felt-tip plotter nib to make the lines look looser, less formal, and more open to change. We have also used various color nibs; when we later print out the tracing, the different colors each give off a different intensity, creating a more varied visual appearance, once again, more open to change. If you are using a bubble jet plotter, you may purchase software that will

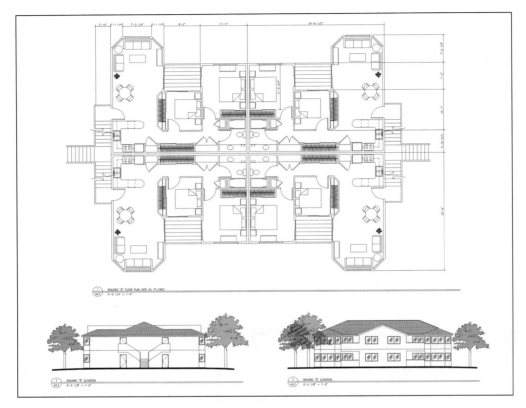

Figure 3.12 Preliminary drawings progress to design development drawings.

distort exact CAD lines and make them look more like a hand drawing. Yes, I know it is sort of strange that you may want to obscure the accuracy, but at times you may not want the exactness of a CAD drawing.

Internal Design Review

During the design development phase, the drawings are constantly being reviewed (see Figure 3.12). In the past, we marked hand drawings up with a red pen and the next day a draftsperson would make the corrections. This process would be repeated until the design was acceptable. With CAD, it is most efficient to have the principal or project architect look at the electronic version of the solution and make the corrections directly on the drawings (see Figure 3.13). At other times, we write the notes for correction on a special note layer. The draftsperson then erases the notes as he or she makes the indicated changes.

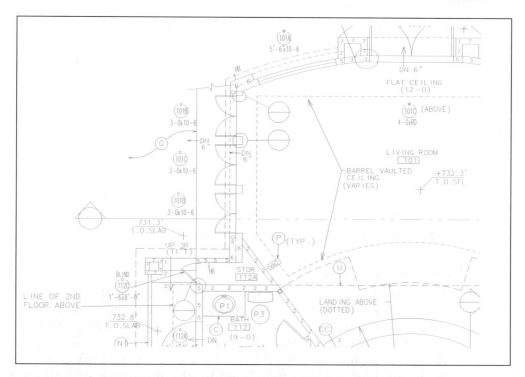

Figure 3.13 Partially completed drawing may be "marked up" electronically.

The Design Development Phase

In the design development phase, the architect makes definite decisions about all aspects of the project. The site plan is finalized and the exterior design and materials are studied and agreed upon. The interior layout and design are also determined. If the project is an interior project, design development drawings now indicate in complete detail the layout, architectural detailing, materials, lighting, and other design elements.

This phase is a time for study. Before CAD, it often required the complete redrawing of the site plans, building plans, and the interior and exterior elevations from the preliminary design. With CAD we have found that the preliminary design drawings can usually be modified to reflect needed changes. In addition, in this phase, the architectural elements are drawn.

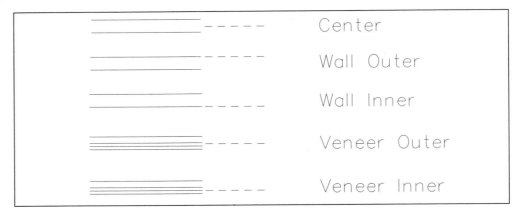

Figure 3.14 The user controls wall settings.

Walls, Doors, and Windows

Walls, doors, and windows are the basic elements of the architectural drawing. Softdesk Auto-Architect gives you several ways to create these essential features. The process, which is quite simple, can be learned in minutes. Softdesk Auto-Architect is a mature software product; the designers have had several years to add the many features requested by users, so don't feel overwhelmed by the multitude of options available. Just start drawing walls and inserting doors and windows by using the Softdesk default settings. Default settings are out of the box settings selected because experience shows that most users choose these basic settings. The software could be shipped with no default setting, but this would require new users to make a number of decisions while they are still unfamiliar with the software. After you have some experience with the software, you can use the settings and toggles to set up the software to your exact specifications.

You can modify the width of the walls and set their height. You can decide if the walls should be drawn based on the centerline or on either the inside or outside face of stud (FOS) or face of material. You can automatically indicate veneers and preselect hatching patterns (see Figure 3.14). With doors, you can set the swing and the attribute, or specifications, prompts. Finally, you can also choose to draw in two or three dimensions. With both doors and windows you can add detail that will be displayed in elevation and perspective views. Windows can be selected for window type, sash size, mullion layout, and size and trim. Doors can be selected for size and style as well as paneling layout and trim.

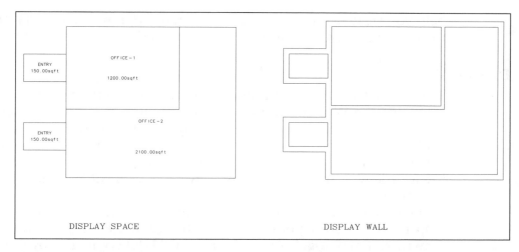

Figure 3.15 Single-line diagram is automatically converted to a wall drawing.

Space Diagrams

Spaces can be created (1) by defining the space by length and width or by length and square footage; (2) dynamically by forming a rectangle on the screen; or (3) free-form with lines and arcs. There are several advantages to creating spaces instead of drawing walls one at a time (see Figure 3.15).

During the early design phase, you can use the space diagrams just as you would use a hand-drawn bubble diagram. Working from your program, you can quickly create the spaces in the approximate size you want and then electronically move them around until you have the most favorable layout. Just as you can save the hand-drawn studies, you can save the electronic studies, either as views inside the drawing or as separate drawing files.

As you work with the spaces, the lines will probably overlap. When you have your desired layout, you have several ways to convert the diagram to a floor plan with walls. First, you can use the basic WALL command and trace over the diagram. Second, you can also change the overlapping diagram to a block, then lay out the space again based on the diagram, taking care not to overlap the spaces.

If the completed space diagram has been carefully created and the lines of the various diagrams do not overlap, you can take advantage of a great time saver. The software can automatically convert the space diagram to a floor plan with wall thickness. You now have the choice of an interior wall thickness and an exterior wall thickness. This feature can help you create a plan in a matter of minutes that would have taken hours to create with just basic AutoCAD alone and days if drawn by hand.

Drawing Walls

To draw walls with the pull-down interface, move the pointing device to highlight the Walls option on the top menu bar. When you select this heading, a pull-down menu is displayed which allows you to select a wall type to draw or to set up a new wall type. You have tremendous control over the wall which includes thickness, veneers, height, hatching for the wall and veneers, base elevation, wall color, layer assignment, and more.

Once you select a wall type to draw, you simply indicate a start and stop point, or start point and length and angle, and the wall will be drawn. You may toggle on and off the ORTHO command by pressing F8 or by selecting from the button at the bottom of the monitor. You may draw walls in free-form, have them snap to a preset grid, or enter exact dimensions and angles. You may also draw in 2D or 3D.

Cleaning Up

Periodically, you will end up with walls that are crossing each other and the lines go through the intersection. Softdesk's automatic cleanup commands result in the desired intersection, as shown in Figure 3.16.

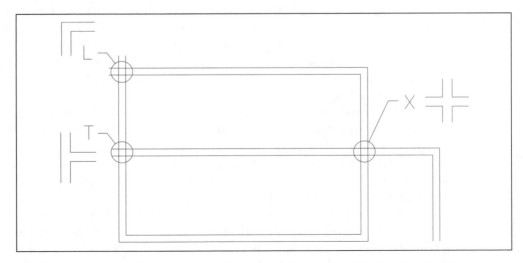

Figure 3.16 Special commands automatically "clean up" wall conditions.

Add two Walls and Add three Walls (Chaining)

When you are drawing repetitive spaces, the chaining offers you speed. With these commands, you can easily add walls between walls and add L or U shapes. The dimensions given for the spaces created may be based on the centerline or on clear dimensions. This is an ideal command for laying out offices (see Figures 3.17 and 3.18).

Doors and Windows

You can choose from two methods by which to insert the doors and windows into your drawing. You can insert these features into walls one at a time or you can select the Quick Doors and Windows option. With Quick option, you insert one symbolic door or window and then simply copy the symbol without stopping to actually insert the symbol into the wall (see Figures 3.19 and 3.20). The advantage of the Quick Mode

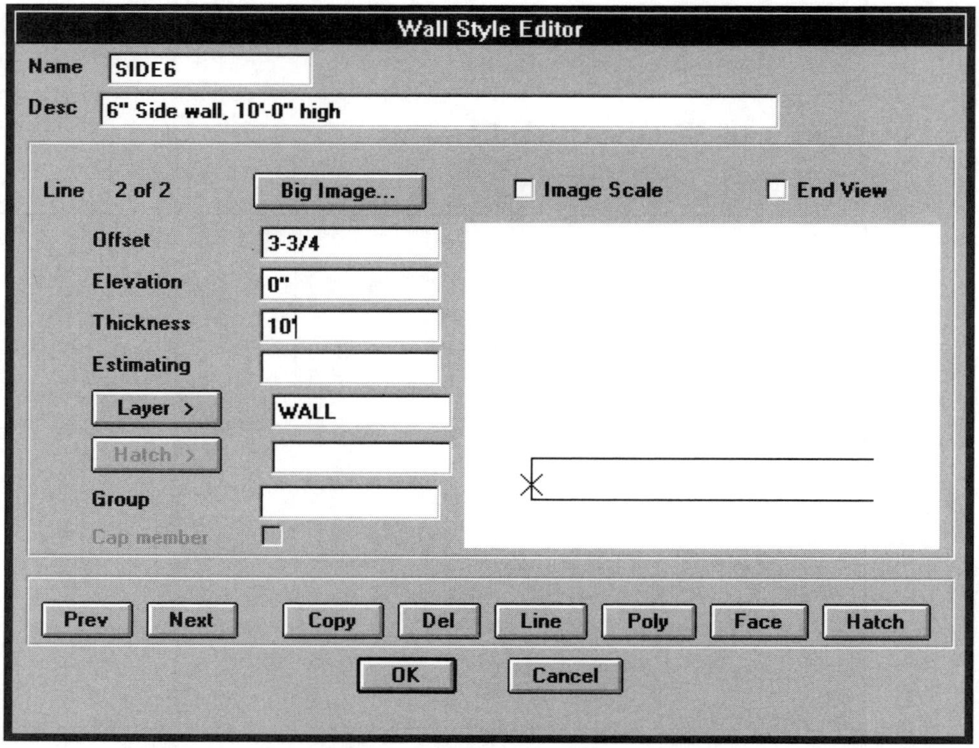

Figure 3.17 Dialog box is used to set the wall environment.

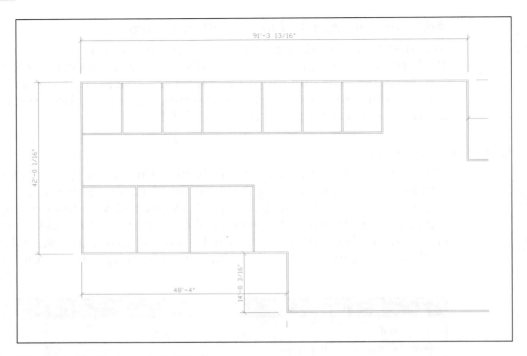

Figure 3.18 Series of chained spaces.

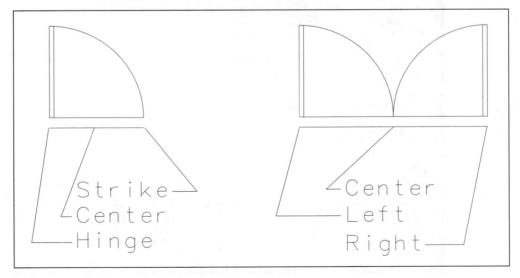

Figure 3.19 Many symbols have multiple insertion points.

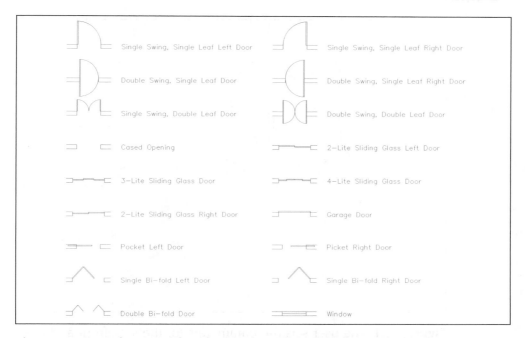

Figure 3.20 Under many headings—for example, "Doors"—there are multiple symbols to pick from.

option is that you can easily COPY or ARRAY the symbol before the automatic insertion. The actual insertion operation is then accomplished at one time, thereby saving you a great deal of time.

Just as with walls, you have a multitude of options to chose from for the actual graphic representation of doors and windows. The doors may be drawn as either two- or three-dimensional representations. The door can be shown as closed or open 45 degrees or open 90 degrees. When drawing three-dimensional doors, you can also indicate door height.

The software maintains a database on each door. Some of the data are by-products of the drawing process, such as the width and height; that is, height when it has been inserted as a three-dimensional door. The software has built-in prompts to request additional door specifications. In AutoCAD, these specifications are known as attributes. If you have indicated to the software that you want to be prompted for attributes, you will be asked for door type, door material, fire rating, thickness, door finish, frame material, frame finish, hardware group, cost, and several other attributes. These attributes can also be used to auto-

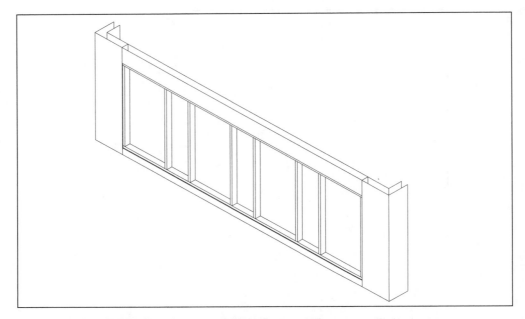

Figure 3.21 The user sets the parameters for the storefront and it is automatically drawn.

matically create schedules which may be displayed in the drawing or printed out on your printer.

Storefronts and Curtain Walls

Storefronts and curtain walls can be easily created. You have two options: the first allows for any design for the placement of the elements; the second option uses a preset pattern (however, you are allowed to modify the dimensions on the pattern). You can insert a rectangular mullion with the dimensions of your choice or a customized shape that you have predrawn (see Figure 3.21).

Roofs

Softdesk Auto-Architect can create roof plans for roof plan drawings, for the elevations sections, and for perspectives (see Figure 3.22). The creation of a roof is an easy process. Simply outline the perimeter of the roof and answer the prompt for overhang, fascia depth, and slope. The roof creation is automatic. This is a very powerful tool and will save you countless hours in both design studies as well as in the documentation phase.

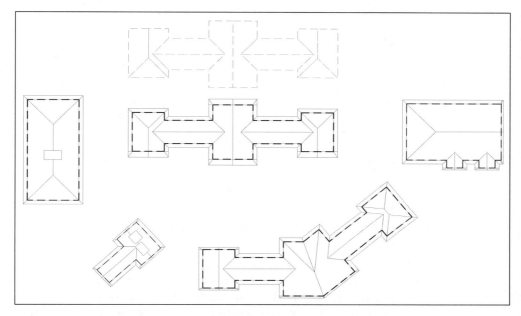

Figure 3.22 Roof studies.

The Multistory Features

A few years ago, no one would ever have considered trying to create a multistory building in one drawing file on the PC. The software and hardware were not fast enough to handle large files and the speed of the drawing manipulation would have been unacceptable. Today, the software and hardware have significantly improved in speed, and it is quite feasible to study multiple floors of a building in one drawing file (see Figure 3.23). The advantages of this feature are many. Alignments can be studied, as well as the massing of the building, and presentation drawings are easy to create using the multistory features.

When starting a multistory drawing, it is easiest to first define the number of stories and the floor heights. You are prompted for the floor name and its elevation above the data. For each additional floor, you are prompted for the floor-to-floor height. You can specify split or partial-height floors. After you have created a floor drawing, you can copy all or part of that drawing onto other floors.

Once the multistory building has been created, you may choose the floor that you want to work on. You can leave all the other floors visible as you work, select certain floors to be visible, or display only the floor

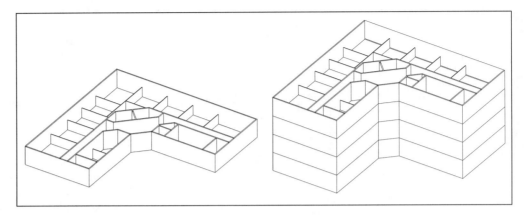

Figure 3.23 Multiple stories may be stacked in one drawing.

you are working on. The drawing can be dissected floor-by-floor and made into individual drawing files to allow for multiple drafting stations to work on the project. The individual drawing files may also be reassembled at any time to study alignments and present the multistory solution.

Symbol Insertion

Softdesk Auto-Architect has a complete selection of 2D and 3D symbols, including landscaping, automobiles, boats, playing fields, plumbing, electrical, mechanical, structural, furnishings, and even people.

Two and Three Dimensions

One of the most powerful features of Softdesk Auto-Architect is its ability to draw with either 2D or 3D symbols (see Figure 3.24). An even more powerful feature is the automatic swapping of the 2D symbols for 3D, or vice versa. You can change a working drawing into a 3D presentation drawing in minutes, automatically, and you have the option of converting the whole drawing or just parts of it.

Exterior Elevations

Softdesk Auto-Architect can create elevations (see Figure 3.25). You start with a plan that has been created with walls that have height. The software prompts you to indicate the wall that is drawn in elevation. The automatically drawn elevation can be put on the drawing you are work-

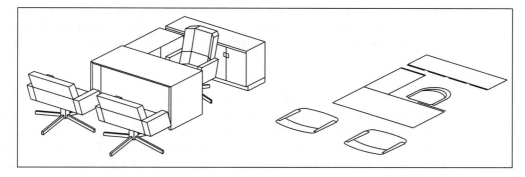

Figure 3.24 Most symbols may be drawn as either a 2D or a 3D symbol. The software will automatically convert back and forth.

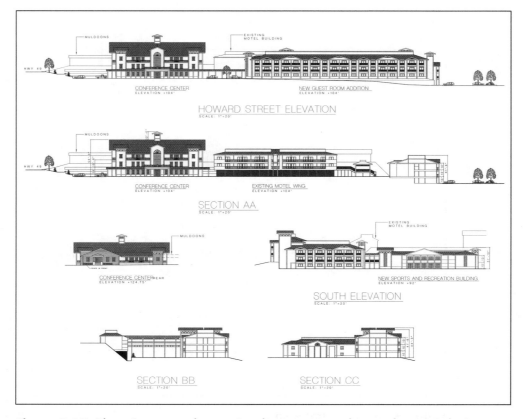

Figure 3.25 Elevations may be as simple or as complex as the user desires.

ing on or onto another drawing. You indicate the location on the sheet and the software proceeds to draw the elevation. Softdesk Auto-Architect contains detailed elevation symbols for doors, windows, and frames.

Consultants

During the design development process, consultants become involved in helping to determine the form and structure of the building (see Figure 3.26). CAD is an ideal tool to use with consultants; it increases the accuracy of the process and decreases the time required to complete the project. The first step in working with consultants is to give them the architectural drawings which they can use both for dimensional information and for backgrounds.

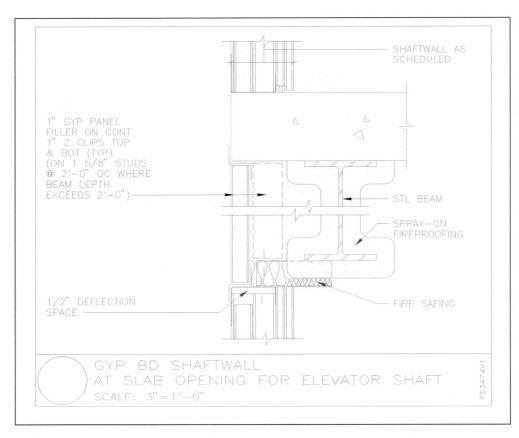

Figure 3.26 Structural detail.

The Civil Engineer

The civil engineer may have started the entire design process by giving you the CAD survey drawing. Now the architect sends the site design back to the civil engineer, who overlays the site drawing onto the civil drawings to study utilities, grades, streets, and boundaries. This additive process is very efficient compared with the redrawing process of hand drawing. Softdesk has a excellent series of civil software applications.

The Landscape Architect

The landscape architect is given both the architectural site plan as a base for the planting, irrigation, and hard-surfaces drawings, and the necessary civil engineering drawings. CAD is a fantastic tool for the landscape architect, who always has to deal with repetitive elements and presentation drawings. Softdesk Auto-Architect provides several landscape symbols.

The Structural Engineer

The software can draw steel, wood, and concrete shapes depending on your input. Dimensions are crucial to the structural engineer. Using Softdesk Auto-Architect, CAD drawings that have accurate dimensions for the shapes and their locations can be passed to the engineer. Just as with the civil engineer, the structural engineer can pull the electronic architectural drawings apart to prepare the structural backgrounds. As the structural drawings are being developed, the engineer can pass electronic drawings back to the architect; these can be laid over the architectural drawings to check for conflicts and to insert final structural elements.

The Electrical Engineer

At times the architectural drawings show the locations of electrical receptacles, as well as telephone and lighting fixtures. An extensive library of electrical symbols is included with Softdesk Auto-Architect. This information may also be used by the electrical engineer to create the base electrical drawings (see Figure 3.27). Softdesk also has specifically designed software for electrical engineers which contains hundreds of electrical symbols and automated routines, including schedule generation.

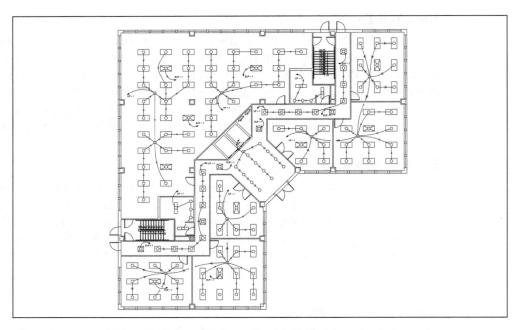

Figure 3.27 A lighting floor plan supplied by the electrical consultant.

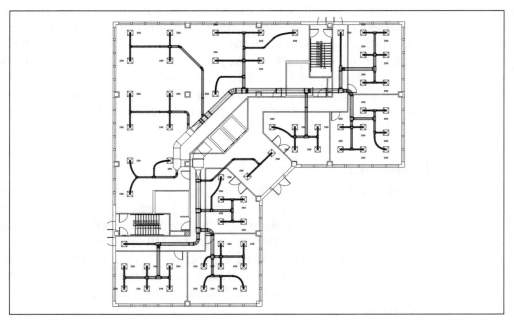

Figure 3.28 HVAC plan.

The Mechanical HVAC Engineer

Softdesk Auto-Architect contains symbols for diffusers and returns to be used in creating reflected ceiling plans. Softdesk also has software designed specifically for mechanical engineers which automates the creation of heating, ventilation, and air-conditioning (or HVAC) drawings (see Figure 3.28). Softdesk professional HVAC application has an interface with analysis software which automates the drawing operation (see Figure 3.29).

Softdesk in conjunction with the U.S. Department of Energy (DOE), Pacific Northwest Laboratory (PNL), and the University of Oregon has created an energy analysis software application that works in conjunction with Auto-Architect to calculate heat gains and heat losses for the structure you are designing. This module is free for the asking. The software is easy to use and fast. It was specifically designed to be used during the preliminary design phase to provide the designer with energy information at a time when design modifications will have tremendous influences upon the final energy efficiency of the structure.

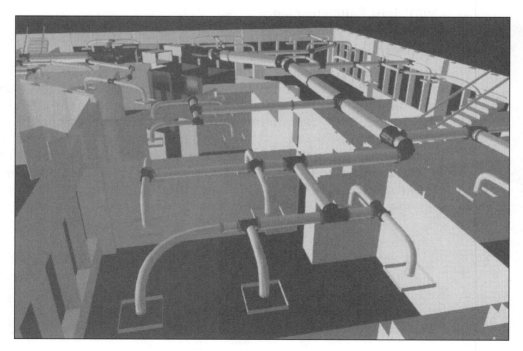

Figure 3.29 3D rendering of the HVAC system.

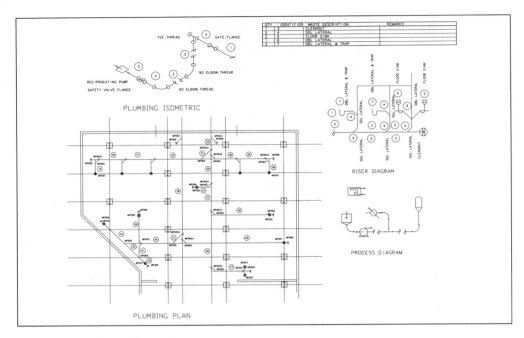

Figure 3.30 Plumbing plan.

The Mechanical-Plumbing Engineer

Softdesk Auto-Architect provides a complete set of architectural plumbing symbols. There are several automated routines for the drawing of plumbing layouts (see Figure 3.30). Toilet room drawing is simplified and automated by parametric commands that create a row of toilets and urinal stalls automatically. A similar command creates the lavatory counter and automatically inserts the desired number of lavatories. Softdesk also has a software application created specifically for mechanical engineers that can be used in designing plumbing and fire protection systems.

CHAPTER FOUR

VISUALIZATION AND PRESENTATIONS

How did you do that?

Those were the first words from the design review board after we had presented our project, using electronic presentation tools. Each of the board members—all architects—had stood before similar design review boards, knowing that the fate of months of work would be decided within the next few minutes. So, in this review their main interest had instantly moved from the project at hand to the method we had used to make the presentation.

For years, I had come to such meetings carrying rolls of colored elevations and perspectives. I would stand in front of our design, which would be pinned to the wall several feet away from the members of the review board, and even farther away from the public. The details we had worked on for hours could only be seen by close review and thus would never be appreciated from 30 feet away. Although we had always sent copies of the drawings to the board in advance, often the members wouldn't have studied the project before the meeting. In truth, even if they had studied the design, they still lacked the personal explanations

Figure 4.1 Electronic design studies are faster to create than conventional physical models or renderings.

needed to understand the concept of many architectural designs (see Figure 4.1).

In this case, I had used drawings at our previous meeting. The review board was ready to deny the project when I asked for a continuance to prepare a slide presentation. I was sure our design was good, but this would be my last chance.

This current session marked the first time I had arrived at a design review meeting with no colored drawings, only slides. This was early 1985 and electronic presentations were new.

The presentation easily convinced the review board to accept our design, not because we had changed it, but because this electronic presentation more clearly indicated the many facets of our project, the details, and how the project would fit into the neighborhood.

In the past, if the neighbors could not understand how the project would specifically affect them, they would give lukewarm acceptance or

Figure 4.2 Electronic 3D models may be easily viewed from any location.

would oppose it. Today, with CAD, we can show them how our project will impact on their neighborhood, often gaining them as our allies in the process. Better than ever, we can now show design review boards and other city commissions more clearly how projects will affect the visual environment. The result is more approvals and that is very good for business. It is becoming harder and harder to get projects approved, but CAD, electronic photo creations, electronic renderings, and animations are tools that will definitely help with the task.

I showed the design review board how I had created the slide presentation with video capture software. While these techniques are no longer new, such presentations are still the exception. In the future, video presentations will become standard. The rest of this chapter explores the visualization and presentation possibilities available through your computer. These tools will continue to grow in capability and usefulness and will be a major part of all architects' work (see Figure 4.2).

Overview

CAD is a powerful tool that can be used in all phases of the architect's work. The first versions of architectural CAD software were meant to be working drawing and drafting products. As the technology improved over the years, more features were added. Today, Auto-Architect continues to be a strong drafting package, but it's now also a powerful visualization and presentation product. The early CAD users tended to be the draftspeople, but now CAD is also a design and presentation tool, with the ability to automatically create 3D geometry and the ability to easily view the design.

Presentations

At several steps along the design process it is necessary to present the design ideas and concepts for review by the client and design review boards. The better the imaging is, the better the reviewer will understand the architect's intentions (see Figures 4.3 and 4.4).

In non-CAD offices, the architect draws thumbnail perspectives for early presentations to a client. Later, the architect draws more formal perspectives—sometimes plain line drawings, sometimes colored. Site plans, floor plans, and elevations are colored to show texture, colors, and shadow patterns (see Figures 4.5 and 4.6).

These drawings are intended first to convince the designer that the design is correct, then to show the client that it is appropriate for the project. Often the result of such client presentations is design modification, then another presentation. It has always seemed strange to see a large portion of the office staff spending their day coloring drawings, yet it is crucial that the client understand the project.

As a hand-drawn project proceeds, it is common to hire someone to do a professional rendering. Such drawings may be in pencil or pen, although most often they are in watercolor. The professional rendering shows the design, materials, and character of the project. But, if the design is changed or if a change is required by a design review board, that hand-drawn perspective becomes out-of-date and often is rendered unusable.

Figure 4.3 Hand sketch.

Figure 4.4 Study from a 3D model base sketch.

Figure 4.5 Architect's rendering based on wireframe model.

Figure 4.6 Professional rendering based on a 3D model.

Perspectives

The perspective is the traditional drawing that best represents the proposed design. The drawing can take on a multitude of representations, from the quick thumbnail sketch to the line drawing to the rendered perspective to, finally, the colored perspective drawing. Before CAD, the process of mechanically creating the accurate perspective was laborious. Often, once the layout was completed, the designer would realize that the view from another location was better and the process would begin all over again.

CAD has greatly simplified this process of creating the perspective. After the 3D geometry has been created, the perspective is generated in a matter of seconds. If the location isn't right, it is simple and equally quick to select another location and flip the new perspective up on the screen. You can look at the perspective as a wire frame, a wire frame with the hidden lines removed, a simply shaded rendering, or a sophisticated shaded rendering (see Figures 4.7 and 4.8).

The perspectives can be used as the equivalent of thumbnail sketches or they can be used as presentation perspectives. Many architects use the CAD perspective as a base drawing for their hand-drawn perspective, a process that saves hours of work that would have been required for a mechanical layout.

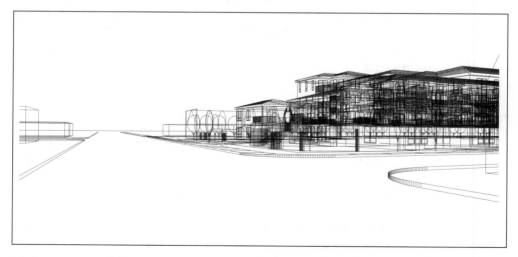

Figure 4.7 Models with lines shown allow the designer to study massing.

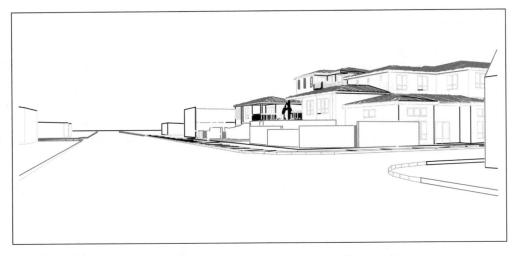

Figure 4.8 Models with hidden lines removed provide excellent representations of the design.

The View Commands

When you are designing with Auto-Architect you have access to several commands—found in Softdesk Core under the heading View—that simplify the creation of quick perspective studies and animations. These View commands let you pick a point you want to look toward, then a point you'd like to look from; Automatically, the perspective jumps into view on the screen (see Figure 4.9) You are able to set the height of the camera, the height of the target point, the lens of the camera, and much more as you will see in the following discussions.

The WALK Command

To evaluate the design during the design process, you will often want to study several views. The WALK command automatically displays step-by-step views along a straight line or a polyline (see Figure 4.10). The camera can be set to stay fixed upon an object to change target points as the camera moves along the path. The perspective views can either display or remove hidden lines. You may also have each step, or frame, shaded or rendered (a more accurate form of shading). You determine the number of steps created; the more steps, the smoother the animation.

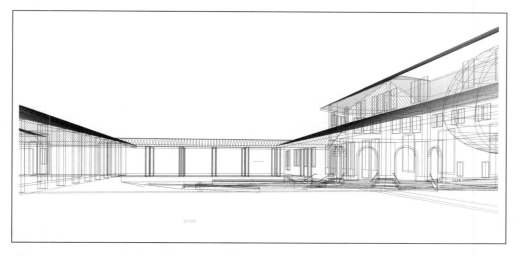

Figure 4.9 Auto-Architect includes commands to allow users to easily generate perspective views of the model.

Depending on the complexity of the drawing, this automatic process may take several minutes or several hours. You can also indicate that you want to create a script file, which you can then play back to study the design. With this process, you can study massing and space.

In addition to following a straight line or a polyline you can also circle around an object. The camera always looks toward the target point. For interior perspectives, draw a small circle around the target location and you will end up with an impressive interior animation. For the exterior draw a circle around the building with the target at the center. Once again, you determine the number of steps or viewpoints that will be taken. You can easily create an impressive basic animation. The playback speed will be dependent upon the speed of your computer and will vary from one view every second to several views per second. (Smooth motion animation takes 30 frames per second.)

AutoShade®

Autodesk's AutoShade is a software color shading product that imports 3D geometry from an AutoCAD drawing and shades an image that appears in perspective view. AutoShade is relatively easy to use and produces images that will help you and your client better understand the design (see Figure 4.11).

Figure 4.10 The software will automatically generate a walkaround the model.

AutoCAD Animator®

You can import AutoCAD AutoShade drawings into Animator, which sequentially replays the AutoShade images, animating your design presentation. In addition to the playback, AutoShade has many tools for the creation of impressive presentations using text and movement. The introduction of Autodesk 3D Studio, with substantially higher quality images, provides more appropriate tools for the creation of architectural animations.

Figure 4.11 The model may be further enhanced with rendering software.

Autodesk 3D Studio

3D Studio is a rendering and animation software application that lets you put together photorealistic and dynamic presentations. The renderings can be based on the geometry produced by Auto-Architect, Auto-CAD, or geometry created using 3D Studio. The interface has been designed to allow ease of use.

This software creates spectacular renderings and animations for your design studies and client presentations (see Figure 4.12). With 3D Studio you may texture map surfaces, show reflections, cast shadows, light, and even spotlight an image. You may view the model from any location. There are software routines available for fog, fire, and water reflections to make your renderings and animations realistic.

The primary use of 3D Studio is to animate your design presentations. Simply indicate the path through the space and the software will automatically step along the path, creating a photorealistic rendering for every thirtieth of a second. You can have the camera rotate and tilt as it

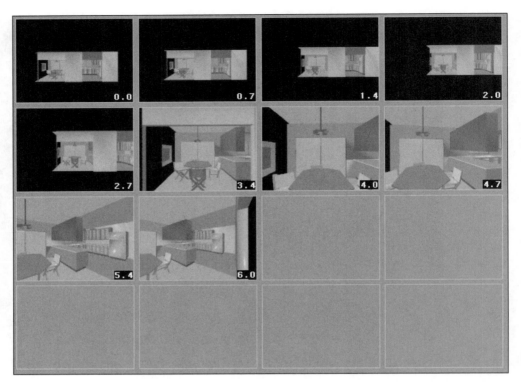

Figure 4.12 The rendered model may be animated for a spectacular presentation.

follows the path and you change the lens aperture. When the automatic process ends, you can play back the animations. The creation of a single photorealistic rendering may take several minutes, so just one second of animation may take several hours to create. The playback speed of the animation, once again, depends upon the speed of your computer. Unless the animation is very simple, most computers cannot yet play back animations at the 30 frames per second that is necessary for smooth motion. To see the animation at 30 frames per second it will most likely be necessary to transfer the images to video tape or a computer that has been specifically configured with hardware and software designed to capture and play back animations.

With 3D Studio you may animate objects within animation: Doors can open; automobiles can move; and the assembly of parts can be demonstrated. Using this feature, you can represent the reality of the design, study the spaces, study textures, and move yourself and objects within the spaces. The quality is very good and the results are very professional and spectacular if you take your time.

I recommend that every designer learn to master 3D studio; certainly every student should learn to master 3D studio.

Video Capture

As you work with AutoCAD, you are dealing with vector-based drawings. When a line is drawn from one point in space that has exact coordinates to another point that has yet another set of exact coordinates, these exact locations are recorded in the database. The coordinates are phrased as numerical locations so that you can summon up the exact length, angle, and slope of any line.

When you look at an AutoCAD drawing, the software builds the lines from the database. Therefore, it can be viewed from any location in space. Clearly, however, as the drawing becomes more complicated—such as one tree, elaborating into a forest—the amount of information that the software must maintain and that the computer must manipulate becomes ever greater, eventually exceeding the capacity of present-day computers.

This overload problem is recognized by software designers. Thus, they have developed another approach to dealing with computer graphics that is not based on vectors or on a numerical database. This system is similar to television. At any given moment on your television or monitor, thousands of dots, or pixels, display a color. The computer or television signal indicates which dots will be which color. Images created by this approach are known as *raster* images. Raster images are much simpler to store and display. Raster images are not based upon geometry, so you cannot accurately measure the distance between two points as you can on a vector-based drawing (see Figure 4.13).

The image you see has been predetermined by camera location. You can't, in short, summon a video (raster) image onto a monitor screen showing the east side of a building, then tell the computer to show you the building from a point 50 feet to the right unless someone has already taken a picture from 50 feet to the right. (With vector-based graphics, though, the computer has absorbed the entire database of the building, so it can grant you this request.)

The advantage of raster images is that they can handle the picture of the tree or the forest. Every picture is of equal complexity in the raster

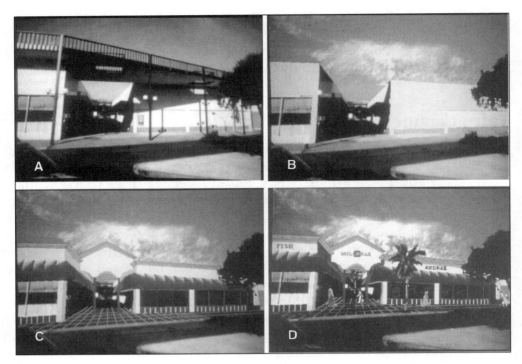

Figure 4.13 A: Existing building. B: Electronically cut away unwanted
sections of existing building and addition of background sky.
C: Electronically add proposed architectural elements.
D: Electronically add people and signage.

system. It simply lights up the dots on the monitor screen with the correct colors. Raster graphics is used on programs with the headings of
"paint" and "video capture." If raster images are made to show animation, such as a video, they present the same problems to the computer as
trying to move through the 3D model of the vector system or playing
back the animations. Depending upon the computer, the display hardware, and the file format of the video, you may or may not be able to
view the video at full monitor size and at the full 30 frames per second
through your computer.

Let's create a raster image to demonstrate how it works. With a paint
package, you can create a foreground using a green base color and a
background using a blue and, presto—you have a field with a blue sky.
Let's say your design is for a schoolhouse building. You can locate a red

square on the horizon line, put a red triangle on top of the red square, and you have a little red schoolhouse. You can add text with a yellow line to label your drawing. If you like, you can now go in and modify individual dots.

Depending on your skill and time, you can make the field look just like grass, dot the sky with beautiful white clouds, and give your schoolhouse clapboard siding, windows, doors, and even shadows. Although this is possible, only artists can really use the paint package in this manner.

Using the same example, you can take the first drawing of the schoolhouse with the blue sky and green grass and easily modify the image with video pictures. You can go outside with a video camera and take a picture of the sky, a grass field, and a red schoolhouse; then you cut in the real pictures.

If you now want to show your design but the project is not yet built, you have several options. You can build a model or make a sketch and take a video image of that model or sketch, then cut this image into the image of the sky or field. Once the image is in the drawing, you can color, tint, or even add other images. Maybe your schoolhouse isn't out in the country but in an urban setting. This is easy to handle: Simply go to the site and photograph it from the angle at which you want to show your building.

There is, in fact, an easier approach than building a physical model or drawing a sketch of the school: Create the drawings of the building with Auto-Architect. Photograph the site and transfer the image to the video capture software. Pinpoint the view on your CAD drawing and use the View command to display a perspective view. Capture this line drawing and cut it into the background drawing; use the paint program to color the perspective.

Models

This chapter has discussed electronic images, but CAD can also provide you with physical models. The traditional model sometimes has advantages over the rendering or animation, because it can be studied from millions of vantage points by many people and can be used to great advantage for presentations and sales. Physical models have an aspect of liveliness and life that is hard to reproduce in electronic models.

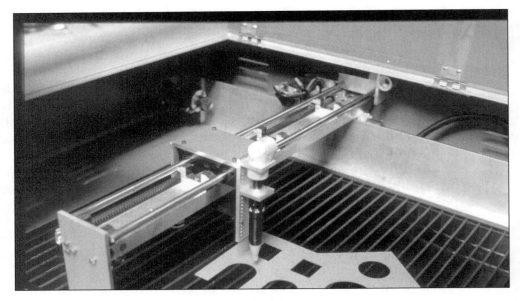

Figure 4.14 Laser cutter creating model piece.

Figure 4.15 The finished model.

With CAD drawings, you no longer need to cut model pieces by hand. The CAD drawing can be used to drive a laser that cuts out the entire model from illustration board or from Plexiglas (see Figure 4.14). Pieces can be cut out with very fine detail. The laser power can be reduced and then used to etch texture on the surface of the material. The laser cutter moves at a rate of several inches per second and can quickly cut out a model (see Figure 4.15).

CAD and Visualization

Electronic data forms the foundation for spectacular presentations. The use of animation by architects will increase the quality of building design more than any other single CAD tool. Designers now can pretest their designs; the clients can preview the designs and provide more meaningful critiques; and review agencies can make more informed decisions because they have more graphical information.

CHAPTER FIVE

CONTRACT DOCUMENTS

CAD is the ultimate overlay drafting system.

With CAD you start the contract document phase with a running start.

In the hand-drawn architecture practice, the contract document phase started with a redrawing to reflect the final decisions made in the design development phase. If the contract document phase did not start with new drawings, you often had to erase almost as much as you drew. With CAD, you can use the ERASE, STRETCH, TRIM, ROTATE, MOVE, and COPY commands to modify the design development drawings in order to start the contract document phase. Thus, much of the drawing is already done by the time you begin the contract document work.

The purpose of the contract document phase is to generate the drawings, schedules, and specifications that provide the information necessary for building departments to check the drawings and for contractors to bid and eventually construct the project. The design development drawings show design, materials, and spatial relationships; the contract documents add dimensions, notes, specifications, and details.

Now schedules are created for doors, windows, finishes, hardware, plumbing, lighting, beams, columns, reinforcing bars, landscaping materials, duct work, and many other items. The specifications describe in minute detail both the materials and the process to be used in supplying, storing, assembling, and applying the materials.

Dimensions

Dimensioning the drawing is simple and accurate with CAD. The Auto-CAD OSNAP commands accurately locate the dimension points. AutoCAD gives you the choice of a running dimension or repetitive dimensions from the same base point. Dimensions can also be made at an angle. AutoCAD has associative dimensioning, which means that if you STRETCH the length of a room and if you have included the actual dimension text in the window of the items to be STRETCHed, the dimension is automatically recalculated and the new text displayed.

Softdesk Auto-Architect has several features to make dimensioning the drawings very efficient. You can set to dimension to face of wall or centerline and the software will automatically follow your instructions. Select a point on a wall then move to another wall and the software will automatically draw in the leader lines, the dimension line, the arrow heads (or tick marks), and the dimension. Pick the next wall and the process is repeated. Even this process can be automated; you can set the software to automatically dimension, in which case the software will pick logical points within the drawing to dimension.

You have the option of setting the design of the tick mark and the location of the dimension text. Before AutoCAD puts the dimension into the drawing, you are given the chance to override the calculated dimension. However, never override the calculated dimension without the clear understanding that you could be defeating the inherent accuracy of the CAD drawing. I have talked with several contractors that have learned to rely on the accuracy of CAD drawings, a confidence that is destroyed when a draftsperson has overridden a dimension without making all the necessary following corrections.

Notes

There are several different recommendations on the best way to annotate the drawings. Some architects put their notes next to the object being noted and then point to the object with a leader line with an arrowhead. Other architects use numbers or alphabet letters near the object and again use an arrow to point to the object; then they organize the notes in one location on the drawing.

In a variation of this latter keynoting technique, the note near the object uses a specification number that refers to standard notes found both on the drawing and in a standard notebook. The notes are numbered to correspond to the CSI format and are also consistent with the numbering used in the specifications.

All of these forms of notation are possible with Softdesk Auto-Architect. Notes can easily be typed and placed near the object (see Figure 5.1). The command prompts you for the start and end points of the pointer line and automatically places an arrowhead at the end. If you want to use numerical or alphabetic notes, you are prompted to give the letter or number, then the pointer line and the arrowhead locations.

At times, you may want to use standard notes that are typical for your office. It wastes time to type these out for every project or every sheet. Softdesk Core has a Text In and Text Out feature that lets text be brought into the drawing from an outside text file. This feature is extremely useful, as you also can take text out of the drawing, modify the text using a text editor, and then bring the text back into the drawing.

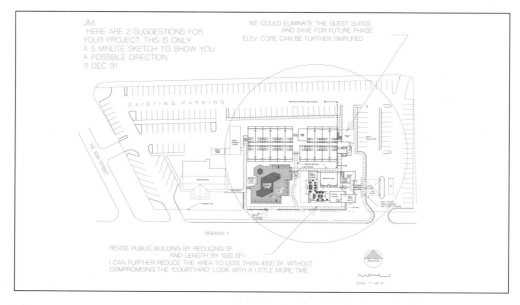

Figure 5.1 Site plan with client's electronic design review notes.

Using Data Link (found in Softdesk Productivity Tools) you may dynamically link the note to the objects in the drawing. After creating the link, when you select a note the objects in the drawing connected to it will be highlighted. Also, if you use Data Link to create your note table, the table will automatically be regenerated with the note inserted in the correct position when you add a new note.

Schedules and Attributes

The single most powerful feature of CAD is not its ability to draw lines, but its ability to attach attributes, or specifications, to an object in the drawing. As you work, you are creating both graphic and alphanumeric databases. You are also creating schedules for doors, windows, lighting fixtures, plumbing fixtures, and many other building components (see Figure 5.2). These alphanumeric data can be extracted from the drawing and collected into a database or a text file or even diffused back into the drawing and plotted out on the drawing sheet.

In the coming years, the database aspect of CAD will flex more and more muscle. Some Softdesk products already let you modify the data-

Qty	Description	Manufacturer	Part Number	Lamp Type
4	FL. FIXT. – 1X4	LITHUANIA	1PM2-2CF30-12	F208X/SPX32
15	FL. FIXT. – 2X2	LITHUANIA	2PM4-2CF40-26	F40BX/SPX35
5	FL. FIXT. – 2X2 EM	LITHUANIA	2PM6-4CF60-18	F408X/SPX45
85	FL. FIXT. – 2X4	LITHUANIA	2PM3-2CF40-16	F40BX/SPX35
10	FL. FIXT. – 2X4 EM	LITHUANIA	2PM4-3DF40-20	F40BX/SP63A
11	INCAND. FIXT. – CLG. MT	HIGHTECH	28401	15W A15
6	INCAND. FIXT. – WALL MT	WIEGHTOLIER	7052	(1)100WT4 CLR LMP

2X2 Standard Fluorescent Fixture — Junction Box – Ceiling Mount
2X4 Standard Fluorescent Fixture — Panelboard – Flush Mount
1X4 Standard Fluorescent Fixture — Double Conduit Tick Mark
2X2 Emergency Fluorescent Fixture — Single Conduit Tick Mark with Neutral
2X4 Emergency Fluorescent Fixture — Double Conduit Tick Mark with Neutral
Ceiling Incandescent Fixture — Double Conduit Tick Mark with Switch Leg
Wall Incandescent Fixture

Figure 5.2 A light fixture schedule.

base and redraw automatically with the database changes now incorporated into the drawing.

With Softdesk Auto-Architect, several symbols have preassigned attributes that you may elect to have prompted. You can insert a symbol and (1) not be prompted for attributes, (2) be prompted for some attributes, or (3) be prompted for all the preassigned attributes. You can create symbols and assign the attributes that you want to associate with that symbol.

You may also modify the attribute prompts and add your own. For example, you can insert a door by indicating only the width and the height, if the 3D toggle is turned on. You can also have the software prompt you for the door number or designation, or you can switch on all the attributes and be prompted for the door type, finish, fire rating, glass type, frame type, frame finish, hardware group, and cost. By making your selection from the settings menu, you control which prompts are requested.

With Softdesk Auto-Architect, you can choose to be prompted for specification information when you insert doors, windows, plumbing fixtures, structural elements, lighting fixtures, appliances, and furnishings. This information can be automatically arranged into a schedule by Softdesk Auto-Architect and printed on notebook paper or plotted onto the drawing.

Details

Softdesk Auto-Architect is primarily designed to create plans, elevations, and sections. Other Softdesk applications may be used to create complete sets of details. Softdesk Structural contains hundreds of components for structural and architectural detailing, including the complete AISC database, wood members, reinforcing steel, and other components.

Softdesk Details is designed to create architectural details by selecting and arranging components; it contains thousands of components that you can select and arrange into details. Attached to each are CSI numbers, standard notes, and information about the component (see Figure 5.3).

Cover Sheet

Softdesk Auto-Architect offers several features that help you compose and fill in the information that is found on a cover sheet. The software

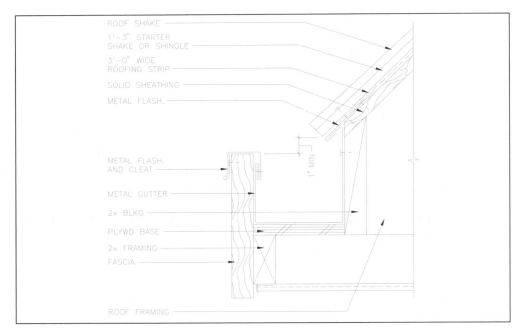

Figure 5.3 Eave with concealed gutter, and wood shakes.

includes box makers that can be used to include location maps, city information, or consultant names. One box is designed to automate your creation of the list of drawings.

The abbreviation feature automatically scans all the drawings in the set for abbreviations, then builds an abbreviation schedule. The Symbol maker performs the same function, looking for all the symbols used in the set and automatically generating a symbol schedule. Wall legends are automatically created by the software searching the drawings and generating a schedule. These automated routines tremendously increase the draftsperson's productivity and accuracy.

Site Plans

The site plan is brought into the contract document phase full of information from the previous phases. Now you add notes on slopes for drainage, utility information, construction phasing information, and references to details. Softdesk's full line of civil applications is available for professionals doing this type of work (see Figure 5.4).

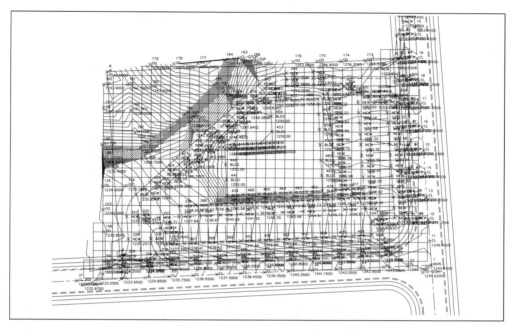

Figure 5.4 Topographic drawing done with civil applications.

Roof Plans

I have spent days working on the roof plans of complicated designs prior to the use of CAD. Using the automated roof routines during the design development phase will have taught you that roofs may be specified and created in a matter of moments. The software draws both the 2D representation of the specified roof as well as the full 3D layout (see Figure 5.5). In the contract document phase, you add notes on material, slopes, and detail designations. You also indicate the location for penetrations and any mechanical equipment mounted on the rooftop.

Floor Plans

In addition to notes, detail designations, and dimensions, you can add hatching to the walls to differentiate wall types in the contract phase. The wall-hatching function included with the software is quite simple to use. If you add a window, door, or opening to a wall that has been

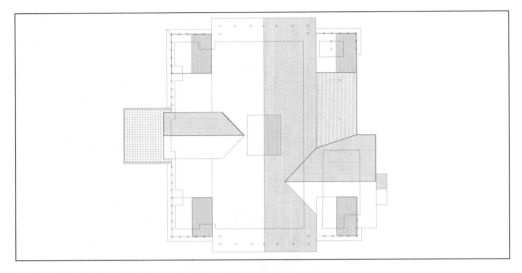

Figure 5.5 Design development roof plan.

hatched, the software will automatically take out the hatching at the location of the opening.

Sometimes one section of the plan has considerable detail (see Figure 5.6), but the drawing scale doesn't let you clearly indicate this detail. In this case, you need to draw the particular area at a larger scale. With CAD, the process is easy because all you do is copy the designated area and increase its size. AutoCAD allows you to combine drawings of various scales on the same sheet.

Exterior and Interior Elevations

Softdesk Auto-Architect can create elevations automatically from the plans and the three-dimensional information on wall heights, door and window locations, and even door and window designs. The elevations are therefore created almost automatically based on the plans that you have drawn (see Figure 5.7).

Sections

Just as you could designate the information to be included in the exterior and interior elevations, you can also indicate a section line through

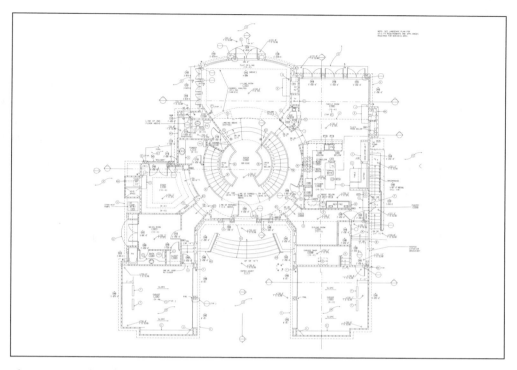

Figure 5.6 The drawing progresses from the preliminary design to design development to contract documents.

Figure 5.7 Exterior elevation.

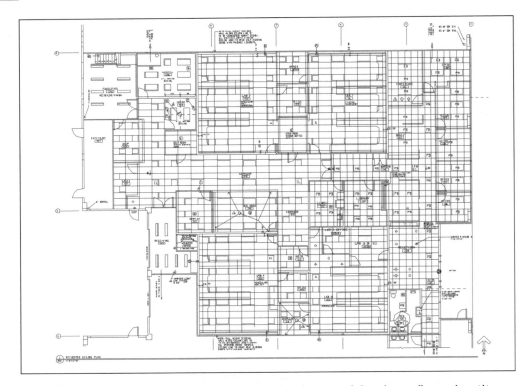

Figure 5.8 The floor plan drawing is the background for the reflected ceiling drawing.

the drawing. AutoCAD and the Softdesk software then create a section of your design. As with the elevation routines, you indicate where the section is to be drawn, the layers to be included, and the direction of the cut; the section is then drawn automatically. You can create *clipping* boundaries that limit the information shown to only those objects found within the boundary.

Reflected Ceiling Plans

Softdesk Auto-Architect has a complete set of functions to automate the creation of reflected ceiling plans. Use the floor plan to create the background drawing (see Figure 5.8). The ceiling grid function can insert a grid ceiling into a room of any size and at any angle. The software also provides symbols for light fixtures, air supplies, and returns.

CHAPTER SIX

FACILITIES MANAGEMENT

Combining CAD and the database created from the CAD drawings with facilities management software is one of the best and most intensive uses of automation that will flourish in the coming years.

Background

The cost of the building design and construction—that cost about which all designers and owners spend so much time worrying—is less than 10 percent of the cost of operating the building over a 40 year life span. Facilities management is, in fact, one of the major operations of business.

Most companies have much of their capital tied up in buildings they own or rent. Equipment and furnishings add another major investment to their balance sheets. Yet most companies today do not know how much space they rent or own, where the people sit, how much equipment they own, where it is, or when it must be maintained. They should know this information.

The term *facilities management* is a catchall phrase that has as many definitions as there are facilities. To the architect, it means area calculations, department layouts, employee locations, and equipment inventories. To the electrical engineer, it means dealing with energy use and equipment maintenance. To the mechanical engineer, it denotes the operation of the facility, energy usage, repairs, and preventive maintenance. To the owner of the building, it means repainting, leasing information, taxes, and depreciation. To the tenant, it means employees, equipment and furnishings, growth and shrinkage, telecommunications systems, and everything connected with the tenant's operations.

Facilities management is the collection, storage, and manipulation of data about the physical facilities, the existing conditions, and changes expected in the future. The quantity of data needed is staggering and it must be coordinated well among the various players. Surprisingly, at the end of construction, everything about the structure is known by only a relatively few people. For example, the architect and the contractors truly know the facility, but in traditional practice, they now roll up the drawings and move on to their next projects.

At this point, the facilities manager unrolls the drawing, opens the specifications and equipment manuals, and sets out to manage the facility, hoping that he or she doesn't miss anything big. The tenant moves in and adds walls, requiring modifications to the electrical and mechanical systems. Sometimes these changes are noted; sometimes not. Over time, remodeling changes even the changes and often all knowledge of what is owned and how it works is lost.

The area requirements, furnishings, and equipment of the tenant often follow much the same twisty path. Departments overflow beyond their original boundaries, others shrink, and soon the original areas devoted to specific departments become a mystery. Equipment and furnishings are bought, need maintenance, or break; equipment is hauled off; new equipment is leased or purchased; and soon accurate information is no longer available.

Accurate knowledge of what is owned, however, is crucial for management decisions and the economic operation of the company. I know of several firms that purchased vast quantities of furnishings, only to later find out that they already had warehouses full of furnishings stashed away; others have rented space only to find out that they already had space or that another department was being reduced and a month later the space would have been available.

Not only are there many definitions of facilities management, but there are equally as many different approaches as to whom should be in charge of the department. In some companies, it is managed by the accounting department; in others, it is managed by the database expert; in still others, it is managed by someone familiar with construction or architecture.

No matter what the background of the manager, each one is looking for a better way to perform his or her responsibilities. Here CAD is proving to be very helpful indeed.

Facilities Management and CAD

The one thread that ties the entire facilities management process together is the need to collect, store, and manipulate data. The computer is good at storing and manipulating data, while CAD is good at collecting graphic data. Before CAD, graphic information belonged to the world of the draftsperson, but with CAD, this is no longer true. CAD is easy to use when set up properly, and graphic information is often easier to understand than textual information.

Adjacency Requirements

The first step in facility design is to list the required spaces, then organize them with the optimum adjacency relationships. CAD can help in this process in a number of ways. Several software products available allow you to create an adjacency matrix, then sort the spaces into an optimum layout. An *adjacency matrix* is a layout or map of what must or must not be adjacent to something else. For example, some codes require that kitchens and bathrooms be separated by halls. At a basic level you can use the CIRCLE command to create bubbles and label them. Colors can be assigned to represent different uses. You can use the SPACE to WALL commands of the Softdesk Auto-Architect application to accurately create bubbles of the correct size (see Figure 6.1).

Stacking and Blocking

The term *stacking* refers to the layout of the spaces on several floors of a multi-floor building. The optimum layout uses each floor to maximum efficiency while putting the uses or departments in the best places. Most designers do this by hand, although several software applications can automate the process. Interviews with designers and facilities managers make clear that the optimum product has not yet reached the market. A desirable one would put the departments on the appropriate floor based on adjacency needs, the projected growth of the use or department, and its relationship to the elevators.

The term *blocking* refers to the layout of spaces on a given floor based on adjacency requirements. Most designers still do this process manually. However, several software programs automate the process. The better programs take into account the layout of the building and the core space. In the coming years, great advances in blocking programs will decrease the time necessary for blocking design.

Attributes

Today, thousands of Softdesk users are entering facilities information into the CAD system. This ability to add attributes to items in the CAD drawing is the basis of CAD facilities management. As a symbol is inserted into the system, you may also add textual information to the symbol, either automatically or manually.

If the system has been programmed to add information automatically, the attributes or specifications are added to the database. For instance, if the symbol is a specific chair and the attributes are already attached to the symbol, the database adds the chair information automatically every time you put the chair into the drawing.

You can also insert a generic chair, then preset the software to prompt you for information about it. For example, when you insert a chair and have turned on the attribute prompting, Softdesk Auto-Architect asks you to enter information on the manufacturer, model, size, color, and several other items about the chair. You have the option of answering all the questions or only those that interest you, or you can modify the prompts to ask only the questions of interest. You can search either the database or the drawing. With the chair example, you can either search the database or you can select the chair in the drawing and display the attributes on the monitor screen.

Users can insert any imaginable object into drawings and attributes to these symbols. On walls, you can indicate the assembly, finishes, and even paint colors or mixing formulas. Ceilings can carry information about the mounting height, assembly, and finishes. Floors can include

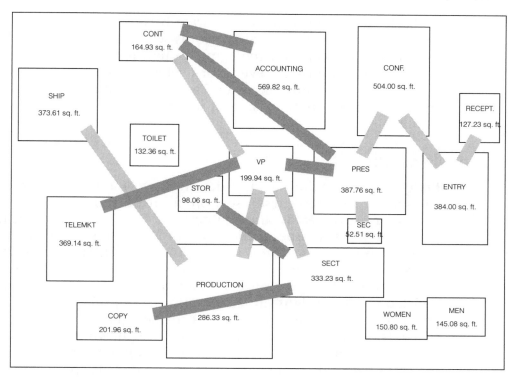

Figure 6.1 Adjacency diagram.

information about the area of the space and finishes. Symbols for structural, plumbing, lighting, furnishings, equipment, electrical, and mechanical elements are all included in Softdesk applications and you can easily add additional unique symbols.

Area Calculations

One of the major reasons for using CAD to manage facilities is its ability to accurately calculate areas. Throughout my architectural career before CAD, we used to have several employees each calculate the area of the project building, then average the results to get the information we put on the drawings. To make matters even worse, areas must be calculated differently for (1) the building department, (2) the planning department, (3) the contractor, and (4) leasing.

Each calculation must be accurate because errors can have terrible results. I've talked to several landlords who have been startled to learn that they have been undercharging on rent for years because of inaccurate area calculations; it's even worse when the tenant discovers that he or she has overpaid for years. In large buildings area errors have amounted to tens of thousands of square feet.

Standard Facilities

Many facilities managers and designers work on projects that have a well-defined scope. These users often create standard facilities documents for plans, details, and equipment. Many projects can be modified slightly to meet site-specific details without making major changes.

In such cases, the AutoCAD STRETCH and TRIM commands may be all that's needed. Companies that have standardized retail stores are logical users of CAD and realize substantial savings. Standardized kitchen and laboratory designs are also logical CAD projects. With attributes attached to equipment, it is easy to make equipment changes; related schedules are automatically created from the drawings.

AutoCAD also allows sophisticated programming that can create drawings with minimal or no drawing input. This approach is ideal for an employee who is not trained in drafting. Software has also been written that automatically creates plans and elevations, and even assembles details based on a question-and-answer sheet.

Facilities managers who work with repetitive projects can now get graphic information without needing a draftsperson to enter and modify the information. With automated applications, the attributes attached to symbols in the drawing can be modified by changing the database table, with the resulting changes made in the drawings.

In the area of facilities management, spectacular applications are about to step over the threshold. These software applications are already providing new opportunities for professionals. By creating your drawings, schedules, and specifications electronically, you will have the foundation of information that will allow you to be involved with the management of your creations.

CHAPTER SEVEN

ZOOMING IN ON THE FUTURE OF CAD

We have just begun to see the changes that are being brought into our lives by the PC workstation and CAD. The designing, building, and management process has traditionally been a fragmented process filled with hundreds of players working with bits of information. Sometimes the information is correctly passed from one player to the next, but, more often, it has to be rediscovered by each person as he or she needs it.

For example, a client may ask for a certain size window in a room and the architect draws that window. The mechanical engineer later measures the window and looks up the type of glass to determine the heat gain. An electrical engineer measures the window and looks up the type of glass to determine the contribution from natural lighting and the artificial lighting necessary in the room. The structural engineer repeats the process to calculate the weight of the window on the building frame and the wind load on the window. The contractor measures the window and looks up the type of frame and the type of glass to estimate the cost for the bid.

Later, the fabricator repeats the process to manufacture the window and to cut the glass. At the job, the carpenter looks for the window schedule for the size of the rough opening and, because he or she has had past bad experiences with schedule accuracy, also checks the window size with the manufacturer. Finally, after the window is installed, the blind installer visits the site and measures the window before making the blinds. If the window ever breaks, the glass installer drives out to measure the window to cut the new glass.

Repeat this process—or a similar one—for each and every item in a building and you have an accurate picture of the inefficiencies associated with traditional non-CAD design, construction, and facilities management. Imagine the cost savings of a reliable storage location for the accurate information about the window and all the rest of the building parts. That's what CAD offers.

Before CAD, these cost savings were unattainable because the data storage contained only alphanumeric information and not graphic information, which is necessary to indicate location, exposure, geometry, and relationships to other elements. Today, we are just at the beginning of database developments. The bad news is stepping-stones are still being placed on the path. The good news is that we can use parts of the path as soon as they are completed.

In the near future, a master database will be ready to be filled in as statistical or graphical information is added. There is a proper location for every bit of information, just as if the CAD program were an electronic file cabinet. Once that information is put in, you will be able to access and update it throughout the entire design, construction, and management process. The amount of control you will gain will be enormous; the quantitative gains will be so great that we will truly be moving into a new era.

Architects often ask me what their future holds in this digital era. Will the electronic tools make it so easy to design and draw that business owners, contractors, and homeowners will replace the profession? While this is certainly possible if architects do not grasp the tools and the opportunity, I seriously doubt if the profession is in jeopardy. In fact, the digital era will expand the opportunities for architects while reducing much of the drudgery and fear of errors and omissions. We are in a time of tremendous change. If you are not changing—no matter if you are a student, a school, an architect, or a draftsperson—you should be concerned for your future. Read on!

Into the Time Machine

When I entered the University of California in 1962 to begin my education in architecture, the computer and the automation of the architectural design and drafting process were not even remote concerns. Architecture had been practiced virtually unchanged for thousands of years. I knew I had much to learn about design, color, textures, materials, manufacturers' products, engineering, drawing and drafting, and the profession of architecture. Clearly, it was a profession of both creative ability and experience.

Around 1965, several of my classmates started taking computer classes. I saw them writing routines and transferring their work to cardboard punch cards that they would take to the computer center; they would hand their cards through a window so that the operator could run their programs. In 1965, however, computers still had no place in my study of architecture.

Less then 29 years later, the PC provided the catalyst for the revolutionary change that is now taking place in the practice of architecture. The profession will never be the same. Architectural education will change in the near future; your practice, if it has not already started to change, will certainly be altered in the next few years. The changes will be for the better and the changes will be dramatic.

While writing this chapter, the main question I asked myself was, "How far into the future should I look?" Obviously, 25 years from now, the computer will have caused changes so revolutionary that they are impossible to predict. Twenty-five years is thus too far forward to have any real meaning today. Also, who will remember then if I was right or wrong? As recently as 1992, a 10-year projection would have been my choice, but some events that I thought would not occur for several more years have already touched down! The future is flying toward us even faster than I had ever imagined, so this chapter looks only four years into the future, to the year 2000.

As noted, architecture is a profession that requires creative ability, knowledge, and experience. The PC gives you tools to improve in these areas. So far, this book has followed the design process and the uses of PCs and PC software available today. This chapter now looks at the hardware and software that will be available by the year 2000 and at the changes they will make in the education and practice of the architect.

Education

Education of the architect faces a great challenge and an even greater opportunity. Architectural education has remained static for hundreds of years, that is until the last few years. Curriculum has started to change with the realization that the architect must be much better versed in areas such as environmental concerns, design and construction technology, and, of course, CAD and computers. The universities teaching architecture have been painfully and unfortunately slow to change, but they are changing.

The future will find every student with a computer that he or she has purchased. The schools will be responsible for the specialty software, plotters, printers, and the infrastructure. Schools will be completely networked. Multimedia rooms will be provided to allow for spectacular presentations.

The curriculums will be modified to eliminate courses that are no longer necessary. Other classes will be combined and reworked to allow for the addition of new classes. Time will be saved in design classes as students no longer need to spend nights on end hand-coloring, drawing trees and automobiles, tracing city maps, and making topography drawings. The new classes will include multimedia, CAD, and digital presentations, as well as classes in office management and marketing. There is an increasing awareness on the parts of educators and students that the practice of architecture is changing and the pressure for change within schools is increasing.

If you are in a school that is not teaching you about computers, CAD, databases, and electronic presentations, demand that they do. If they do not change, find another school. This knowledge is your future; your time in school is too valuable and important to waste a single moment. Just as there is minimal need for the blacksmith in our current era, there will be diminishing need for the digital uninformed. A good designer with a mastery of the digital tools will outperform a very good designer without the tools. A very good designer with a mastery of the electronic tools will be unbelievable.

Education through its foundation in research has a golden opportunity to make significant contributions to the knowledge of architectural information. Prior to the Internet most information had, at best, a chance to be published and placed upon a shelf. Most information just disappears. The Internet offers the opportunity for information to be made available for the asking. Schools have a tremendous opportunity to substantially contribute to the knowledge base. Instead of independent research projects I foresee a day when research is coordinated world-wide with each student and each school adding to a collective database of information. Instead of hundreds of students looking into the same information, then throwing the information away, they will all look into a different part of the information, then file the data in its proper place. Currently the master indexing system is missing, but I am confident that will arrive soon.

By the year 2000 we will see practicing professionals heavily influencing the architectural schools. The schools provide the workforce for the profession and it is critical to the future of the existing offices to be able to identify and hire their future. Interestingly, students graduating with this digital knowledge will be able to move quickly into important positions as their knowledge will be greater in these matters than most of the other employees of the firm.

Hardware

From 1986 to 1996, PC hardware has advanced in processing speed several times over. Graphic operations that took 20 to 30 seconds in 1986 now take a fraction of a second; in four more years, they will just happen. Processing speed has always been one of the main weak links in using a PC for CAD. Ideally, you want the computer to keep pace with your mind. Although PCs may not get that fast in the next few years, they will be close enough that I don't think anyone will pass up the computer because of its lack of processing speed.

The computer is a warehouse for information. The more information that may be stored and accessed easily, the more useful the computing tool. In the mid-1980s we had just moved from storage on 360 Kb, or 0.36 Mb floppy disks, to hard-disk storage in the 20 to 40 Mb range. Today, 500 to 9,000 Mb (9 gigabytes) disks are common. 650 Mb CD-ROM disks are available and can be made in the office with machines costing less than $1,500. Five years from now, you will have access to thousands of gigabytes of information through your PC, either on your hard disk, on CD-ROMs or from a network such as the Internet or the Microsoft® Network.

Such speed, combined with new storage and access capabilities, will give you the most powerful productivity tool you have ever had. Costs will continue to decrease on every component—computers, software, printers, and the cost of information.

Software

The advances in software will be even more remarkable than the advances in hardware. CAD software may continue to fall into two main categories: the graphic engine software (AutoCAD) and the applications software, such as the suite of applications offered by Softdesk. It is easy to believe that the future will bring a combination product that includes both the graphic engine and the application software in one product.

The next generations of graphic engine software will continue to get faster and faster. More and more work will be done in 3D. Databases of information will be tied to the drawings allowing for more automated drawings. The drawing structure will be linked together so changes to one part of the drawing will ripple through the drawings with the necessary corrections. Visualization software will continue to improve in both ease of use and rendering and animation power.

Fantastic advances will also occur in applications software. The goal of the software designer is to weave together the information and drawings that make up the design, construction, and management process. The first step of the process involves gathering and indexing information. With hand drawing throughout the entire process, information is kept in hundreds of files and on thousands of slips of paper. The current process is a constant modification and gathering of information that has been gathered time and time again by other members of the designing and building team. In the future, you'll have a master database for the storing and retrieving of information.

As the process moves along, information will be added and modified, but will continue to be found in a consistent location. The master database will include all the information about the project, including the program, code information, architectural and engineering drawings, and all the statistics contained within the drawings, analysis results, manufacturers' data, specifications, and estimates. Moreover, the master database will be interactive so that as you change one bit of information, either graphically or alphanumerically, the software will adjust accordingly throughout the database. This interactive database will organize the entire process.

The Architectural Phases in the Future

Programming

In the future, you will build both an alphanumeric database as well as a graphic database for the program requirements. Sophisticated adjacency programs will help you lay out the spaces. Stacking programs will look at the vertical layout within buildings. Research papers will be available to you on the subject of your project. You will be able to gather information about equipment graphically so that you will be able to begin the design process graphically.

Preliminary Design Phase

During the design process, you will no longer draw double lines for walls. You won't need to draw in all the detail for doors and windows. You'll create diagrams and the software will create the graphically correct drawing. During this phase, you'll be able to automatically generate cost estimates and construction schedules. You'll be able to study the massing of the design through renderings and animation created automatically by the software, and you'll be able to mold the design and to continue to make studies to refine the design ideas.

Software will provide libraries of buildings to call on for elements and ideas. If you want to experience the spatial feeling of an existing significant building, just call up the geometry and animate it to stroll through the building. Even if you have actually physically visited the building, you'll be able to view the building from many more vantage points with electronic graphics. You'll be able to walk around and even fly around and through the building! In one afternoon, you'll be able to visit scores of buildings electronically.

Codes and ordinances will be stored and searched electronically. You'll be able to enter the location of a site and the applicable codes and planning requirements will be provided. Once you have indicated the type of building and occupancy you are designing, the fire, planning, and other applicable codes will be searched and the pertinent information provided. Converting the codes to electronic format will dramatically point out the inconsistencies and conflicts in today's codes, which will lead to necessary corrections. This one might take more than four years.

Presentations

In the future, architectural presentations will be truly breathtaking. They will jump alive with animation, titles, spectacular renderings, and even digital sound. These presentations will be created by all members of the design team, not just by a highly trained specialist. Prior to design review meetings, you'll be able to give the members of the board the full presentation for the project. You'll have access to databases that will allow accurate information to be provided on environmental issues, similar projects, and traffic studies. Both shadow studies and wind studies will be created electronically.

Design Development and Contract Documents Phases

These two phases—design development and contract documents—will likely merge into one phase because you will automatically move well beyond the traditional preliminary design information in the preliminary design phase. By the time this phase is finished, you will be ready to move into contract documents.

In the future, as you draw you will find displayed: the cost of the project in the lower left-hand corner of the monitor; the time to build the project in the bottom right-hand corner; and the energy requirements for the project in the upper right-hand corner. Manufacturers' data, drawings, photographs, details, specifications, costs, and availability will all be part of the drawing session.

When you select a window, you will see the cost implications and their effect on the schedule based on the manufacturers' information and the construction process. You'll be able to call up photographs of the elements being considered and to study your selections in photorealistic perspective views. You will be able to animate your designs for design studies. Changes to the architectural drawings will be reflected in changes to the engineering drawings. Real-time fly-throughs will be possible so that you'll be free to set your path as you move through the design.

Bidirectional changes will be possible. Change the CFM of the air diffuser in the database and the ducts will be redrawn correctly or add a diffuser to the drawings and the analysis will be rerun and the drawings then redrawn to reflect the changes. Modifying the drawings from the database is the most powerful feature of CAD and alphanumeric data processing. You'll do less drawing and the drawings will be created faster and more accurately.

Specifications will be tied to the drawing. As you add elements, the specifications will be created and tied directly to the products you've used in the project. You'll be able to automatically create either generic or manufacturer-specific specifications. In addition, the specifications software will check for conflicts and inconsistencies.

Most details will be created automatically given the design of the building and the materials specified. You'll have the option of drawing with generic or with manufacturer-specific details. Manufacturers will provide the details for their products.

Electronic code checks will be performed before you submit the drawings and calculations for permits. The code-checking software will review your drawings and point out code violations so that they may be addressed before the permit process or before construction. Using CAD and alphanumeric processing on the PC workstation will greatly reduce errors and omissions; this will result in lower insurance costs for design professionals. Once again, however, this is sadly more than four years away.

Bidding and Negotiation

The contractor and the subcontractors will receive contract documents both in electronic format and in traditional drawing and specification formats. Working with the electronic information, they will be able to accurately determine all the physical characteristics of the project. Square footage, area of walls and ceiling, cubic yards of concrete, and materials takeoff for all materials in the project will be available and accurate. The time required for estimation will shrink as the accuracy sharpens. Direct ties to estimation data services will read your information into their databases. The construction cost will fall because the contractor will estimate more accurately and will spend less time estimating.

Construction

The computer, which will soon be as common a sight on the job as the contractor's pickup truck, will be used to track the building schedule and material deliveries. CAD will be used to record the as-built conditions; progress photographs will be taken and stored digitally for review and transfer. The workers will be able to study any condition electronically before the actual construction; 3D displays and animation will be used to study complicated intersections and details.

CAD will provide exact information on the parts of an assembly so that the individual pieces will fit together. Modifications that used to delay projects will be made at the job site, while cost adjustments will be determined and approvals received after electronic review at the home office. In fact, the entire project database will be available at the construction site.

Facilities Management

After the project is completed, the most important phase in the life of the structure—the management of the facilities—begins. As noted earlier, facilities management is a broad-spectrum concept that includes interior space layout, furniture and equipment inventories, management of the leased areas, maintenance and operations, cable and communications, and renovation.

Today, when the project is completed, the design and construction teams turn over to the owner or facilities manager piles of manuals, specifications, manufacturer literature, and drawings. The facilities manager must then wade through the information and assume responsibility for the building. In the future, this information will be better organized and will be passed on electronically, enabling the facilities manager to search the information electronically and make modifications to the electronic information to keep the database current.

Maintenance manuals will not take the form of paper books, but will be animated instructions on the operation, maintenance, and repair of the equipment, with instructions given by experts in the field.

Managing the growth or shrinkage of a company will be based on the integration of the various databases. For example, growth within a department will be indexed to the available space for expansion and the cost of various possibilities. Tying together the various databases for the building will give the facilities manager tremendous power.

Conclusion

This is not science fiction. Everything discussed in this chapter is possible today. Several of these features are already working in developmental software. The only element separating the future from today is time. New technology will only make the future arrive earlier and with more power.

In the past, the architect sat and drew the same window over and over again by hand, realizing that all of his or her training and knowledge was not being put to good use. The lack of automation and the waste of valuable time were frustrating. Today, architects know the path to the future, but they're still frustrated; they can only run down that path so fast. As you proceed, you will discover and develop more and more of the fantastic tools that you will have to perform your work at peak efficiency.

In 15 years, from 1985 to 2000, the practice of architecture will have undergone a complete transformation. In 1985, the PC arrived in the AEC professions; by the year 2000, it will have changed these professions forever. The PC, with graphic engine software and applications software, will make the work of the design professional more accurate, the designs better, and the construction process more cost-effective and smooth.

The PC and the software of the year 2000 will see a new design professional in the driver's seat. You will be more like a master builder: You'll be responsible for the complete design of the structure; you'll have the power of the best minds in structure, design, electrical, mechanical, plumbing, color, and program information; you won't be distracted by calculations; and you'll be able to imagine an idea and test the idea for every conceivable concern.

If you are a student, you need to start thinking now about this new architectural practice and about what you will need to know to take on the master builder role. If you are already an architect, these predictions may seem farfetched; they aren't. They may even seem somewhat frightening; in many ways, they are. How do we license the architect of the future? How do we educate the students of the future and the architects of today so that they can move into the future?

Actually, these are simple questions, so they will be answered. You need to stay in touch with the technology in the coming years, for it will come quickly. You also need to become involved in helping to mold the future by reviewing products, providing feedback to the designers of the software, and keeping in touch with the licensing boards and the educational institutions.

Architecture is a wonderful profession, a mixture of art and sculpture balanced against the complexity of construction and the realities of business. CAD and alphanumeric data processing will make this profession even better and more enjoyable in the near future.

We are entering the most exciting age ever for architects and engineers. I look forward to seeing what you will do with these fantastic new tools.

PART TWO

SOFTDESK 7 CORE AND ARCHITECTURAL TUTORIAL

B. Robert Callori

PART TWO OVERVIEW

CHAPTER EIGHT

DRAWING SETUP

Starting the Softdesk Environment

Contents

USING AUTOCAD WITH SOFTDESK

This tutorial assumes that you have a basic knowledge of AutoCAD®
and have previously and successfully installed AutoCAD® Release 13
and Softdesk 7 for Windows on your hard drive with default directory
names. To open the Softdesk program select the appropriate Icon.

For first-time users who have not assigned a
named drawing, the drawing editor will open
displaying the AutoCAD [UNNAMED] drawing
and possibly a Softdesk Startup message box
indicating that Softdesk Core is not initialized.

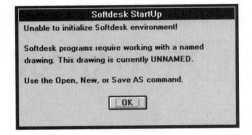

   Pick OK to begin a new drawing.

ASSIGNING A PROTOTYPE DRAWING

ACAD Menu: **FILE ➤ NEW**

Pick **New** from the File pull-down menu
to display the *Create New Drawing* dialog box.
Assign a Softdesk prototype drawing by selecting the **Prototype...** pick box. If an X mark
appears in the box beside **No Prototype**, pick
the box to remove the check mark, then
choose **Prototype....**

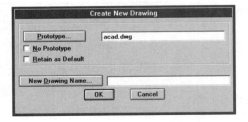

Selecting **Prototype...** opens the *Prototype Drawing File* dialog box.

Locate the installed Softdesk drive and \SDSK
directory then double-click on the SDSK_I
imperial prototype drawing to display it in the
File Name edit box.

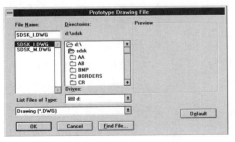

Note: The installed drive letter for this tutorial is D; your drive letter may be C.

Pick OK and return to the *Create New Drawing* dialog box; then select the pick box beside **Retain as Default**, so that an X mark appears.

Type SESSO1 as the **New Drawing Name**, then pick OK. This initializes the Softdesk environment.

Note: The Softdesk program will not initialize unless a new drawing name is specified. The directory and drawing name are not important at this time because the drawing will not be saved.

● ●

STARTING THE SOFTDESK ENVIRONMENT

Once Softdesk Core is initialized from an imperial or metric prototype drawing furnished by Softdesk, additional modules can be integrated into the working environment. Assuming default values were accepted during installation, the \SDSK directory was created with an SDSK_I and SDSK_M drawing.

Note: Depending upon the desired unit of measure, the imperial SDSK_I or metric SDSK_M drawing must be selected as the prototype drawing.

Softdesk Menu: **FILE**

Picking the File pull-down menu displays Core commands that have been appended to the ACAD menu:

> **Softdesk Preferences...**
> **Prototype Manager...**
> **Project Manager...**
> **Prototype Settings...**
> **Project Settings...**
> **Setup Drawing...**
> **Softdesk Products...**

CREATING AN INITIAL PROJECT

FILE ➤ SETUP DRAWING...

If the Softdesk program has just been installed or no project exists in the \SDSKPROJ directory, the *Create Project* dialog box appears for input of a Project Name, Description, and Key Words.

Note: Entering the Project Name creates a subdirectory under the directory \SDSKPROJ. Descriptions and Key Words are not required, but serve as useful information when several projects exist and searches become necessary.

To create a project and initialize the Softdesk environment select **Setup Drawing...** from the File pull-down menu.

Choosing **Setup Drawing...** opens the *Create Project* dialog box to associate the new drawing with a project or named subdirectory under \SDSKPROJ.

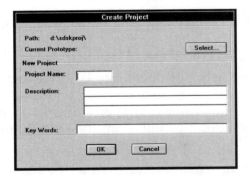

Pick **Select...** to open the *Select Prototype* dialog box.

The drawing must be associated with a project. (A project represents a subdirectory name). During installation the directory \SDSKPROT and subdirectory SOFTDESK were created as a default by Softdesk Core. The **Select Prototype** list box displays the SOFTDESK prototype as shown. The Softdesk environment always maintains a SOFTDESK prototype. If this pro-

totype is deleted, it will be automatically recreated, using the default system settings when the Softdesk environment is initialized. This directory may contain additional prototypes if they were saved by previous users.

Other pick options of this dialog box include **Search by...** and **Statistics...**. Explore the contents of each subdialog box, but do not enter any data at this time.

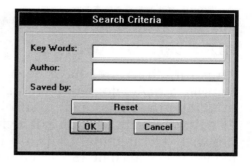

Selecting **Search by...** opens the *Search Criteria* dialog box where keyword information can be saved and retrieved.

Selecting **Statistics...** opens the *Project Statistics* dialog box where project information can be recorded as a management tool.

 Double-click on the name SOFTDESK to close the *Select Prototype* dialog box and return to the *Create Project* dialog box. Enter the **Project Name**, **Description**, and single or multiple **Key Words** as shown, then pick OK.

Project Name: **ARCHTUT** (limited to 8 characters)
Description: **Softdesk default prototype**
                  Architectural tutorial
                  Three Story Building
Key Words: **arch tutorial**

Pick OK.

A message box appears briefly with the words "Creating project...", then the *Drawing Setup* dialog box opens.

SETTING UP A SCALED DRAWING

FILE ➤ SETUP DRAWING ...

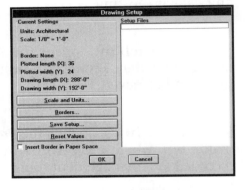

After the directories have been created, the *Drawing Setup* dialog box automatically opens to configure the drawing sheet. Softdesk's default values are set for a 1/8-inch scale drawing with Architectural units, no border, plotted length (X axis) of 36", and plotted width (Y axis) of 24". The corresponding drawing length (X axis) is identified as 288' and width (Y axis) is 192'.

In the following discussions, a 1/8" plotted drawing scale is used with imperial units to set up a predefined 24 × 36 border in paperspace.

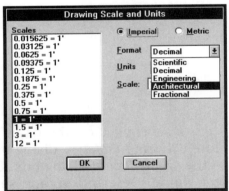

Choose the **Scale** and **Units...** pick box to open the *Drawing Scale and Units* dialog box which displays a list box with default **Scales**, radio buttons to select **Imperial** or **Metric** units of measure, and a pop-up list to set the **Format**. Scales not listed can be entered in the **Scales** edit box. Accept the default values of 1/8"=1'-0", Architectural and Imperial units.

Note: Picking the down arrow beside **Format** opens a pop-up list to choose selections for Scientific, Decimal, Engineering, Architectural, and Fractional units in the drawing.

 Dialog box:

Scale: **1/8"=1'-0"**
Imperial   [radio button]
Format: **Architectural**

Pick OK.

Picking the **Metric** radio button would display the *Drawing Scale and Units* subdialog box for metric units. Pop-up lists provide for Decimal or Scientific Format, settings for Units and edit Scale box as shown.

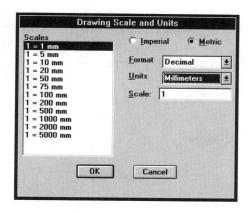

The **Units** pop-up list for metric offers options for millimeters, centimeters, decimeters, and meters.

Note: When working in metric, it is best to start with the SDSK_M prototype drawing.

 Selecting the **Borders...** pick box opens the *Border Sheets* dialog box for **Predefined**, **Free Size**, **No Border**, or **User Border....** Plotted and drawing lengths and widths are displayed in edit boxes to set X and Y coordinates for Free Sizes.

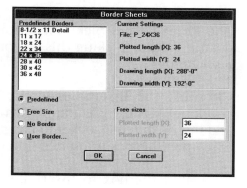

Select the **Predefined** radio button, highlight the 24 × 36 predefined border from the list box, then pick OK.

Dialog box:

Predefined   [radio button]
Predefined Border: **24 x 36**

Selecting **User Border...** from the *Border Sheets* dialog box opens the *Select Border Drawing* dialog box. If a custom titleblock drawing had been created for this tutorial, it would be saved to this \SDSKPROJ\ARCHTUT directory for insertion into modelspace or paperspace.

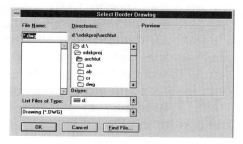

Select **Save Setup...** to display the *Save Setup File* dialog box and type ARCHTUT.SET in the **File Name**: edit box, then pick OK. Setup files are saved to the \SDSK\SETUP directory.

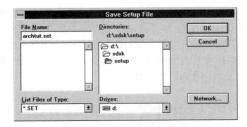

Dialog box:

File Name: **archtut.set**

The saved 1/8-inch scale imperial drawing with a 24" × 34" predefined border and ARCHTUT setup file name appears in the **Setup Files** list box for future retrieval.

The **Reset Values** pick box restores Softdesk's default values. (Picking this button now would reset Border.)

Choosing the **Insert Border in Paper Space** check box sets the tilemode system variable to 1 and inserts the titleblock into paperspace. Otherwise, the titleblock is inserted into modelspace.

 Pick the box to **Insert Border in Paper Space** and a check mark will appear. Select OK to close the dialog box.

The drawing toggles from modelspace to paperspace, inserts the predefined border, then opens a dialog box to enter attribute values in the titleblock specific to the project.

The *Edit Attributes* dialog box opens next, displaying the default values entered during setup. Based on the sheet style selected, Softdesk inserts a titleblock from the \SDSK\BORDERS\LNG directory named ZZ_TITLE into the current drawing.

Default values are:

Drawing scale   1/8"=1'-0"
Drawing date   5-29-95 **[displays current date]**

Enter additional values as shown.

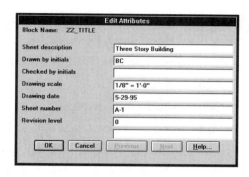

 Dialog box:

Sheet description   **Three Story Building**
Drawn by initials   **[enter your initials]**

Note: Press the TAB key four times to advance downward or click on **Sheet number** edit box.

Sheet number   **A-1**

 Pick OK.

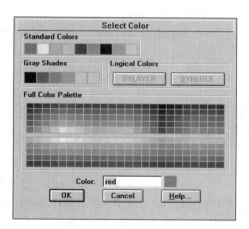

After inserting the border, the command-line prompts appear. Type **YES** and the text screen appears. Enter **2** at the **Choose option (1/2/3) <2>:** prompt to create viewports for plan, elevations (front and side), and isometric views. The *Select Color* dialog box opens to choose a color for the viewports which are inserted on the layer DEFPOINTS.

PROMPTING SUMMARY

Command: sdsk
Entering Paper space. Use MVIEW to insert Model space viewports.
Regenerating drawing.
Create viewports <Yes>: **y**
Loading mvsetup....
Available Mview viewport layout options:

1. Single

2. Plan, Elevations & Isometric

3. Array of Viewports

Choose option (1/2/3) <2>: **2**

Bounding area for viewports:

First corner: [pick point near bottom left corner of titleblock]

Other corner: [pick point near top right corner of titleblock]

Distance between viewports in X direction <1/4">: ↵

Distance between viewports in Y direction <1/4">: ↵

Hint: A dark color will make the active viewport stand out better. [***Select Color* dialog box
      appears to assign color for viewport layer]**

MVSETUP in progress...

Creating Viewport(s)...

View "FRONT" created. UCS "FRONT" created.

View "PLAN" created

View "RIGHT" created. UCS "RIGHT" created.

View "ISO" created.

Regenerating drawing.

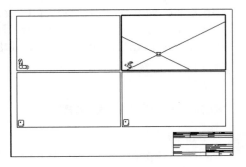

Select first and second points at the lower left and upper right corners of the title block, forming a rectangle to create four viewports spaced 1/4" apart.

The drawing editor now appears with the titleblock, selected border, and viewports. The top right viewport is active, as shown.

Since keyboard macros are the most productive way to work, they will be used extensively in this tutorial. To see a list of available macros enter HE (for Help) at the command line or Appendix A.

CURRENT SETTINGS IN THE DRAWING

Titleblock Layers and Fonts

Now that the drawing setup is complete and a titleblock has been inserted into the drawing, we will review current layers and fonts created with the default Softdesk environment.

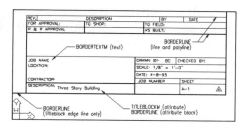

The ZZ_TITLE attribute block identifies only some information relating to the drawing. The figure shows an enlarged view of the titleblock (located at the bottom right corner of the predefined border). Additional textual information can be furnished to complete the titleblock using layers and text styles described and created by Softdesk.

Invoke the Softdesk Macro **TI** and return to modelspace.

     Macro Command: **TI**

(AutoCAD Command: **TILEMODE**)

Command: **ti**
Macro: Tilemode Toggle
Regenerating drawing.

DEFAULT SOFTDESK LAYERS

Open the *Layer Control* dialog box to view Softdesk default layers using any of the following methods: Pull-down menu, Macro, or Tool icon.

Softdesk Menu: **VIEW ➤ LAYER CONTROLS ➤ LAYER...**

     Macro Command: **LD**

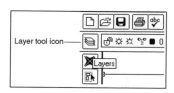

Select the Layer tool icon to open the *Layer Control* dialog box. An enlarged view of the layer tool icon and associated tooltip is shown.

The *Layer Control* dialog box opens, displaying the layers now defined in the drawing. A full list and description are shown in the table titled Default Layering List in Drawing. All linetypes are continuous. Layer NO-PLOT is off. Otherwise, all other layers are on, thawed, and unlocked.

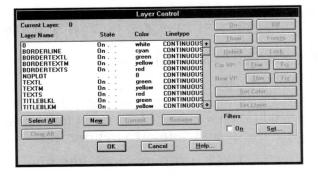

Default Layering List in Drawing

Layer Name	Color		Description
0	white	7	AutoCAD unpurgeable layer
TEXTL	green	3	Not in current drawing, default SDSK_I prototype drawing text style
TEXTM	yellow	2	Not in current drawing, default SDSK_I prototype drawing text style
TEXTS	red	1	Not in current drawing, default SDSK_I prototype text style

All Softdesk products define layers as they are needed. The following layers were created because the border and titleblock have been inserted.

Border and Titleblock Layers

Layer Name	Color		Description
BORDERLINE	cyan	4	Title border lines
BORDERTEXTL	green	3	Border text, large
BORDERTEXTM	yellow	2	Border text, medium (Attributes in ZZ_TITLE block)
BORDERTEXTS	red	1	Border text, small
NOPLOT		8	Layer for reference objects
TITLEBLKL	green	3	Large text
TITLEBLKM	yellow	2	Medium text (Text label in the titleblock)
TITLEBLKS	red	1	Small text (Text label in the titleblock)

DEFAULT TEXT STYLES

The SDSK_I prototype drawing contains the following predefined text styles with the current text style set to DIMTEXT. All text styles are defined with Height: 0'-0", Obliquing angle: 0.0, and Generation: Normal.

Default Text Styles Drawing

Style Name	*Font File*	*Width Factor*
DIMTEXT	DIM.SHX	0.7500
STANDARD	TXT.SHX	1.0000

Note: The use of the DIM.SHX font for the style DIMTEXT is similar to Romans.shx except that there is reduced space around the characters for dash, inch, and foot marks.

Titleblock Text

Style Name	*Font File*	*Width Factor*
BORDERTEXTL	ROMANS.SHX	1.0000
BORDERTEXTM	ROMANS.SHX	1.0000
BORDERTEXTS	ROMANS.SHX	1.0000
TITLEBLKL	ROMANS.SHX	1.0000
TITLEBLKM	ROMANS.SHX	1.0000
TITLEBLKS	ROMANS.SHX	1.0000

SETTING THE CURRENT TEXT STYLE

Invoking the Macro **SY** opens the *Text style* dialog box to set a style as current.

 Macro Command: **SY**

(AutoCAD Command: **DDMODIFY**)

Command: **sy**
Macro: Set Style

Review the list of Macros in Appendix A to enter text using default Softdesk styles. For example, the Macro TM will start the text command using medium text placed on the correct layer.

Note: Be aware that some styles may use a "special" font; these are unique to the Softdesk program and cannot be shared unless consultants that are using Softdesk replace these fonts with AutoCAD font files.

SAVING A DRAWING TO THE PROJECT DIRECTORY

FILE ➤ SAVEAS

Select **Saveas** under the File pull-down menu to open the *Save Drawing As* dialog box.

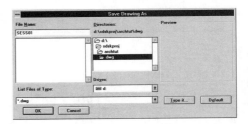

Locate the \SDSKPROJ\ARCHTUT\ DWG directory, then type the name SESS01 in the **File Name**: edit box

Pick OK and the command line returns the prompt confirming the filename and path.

Current drawing name set to D:\sdskproj\archtut\dwg\SESS01.

Note: Selecting **Save** under the File pull-down menu would save the drawing to the \SDSK directory.

WHAT IS A PROJECT?

As the Softdesk products have become more sophisticated, more information relating to a design project has been moved outside the drawing file. Data such as Door and Window styles, Wall styles and program settings are stored externally. To organize these related files, they are stored under a common directory known as the Project Directory. These files, along with the drawing files, are grouped together in a systematic way, simplifying the process of backing up or sharing projects between remote offices.

WHAT IS A PROTOTYPE?

A prototype is a way to save and reuse the Project settings and styles. For example, suppose you have to work on a job called HALSTEAD RESIDENCE. All the program settings and styles used could be saved to a prototype RESIDENCE for future use on similar projects.

THE PROJECT DIRECTORY

During the create project initialization process, Softdesk creates new subdirectories and default files in the \SDSKPROJ directory using the \SDSKPROT\SOFTDESK directory as a source. The Project Name ARCHTUT becomes a subdirectory name in the \SDSKPROJ directory. Project files created or customized for the ARCHTUT project are stored under this directory.

During the installation of the Softdesk program the Main directory structure is created as the following program excerpt shows. The File Manager can be used to compare the \SOFTDESK subdirectory and the newly created \ARCHTUT subdirectory found under the directory \SDSKPROJ.

\SDSK	Contains SDSK_I and SDSK_M prototype drawings
(additional subdirectories...)	
\SDSKPREF	Softdesk settings specific to user
\SDSKPROJ	Project directory
\SDSKPROT	Default prototype directory
\SOFTDESK	Contains Softdesk's environment subdirectories and files
\SDSKTEMP	Softdesk's temporary directory

Microsoft Windows: **FILE MANAGER**

The Microsoft Windows **File Manager** screen shown here displays the default \SDSKPROT directory with the \SOFTDESK subdirectory on the left and newly created \SDSKPROJ directory with the \ARCHTUT subdirectory on the right.

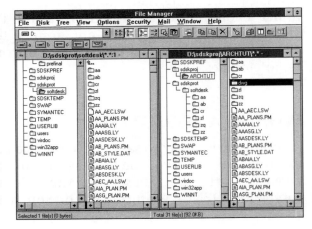

One obvious difference between these directories is that the project contains a directory \DWG to store drawing files while the Prototype does not.

EXITING THE SOFTDESK PROGRAM

FILE ➤ EXIT

Exit from the Softdesk program by selecting **Exit** under the File pull-down menu or continue on to Chapter 9 for a detailed review of the Softdesk environment.

CHAPTER NINE

THE SOFTDESK ENVIRONMENT

*Overview of Core Settings and Preferences,
including Layer and Text Management*

Contents

SOFTDESK PRODUCTS AND COMMANDS

This chapter provides an overview of Softdesk's environment and does not require setting controls. Softdesk Core provides the integrated working environment for all Softdesk modules. Core consists of four pull-down menus: **File**, **Edit**, **View**, and **Tools**, providing both Softdesk and AutoCAD® commands. When most Softdesk modules are loaded, the menus for those modules appear to the right of the Tools pull-down menu. Softdesk Productivity Tools, however, is the exception because it integrates commands within these four pull-down menus.

Experimentation is encouraged for a better understanding of the predefined settings or dialog boxes in the File pull-down menu. The discussions that follow cover Core, Building Base, Productivity Tools, and Auto-Architect® modules.

Basic features of the Softdesk Core environment include:

- System management
- Project management
- Drawing configuration
- Layer management
- Text style management
- Symbol management
- Drawing annotation

Let's look at some of the Softdesk commands located in the File pull-down menu.

OPEN THE SESS01 DRAWING

FILE ➤ OPEN

If you have exited the Softdesk program, pick your Softdesk icon, then select **Open** under the File pull-down menu to display the *Select*

File dialog box. Highlight the SESS01 drawing from the \SDSKPROJ\ ARCHTUT\DWG directory, then pick OK to make it the current drawing.

SOFTDESK PREFERENCES

FILE ➤ SOFTDESK PREFERENCES...

Softdesk Preferences... opens the *Softdesk Preferences* dialog box to view controls that set user interface preferences for the Softdesk environment. All settings saved in this dialog box are stored in the SDSK.DFM file in the \SDSK directory and can be initialized by checking the appropriate boxes.

Login Name displays the name entered when AutoCAD was initially installed.

Note: Make sure that the login name is unique when running on a multiuser network because this is used by Core during file locking.

Current Language specifies the current language used for the Softdesk environment. The Softdesk products have been translated into many languages.

Automatic Initialization controls automatic initialization of the Softdesk environment at the start of a drawing session. When enabled, the Softdesk Startup dialog box appears when AutoCAD first opens with the UNNAMED drawing. If you anticipate opening several drawings just to view them, turning automatic initialization off will save time.

Automatic Menu Macro Loading automatically loads Softdesk's two-letter keyboard macros. Related files that can be customized using the Microsoft Notepad or any ASCII text editor are listed in the table. Entering **HE** at the command line displays a list of the Macros and their definitions. (See MENUS AND TOOLBARS in this chapter for additional information on customizing menus).

Menu Macro Files

File Path and Name	File Type	Description
\SDSK\MACROS.LSP	LISP source code	Macro Definitions
\SDSK\CR\LNG\MACROS.TXT	Text file listing macros	Macros Help Files
\SDSK\CR\LNG\CR_STUB.MNU	Menu file	Menu Files

Snap Off During Object Selection toggles the AutoCAD SNAP command off during object selection when Softdesk commands are invoked. (This option avoids the situation where the object you want to select is between two fixed snap points.)

Display Screen Support Menus controls the visibility of screen menus during execution of AutoCAD commands and requires the loading of Softdesk's Productivity Tools to activate it. This would, for example, show all of the line command options when Line is picked from the pull-down menu or the Macro **L** is invoked. This toggle is also controlled from the AutoCAD *Preferences* dialog box. Select Configure under the File pull-down menu, then check **Screen Menu** in the AutoCAD Graphics Window section.

Third Button Osnap specifies the third mouse button pick commands (for a three-button mouse or digitizer puck). This command is also accessed using the SHIFT key plus the right button on a two-button mouse. In AutoCAD® R13 only the Cursor Menu (Pop 0) is available (unless the menu is customized as discussed later in the chapter).

FILE ➤ SOFTDESK PREFERENCES... ➤ PATH SETTINGS...

Path Settings... displays a list box of current directory paths that can be modified when modules are installed or moved. Path keys are saved to the SDSK.DFM file in the \SDSK directory. The figure shows an example of **Key, Value,** and **Description** for the **Softdesk Program Root** path settings.

Key: SDSK represents an alias name for a directory path on the local system or network. The Key SDSK might be considered a nickname for the actual drive letter and directory path.

Value: The value of the key or the location the key points to. In this case, the directory path D:/SDSK/ is where Softdesk products are installed.

Path: D:\SDSK\ represents the actual path adjusted for the operating system (DOS or UNIX).

The Path Settings dialog box should be modified only by users with customization experience.

FILE ➤ SOFTDESK PREFERENCES... ➤ PATH SETTINGS... ➤ ADD KEYS...

Add Keys... pick box opens the *Add Path* dialog box to identify path locations for new programs. Descriptions and new path keys are appended to the Select Path list (stored in the SDSK.DFM file in the \SDSK directory).

Key: Represents an alias name for a directory path on the local system or network as previously discussed.

Value: Represents the actual drive letter and directory path where related programs or files are stored.

Description: Provides identification which will appear in the Path Settings list previously shown.

TYPES OF KEYS

There are several different types of keys used in the Softdesk system:

Path
Layer
Symbol
Symbol file
Elevation (Building Base)

WHY HAVE KEYS?

Keys provide extra flexibility within the Softdesk environment. Path Keys allow you to install components of Softdesk products on different drives or on a network. Layer keys let you specify in advance what layers are used when a program draws an object. Note that the value of a path key can reference a previously defined key using the percent (%) marks. If the SDSK key points to D:\SDSK\ and the AA key value is %SDSK%AA\, the actual directory used for AA will be D:\SDSK\AA\. Any changes to the SDSK key will thus reference all the other keys which reference it.

A portion of the SDSK.DFM file is shown for reference:

    zz#loginname=bob callori

    [SystemPaths]

    SDSK=(D:\SDSK\,Softdesk Program Root)

    ZZ=(%sdsk%zz\,Programming Tools)

    ZZPROT=(%zz%prot\,Programming Tools Prototype Root)

    ZZPRZZ=(%zzprot%zz\,Programming Tools Prototype)

    ZD=(%sdsk%zd\,Database Tools)

Chapter 8 briefly discussed the Main prototype directory structure; however, a more detailed account is shown here. The files from the \SDSKPROT\SOFTDESK prototype directory are copied to create a project directory named \SDSKPROJ. Only the files and directories needed by the program are created. Although the \DWG subdirectory is not part of the \SDSKPROT directory, it is made when a new project is created.

DIRECTORIES	DESCRIPTIONS
\SDSKPROT	Root directory of project files
\SOFTDESK	**Default subdirectory used to create as project name**
aaaia.ly	AutoArchitect - aia layering convention
aaasg.ly	AutoArchitect - asg layering convention
aasdesk.ly	AutoArchitect - Softdesk layering convention
aa_aec.lsw	Layer conversion - AutoArch to AEC
aa_plans.pm	AutoArchitect - Plan Matrix layer settings
abaia.ly	Architectural Base - aia layering convention - Architectural base

abasg.ly	Architectural Base - asg layering convention - Architectural base
absdesk.ly	Architectural Base - softdesk layering convention - Architectural base
ab_plans.pm	Architectural Base - Plan Matrix
ab_style.dat	Architectural Base - default text style settings
aec_aa.lsw	Layer conversion - AEC to AutoArchitect
aia_plan.pm	AIA - Plan Matrix
asg_plan.pm	ASG - Plan Matrix
bs1192.lsw	Layer conversion (swap files) - Softdesk to British Standard Conversion
project.dfm	Project statistics and descriptions (for dialogue box)
samplepl.pm	Sample Plan Matrix for Core (not needed by Auto-Architect users)
softdesk.ave	Autovision - default materials table
zzaia.ly	Core - aia layering convention
zzasg.ly	Core - asg layering convention
zzsdesk.ly	Core - softdesk layering convention
zzstyle.dat	Core - default text style
\AA	**Auto-Architect module**
aa.dfm	Auto-Architect settings
aabbrev.txt	Abbreviations list
rooms_i.dbf	Imperial room name database, for room schedule
rooms_m.dbf	Metric room name database, for room schedule
walltype.dam	Metric wall style data file
walltype.dat	Imperial wall style data file
\AB	**Building Base module**
ab.dfm	Building Base statistics
abbrev.txt	Abbreviations list
windassi.dbf	Imperial window database, for window schedule
windassm.dbf	Metric window database, for window schedule
windoori.dbf	Imperial door database, for door schedule
windoorm.dbf	Metric door database, for door schedule
\CR	**Core module**
cr.dfm	Core statistics/preferences
\ZL	**Datalink module**
datalink.cfg	Configuration file
\ZQ	**Productivity module**
zone_tag.dwg	Block collection for zone labels/database
\ZZ	**British Standard Units module**
bs1192.ali	BS1192 and AEC layering alias table
bs1192.cat	Layer naming convention catalogue
locale.dat	Locale conventions, for preferences
pens.dat	Used for British Standard system

THE PROTOTYPE MANAGER DIALOG BOX

FILE ➤ PROTOTYPE MANAGER...

Prototype Manager... opens the *Prototype Manager* dialog box to **Create...**, **Copy...**, **Search...** for, edit **Statistics...** , **Rename...**, and **Remove...** Softdesk prototypes. Prototypes store predefined settings for the Softdesk environment. A new project can be created by referencing an existing prototype.

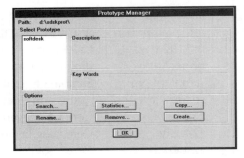

FILE ➤ PROTOTYPE MANAGER... ➤ CREATE...

Create... opens the *Create Prototype* subdialog box to make a new prototype based on the \SOFTDESK prototype. A **Prototype Name** (from 1 to 8 characters) is required. **Description** and **Key Words** are optional.

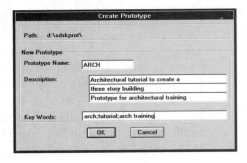

Experiment: Select **Create...**, then type ARCH for the **Prototype Name**. Add additional information as indicated, then pick OK.

 Dialog box:

Prototype Name:	**ARCH**
Description:	**Architectural tutorial to create a three story building**
	Prototype for architectural training
Key Words:	**arch;tutorial;arch training**

Note: Descriptions similar to "Architectural tutorial" or "Creating a three-story building" can provide useful archival information about a project. **Key Words** can help to locate projects. Enter words or phrases using a space, colon(:), semicolon (;), vertical bar (l), or comma (,) as valid delimiters. The figure shows Key Words "arch; tutorial;arch training" typed in the edit box.

The name ARCH then appears in the **Select Prototype** list box in the *Prototype Manager* dialog box. The new prototype name is created under the \SDSKPROT directory. Highlighting the name displays the additional information.

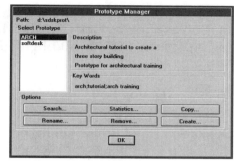

Example of directory structure: \SDSKPROT
                                        | - \ARCH
                                        | - \SOFTDESK

FILE ➤ PROTOTYPE MANAGER... ➤ RENAME...

Rename... opens the *Rename Prototype* subdialog box to rename the selected prototype. The subdirectory name under \SDSKPROT is shown renamed from ARCH to STRU.

Example of directory structure: \SDSKPROT
                                        | - \SOFTDESK
                                        | - \STRU

Experiment: Highlight ARCH, pick **Rename...**, then type STRU. Pick OK.

Renaming the prototype replaces the name in the list box.

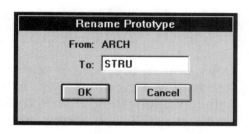

FILE ➤ PROTOTYPE MANAGER... ➤ STATISTICS...

Statistics... opens the *Prototype Statistics* subdialog box to display or edit the name of the selected prototype **Path**, **Current Project**, **Description**, and **Key Words**. The **Author** (individual who created the prototype) and person whom the file was **Last Saved By** is identified. Revising information in the *Prototype Statistics* dialog box updates the *Prototype Manager* dialog box.

Experiment: Highlight STRU, pick **Statistics...**, then edit the information as shown. Pick OK, and the new information appears in the dialog box when STRU is highlighted.

    Dialog box:

current Project: **STRU**
Description: **Structural tutorial to create framing**
                   three story building
                   Prototype for structural training
Key Words: **stru;tutorial;struct training**

FILE ➤ PROTOTYPE MANAGER... ➤ COPY...

Copy... opens the *Copy Prototype* subdialog box for creating a prototype with a new directory name by duplicating subdirectories. The figure shows the STRU prototype copied to MECH under the \SDSKPROT directory.

Example of directory structure: \SDSKPROT
                                    | - \MECH
                                    | - \SOFTDESK
                                    | - \STRU

    Experiment: Highlight STRU, pick **Copy...**, then type MECH. Pick OK.

Copying the prototype appends the name to the list box.

FILE ➤ PROTOTYPE MANAGER... ➤ REMOVE...

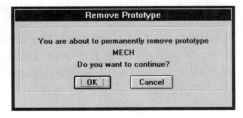

Remove... opens the *Remove Prototype* subdialog box to remove the selected prototype. The subdirectory name under \SDSKPROT and all related files and directories under \MECH are deleted when OK is chosen.

Example of new directory structure: \SDSKPROT
                                                                        | - \SOFTDESK
                                                                        | - \STRU

Experiment: Highlight MECH, pick **Remove...**, then pick OK. MECH is removed from the list box.

Note: This pick box option should be used with caution.

The list box is shown with the MECH prototype removed.

(If the description still appears in the *Prototype Manager* dialog box, select another prototype name to update the dialog box.)

FILE ➤ PROTOTYPE MANAGER... ➤ SEARCH...

Search... opens the *Search Criteria* subdialog box to find prototypes in the current prototype directory. Searches can be made with **Key Words**, **Author** (individual who created the prototype), and the last person whom the prototype drawing was **Saved by**. Edit boxes that do not apply can remain blank. **Reset** removes all values from the dialog box, enabling a new search.

Experiment: Pick **Search...**, enter the key word STRU, then pick OK.

The list box displays the specific prototype name being searched along with the information entered when the prototype was created or edited.

Choose **Search...**, select **Reset**, then pick OK to restore the list box information and return to the *Project Manager* dialog box.

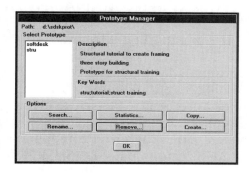

Highlight STRU, then pick **Remove**... to remove the STRU prototype. Pick OK to close the *Prototype Manager* dialog box and conclude your experimentation.

THE PROJECT MANAGER DIALOG BOX

FILE ➤ PROJECT MANAGER...

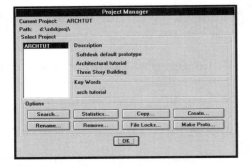

Project Manager... opens the *Project Manager* dialog box to **Create...**, **Search...** for, **Copy...**, **Rename**, edit **Statistics**, create **File Locks**, **Remove...**, **and Make Prot...** (Prototype) projects. The **Current Project** name ARCHTUT and directory path D:\SDSKPROJ\ appear at the top. Projects from the current directory, such as \ARCHTUT, created in Chapter 8, appear in the list box. Projects control the default settings for all associated drawing files and serve as a repository for data created by and shared between drawings in a project.

Example of directory structure: \SDSKPROJ
                                       | - \ARCHTUT

Experiment: Pick **Project Manager**... under the File pull-down menu and pick each button as discussed to view or experiment further.

Note: Softdesk requires that every drawing be associated with a project and automatically verifies this each time the drawing opens. If a project has been renamed or deleted, you will be prompted for a new project name.

FILE ➤ PROJECT MANAGER... ➤ SEARCH...

Search... opens the *Search Criteria* subdialog box to locate projects in the current project directory using **Key Words**, **Author**, or name of the last person the prototype drawing was

Saved by. Reset will remove all values from the dialog box to enable a new search.

After specifying the search criteria, picking OK displays all projects that meet the criteria in the *Project Manager* dialog list box. Values for edit boxes that do not apply can remain blank.

FILE ➤ PROJECT MANAGER... ➤ STATISTICS...

Statistics... opens the *Project Statistics* subdialog box to view or edit names of the **Path, Current Project, Description,** and/or **Key Words**. The **Author** and the person who the project was **Last Saved By** are identified.

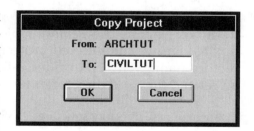

FILE ➤ PROJECT MANAGER... ➤ COPY...

Copy... opens the *Copy Project* subdialog box to create a new project with the default settings that match the selected project. Entering a new directory name, such as CIVILTUT, will cause it to be duplicated along with subdirectories and files under the root directory name \SDSKPROJ. The figure shows the ARCHTUT project under the \SDSKPROJ directory copied to the name CIVILTUT in the same root directory.

Use Copy Project where two projects are very similar. Use the first as a starting point for the second.

```
Example of directory structure:   \SDSKPROJ
                                    I - \ARCHTUT
                                    I - \CIVILTUT
```

Experiment: Highlight ARCHTUT, pick **Copy...**, then type CIVILTUT. Pick OK.

FILE ➤ PROJECT MANAGER... ➤ CREATE...

Create... opens the *Create Project* directory to create a new project as discussed in Chapter 8.

FILE ➤ PROJECT MANAGER... ➤ RENAME...

Rename... opens the *Rename Project* subdialog box to rename selected projects. The subdirectory name under \SDSKPROJ is shown renamed from CIVILTUT to STRUTUT.

Example of directory structure: \SDSKPROJ
      | - \ARCHTUT
      | - \MECHTUT
      | - \STRUTUT

Experiment: Highlight CIVIL, choose **Rename...**, enter STRUTUT. Pick OK.

FILE ➤ PROJECT MANAGER... ➤ REMOVE...

Remove... opens the *Remove Project* subdialog box to remove the selected project. The subdirectory name STRUTUT under \SDSKPROJ and all related files and directories are deleted.

Example of new directory structure: \SDSKPROJ
      | - \ARCHTUT
      | - \MECHTUT

Note: This pick box option should be used with caution.

Experiment: Highlight STRUTUT, choose **Remove...**, then pick OK to remove the STRUTUT project.

FILE ➤ PROJECT MANAGER... ➤ FILE LOCKS...

If the Softdesk environment has locked files for specific project data, this pick box allows viewing and deletion (if necessary) of information relat-

ing to the lock files. Locks are placed to control multiple-user access to project data on a network and should be deleted if they do not serve a valid purpose. (For example, locked files remaining on your hard drive due to a system crash should be erased.) Picking this button will otherwise display the error message dialog box shown.

Note: Make sure no one is currently accessing a drawing on the project selected for unlocking.

FILE ➤ PROJECT MANAGER... ➤ MAKE PROTO...

Make Proto... opens the *Make Prototype* subdialog box to create a new prototype based on default settings in the selected project.

Entering the name MECH2D in the **Prototype Name** edit box would create a MECH2D subdirectory under the root directory \SDSKPROT containing duplicate files and directories.

Example of directory structure: \SDSKPROT
          | - \MECH2D
          | - \SOFTDESK
          | - \STRU

SOFTDESK PRODUCTS

The **Softdesk Products...** command allows you to load installed Softdesk modules.

FILE ➤ SOFTDESK PRODUCTS...

Select **Softdesk Products...** from the File pull-down menu to display the *Softdesk Prod-*

ucts dialog box. Highlight Softdesk's Auto-Architect product to load the module, then pick OK. This switches menus to the AA.MNC menu found in the \SDSK directory and initializes the module.

Note: The asterisk (*) indicates that the module is loaded into memory. Selecting **Clear** removes the selected module from memory to free-up system resources. Clearing a module can free-up a floating network license, if any.

MENUS AND TOOLBARS

Installing the Auto-Architect module appends the Core pull-down menus File, Edit, View, and Tools with the Auto-Architect pull-down menus Walls, Door/Wind, Design, Symbols, and ArchTools. Commands specific to the Auto-Architect menus are discussed in each chapter.

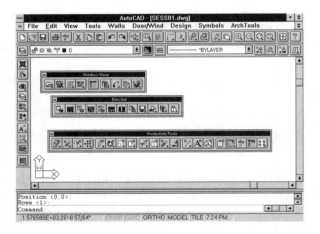

Database_Query, Data_Link, and Productivity_Tools are shown as floating toolbars and the Softdesk Core toolbar is docked along the left side. Clicking once on the hyphen at the top left of each floating toolbar hides it.

To display floating toolbars, type the AutoCAD **Toolbar** command and enter the name (including the underscore) at the command line as shown:

Command: sdsk

Command: toolbar

Toolbar name (or ALL): **productivity_tools**

Show/Hide/Left/Right/Top/Bottom/Float: <Show>: **f**

Position <0,0>:↵

Rows <1>:↵

FILE ➤ UTILITIES ➤ MERGE MENUS...

Merge menus... combine Core or Productivity Tools menus with Softdesk applications. Each Softdesk module has an editable stub menu which can be spliced with Core (or Protools) and AutoCAD menus to create the full module menu. The stub menu can be edited with an ASCII text editor to modify an application menu, then recompiled with **Merge menus...** to initialize the changes.

Menus are merged automatically the first time a module is used after installation, so this command is only needed if any of the component menus such as Protools, Core, Acad, or Applications have been changed.

Softdesk Menus

Menu File Name	Directory	Application
CR.MNC	\SDSK	CORE
AB.MNC	\SDSK	BASE BUILDING
AA.MNC	\SDSK	ARCHITECTURAL
PP.MNC	\SDSK	PRODUCTIVITY TOOLS
CR_STUB.MNU	\SDSK\CR\LNG	CORE
AB_STUB.MNU	\SDSK\AB\LNG	BASE BUILDING
AA_STUB.MNU	\SDSK\AA\LNG	ARCHITECTURAL
PP_STUB.MNU	\SDSK\PP\LNG	PRODUCTIVITY TOOLS

PROTOTYPE SETTINGS

FILE ➤ PROTOTYPE SETTINGS...

Prototype Settings... opens the *Select Prototype* dialog box to select a prototype for editing. Use the command to configure settings for Softdesk prototypes, then copy the changes to new projects using the *Prototype Manager* dialog box. Choosing **Search by...** and **Statistics...** pick boxes opens subdialog boxes as previously discussed. Double-clicking a prototype or picking OK opens the *Prototype Settings* dialog box.

Core and Application Settings will be discussed in the PROJECT SETTINGS section.

Note: Commands in this section are only informational; no changes will be made to the prototype settings.

Experiment: Pick **Prototype Settings...** from the File pull-down menu, then double-click the Softdesk name to open the *Prototype Settings* dialog box.

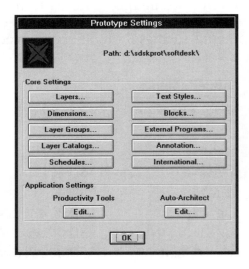

The *Select Prototype* dialog box is used for viewing and editing default values of the selected prototype.

Prototype and project dialog boxes have the same setting pick boxes and will be discussed in detail later in the Project Settings section. Picking and editing any of the 10 **Core Settings** pick boxes in the *Prototype Settings* dialog box allows modifications only to prototypes, not projects.

Note: The current Softdesk application (other than Core) appears at the bottom of the Prototype Settings and Project Settings dialog boxes, along with Productivity Tools, if installed. If the module is grayed, there is no current Application. Selecting Softdesk Products... from the File pull-down menu will load an Application.

. . . .

PROJECT SETTINGS

The following describes the top 10 buttons (shown in the *Project Settings* dialog box) which apply to both Prototypes and Projects. Prototype Settings affect future projects, whereas Project Settings only alter the current project.

FILE ➤ PROJECT SETTINGS...

Project Settings... opens the *Project Settings* dialog box to view and edit settings for the current drawing's project. The dialog box displays the location of the drive letter and current project path D:\SDSKPROJ\ARCHTUT.

The dialog box also contains **Load from Prototype...** and **Save to Prototype...** pick boxes used for retrieving and saving prototype settings.

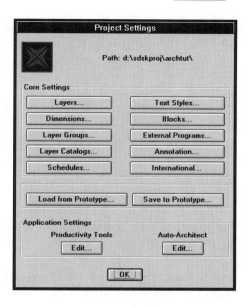

FILE ➤ PROJECT SETTINGS... ➤ LAYERS... (Color/Linetype option)

Layers... opens the *Layer Settings* dialog box displaying descriptions, layer names, colors, and ltypes (linetypes). The contents of the list box change based on the current radio button selected in the **Options** section. When the **Groups** radio button is active, the list box displays layer group controls.

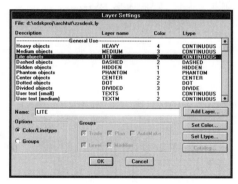

Layer descriptions identify the types of entities placed on a given layer and cannot be changed. However, layer names, which Softdesk calls *root layer names*, can be edited.

Highlighting text names TEXTS, TEXTM, and TEXTL, then entering the new name TEXT in the **Name:** edit box would rename all selected layers to the single layer name. This allows you to simplify the layer system to match personal needs.

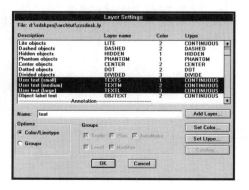

Duplicate layer names then appear for small, large, and medium annotation text as shown.

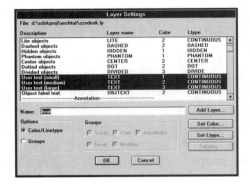

FILE ➤ PROJECT SETTINGS... ➤ LAYERS... ➤ SET COLOR...

Layer colors can also be changed by selecting the **Set Color...** pick box and opening the *Select Color* dialog box.

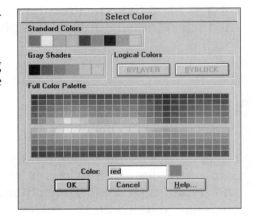

FILE ➤ PROJECT SETTINGS... ➤ LAYERS... ➤ SET LTYPE...

Layer linetypes can be modified by selecting the **Set Ltype...** pick box and opening the *Select Linetype* dialog box displaying more than 100 different linetypes.

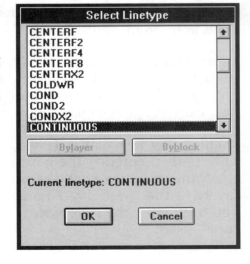

FILE ➤ PROJECT SETTINGS... ➤ LAYERS... ➤ ADD LAYER...

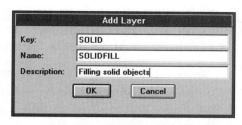

Add Layer... opens the *Add Layer* dialog box to append new layers to the current ZZSDESK.LY layer file stored in the \SDSKPROJ\ARCHTUT directory. The figure shows SOLID entered as the **Key**, SOLIDFILL as **Name**, and "Filling solid objects" as the **Description**.

The new layer is shown appended to the layer list. New layers always appear at the bottom of the list unless rearranged by editing the layer file (ZZSDESK.LY) using the Notepad or similar ASCII text editor.

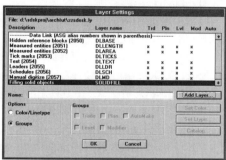

Note: The Key serves as a label or word describing the layer name. A new key that you create could be used in the Symbol Manager to set the layer used for a symbol or in the Wall Style editor to specify a custom layer for a wall component.

The layer SOLID, for example, can be used for any symbol in the Symbol Manager dialog box. Choosing **Tools ➤ Symbol Manager... ➤ Edit ➤ Layer Key...** would open the *Layer Key Name Descriptions* dialog box where the new layer can be highlighted and assigned to the current symbol.

THE ZZSDESK.LY FILE

The following list shows the beginning structure of the ZZSDESK.LY file which stores Core layer information. Particular attention should be focused on the lines after the group heading "General Use," as this information appears similar to the actual contents of the *Layer Settings* dialog box.

The entry "Heavy objects,HEAVY,HEAVY,4,CONTINUOUS,1,1,1,1,0" follows the explanations shown on the second line of the file. Values for **Trade** through **AutoCreate** refer to status in layer groups (0=off, 1=on).

```
*Softdesk Layer Default File: zzsdesk.ly
*Description,Keyname,Layername,Color,Linetype,Trade,Plan,Level,Modifier,AutoCreate
*VERSION:12.0
*DELIMITER:,
*FNAME:zzsdesk.ly
*UNITS:Imperial
*TITLES:Layer Defaults,Description
*FIELD:Description,,2,17,0,0,0,,Description
*FIELD:Keyname,,2,1,0,0,0,,Program key name
*FIELD:Aliasname,,2,17,0,0,0,,User assigned name
*FIELD:Color,,2,1,0,0,0,,Color
*FIELD:Linetype,,2,17,0,0,0,,Linetype
*FIELD:Bitcode,,2,1,0,0,0,,Mask setting 1
*FIELD:Bitcode,,2,1,0,0,0,,Mask setting 2
*FIELD:Bitcode,,2,1,0,0,0,,Mask setting 3
*FIELD:Bitcode,,2,1,0,0,0,,Mask setting 4
*FIELD:Create,,2,1,0,0,0,,Create bit
~General Use
Heavy objects,HEAVY,HEAVY,4,CONTINUOUS,1,1,1,1,0
Medium objects,MEDIUM,MEDIUM,3,CONTINUOUS,1,1,1,1,0
Lite objects,LITE,LITE,2,CONTINUOUS,1,1,1,1,0
```

The ending portion of the ZZSDESK.LY file is significant because it shows the actual location of the SOLIDFILL layer previously discussed.

```
Text (2054),ZLTEXT,DLTEXT,4,CONTINUOUS,1,1,1,1,0
Leaders (2055),ZLLDR,DLLDR,2,CONTINUOUS,1,1,1,1,0
Schedules (2056),ZLSCH,DLSCH,4,CONTINUOUS,1,1,1,1,0
Manual digitize (2057),ZLMD,DLMD,2,CONTINUOUS,1,1,1,1,0
Filling solid objects,SOLID,SOLIDFILL,7,CONTINUOUS,0,0,0,0,0
```

Repositioning new layer names under group headings (marked with "~") or deleting a layer from the ZZSDESK.LY file, requires *cut-and-paste* of complete lines using a text editor. Saving the modified file and reopening the *Layer Settings* dialog box displays the modifications.

DEFAULT LAYERS IN CORE

The following partial list identifies Softdesk's default layering information. Layering groups include:

- General Use (see Table 1)
- Annotation (see Table 2)
- Borders and Schedules (see Table 3)
- Miscellaneous (see Table 4)
- Productivity Tools (see Table 5)
- Data Link (see Table 6)

Table 1 General Use

Description	Layer Name	Color	Linetype
Heavy objects	HEAVY	4	CONTINUOUS
Medium objects	MEDIUM	3	CONTINUOUS
Lite objects	LITE	2	CONTINUOUS
Dashed objects	DASHED	2	DASHED
Hidden objects	HIDDEN	1	HIDDEN
Phantom objects	PHANTOM	1	PHANTOM
Center objects	CENTER	2	CENTER
Dotted objects	DOTTED	3	DOT
Divided objects	DIVIDED	3	DIVIDE
User text (small)	TEXTS	1	CONTINUOUS
User text (medium)	TEXTM	2	CONTINUOUS
User text (large)	TEXTL	3	CONTINUOUS
Object label text	OBJTEXT	2	CONTINUOUS

Table 2 Annotation

Description	Layer Name	Color	Linetype
Hatch patterns	HATCH	5	CONTINUOUS
Annotation, leaders, etc	ANNOBJ	2	CONTINUOUS
Annotation text	ANNTEXT	2	CONTINUOUS

(continues)

Table 2 Annotation (*Continued*)

Description	Layer Name	Color	Linetype
Dimension lines	DIMLINE	1	CONTINUOUS
Dimension text	DIMTEXT	2	CONTINUOUS
Plan grid lines	GRIDLINE	2	CONTINUOUS
Plan grid bubbles	GRIDBUB	2	CONTINUOUS
Plan grid bubble text	GRIDTEXT	2	CONTINUOUS
Section marks	ANNSXOBJ	2	CONTINUOUS
Section mark text	ANNSXTEXT	2	CONTINUOUS
Detail marks	ANNDTOBJ	2	CONTINUOUS
Detail mark text	ANNDTTEXT	2	CONTINUOUS
Miscellaneous annotation symbol	ANNSYMOBJ	2	CONTINUOUS
Miscellaneous annotation text	ANNSYMTEXT	2	CONTINUOUS
Table annotation text	ANNTABLE	4	CONTINUOUS

Table 3 Borders and Schedules

Description	Layer Name	Color	Linetype
Border line	BORDERLINE	4	CONTINUOUS
Border text (small)	BORDERTEXTS	1	CONTINUOUS
Border text (medium)	BORDERTEXTM	2	CONTINUOUS
Border text (large)	BORDERTEXTL	3	CONTINUOUS
Title block text (small)	TITLEBLKS	1	CONTINUOUS
Title block text (medium)	TITLEBLKM	2	CONTINUOUS
Title block text (large)	TITLEBLKL	3	CONTINUOUS
Title text	TITTEXT	2	CONTINUOUS
Heavy schedule lines	SCHLINEH	4	CONTINUOUS
Schedule lines	SCHLINE	2	CONTINUOUS
Schedule rule lines	SCHLINER	3	CONTINUOUS
Schedule text (titles)	SCHTEXTL	3	CONTINUOUS
Schedule text (entries)	SCHTEXTM	2	CONTINUOUS
Schedule text (notes)	SCHTEXTS	2	CONTINUOUS

Table 3 (*Continued*)

Description	Layer Name	Color	Linetype
Legend lines	LGDLINE	2	CONTINUOUS
Legend text (small)	LGDTEXTS	1	CONTINUOUS
Legend text (medium)	LGDTEXTM	2	CONTINUOUS
Legend text (large)	LGDTEXTL	3	CONTINUOUS

Table 4 Miscellaneous

Description	Layer Name	Color	Linetype
Reference objects	REFERENCE	8	CONTINUOUS
Noplot layers	NOPLOT	8	CONTINUOUS
Boundary lines	BOUNDLINE	3	CONTINUOUS
Zone boundaries	ZONE	6	CONTINUOUS
Match lines	MATCHLINE	3	CONTINUOUS
Match line text	MATCHTEXT	2	CONTINUOUS

Table 5 Productivity Tools

Description	Layer Name	Color	Linetype
Day stamp layer	DAYSTAMP	8	CONTINUOUS
Detail layer	DETAILS	6	CONTINUOUS

Table 6 Data Link (ASG alias numbers shown in parentheses)

Description	Layer Name	Color	Linetype
Hidden reference blocks (2050)	DL_BASE	4	CONTINUOUS
Measured entities (2051)	DL_LENGTH	1	CONTINUOUS
Measured entities (2052)	DL_AREA	1	CONTINUOUS
Tick marks (2053)	DL_TICKS	2	CONTINUOUS
Text (2054)	DL_TEXT	1	CONTINUOUS
Leaders (2055)	DL_LDR	4	CONTINUOUS
Schedules (2056)	DL_SCH	2	CONTINUOUS
Manual digitize (2057)	DL_MD	4	CONTINUOUS

Note: Colors 1 through 7 are often described by color name: 1=red, 2=yellow, 3=green, 4=cyan, 5=blue, 6=magenta, and 7=white.

FILE ➤ PROJECT SETTINGS... ➤ LAYERS... (Groups option)

The **Groups** radio button in the **Options** section of the *Layer Settings* dialog box activates **Trade, Plan, AutoMake, Level,** and **Modifier** check boxes in the **Groups** section. Groups consist of five components which can be combined with every layer in the Softdesk layering system, each controlled by a toggle:

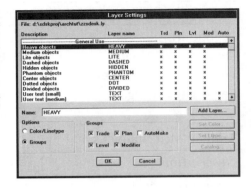

Discipline	=	Trade
Primary Code	=	Plan
Secondary Code	=	Level (or Floor)
Refining Code	=	Modifier
Layer type	=	AutoMake

If a toggle is set, the corresponding layer component (if defined and enabled) will be combined with the *root layer name* for the placement of objects in the drawing.

AutoMake creates layers automatically when invoking **Setup Drawing...** from the File pull-down menu. The current layer group is applied when this setting is toggled on. Layer groups are used to set up or facilitate the plotting of various modelspace drawing types, such as floor plans, demolition plans, reflected ceiling plans, and so on. Softdesk offers this layer naming tool as a feature to more effectively manage the CAD drafting and plotting process. Layer names can be combined with components defined as Trade, Level, Plan, Root, and Modifier. The order or sequence of each group name plus the inclusion or exclusion of any or all group names must be set by the user at the start of a project. Users can choose to apply all or only some group names to a root layer name.

The order in which the layer components appear is controlled by the layer format mask. Each group name is defined by a single letter enclosed by curly brackets ({ }) to create the format mask. As an example, the format mask {T}{R}{P}{L}{M} represents group names in the order TRADE, ROOT LAYER NAME, PLAN, LEVEL, and MODIFIER. Using a dash (-) deliminiter, would insert annotation text on the layer A-ANN-TEXT-RCP-FLO1-N.

Example:

Order of Format Mask **{T}{R}{P}{L}{M}** with a dash **(-)** as the delimiter

Layer Name: **A-ANNTEXT-RCP-FL01-N**

Mask	Name	Example	Description
{T}	Trade	A	Architectural
{R}	Root layer name	ANNTEXT	Annotation text
{P}	Plan	RCP	Reflected Ceiling Plan
{L}	Level	FL01	First floor
{M}	Modifier	N	New

Note: When MODIFIER is used, it must be the last component in the mask for proper operation.

LAYER GROUP SETTINGS

FILE ➤ PROJECT SETTINGS... ➤ LAYER GROUPS...

Layer Groups... opens the *Layer Group Settings* subdialog box to specify layer group components separated by a delimiter. Valid delimiter types include a dash (-), dollar sign ($), and underscore (_). The dialog box displays a format mask that includes components as described.

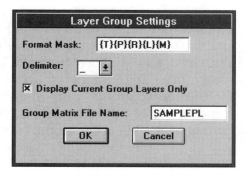

Trade Name identifies disciplines such as Architectural, Structural, Mechanical, Plumbing, and so forth. This component can be included in the mask when drawing information is shared by an Architect and Structural Engineer.

Plan Type identifies drawing types such as Floor Plan, Reflected Ceiling Plan, Elevations, and so forth. Softdesk provides a sample Plan Matrix file stored in a spreadsheet called SAMPLEPL.PM containing layer information for various plan types.

Level Name identifies working levels based on a UCS and elevation. They can represent floor names and/or floor numbers.

Modifier Name identifies building construction phase information such as demo, existing, or new. It can also represent a project's construction phase, such as Phase I, Phase II, and so forth.

Display Current Group Layers Only forces the appearance of only those layer names that are relevant to the current layer group components during Softdesk layer commands such as Layer Set, Layer Thaw, and so forth.

Group Matrix File Name specifies the name of the current Layer Plan Matrix file.

FILE ➤ PROJECT SETTINGS... ➤ LAYER GROUPS...

A format mask for Level and Root layer name, for example, is set by entering {L} and {R} in the **Format Mask:** edit box enclosed with curly brackets as shown.

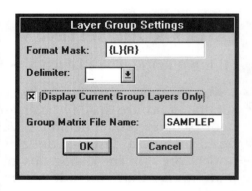

The Format Mask is considered a high-level enable for the use of layer group components. The Groups options, set from the Layer Settings dialog box, are considered a low-level enable for the use of group components. They determine which of the components enabled by the Format Mask will apply to the current layer.

A dash can be assigned from the **Delimiter:** pop-up list as the separator between Level and Root layer names.

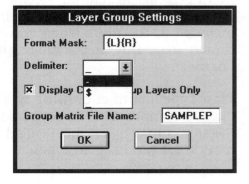

Once a Format Mask has been defined and Groups is turned ON (by invoking the Macro **GX**) , choosing **Layers...** in the *Project Settings* dialog box or the *Softdesk Auto-Architect Settings* dialog box and removing check marks for highlighted layer names in the list box excludes the component from the layer name for inserted objects.

A Format Mask with Level and Root layer names is defined and discussed in detail in Chapter 10.

FILE ➤ PROJECT SETTINGS... ➤ DIMENSIONS...

Dimensions... opens the *Dimension Settings* dialog box. **Suppress Inch Mark**s sets the appearance for Imperial units of measurement values and Architectural unit display to include or suppress inch marks for Structural modules only. When enabled, **Use Special Fractions** displays dimensions stacked.

FILE ➤ PROJECT SETTINGS... ➤ LAYER CATALOG...

Layer Catalog... opens the *Layer Catalog Settings* dialog box to set preferences for layering name systems, including SDESK, AIA, ASG, BS1192, and User. Changes made to the Standard Catalog Name are immediately reflected in the *Layer Settings* dialog box when choosing the **Layers...** pick box. Selection of a catalog name sets the layering standard for all Softdesk modules.

The **Alternate Catalog File** and **Alternate Alias File** can be ignored as they are only used in the British BS1192 layer system.

FILE ➤ PROJECT SETTINGS... ➤ SCHEDULES...

Schedules...opens the *Schedule Settings* dialog box to set a format for creating and printing schedules.

FILE ➤ PROJECT SETTINGS... ➤ TEXT STYLES...

Text Styles... opens the *Text Style Settings* dialog box to set or edit text styles for the Softdesk environment. Highlighting one or more text styles displays a text style name and associated height in their appropriate **Style:** and **Height:** edit boxes for modification.

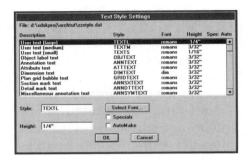

Picking **Select Font...** opens the *Select Font File* dialog box to choose a font shape file for the selected text style. AutoCAD (c4 release) fonts can be selected from the default \R13\ COM\FONTS directory and Softdesk fonts can be chosen from the SDSK directory.

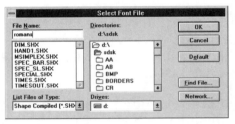

If drawings are shared by consultants that do not use Softdesk products, special characters should not be used. Font files that read "Style name: DIMTEXT Font files: romans.shx,special" can be replaced with the AutoCAD romans.shx font in the Select Font File dialog box by invoking the Style command.

Specials provide special characters such as stacked fractions, centerline characters, and so on.

AutoMake appears in the Layer Settings dialog box and was previously discussed.

FILE ➤ PROJECT SETTINGS... ➤ BLOCKS...

Blocks... opens the *Block Settings* dialog box to set aspects of block insertion in the Softdesk environment.

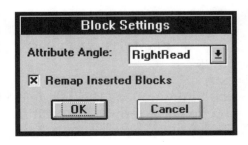

The **Attribute Angle** pop-up list has these two settings — **RightRead** and **Horizontal**.

RightRead inserts attributes within some blocks (such as annotation or identification blocks) so they read from the right and not upside-down.

Horizontal inserts attributes with zero degrees rotation relative to the current UCS.

Remap Inserted Blocks... check box assigns group component settings to the root layer names of entities in blocks.

FILE ➤ PROJECT SETTINGS... ➤ EXTERNAL PROGRAMS...

External Programs... opens the *External Program Settings* dialog box to enter names of a user-supplied **Text Editor, Image Viewer**, and **Spreadsheet** software.

For example, by typing the path and filename C:\DOS\EDIT.COM in the **Text Editor:** the edit box will invoke the MS-DOS text editor file as an ASCII text editor for Productivity Tools applications.

FILE ➤ PROJECT SETTINGS ➤ ANNOTATION...

Annotation... opens the *Annotation Settings* dialog box to set the plotted size for scaling of all annotation symbols and specific display controls for leader symbols. Picking a pop-up list in the **Leaders** sections displays choices for **Type, Pointer, Terminator**, and **Symbol**.

All Text Left-Justified sets text placement as left justified when invoking the Softdesk **Text Leader** command.

FILE ➤ PROJECT SETTINGS... ➤ INTERNATIONAL...

International... opens the *Internal Settings* dialog box to choose among **Date, Time**, and **Currency** Format edit boxes.

Change... in the **Date Format** section opens the *Date Formats* dialog box to control how dates appear in drawings. The Short Date Format section offers radio button options for **Order** and **Separator**. The **Long Date Format** offers radio button options for **Order** with additional pop-up lists for **Day**, **Date**, **Month**, and **Year** variations.

An example of the date format will appear when a Softdesk Title block is inserted into a drawing.

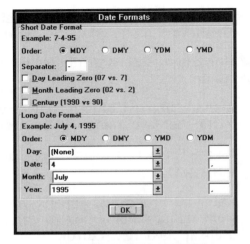

Change... in the **Time Format** section opens the *Time Formats* dialog box to set a 12 or 24 hour clock plus a **Notation** section to classify time designations.

Leading Zeros displays numbers from 1 through 9 as " 01" by including a leading zero.

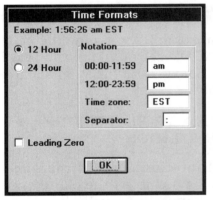

Change... in the **Currency Format** section opens the *Currency Formats* dialog box to set various currency styles by selecting pop-up lists and edit boxes in the **Monetary Formats** section.

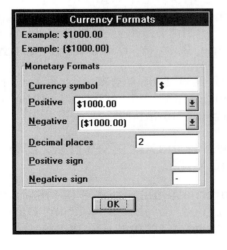

EDITING APPLICATION SETTINGS FOR AUTO-ARCHITECT

FILE ➤ PROJECT SETTINGS... ➤ (AUTO-ARCHITECT) EDIT...

Auto-Architect Edit... at the bottom of the *Project Settings* dialog box opens the *Softdesk Auto-Architect Settings* subdialog box to set controls specifically for the Auto-Architect module.

This subdialog box has additional pick boxes for **Layers...**, **General...**, **Symbols...**, **Walls...**, **Doors and Windows...**, and **Stairs...** which will be discussed later.

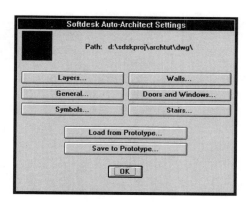

FILE ➤ PROJECT SETTINGS... ➤ (AUTO-ARCHITECT) EDIT... ➤ LOAD FROM PROTOTYPE...

Load from Prototype... opens the *Select Prototype* dialog box to retrieve default settings and style libraries from a selected prototype. **Search by...** and **Statistics...** pick boxes are available as previously discussed.

FILE ➤ PROJECT SETTINGS... ➤ (AUTO-ARCHITECT) EDIT... ➤ SAVE TO PROTOTYPE...

Save to Prototype... opens the *Select Prototype* dialog box to save current Auto-Architect project settings to a selected prototype. **Search by...** and **Statistics...** pick boxes are also included as choices.

This completes the overview of the Core and Softdesk commands in the File pull-down menu. The File pull-down menu also offers cascading **Import, Export, Utilities**, and **Configure** menus with additional commands.

In some of the following chapters, controls will be set for the Softdesk environment to draw a three-story building. Starting from a space plan, walls are converted to a three-dimensional floor plan, with doors, windows, and plumbing fixtures added, then all objects are copied to different UCS levels to create the final design.

CHAPTER TEN

PROJECT SETTINGS

Set Controls for the Architectural Tutorial; Helpful
Hints to Launch Softdesk; Loading menus and Toolbars

Contents

Before we start to set controls for this Architectural tutorial, topics in this chapter will include some helpful Windows techniques for launching the Softdesk software. Next, information is introduced concerning procedures for loading Softdesk modules, associating a menu with a drawing, and loading Toolbars. In the later part of the chapter, project settings are reviewed and set for creating floor plans with several level (floors) that are all stored in one drawing.

STARTING SOFTDESK—CUSTOMIZING THE ICON

If you have not exited from the Softdesk program, save the SESS01 drawing and return to the Program Manager.

The Program-item icon used to launch AutoCAD® with S7 from the Group window may appear as shown here or in Chapter 8. The icon description and working directory for an icon can be customized to save time later when opening and saving files.

Copy your Softdesk icon by picking it and dragging the icon while pressing the CTRL key. Next, pick the copied icon so that the description is highlighted. Press Alt + Enter and the *Program Item Properties* dialog box will appear.

Change the description and working directory created in Chapter 8 by entering your drive letter and the project directory created for the architectural tutorial. Type a description, such as Arch Tutorial and the name of the directory where the SESS01 drawing was saved. In Chapter 8, the SESS01 drawing was saved to <drive> \SDSK\ARCHTUT\DWG.

   Dialog box:

Description: **Arch Tutorial**
Working Directory: **<drive>\SDSKPROJ\ARCHTUT\DWG**

Pick OK, then double-click the icon to start the Softdesk program.

OPENING THE DRAWING

FILE ➤ OPEN

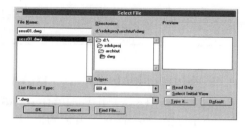

Pick **Open** from the File pull-down and the project directory immediately appears in the *Select File* dialog box with the SESS01 drawing. Highlight SESS01 in the \SDSKPROJ\ ARCHTUT\DWG directory, then pick OK. Core, Productivity Tools, and Auto-Architect modules should initialize automatically.

Initializing...
Current project is ARCHTUT.
       Softdesk Core Version 7.2
  Copyright 1994 Softdesk, Inc. All Rights Reserved.
      Loading... Please wait.
   Softdesk Productivity Tools Version 7.2
 Copyright 1992-1994 Softdesk, Inc. All Rights Reserved.
     Loading... Please wait.
Loading Softdesk Building Base... Please wait
   Softdesk Auto-Architect Version 7.2
  Copyright 1994-1995 Softdesk, Inc. All Rights Reserved.
     Loading... Please wait.

LOADING MODULES

FILE ➤ SOFTDESK PRODUCTS...

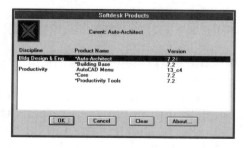

Some of the Softdesk modules include Core, Productivity Tools, Auto-Architect, Details, Landscape, CAD Overlay ESP, and CAD Overlay LFX. When installed, these Softdesk modules can be initialized from the *Softdesk Products* dialog box.

If the Auto-Architect, Building Base, Core, and Productivity Tools modules have not been loaded, select **Softdesk Products...** from the File pull-down menu (or type "SOFTDESK" at command line) to open the

Softdesk Products dialog box and highlight the Product name, then pick OK. Only one module can be loaded each time.

Note: An asterisk (*) appears with the name of the modules loaded in memory. Other modules may be loaded in memory, but the main focus of this tutorial is Core with the Auto-Architect module.

Softdesk Menu: AUTO-ARCHITECT

Loading Auto-Architect displays pull-down Core menu headings for File, Edit, View, and Tools, as well as Auto-Architect menu headings for Walls, Door/Wind, Design, Symbols, and ArchTools. The default Softdesk installation may appear with the Core toolbar docked along the left side of the screen and the Database Query, Data Link, and Productivity toolbars floating.

Depending on the modules loaded, the pull-down menus along the menu bar (at the top of the screen) are different. Windows and Windows for Workgroups operating systems have memory limitations, which do not allow display of the Edit, View, and Tools pull-downs in Auto-Architect. Windows® 95 and Windows® NT do not have these limitations.

ASSOCIATING A MENU WITH A DRAWING

FILE ➤ CONFIGURE ➤ PREFERENCES...

In AutoCAD Release 13 there is an option to associate a menu file with a drawing file. Selecting **Preferences...** under **Configure** in the File pull-down menu opens the *Preferences* dialog box. Picking the tab labeled Misc. then placing a check mark at **Use Menu in Header** enables this option for the Softdesk prototype drawing SDSK_I ,causing the desired Softdesk menu to display. When this toggle is off, it may be necessary to manually load a menu file from the *Softdesk Products* dialog box. However, if you will primarily be using only one Softdesk Application (such as Auto-Architect), it is better to turn off **Use Menu in Header** to avoid extra regens when opening a drawing.

LOADING TOOLBARS

FILE ➤ CONFIGURE ➤ TOOLBAR

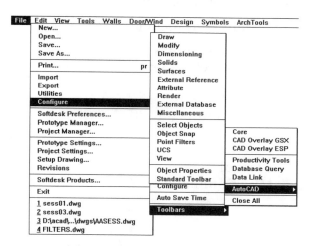

Toolbars for specific modules can be loaded by invoking the AutoCAD Toolbar command or selecting **Configure**, then **Toolbar** under the File pull-down menu. Typing the command or selecting it from the pull-down menu requires inclusion of the underscore (_) in titles, such as Database_Query and Data_Link.

Note: To identify Toolbar names, pick any tool icon with the right mouse button and the *Toolbar* dialog box opens to display the names in the **Toolbars** list box.

(AutoCAD Command: **TOOLBAR**)

 Command line:

Command: **toolbar**

Toolbar name (or ALL): **productivity_tools**

Show/Hide/Left/Right/Top/Bottom/Float: <Show>: ↵

To close a floating toolbar, pick the hyphen in the rectangular box at the top left corner of the toolbar.

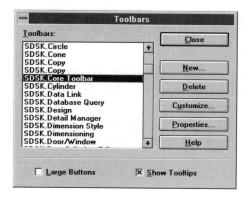

DOCKED CORE TOOLBAR

Commands can be selected from the Softdesk Core Toolbar positioned along the left of the display screen or from the pull-down menu. All tools have tooltips and some have flyouts with additional icons. Holding the mouse button over a tool displays the tooltip as shown for the first icon, Softdesk Products.

Core commands include:

> Softdesk Products
> Build Selection Set
> Eye Tools
> Layer Controls
> Layer Group Edit
> Annotation
> Hatch
> Schedules
> Misc Commands

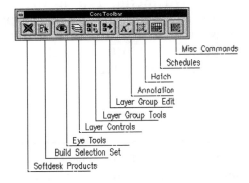

FLOATING CORE TOOLBAR

The floating Core toolbar is shown with names of tooltips.

SETTING A COMPOUND LAYER GROUP—THE FORMAT MASK

VIEW ➤ LAYER GROUPS ➤ EDIT GROUP ➤ EDIT FORMAT MASK

Select **Edit Format Mask** from **Edit Group** under **Layer Groups** in the View pull-down menu. Create compound layer names by setting a Format Mask for Level and Root components as described next.

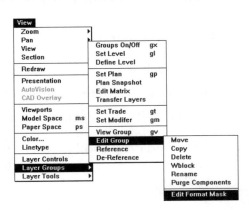

Mask	Component	Description
{L}	Level	Represents floor level
{R}	Root layer name	Represents default layer name

Enter {L}{R} at the prompt to set a mask for components Level and Root, then type D to use a dash line as the separator.

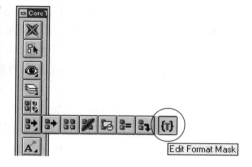

Note: Alternate methods for setting the Format Mask include: (1) picking the **Layer Group Edit** flyout and choosing the **Edit Format Mask** tool or (2) selecting the **Layer Groups...** button in the *Project Settings* dialog box. (Although Alternate 2 was discussed in Chapter 9, it is not available in the current Softdesk version.)

The prompting sequence is:

```
Command: sdsk
Set new layer mask format (or . for none) <{T}{P}{R}{L}{M}>: {L}{R}
Set new layer delimiter ($/Dash/Underscore) <Underscore>: D
```

. . . .

DEFINING A LEVEL

VIEW ➤ LAYER GROUPS ➤ DEFINE LEVEL

Define level names FL01, FL02, and FL03 for the First, Second, and Third Floors with heights set to 10' above the previous floor level. Next, initialize the format. Set FL01 as the current level to begin the space planning process of the design for the three-story building.

Select **Define Level** from the View pull-down menu under **Layer Groups** using the level information described in the table.

Level Information

Level name	Height of level above current UCS	Description
FL01	0	First Floor
FL02	10'	Second Floor
FL03	10'	Third Floor

PROMPTING SUMMARY

Command: sdsk
Level name: **FL01**
Height of level above current UCS <0">: **0**
Description: **First Floor**
Level name (or . for none) <FL02>: **FL02**
Height of level above previous level <10'>: **10'**
Description (or . for none) <First Floor>: **Second Floor**
Level name (or . for none) <FL03>: **FL03**
Height of level above previous level <10'>: **10'**
Description (or . for none) <Second Floor>: **Third Floor**
Level name (or . for none) <FL04>: **. [type a period]**
Restore layers now? <Yes>: **n**
Group settings are ON.
Level: FL01 Description: First Floor (Elev. 0")

CORE AND AUTO-ARCHITECT LAYER NAMES

Compound layer names can be created by combining the Core or Auto-Architect Root layer name with any or all of the Trade, Plan Type, Level, Root, or Modifier layer group components.

FILE ➤ PROJECT SETTINGS... ➤ LAYERS...

Root layer names are stored in separate files for Core and each Softdesk module in the project directory. Core layer names are found in the *Layer Settings* dialog box when **Layer...** is chosen from the **Core Settings** section of the *Project Settings* dialog box.

The path and filename for core layers for this architectural tutorial is D:\SDSKPROJ\ARCHTUT\ZZSDESK.LY.

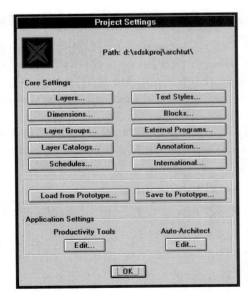

FILE ➤ PROJECT SETTINGS... ➤ (AUTO-ARCHITECT) EDIT... ➤ LAYERS...

As previously discussed, the layers specific to the architectural module are accessed from the *Project Settings* dialog box under **Auto-Architect Edit....** Choosing the **Layers...** button shows the path and filename of architectural layers (at the top of the dialog box) as D:\SDSKPROJ\ARCHTUT\AASDESK.LY.

Note: The drive letter may be different, but the path and filename should be the same.

SETTING LAYER ELIGIBILITY FOR GROUPS

Picking the **Groups** radio button in the **Options** section of either the Core or Architectural layer dialog boxes displays the component heading names Trd, Pln, Lvl, and Mod (along the top of the list box) and the associated toggles Trade, Plan, Level, and Modifier names in the **Groups** section (at the bottom of the dialog box).

Since a Format Mask for the layer group Level and Root layer name was set previously, the next step is to determine the eligibility of those layers that you wish to accept or ignore for the Format Mask.

The figure shows the layer VEHICLES highlighted and X marks placed in columns Trd, Pln, and Mod. In the **Groups** section, X marks appear for Trade, Plan, and Modifier. Since no mark has been placed under the Lvl column in the list box, VEHICLES is not eligible to draw objects using the Format Mask. Since the format mask has been set for Level and Root, layers will only be drawn on the root layer name VEHICLES. If the check box adjacent to Level in the Groups section had a check mark for the VEHICLES layer and the Level name was defined FL01, objects would be drawn on FL01-VEHICLES.

Note: Trade, Plan, and Modifier have not been included in the Format Mask and therefore are ignored. Checks can remain in these boxes as long as their components are not defined in the Format Mask.

SETTING THE CURRENT LEVEL

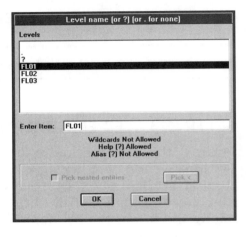

Select **Set Level** from the View pulldown menu under **Layer Groups** to open the *Level name (or?) (or.for none)* dialog box. Highlight FL01 to set the First Floor as the current UCS level 0, then pick OK.

All objects such as walls, doors, and windows will now be drawn using Format Mask on UCS level 0.

The prompting sequence is:

Command: sdsk

Restore layers now? <Yes>: **n**

Group settings are ON.

Level: FL01 Description: First Floor (Elev. 0")

SAVE THE DRAWING

Invoke the Macro **SA** to save the SESS01 drawing, then proceed to the next chapter to review the space design program and begin drawing the three-story building.

Macro Command: **SA**

(AutoCAD Command: **SAVE**)

Command: **sa**
Macro: Save
Save Drawing As <D:\sdskproj\archtut\dwg\SESS01>:↵

CHAPTER ELEVEN

CREATING SPACES

Creating and Annotating Space Diagrams

CONTENTS

THE DESIGN PROGRAM

The three-story building design will commence by drawing spaces of areas as outlined in the table. The design process will start with a space diagram, a single-line diagram of areas that will be converted into rooms enclosed with double-line walls of varying thickness. The program requirements include creating a three-level structure with 10' floor-to-floor heights and a hip roof. This drawing will contain annotation notes, reference symbols, and exterior elevation.

The chapter will focus on the creation of the space diagram. The following table describes spaces that will comprise the building plan.

Program: Three-Story Building

Space name	Size or Area/SF	Comments
OFFICE-1	60' X 45' (2,700 SF)	Includes storefront window
ENTRY	30' X 30' (900 SF)	Includes custom curved wall
OFFICE-2	60' x 45' (2,700 SF)	Includes 3 additional rooms: OFFICE 2A, 2B and 2C
CORRIDOR	10' wide	Includes exterior exit door
OFFICE-3	(approx 5,500 SF)	Includes exterior exit door
SERVICE	(approx 2,000 SF)	Includes men's and women's restrooms
Total	13,650 SF	

SAVING THE DRAWING FOR EACH SESSION

FILE ➤ SAVEAS

If you wish to save each session as a separate drawing file, select **Saveas** from the File pull-down menu to open the *Save Drawing As* dialog box and enter the name SESS02. As discussed in Chapter 10, the path has been set to save drawings directly to the \SDSKPROJ\ARCHTUT\DWG working directory.

Note: As the tutorial progresses, save the drawing frequently using the AutoCAD **QSAVE** or Softdesk **SA** macro.

Drawings can also be saved as another name in the same (or other) directory and still retain all related file information. Settings are stored in a <drawing>. dfm file such as SESS02.DFM. If the drawing is saved as SESS03, the settings file SESS03.DFM will be created automatically.

CREATING A SPACE DIAGRAM

DESIGN ➤ SPACES AND ROOMS ➤ CREATE SPACES OR LABELS...

Selecting **Create Spaces or Labels...** from the Design pull-down menu under **Spaces and Rooms** opens the *Space Planning* dialog box. Controls are set by picking from radio buttons, list boxes, edit boxes, and image boxes to draw space diagrams.

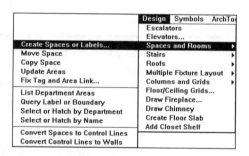

Space diagrams can be created using **Boundary Options** with various **Shapes**. The **Create Spaces or Labels...** command can create space diagrams by drawing a new boundary, selecting an existing polyline or choosing one or more interior points within an enclosed space.

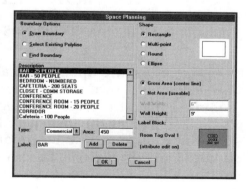

Note: The **Find Boundary** option has limitations imposed by AutoCAD Release 13 and cannot be used with this version of Softdesk.

New spaces can be created by copying or moving existing spaces, then editing them as needed. The aspect ratio or size of a space can be changed at the **Edge point (or Done) <Done>:** prompt by picking alternate points or entering a length and direction. The prompting sequence and figure shown provide an example.

The prompting sequence is:

First corner point: [pick a point]

Edge point: <Ortho on> [if desired, press F8 to set
orthomode on]

Size = 27'-10 41/64" x 96'-9 55/64"

Edge point (or Done) <Done>: [pick point as shown in figure to set aspect ratio (proportions)
of space or enter a value]

Size = 44'-11 25/32" x 60'-0 19/64"

Edge point (or Done) <Done>: [pick another point, enter another value or press enter to
accept proportions of the defined area]

Place label block.

Area = 388800.00 square in. (2700.0000 square ft.), Perimeter = 210'-0 9/64"

Inserting Room Tag Oval 1 at Floor elevation=0".

Note: Based on the value set for the dimension variable
DIMZIN, values for feet and inches may appear as 30'
or 30'-0" in dialog boxes and at the command line.

DRAWING THE FIRST SPACE—OFFICE 1

DESIGN ➤ SPACES AND ROOMS ➤ CREATE SPACES OR LABELS…

Select **Create Spaces or Labels…** from
the Design pull-down menu under **Spaces and
Rooms** to open the *Space Planning* dialog box.
Draw OFFICE-1 as the first space by choosing
radio buttons for **Draw Boundary** and **Rectangle**. Scroll through the **Description** list box
and highlight OFFICE-SMALL. Enter 2700 as
the **Area** and 10' as the **Wall Height**. Accept
the defaults for the **Type** of space as Commercial and the **Room Tag Oval 1** for the **Label
Block**. The name OFFICE-1 automatically
appears as the default in the **Label** edit box.

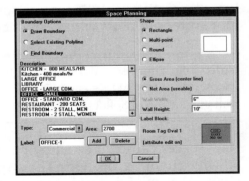

Dialog box :

Boundary Options:	**Draw Boundary**
Shape:	**Rectangle**
Description:	**OFFICE-SMALL**
Type:	**Commercial**
Area:	**2700**
Label:	**OFFICE-1**
Gross Area (centerline):	**[pick radio button]**
Wall Width:	**[disabled/greyed out]**
Wall Height:	**10'**
Label Block for room tag	**(attribute edit on)**

Double-clicking on the image box in the **Label Block** section of the *Space Planning* dialog box opens the *Symbol Manager* dialog box to choose alternate room tags.

The Room Tag Oval 1 highlighted in the *Symbol Manager* dialog box is the default setting. Picking another image button, then picking OK replaces the Label Block in the *Space Planning* dialog box.

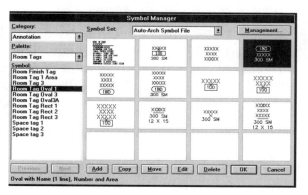

PROMPTING SUMMARY

First corner point: **38',34'**

Edge point: **@60'<0**

Size = 60' x 45'

Edge point (or Done) <Done>: ↵

Place label block.

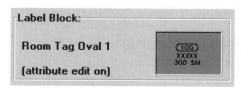

Area = 388800.00 square in. (2700.0000 square ft.), Perimeter = 210'-0"

Inserting Room Tag Oval 1 at Floor elevation=0

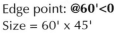 Draw the first space by picking a start point at the X,Y coordinate 38',34' when prompted for **First corner point:**

First corner point: **38',34'**

 Set the distance (width of space) as 60' in the horizontal (0) direction when prompted for **Edge point:**. Pressing enter at the **Edge point (or Done):** prompt draws the rectangular space, then opens a dialog box to specify room tag values.

Edge point: **@60'<0**
Size = 60' x 45'
Edge point (or Done) <Done>: ↵

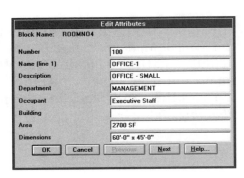 When the *Edit Attributes* dialog box opens, edit the values as shown. The *Edit Attributes* dialog box displays values previously entered from the *Space Planning* dialog box.

Place label block.
Area = 388800.00 square in. (2700.0000 square ft.),
Perimeter = 210'-0"
Inserting Room Tag Oval 1 at Floor elevation=0".

Dialog box:

Number:	100
Name:	OFFICE-1
Description:	OFFICE-SMALL
Department:	**MANAGEMENT**
Occupant:	**Executive Staff**
Building:	(leave blank)
Area:	2700 SF
Dimensions:	60'-0" x 45'-0"
Net Offset:	0

Additional dialog box screens may appear depending on the number of attributes assigned to the specific Room Tag symbol selected.

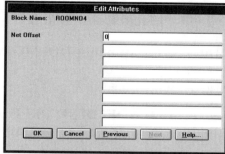

The first space diagram is drawn as shown.

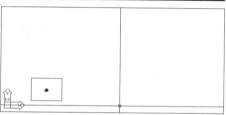

A closer view of the Callout or Room Tag displays visible attribute values for Number, Name, and Area.

Normally invisible attributes appear when the AutoCAD commands **Attdisp** and **Regen** are invoked. (If you wish to invoke these commands, use **Undo** to restore the previous conditions.)

OPENING THE LAYER CONTROL DIALOG BOX USING A MACRO

Invoking the Softdesk Macro **LD** opens the *Layer Control* dialog box to view the new layers formatted with their layer group components for Level and Root layer name FL01-ROOM-TAG and FL01-SPACE created respectively for the Room Tag attribute and Space diagram.

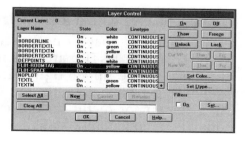

Macro Command: **LD**

(AutoCAD Command: **DDLMODES**)
Command: **ld**
Macro: Layer Dialogue

See **FILE** ➤ **SOFTDESK PREFERENCES** ➤ **Automatic Menu Macro Loading** in Chapter 9 for additional information on Softdesk Macros.

CREATING SPACES BY USING AN EXISTING POLYLINE—ENTRY

Use the **Select Existing Polyline** option in the **Boundary Options** section of the *Space Planning* dialog box to draw the ENTRY area as the next space. Set the current layer to NOPLOT and invoke the AutoCAD REC-TANG command so that these objects can later be easily erased.

Setting Layer Noplot On

Invoke the Macro **LS** and highlight the NOPLOT layer, then pick OK. The command turns the layer on and sets it current. This is a default Softdesk layer used to hold objects that are never plotted.

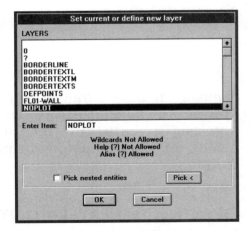

 Macro command: **LS**

Command: **ls**
Macro: Layer Set

Creating Shapes with a Rectangle (Polyline)

Draw the next space on the current layer NOPLOT as the ENTRY area using the Macro **RC**. Start at the upper right intersection of OFFICE-1 defining a width and depth of 30' using the cursor menu for object snap selections.

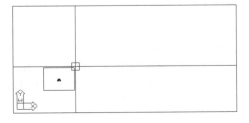

Macro Command: **RC**

(AutoCAD Command: **RECTANG**)

Command: **rc**
First corner: **int** of [**top right intersection of OFFICE-1**]
Other corner: **@30',-30'**

DESIGN ➤ SPACES AND ROOMS ➤ CREATE SPACES OR LABELS...

   Select **Create Spaces or Labels...** from
the Design pull-down menu again to open the
Space Planning dialog box. Use the rectangle
(drawn as a polyline) to create a space diagram
for the ENTRY.

The prompting sequence is:

Select polyline: [**pick polyline**]
Place label block.
Area = 129600.00 square in. (900.0000 square ft.), Perimeter = 120'-0"
Inserting Room Tag Oval 1 at Floor elevation=0".
Insertion point:

   Choose **Select Existing Polyline** and highlight ENTRY in the
Description list box. Accept the defaults Commercial, ENTRY, and 10'
for **Type**, **Label**, and **Wall Height**, respectively.

   Dialog box:

Boundary Options:	**Select Existing Polyline**
Shape:	**[disabled/greyed out]**
Description:	**ENTRY**
Type:	**Commercial**
Label:	**ENTRY**
Area:	**[disabled/greyed out]**
Gross Area (centerline):	**[pick radio button]**
Wall Width:	**[disabled/greyed out]**
Wall Height:	**10'**
Label Block for room tag	**(attribute edit on)**

Select the polyline using your pick box as shown. Pick a point in the middle of the space to place the room tag.

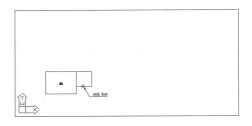

When the *Edit Attributes* dialog box opens, edit the values as shown for the ENTRY space.

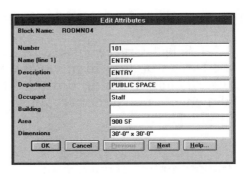

Dialog box:

Number: **101**
Name: ENTRY
Description: ENTRY
Department: **PUBLIC SPACE**
Occupant: **Staff**
Building: (leave blank)
Area: 900 SF
Dimensions: 30'-0" x 30'-0"
Net Offset: 0

The space diagram is now shown with the ENTRY space.

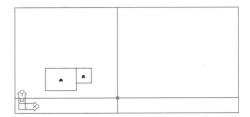

CREATING SPACES BY COPYING EXISTING SPACES—OFFICE-2

DESIGN ➤ SPACES AND ROOMS ➤ COPY SPACE...

Select **Copy Space** from the Design pull-down menu under **Spaces and Rooms**.

Draw OFFICE-2 as the next space along the right side of the ENTRY area with the same 2,700 sq.ft. requirements as OFFICE-1, using Softdesk's **Copy Space** command to duplicate the area.

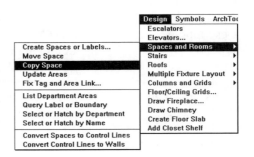

Pick a point at the edge of the single-line space diagram of OFFICE-1 as shown. After the space appears highlighted, select a base point at the top left corner of OFFICE-1 and second point of displacement at the top right corner of ENTRY.

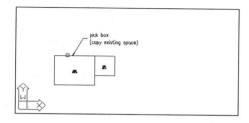

 Command line:

Command:
Pick room boundary or label: **[pick as shown]**
Base point or displacement: **int** of **[top left corner of OFFICE-1]**
Second point of displacement: **int** of **[top right corner of ENTRY]**

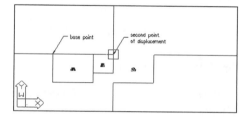

The *Edit Attribute* dialog box opens. Modify the values as shown.

Dialog box:

Number:	**103**
Name:	**OFFICE-2**
Description:	OFFICE-SMALL
Department:	MANAGEMENT
Occupant:	**Support Staff**
Building:	(leave blank)
Area:	2700 SF
Dimensions:	60'-0" x 45'-0"
Net Offset:	0

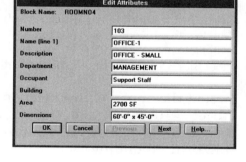

The drawing now appears with space diagrams and room tags for OFFICE-1, ENTRY, and OFFICE-2.

● ●

CREATING A SPACE BY DRAWING A BOUNDARY WITH MULTI-POINT—OFFICE-3

DESIGN ➤ SPACES AND ROOMS ➤ CREATE SPACES OR LABELS...

   Select **Create Spaces or Labels...** and add OFFICE-3 to the diagram by drawing the space as a multi-point shape, with the values shown. Choose **Draw Boundary** in the **Boundary Options** section, then **Multi-point** in the **Shape** section and the image will appear as an irregular outline. Highlight OFFICE-LARGE COM. in the list box and accept the defaults for **Type** and **Label**. Enter 10' as the **Wall Height**.

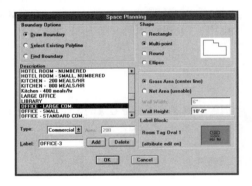

Dialog box

Boundary Options:	**Draw Boundary**
Shape:	**Multi-point**
Description:	**OFFICE-LARGE COM.**
Type:	**Commercial**
Area:	**[enabled/greyed out]**
Label:	**OFFICE-3**
Gross Area (centerline):	**[pick radio button]**
Wall Width (greyed out):	**[accept 6"]**
Wall Height:	**10'**
Label Block for room tag	**(attribute edit on)**

Start at the upper left intersection of OFFICE-2 to create the next space. Proceed@10'<90 upward, then continue a distance @50'<180 to the left, then @45'<90 upward and a horizontal length of 110'<0 toward the right side of the building. Select the upper right corner of OFFICE-2 and CLOSE by entering C at the command line.

═══

PROMPTING SUMMARY

Command:
** Hint: First two points establish room orientation.
Trace room perimeter with polyline...
From point: **int** of **[upper right intersection of ENTRY area]**
Arc/Undo/next point (or Arc): <Ortho off> **@10'<90**
Arc/Undo/next point (Arc/Undo): **@50'<180**
Arc/Undo/next point (Arc/Undo/Close) <Close>: **@45'<90**
Arc/Undo/next point (Arc/Undo/Close) <Close>: **@110'<0**
Arc/Undo/next point (Arc/Undo/Close) <Close>: **int** of **[top right intersection of OFFICE-2]**

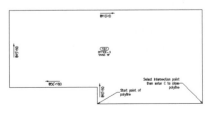

Arc/Undo/next point (Arc/Undo/Close) <Close>: **c**
Place label block.
Area = 799200.00 square in. (5550.0000 square ft.), Perimeter = 330'-0"
Inserting Room Tag Oval 1 at Floor elevation=0".
Insertion point: **[pick point to locate tag]**

Edit the values for **Number, Department,** and **Occupant** as shown, then place the Room Tag in the middle of the space.

    Dialog box:

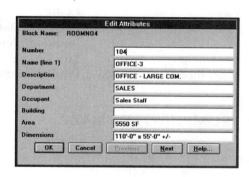

Number:	104
Name:	OFFICE-3
Description:	OFFICE-LARGE COM.
Department:	**SALES**
Occupant:	**Sales Staff**
Building:	(leave blank)
Area:	5550 SF
Dimensions:	110'-0" x 55'-0" +/-
Net Offset:	0

The completed OFFICE-3 space diagram is shown.

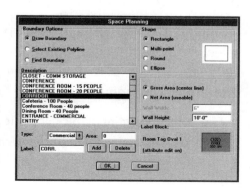

CREATING SPACES BY DRAWING A RECTANGLE WITH AREA ZERO (0)—CORRIDOR

DESIGN ➤ SPACES AND ROOMS ➤ CREATE SPACES OR LABELS...

Draw the CORRIDOR as the next space. Pick **Create Spaces or Labels...** from the pull-down menu. Select **Draw Boundary** using a **Rectangle** and enter a zero for the **Area**. Highlight CORRIDOR in the list box and accept the default values for **Type** and **Label**. **Wall Height** should already be set to 10'.

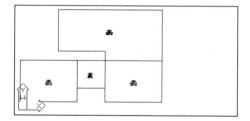

Dialog box:

Boundary Options:	**Draw Boundary**
Shape:	**Rectangle**
Description:	**CORRIDOR**
Type:	**Commercial**
Area:	**0**
Label:	**CORR.**
Gross Area (centerline):	**[pick radio button]**
Wall Width:	**[enabled/greyed out]**
Wall Height:	**10'**
Label Block for room tag	**(attribute edit on)**

PROMPTING SUMMARY

First corner point: **int** of

Second corner point: **int** of

Size = 90'-0" x 10'-0"

Area = 900 SF

Second corner point (or Done) <Done>: ↵

Place label block.

Area = 129600.00 square in. (900.0000 square ft.), Perimeter = 200'-0"

Inserting Room Tag Oval 1 at Floor elevation=0".

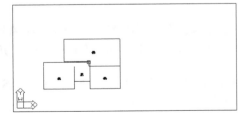

Start by selecting the upper left corner of OFFICE-1, then the lower left inner corner of OFFICE-3 as shown. Press enter when the prompt **Second corner point (or Done) <Done>:** appears after choosing the second corner. (This prompt offers you the choice to select a different second point.)

The prompting sequence is:

First corner point: **int** of **[pick upper left corner of OFFICE-1]**

Second corner point: **int** of **[pick lower left inner corner of OFFICE-3, as shown]**

Size = 90'-0" x 10'-0"

Area = 900 SF

Second corner point (or Done) <Done>: ↵

Place label block.

Area = 129600.00 square in. (900.0000 square ft.), Perimeter = 200'-0"

Inserting Room Tag Oval 1 at Floor elevation=0".

Edit the values for the CORRIDOR space as shown.

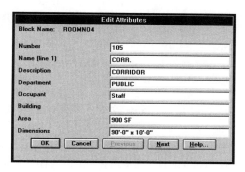

 Dialog box:

Number:	105
Name:	CORR.
Description:	CORRIDOR
Department:	**PUBLIC**
Occupant:	**Staff**
Building:	(leave blank)
Area:	900 SF
Dimensions:	90'-0" x 10'-0"
Net Offset:	0

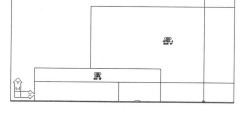

The corridor space is drawn as shown with the Room Tag.

DESIGN ➤ SPACES AND ROOMS ➤ CREATE SPACES OR LABELS...

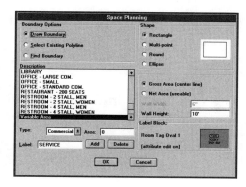

Now that several **Boundary Options** have been used, pick **Create Spaces or Labels...** and draw the last space using any of the previous procedures discussed assigning the label name SERVICE.

As an example, the figure shows the SERVICE space created using **Draw Boundary** and Rectangle. Variable Area has been selected from the **Description** list box causing **Area** to be set at 0 and **Label** appearing without a name. The **Wall Height** is 10'.

 Command line:

Command:
First corner point: **int** of [**top left corner of CORRIDOR**]
Second corner point: **int** of [**top left corner of OFFICE-3**]
Size = 40' x 45'
Area = 1800 SF
Second corner point (or Done) <Done>: ↵
Place label block.
Area = 259200.00 square in. (1800.0000 square ft.), Perimeter = 170'-0"
Inserting Room Tag Oval 1 at Floor elevation=0".

The rectangle's first point starts at the top left corner of the CORRIDOR and stretches (at the opposite diagonal side) to the top left corner of OFFICE-3.

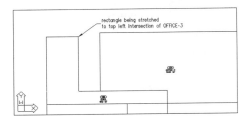

 Dialog box:

Number: 106
Name: SERVICE
Description: RESTROOM
Department: **PUBLIC**
Occupant: **Staff**
Building: (leave blank)
Area: 1800 SF
Dimensions: 40' x 45'
Net Offset: 0

The completed drawing space diagram drawing is shown.

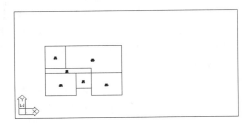

STRETCHING WALL SEGMENTS—ENTRY

Zoom into the ENTRY space as shown to enlarge the view.

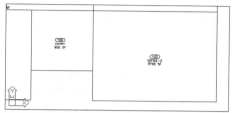

WALLS ➤ WALL EDIT ➤ STRETCH WALL SEGMENTS

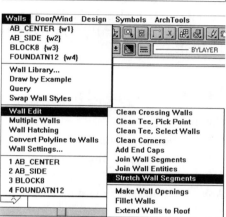

 Select **Stretch Wall Segments** from the **Wall Edit** submenu under Walls or invoke the Macro **ST**.

 Pick **First corner** and **Other corner** as crossing window points around the lower portion of the ENTRY as shown to enlarge the space 4'.

Macro Command: **ST**

(AutoCAD Command: **STRETCH**)

Command:
Building Base Stretch...
Select objects with Crossing window.
First corner: [**bottom left corner of entry area**]
Other corner: [**top right corner of entry area**]
Remove objects: ↵
Base point: [**pick display screen**]
New point (press Enter to drag): **@4'<270**

The enlarged area is shown.

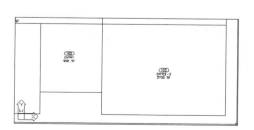

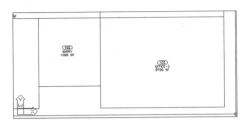

UPDATING SPACES—ENTRY

DESIGN ➤ SPACES AND ROOMS ➤ UPDATE AREAS

   Select **Update Areas** from the Design pull-down menu under **Spaces and Rooms** to update the Room Tag information for the ENTRY. Pick the ENTRY Room Tag and the value automatically changes from 900SF to 1020SF.

   Command line:

Command:
Select labels to fix (RETURN for all)...
Select objects: **[pick the room tag]** 1 found
Select objects: ⏎
Area = 146880.00 square in. (1020.0000 square ft.), Perimeter = 128'-0"

QUERYING SPACES

DESIGN ➤ SPACES AND ROOMS ➤ QUERY LABEL OR BOUNDARY

Selecting a Room Tag displays the *Edit Attributes* dialog box to view or edit information entered when spaces were created. The updated ENTRY Room Tag is shown as an example.

   Command line:

Command:
Pick room boundary or label <Done>: **[pick room tag]**
Pick room boundary or label <Done>: ⏎

CREATING A LIST OF SPACES

DESIGN ➤ SPACES AND ROOMS ➤ LIST DEPARTMENT AREAS

 Create a list of the department areas by selecting **List Department Areas** from **Spaces and Rooms** under the Design pull-down menu. Pick a start point at the right side of the space diagram to insert the list.

PUBLIC SPACE	1020	7%
MANAGEMENT	5400	37%
SALES	5650	38%
PUBLIC	2700	18%
TOTAL AREA	14670	100%

Command line:

Command:
PUBLIC SPACE 1020
MANAGEMENT 5400
SALES 5550
PUBLIC 2700
Total Area = 14670
Place results on drawing <Yes>: **y**
Include percentages <Yes>: **y**
Line spacing <auto>: ↵
Show upper left starting point: **[pick a point]**

The schedule is placed into the drawing on layer FL01-SCHTEXTM.

HATCHING SPACES BY DEPARTMENT

DESIGN ➤ SPACES AND ROOMS ➤ SELECT OR HATCH BY DEPARTMENT

Selecting the Softdesk commands **Select or Hatch by Department** and **Select or Hatch by Name** from the Design menu under **Spaces and Rooms** places a hatch pattern within the designated space or spaces. Invoking the command prompts for department or space name(s), which can be separated by commas. Next, the command displays the *Select Hatch Pattern* dialog box for selection with additional prompts as illustrated.

PROMPTING SUMMARY

Department to highlight <SALES>: **management**
Hatch highlighted areas <Yes>: ↵
Hatching to avoid labels <Yes>: ↵
Hatch scale <96>: ↵
Hatch angle <0>: ↵
Select new base point (Angle/Scale/Pattern): ↵
Select new base point (Angle/Scale/Pattern): ↵

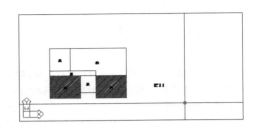

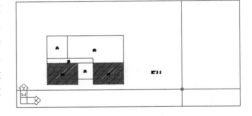
Choose **Select or Hatch by Department** under **Spaces and Rooms**, invoking prompts to hatch the Management spaces. Enter the department name MANAGEMENT at the command-line prompt **Department to highlight** and accept all the default values. The current layer will change to FL01-HATCH.

Department to highlight <SALES>: **management**
Hatch highlighted areas <Yes>: ↵
Hatching to avoid labels <Yes>: ↵

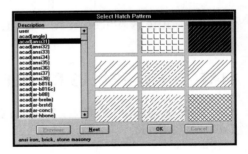
Select the ANSI31 hatch pattern when the dialog box opens, then pick OK.

Hatch scale <96>: ↵
Hatch angle <0>: ↵
Select new base point (Angle/Scale/Pattern): ↵
Select new base point (Angle/Scale/Pattern): ↵

Each space is highlighted then hatched as shown.

The space diagram for the three-story building is now complete. Continue on to the next chapter where you will learn how to convert the spaces to control lines then to walls.

CHAPTER TWELVE

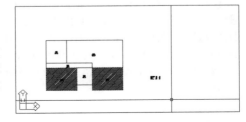

CONVERTING SPACES TO WALLS

*Converting Areas with Single Lines
to Spaces with Double-line Walls*

CONTENTS

This chapter continues to the next step of the CAD design process by first converting spaces to control lines, then converting the control lines to walls. The **Convert Spaces to Control Lines** command changes space boundary polylines to wall control lines on the Wall Control lines' layer and includes automatic erasing to eliminate lines on top of each other. The space polylines, on layer FL01-SPACE with linetype Continuous, are copied to control lines on layer FL01-WALLCL using linetype Center2.

After completing this first conversion process, the interior and exterior single lines can then be converted again with the **Convert Control Lines to Walls** command to double lines of selected widths and height (thickness). The command creates double-line walls following control lines which can actually be lines, arcs, and circles drawn on any layer as control lines for the walls style routine.

CONVERTING SPACE AREAS INTO WALL CONTROL LINES

DESIGN ➤ SPACES AND ROOMS ➤ CONVERT SPACES TO CONTROL LINES

Select **Convert Spaces to Control Lines** under **Spaces and Rooms** in the Design pull-down menu to copy space boundary polylines to wall control lines.

Convert Spaces to Control Lines copies the space polylines to line entities, places them on the FL01-WALLCL layer, and turns off the FL01-SPACE layer as shown in the *Layer Control* dialog box.

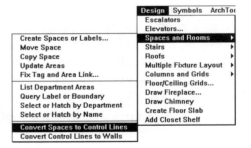

The prompting sequence is:

    Select space boundaries to convert...
    Select objects: [select corner points, placing a window around the space diagram]
    First corner: Other corner: 14 found
    8 were filtered out.
    Select objects: ↵

Using a window selection, set pick points at the lower left and upper right corners of the space diagram to include all objects. The command confirms that 14 objects, including the polylines and room tags, were selected. The six Room Tags and two hatch patterns were filtered out.

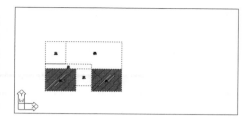

- -

VIEWING CURRENT DEFAULT LAYERS

    Invoke the Macro **LD** to open the *Layer Control* dialog box. Set the current layer to 0, then turn off the FL01-HATCH and NOPLOT layers. The **Layer Name** list box shows FL01-ROOMTAG for the room tags, FL01-SCH-TEXTM for the list, FL01-HATCH for the hatch patterns of the Management department, and FL01-SPACE for the space diagram lines generated from the **CREATE SPACES AND LABELS...** command. The FL01-SPACE layer was automatically turned off.

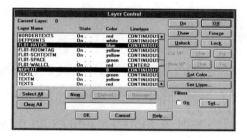

    Pick OK.

    Macro Command: **LD**

(AutoCAD Command: **DDLMODES**)

Command: ld
Macro: Layer Dialogue

- - - - - - - - - - - - - - - -

BREAKING LINES

Zoom into the ENTRY as shown to break the vertical control lines that will define the interior and exterior walls. The control lines should be broken at each intersection to delineate the interior and exterior portions, before converting to walls.

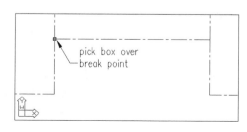

Enter the Macro **BA**; then, using the intersection object snap mode, place the pick box directly over the control line intersections as on previous page. Invoke the macro at both control line intersections.

Note: The pick box turns into a double pick box during intersection snap mode.

 Macro Command: **BA**

(AutoCAD Command: **BREAK**)

Command: **ba**
Macro: Break @ **int [pick intersection of control lines]**

CONVERTING SINGLE CONTROL LINES TO DOUBLE LINES AT EXTERIOR WALLS

DESIGN ➤ SPACES AND ROOMS ➤ CONVERT CONTROL LINES TO WALLS

The **Convert Control Lines to Walls** command turns single control lines into double-line walls. Specify a tolerance factor of 0 (zero) since all lines intersect. Otherwise, Softdesk searches for lines that are not connected at intersections. The command prompts to **Select objects to convert...**, then opens the *Wall Style Definitions* dialog box to select a wall style.

Select all the exterior control lines at the perimeter of the building except for the two vertical lines near the ENTRY as shown.

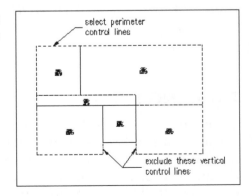

The prompting sequence is:

Command:
Convert single lines to a Wall Style...
Select objects to convert...
Select objects: [**selected at OFFICE-1**]1 found
Select objects: [**selected at OFFICE-1**]1 found
Select objects: [**selected at ENTRY**]1 found

Select objects: [**selected at OFFICE-2**]1 found

Select objects: [**selected at OFFICE-2**]1 found

Select objects: [**selected at OFFICE-3**]1 found

Select objects: [**selected at OFFICE-3**]1 found

Select objects: [**selected at SERVICE**]1 found

Select objects: [**selected at SERVICE**]1 found

Select objects: [**selected at CORRIDOR**]1 found

Select objects: ↵

Tolerance distance <1'-0">: **0**

Working...

Choose wall style... [**Wall Style Definitions dialog box opens, select AB_CENTER**]

Wall width <6">: **6**

Wall thickness <8'-0">: **10'**

The *Wall Styles Definitions* dialog box opens after all lines are selected to choose a Style Name. Select AB_CENTER, a special predefined wall style, considered by Softdesk to be a general purpose wall. Enter 6" for **Wall width** and 10' for **Wall thickness** (height) at the command line.

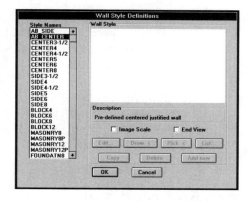

Choose wall style...
Wall width <6">: **6**
Wall thickness <8'-0">: **10'**

An enlarged view of the ENTRY space shows the walls converted from single lines to 6 inch-wide double lines.

LISTING AN ENTITY

Enter the Macro **LI** then pick both a wall line (shown continuous) and wall centerline (shown dashed). The layer displays FL01-WALL to identify and confirm the 10' double-line wall's height.

Macro Command: **LI**

(AutoCAD Command: **LIST**)

Command: **LI**
Macro: List
Select objects: **[pick wall line]** 1 found
Select objects: **[pick wall centerline]** 1 found
Select objects: ↵
        LINE   Layer: FL01-WALL
            Space: Model space
      Thickness =   10'-0"
      Handle = 614
    from point, X= 98'-3" Y= 33'-9" Z=   0'-0"
     to point, X= 98'-3" Y= 44'-9" Z=   0'-0"
 Length = 11'-0", Angle in XY Plane = 90.00
     Delta X =   0'-0", Delta Y =   11'-0", Delta Z =   0'-0"

        LINE   Layer: FL01-WALLCL
            Space: Model space
      Thickness =   10'-0"
      Handle = 5B5
    from point, X= 98'-0" Y= 34'-0" Z=   0'-0"
     to point, X= 98'-0" Y= 45'-0" Z=   0'-0"
 Length = 11'-0", Angle in XY Plane = 90.00
     Delta X =   0'-0", Delta Y =   11'-0", Delta Z =   0'-0"

CONVERTING THE VERTICAL ENTRY AREA CONTROL LINES TO WALLS

DESIGN ➤ SPACES AND ROOMS ➤ CONVERT CONTROL LINES TO WALLS

Select **Convert Control Lines to Walls** from the Design pull-down menu under **Spaces and Rooms** to convert the two vertical exterior control lines at the ENTRY space to 6 inch-wide double-line walls using the SIDE6 wall style. The control lines are shown highlighted.

The prompting sequence is:

Command:

Convert single lines to a Wall Style...

Select objects to convert...

Select objects: **[pick vertical control line]** 1 found

Select objects: **[pick vertical control line]** 1 found

Select objects: ⏎

Tolerance distance <0">: ⏎

Working...

Choose wall style... **[Wall Style Definitions dialog box opens]**

Pick side: **[pick point outside building plan]**

Pick side: **[pick point outside building plan]**

The *Wall Style Definitions* dialog box opens for selection of a Style Name from the list box. Select a wall style from the list box that draws a 6 inch-wide exterior wall aligned with the interior walls with a 2 1/4" offset distance.

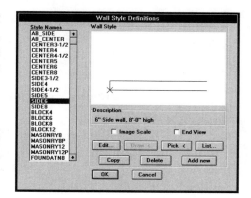

 Highlight the SIDE6 style name, then choose the **Edit...** pick box to open the *Wall Style Editor* dialog box and modify values for offset distance, description, and thickness.

The image tile displays the wall as two lines that represent each face or side of the wall and an end cap with an X marking its insertion point. Line 1 represents the top line and Line 2 represents the bottom line.

The SIDE6 wall style defines each line in separate dialog boxes as **Line 1 of 2** and **Line 2 of 2**. Notice that the SIDE6 wall style offset distance for **Line 1 of 2** is a negative value.

Enter values as specified, then pick OK to close all dialog boxes.

Dialog box:

Line 1 of 2

	Existing values	New values
Name:	SIDE6	
Desc:	6" Side wall,	**6" Side wall,**
	8'-0" high	**10'-0" high**
Offset:	0	**-2-1/4**
Elevation:	0"	
Thickness:	8'	**10'**
Estimating:	(blank)	
Layer	WALL	
Group	(blank)	

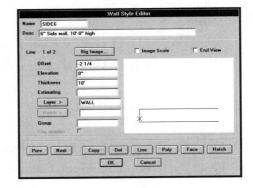

 Pick **Next**, then edit the values for **Line 2 of 2**.

 Dialog box:

Line 2 of 2

	Existing values	New values
Name:	SIDE6	
Desc:	6" Side wall,	
	10'-0" high	
Offset:	6	**3-3/4**
Elevation:	0"	
Thickness:	8'	**10'**
Estimating:	(blank)	
Layer	WALL	
Group	(blank)	

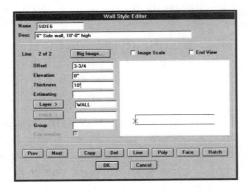

 Pick OK twice.

Select points outside the building as the offset side. The figure shows the 6 inch side wall drawn at the right side of the ENTRY and the outside offset point being selected at the left side.

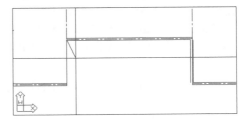

The prompting sequence is:

Convert single lines to a Wall Style...
Select objects to convert...
Select objects: 1 found **[select control line]**
Select objects: 1 found **[select control line]**
Select objects: ⏎
Tolerance distance <0">: ⏎
Working...
Choose wall style...
Pick side: **[pick point outside of building]**
Pick side: **[pick point outside of building]**

As walls are drawn, the figure shows that the intersections will require cleanup to connect interior and exterior wall lines. We will clean up the intersections after converting the interior control lines.

CONVERTING SINGLE CONTROL LINES TO DOUBLE LINES AT INTERIOR WALLS

DESIGN ➤ SPACES AND ROOMS ➤ CONVERT CONTROL LINES TO WALLS

Select **Convert Control Lines to Walls** under **Spaces and Rooms** in the Design pull-down menu to convert the interior control lines to 4-1/2" double-line walls. Pick all the interior control lines.

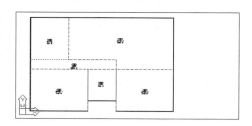

The prompting sequence is:

Command:
Convert single lines to a Wall Style...
Select objects to convert...
Select objects: **[selected between OFFICE-1 and ENTRY]** 1 found
Select objects: **[selected between OFFICE-2 and ENTRY]** 1 found
Select objects: **[selected between OFFICE-2 and OFFICE-3]** 1 found
Select objects: **[selected between OFFICE-3 and CORRIDOR]** 1 found

Select objects: **[selected between OFFICE-3 and CORRIDOR]** 1 found
Select objects: **[selected between OFFICE-3 and SERVICE]** 1 found
Select objects: **[selected between CORRIDOR and OFFICE-1]** 1 found
Select objects: ↵
Tolerance distance <0">: ↵
Working...
Choose wall style... **[dialog box opens; edit CENTER 4-1/2 wall style]**

The *Wall Style Definitions* dialog box opens after all the control lines are selected. Highlight CENTER4-1/2 in the **Style Names** list box to display 4-1/2" Centered wall, 8'-0" high in the **Description** section. The image box section also identifies the wall style insertion point with an X.

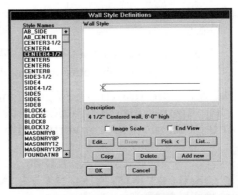

Highlight CENTER4-1/2 in **Style Names** list box.

Pick the **Edit...** box to open the *Wall Style Editor* dialog box displaying information about the current wall style. The current wall values are shown for **Line 1 of 2**.

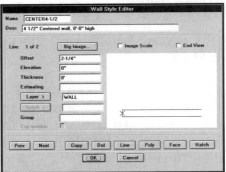

Edit the **Description** and **Thickness** for **Line 1 of 2** as shown.

 Dialog box:

	Existing values	New values
Name:	CENTER4-1/2	
Desc:	4 1/2" Centered wall, 8'-0" high	**4 1/2" Centered wall, 10'-0" high**
Offset:	2-1/4	
Elevation:	0"	
Thickness:	8'	**10'**
Estimating:	(blank)	
Layer	WALL	
Group	(blank)	

Note: Other items can be edited in the *Wall Style Editor* dialog box, including renaming the wall style. Entering a new name in the **Name** edit box creates a new wall style and adds it to the **Style Name** list box in the *Wall Style Definitions* dialog box.

Select **Next** near the left bottom corner of the dialog box to edit the lower wall line. The upper left corner of the dialog box shows the lower line being edited as **Line 2 of 2**.

The offset distance shows a negative number for **Line 2 of 2** and **Thickness** as 8'.

Change the **Thickness** for **Line 2 of 2** .

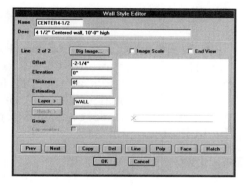

    Dialog box:

	Existing values	New values
Name:	CENTER4-1/2	
Desc:	4 1/2" Centered wall, 10'-0" high	
Offset:	2-1/4	
Elevation:	0"	
Thickness:	8'	**10'**
Estimating:	(blank)	
Layer	WALL	
Group	(blank)	

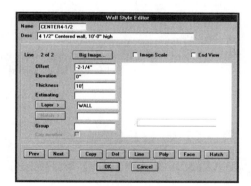

Pick OK and return to the *Wall Style Definitions* dialog box. Changes can be confirmed by selecting **List** and opening the *List Style Definitions* dialog box.

Pick OK to close the dialog boxes, noting the updated description in the *Wall Style Definitions* dialog box.

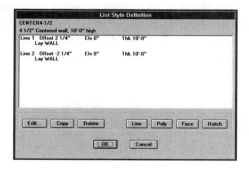

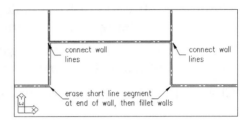

An enlarged view of the exterior and interior walls in the CORRIDOR space are shown mended, glued, and cleaned up at intersections. Unfortunately, not all lines are cleaned up.

CLEANUP

 Next, invoke the Macro **ER** to remove the short line segments that cap the existing exterior corner walls at the ENTRY. The horizontal and vertical wall lines on layer FL01-WALL should intersect at the exterior corner of the building.

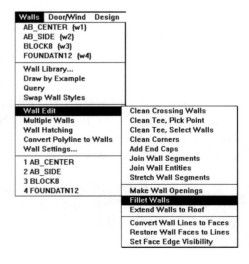

Macro Command: **ER**

(AutoCAD Command: **ERASE**)

Command: **er**
Macro: Erase
Select objects: 1 found [**left horizontal wall endcap**]
Select objects: 1 found [**right horizontal wall endcap**]
Select objects: ↵

FILLET WALL LINES

WALLS ➤ WALL EDIT ➤ FILLET WALLS

Zoom into the ENTRY, then select **Fillet Walls** from the Walls pull-down menu under **Wall Edit** to connect wall intersections. Fillet the exterior horizontal and vertical wall lines (on layer FL01-WALL) at the left and right corners of the building entrance area.

The prompting sequence is:

Command:
Wall maximum fillet radius <0">:

Select all wall objects to fillet: [**pick horizontal wall line**] 1 found
Select objects:[**pick vertical wall line**] 1 found
Select objects: ⌐

JOIN WALL SEGMENTS

WALLS ➤ WALL EDIT ➤ JOIN WALL SEGMENTS

Some additional cleanup is also required at the interior wall lines of the ENTRY. Select **Fillet Wall Segments** from the Wall pull-down menu under **Wall Edit** and pick the two interior vertical lines at the ENTRY. The command prompts for **First** and **Other** corners to create a crossing window (as shown) to heal the line segments.

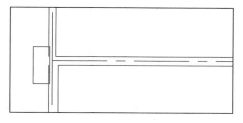

The prompting sequence is:

Erase inside selection window and heal gap...
First corner point: [**pick a point**]
Other corner point: [**pick a point**]

The completed drawing is shown in plan.

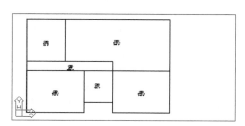

CREATING AN ISOMETRIC VIEW

VIEW ➤ VIEW ➤ VIEW PRESETS...

To view the drawing in isometric view, select **View Presets...** from the **View** command in the View pull-down menu.

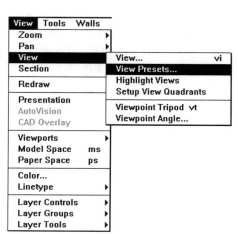

The *Preset and Currently Defined Views* dialog box opens, displaying a list box with default view choices. Select **South West Isometric**, then pick **Preview<** to review the image prior to final selection.

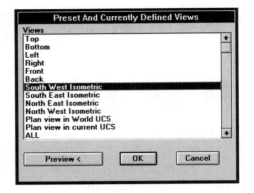

    Pick OK to close the dialog box for the drawing to change from plan to the isometric view.

The isometric view displays the plan with 10-foot high walls.

Enter the Macro **PN** to change to the plan view.

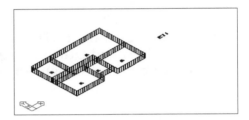

Macro Command: **PN**

(AutoCAD Command: **PLAN**)

Command: **pn**
Macro: Plan
<Current UCS>/Ucs/World: ↵
Regenerating drawing.

Save the completed plan of the First Floor, In the next chapter, additional interior walls will be added to create spaces for restrooms and several small office spaces. A custom curved wall will also be drawn at the rear portion of the ENTRY space.

CHAPTER THIRTEEN

WALL SETTINGS

Overview of Wall-related Settings

Contents

The Softdesk Auto-Architect® module provides four command-line shortcut key macros for drawing walls. Macro default names appear within curly brackets { } next to the wall style name in the Walls pull-down menu. Walls can be created as lines and/or polylines of any elevation and thickness (height) with 3D faces and hatch patterns from a center point or offset from a side. In Chapter 14 interior walls will be drawn in the floor plan to create spaces for men's and women's restrooms and three smaller offices within the OFFICE-2 space. Before proceeding, however, it will be helpful to understand how to set controls for drawing walls.

THE PRESET WALL STYLES

WALLS ➤ (top portion of menu)

Selecting the Walls pull-down menu displays the four preset wall styles with their associated shortcut keys at the top of the pull-down menu. These preset styles are controlled by wall settings and should be modified to show styles used most often in a project. At the bottom of the pull-down menu are listed the four most recently used styles already in the Preset style list.

SETTING CONTROLS FOR WALLS

ARCHTOOLS ➤ AUTO-ARCHITECT SETTINGS... ➤ WALLS

To set controls for walls, pick **Auto-Architect Settings...** from the ArchTools pull-down menu.

The *Softdesk Auto-Architect Settings* dialog box appears with **General...** and **Walls...** buttons used to set the wall controls discussed in this chapter.

Walls　Door/Wind　Design
AB_CENTER {w1}
AB_SIDE {w2}
BLOCK8 {w3}
FOUNDATN12 {w4}

Wall Library...
Draw by Example
Query
Swap Wall Styles

Wall Edit　▶
Multiple Walls　▶
Wall Hatching　▶
Convert Polyline to Walls
Wall Settings...

1 AB_CENTER
2 AB_SIDE
3 BLOCK8
4 FOUNDATN12

ArchTools
Draw Symbol by Example
Query Symbol
Block Swap
Adjust Symbol
Symbol 2D<->3D

Place Wall Dimensions
Framing Notation...
Calculate Wall Area
Draw Shadows

Extract 2D Elevation
Extract 2D Section
Schedules　▶
Annotation　▶

Auto-Architect Settings...

Select **Walls...** to open the *Wall Settings* dialog box and view the four Shortcut keys plus other options for specifying wall styles. Although no controls will be set, discussions include descriptions of wall styles as well as prompt sequences and responses when drawing walls. Pick Cancel to exit the dialog boxes after your review.

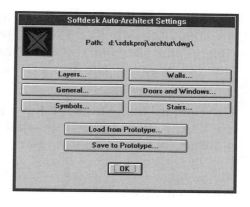

Note: Choosing Wall Settings... under the Walls pull-down menu or picking the Auto-Architect Edit... button from the Project Settings dialog box under Project Settings... in the File pull-down menu also opens the Wall Settings dialog box.

SHORTCUT KEYS (MACROS)

The *Wall Settings* dialog box displays the four shortcut keys in edit boxes along the left side of the **Menu Styles and Keyboard Macros** section. These settings are saved to the file-name <drawing>.DFM in the \SDSKPROJ\ ARCHTUT\ project directory.

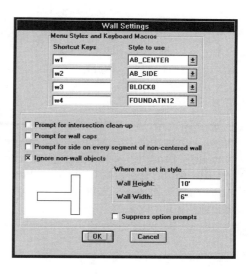

Note: Every drawing can have its own Preset wall styles. <drawing> refers to the current drawing.

The **Menu Styles and Keyboard Macros** section contains **Shortcut Keys** in edit boxes that can be modified or replaced with any user-defined combination of letters and/or numbers. Selecting the down arrow under the **Style to use** section opens a pop-up list displaying a list of predefined wall styles stored in the WALLTYPE.DAT file. Choosing another style reassigns the shortcut key.

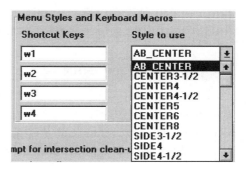

For example, selecting CENTER4 would replace AB_CENTER with CENTER4 as the new wall style for the shortcut key w1. These wall styles always appear at the top of the Walls pull-down menu.

The default wall **Shortcut Keys** and **Style to use** names listed in the following table can be modified as needed to suit the current project.

Menu Styles and Keyboard Macros	
Shortcut Keys	**Style to use**
w1	CENTER4
w2	AB_SIDE
w3	BLOCK8
w4	FOUNDATN12

Preset Wall Styles

Shortcut Key	*Wall Style*	*Description*
w1	AB_CENTER	6" wide, 8'-0" high centered wall
w2	AB_SIDE	6" wide, 8'-0" high offset wall
w3	BLOCK8	8" wide, 8'-0" high block wall
w4	FOUNDATN12	12" Concrete foundation, 24" Footing with top caps

Note: Walls that are symmetrical about their working point are considered *centered* with no prompt for side offset when placed in a drawing. The points picked in a drawing determine the path of the wall's working point. Layer names are defined in the *Auto-Architect Layer Settings* dialog box and stored in the AASDESK.LY file in the \SDSKPROJ\ARCHTUT directory.

- -

DRAWING CENTERED WALLS

The default AB_CENTER wall is symmetrical about its working point; thus, the points selected in the drawing represent the wall's centerline.

The prompting sequence is:

Command:
Wall style - AB_CENTER
Wall width <6">: **[enter wall width]**
Wall thickness <8'>: **[enter wall height]**

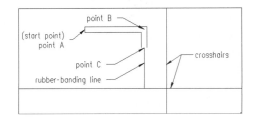

From point: [**point A**]
To point: [**point B**]
To point: [**point C**]
To point: ⏎

Note: AutoCAD defines thickness to mean the Z-axis thickness of objects being drawn. Therefore, objects that represent walls are identified with a command line prompt for **Wall thickness** which is interpreted (for architectural applications) as wall height.

DRAWING NON-CENTERED WALLS

The default AB_SIDE is not symmetrical about its working point. The command starts by prompting for two points, then prompts to **Pick side:** to set the offset direction. Additional wall lines continue to be offset on the same side if the **Prompt for side on every segment of non-centered wall** is not checked in the Wall Settings dialog box as shown in the following three figures.

The prompting sequence is:

Command:
Wall style - AB_SIDE
Wall width <6">: [**enter wall width**]
Wall thickness <8'>: [**enter wall height**]
From point: [**point A**]
To point: [**point B**]
Pick side: [**point C**]
To point: [**point D**]
To point: ⏎

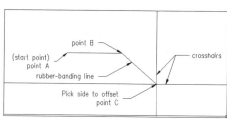

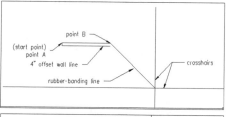

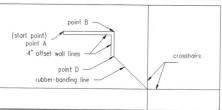

The adjacent figure shows a 4" offset wall with an endcap at the start point (point A). The *Wall Setting* dialog box offers the option to close walls at their start and end points when **Prompt for wall cap** is checked. In other words, once you offset to the right, the program continues offsetting to the right.

SETTING WALL CONTROLS

Before drawing walls, controls can be adjusted to fit a project by checking the appropriate toggles listed here. Each option is described in detail in the sections that follow.

☐ Prompt for intersection clean-up
☐ Prompt for wall caps
☐ Prompt for side on every segment of non-centered wall
☒ Ignore non-wall objects

- Prompt for intersection cleanup
- Prompt for wall caps
- Prompt for side on every segment of non-centered wall
- Ignore non-wall objects

WALL SETTING—PROMPT FOR INTERSECTION CLEANUP

Normally, intersections are automatically cleaned up when one wall starts or ends at another (providing either the styles are the same or the layer and wall heights match). Note that a question mark (?) appears at the wall intersection in the image box to identify the command's application. With the toggle on, the cleanup will not be automatic and a prompt will appear.

☒ Prompt for intersection clean-up
☐ Prompt for wall caps
☐ Prompt for side on every segment of non-centered wall
☒ Ignore non-wall objects

Where not set in style
Wall Height: 8'
Wall Width: 6"
☐ Suppress option prompts

The next three figures show the centered wall with intersections cleaned up at the start (point A) and end (point C). As each wall segment is drawn, the prompt **Clean intersection <No>:** appears after the second point is chosen. Wall lines may temporarily flash as they are adjusted.

The prompting sequence is:

Command: **w1**
Wall style - AB_CENTER
Wall width <6">: [**enter wall width**]
Wall thickness <8'>: [**enter wall height**]
From point: **mid** of [**point A**]

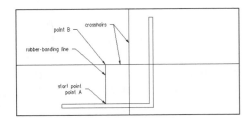

To point: **[point B]**
Clean intersection <No>: **y**
To point: **per** to **[point C]**

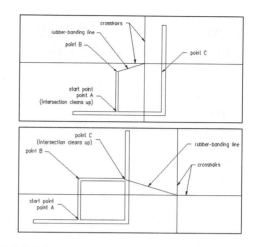

To point: ↵
Clean intersection <No>: **y**

WALL SETTING—PROMPT FOR WALL CAPS

Checking this box displays the **Cap wall <Yes>:** prompt for options to automatically draw a closing line at the end of new walls. The image tile displays question marks identifying open wall ends.

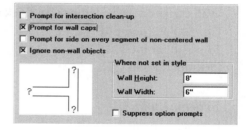

The prompting sequence is:

Command: W1
Wall style - AB_CENTER
Wall width <6">: **[enter wall width]**
Wall thickness <8'>: **[enter wall height]**
From point: **[point A]**

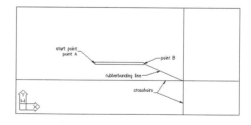

To point: **[point B]**
Cap wall <Yes>: **y**
To point: **[point C]**
To point: ↵
Cap wall <Yes>: **N [entering "n" or "no" keeps the wall end open]**

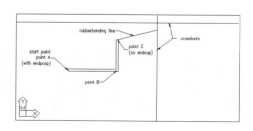

WALL SETTING—PROMPT FOR SIDE ON EVERY SEGMENT OF NON-CENTERED WALL

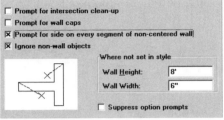

Checking this box prompts to **Pick side:** as each line is drawn then offset to the specified side. The image tile displays an X mark to identify the offset pick side. The next three diagrams show two sequential walls drawn with their offset sides determined along each segment.

The prompting sequence is:

> Command: w2
> Wall style - AB_SIDE
> Wall width <6">: **[enter wall width]**
> Wall thickness <8'>: **[enter wall thickness]**
> From point: **[point A]**
> To point: **[point B]**
> Pick side: **[point C]**
>
> To point: **[point D]**
> Pick side: **[point E]**
>
>
> To point: ↵

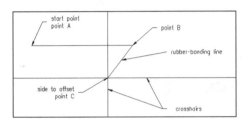

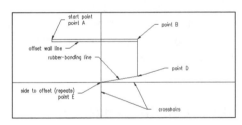

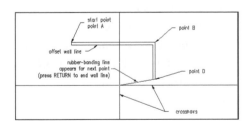

WALL SETTING—IGNORE NON-WALL OBJECTS

Checking this box ignores non-wall entities (lines or objects that are not wall objects) that cross wall lines during cleanup and wall breaks. For example, door blocks will insert into any double lines if not checked. Softdesk recommends not checking this box when editing drawings created by previous versions of Auto-Architect, ASG Architectural, or other software packages.

Note: Softdesk's wall objects have hidden extended entity data marking them as walls. Normally the xdata is used during wall breaks to identify walls.

WALL SETTING—WHERE NOT SET IN STYLE

Entering a value in the current drawing units in the **Wall Height:** and **Wall Width:** edit boxes draws walls with the specified wall width and thickness (height) for the AB_SIDE and AB_CENTER wall styles. For all other styles this value is ignored.

```
Where not set in style
Wall Height:        10'
Wall Width:         4"
☐ Suppress option prompts
```

The prompting sequence is:

Command: **w1**
Wall style - AB_CENTER
Wall width <4">: [**wall width set at 4" in Wall Width: edit box**]
Wall thickness <10'>: [**wall height set to 10' in Wall Height: edit box**]
From point: [**select first point**]
To point: [**select second point**]
To point: ↵

WALL SETTING—SUPPRESS OPTION PROMPTS

This command reduces the prompts that normally appear when drawing walls, including height and width for the AB_SIDE or AB_CENTER wall styles.

Styles with a question mark (?) in the input fields are affected. With prompts suppressed, a style must only be selected the first time a polyline or wall control line is converted in a drawing session.

Following is an example of a W1 wall style command-line sequence when the **Suppress option prompts** box is not checked.

The prompting sequence is:

Command: **w1**
Wall style - AB_CENTER
Wall width <4">:
Wall thickness <10'>:
From point:
To point:
To point:
To point:

Following is an example of a W1 wall style command sequence when **Suppress option prompts** is checked. Notice that the prompt includes a reminder in parentheses.

The prompting sequence is:

Command: **w1**
Wall style - AB_CENTER
Width: 4" Height: 10' (wall prompts suppressed)
From point:
To point:
To point:
To point:

When all boxes are checked, the image tile displays question marks and X marks identifying their application.

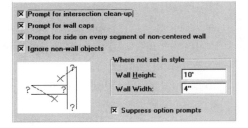

SETTING MORE CONTROLS FOR WALLS

ARCHTOOLS ➤ AUTO-ARCHITECT SETTINGS... ➤ GENERAL...

Selecting **Programs make 3D entities** draws entities as three-dimensional objects as shown in the adjacent image tile. It is important to note that this toggle has no effect on symbol insertion. Deselecting the box displays the image tile as a 2D plan. Entering a value for

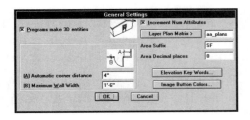

Automatic corner distance sets the corner distance when placing doors or windows in walls with the **<auto>** option. **Maximum wall width** sets how far to look for the other side of the wall. Additional choices include settings: to sequentially **Increment numbered attributes**; set a **Layer plan matrix**, **Area suffixes**, and **Area decimal places** precision; and choose **Elevation Key Words** and **Image Button Colors**.

DEFINING WALL STYLES USING THE WALL LIBRARY

WALL ➤ WALL LIBRARY...

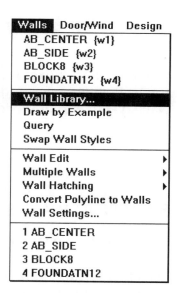

The *Wall Settings* dialog box was previously discussed as a method for assigning shortcut key macros to a wall style. The CENTER4 wall style was also described as a possible replacement to AB_CENTER for the w1 macro. Descriptions for the CENTER4 default wall style are stored in the *Wall Style Definitions* dialog box and can be viewed or edited by choosing **Wall Library...** under the Walls pull-down menu.

A **Style Names** list box appears along the left side and buttons to **Edit...**, **Draw**, **Copy**, **Delete**, or **Add new** wall styles are found along the bottom with **Pick** and **List**. Highlighting a style, then exiting the dialog box, replaces the current name at the bottom of the pull-down menu and displays the command-line prompts for drawing the specified wall style as the new option. (See the section titled, **The Preset Wall Styles** at the beginning of this chapter.)

Highlighting a style in the list box and choosing **Draw<** displays the prompt to **Show placement in empty area:**. Picking a point inserts the highlighted style name into the drawing for editing. After revising the wall style graphically in AutoCAD, save it by reselecting **Wall Library...** in the Walls pull-down menu. Pick OK when the *Confirmation* dialog box appears with the message "**Save changes from Draw?**"

Choosing **Pick<** prompts to **Pick wall entities that make up the style.** After selecting objects, the *Wall Style Editor* dialog box opens to draw the wall style. Picking OK displays the **Changes have been made** message box to accept or discard the changes. This is particularly useful if you received a drawing from another office without the wall style file.

List was discussed briefly in Chapter 12. Pick buttons along the bottom of the dialog box offer options to **Edit..., Copy,** and **Delete** as well as draw lines, polylines, faces, or a hatch pattern.

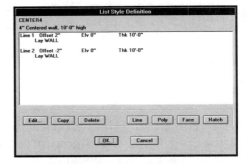

Toggling check boxes for **Image Scale** enlarges the wall style image and **End View** shows the wall style in end or section view.

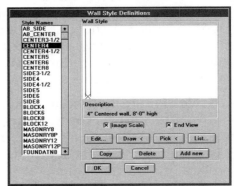

SWAPPING WALL STYLES

WALLS ➤ SWAP WALL STYLES

Selecting **Swap Wall Styles** under the Walls pull-down menu replaces or swaps an existing wall style with another style. The figure shows two interior walls drawn with the CENTER4 wall style.

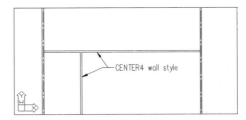

The prompting sequence is:

> Select wall segment to redo...
> Select objects: **c [pick points to create crossing window]**
> First corner: Other corner: 2 found **[left side of horizontal wall style selected with crossing window]**
> Select objects: **c [pick points to create crossing window]**

First corner: Other corner: 2 found (1 duplicate) **[right side of horizontal wall style selected with crossing window]**

Select objects: ⏎

To swap the existing horizontal wall style with CENTER8, choosing **Swap Wall Styles** prompts to select the object, (shown highlighted) then opens the *Wall Style Definitions* dialog box to pick a new wall style. Exiting the dialog box draws the new or replaced wall style.

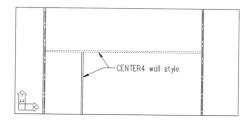

Note: Picking all objects with a crossing window assures that all elements of the wall containing the necessary data for the command to function properly are selected. If the original walls are still visible, invoke the Macro **RD** to refresh the display screen.

To use the command productively, choosing a new wall style with the same *working point* (the 0 offset value) and same wall width is recommended to avoid additional cleanup at intersections of varying wall widths.

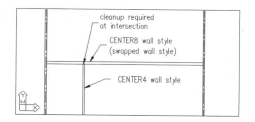

• •

CREATING A WALL LEGEND

ARCHTOOLS ➤ CREATE WALL LEGEND

A legend can be created of existing wall styles defined in the drawing by selecting **Create Wall Legend** from the ArchTools pull-down menu under **Schedules**.

Choosing **Create Wall Legend** creates a chart of all the wall styles used in the drawing, then prompts for a location. The information to draw the chart is retrieved from the WALL-TYPE.DAT file.

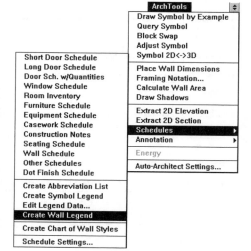

The prompting sequence is:

Command:
Move objects (or ENTER for options): **[pick a point]**
Second point of displacement: **[offers option to select new location for the chart]**
New basepoint (Copy/Xflip/Yflip/Move/Rotate/Done) <Done>: ⏎

WALL LEGEND	
▭	6" width wall, center justified
──	One-sided wall for column enclosures
▭	4 1/2" Centered wall, 10'-0" high
▭	6" Side wall, 10'-0" high

CREATING A CHART OF WALL STYLES

ARCHTOOLS ➤ SCHEDULES ➤ CREATE CHART OF WALL STYLES

Selecting **Create Chart of Wall Styles** under **Schedules** in the ArchTool pull-down menu draws a chart of all the Style Names listed in the Wall Styles Definition dialog box, The chart appears as a series of grids containing the wall style with a title, description, working point (identified by an X node point) as well as the lines, faces, and hatch patterns that define the style.

Styles with color or linetypes not defined in the layer defaults file cause the *Select Color* and *Select Linetype* dialog boxes to open for selection as the chart is drawn.

AB_SIDE	AB_CENTER	CENTER3-1/2	CENTER4	CENTER4-1/2	CENTER5	CENTER6	CENTER8	SIDE3-1/2	SIDE4
SIDE4-1/2	SIDE5	SIDE6	SIDE8	BLOCK4	BLOCK6	BLOCK8	BLOCK12	MASONRY8	MASONRY8P
MASONRY12	MASONRY12P	FOUNDATN8	FOUNDATN10	FOUNDATN12	LOW4	ONELINE	SOFFIT	SOFFITWALL	COUNTER
L2CENTER	L4CENTER	CLINES	GUTTER	WALLEL3	TOPFACE	FACEWALL	FACE2WALL	ALLFACE	MASFACE12
FACESLOPE	FACESLOPE2	MAS12T	POLY6	PLOYOFF	FANCYWALL	NOT DEFINED	NOT DEFINED	NOT DEFINED	NOT DEFINED

The prompting sequence is:

Command:

Show placement in empty area (lower left corner): **[pick a point]**

Defining new layer GUTTER... [*Select Color* or *Select Linetype* dialog box may appear, make a selection or pick OK]

Defining new layer WALL_1... [*Select Color* or *Select Linetype* dialog box may appear, make a selection or pick OK]

Defining new layer WALL_2... [*Select Color* or *Select Linetype* dialog box may appear, make a selection or pick OK]

Defining new layer WALL_3... [*Select Color* or *Select Linetype* dialog box may appear, make a selection or pick OK]

Defining new layer FOOT... [*Select Color* or *Select Linetype* dialog box may appear, make a selection or pick OK]

MORE SCHEDULES

ARCHTOOLS ➤ SCHEDULES ➤ ROOM INVENTORY

The **Schedules** menu offers commands that create the various types of schedules as listed. Choosing a schedule type opens one or more dialog boxes to choose appearance and content of the information. An example of a schedule and prompting sequence for **Room Inventory** follows.

ROOM INVENTORY		
NUMBER	NAME	AREA
100	OFFICE—1	2700.00
101	ENTRY	1020.00
103	OFFICE—1	2700.00
104	OFFICE—3	5550.00
105	CORR.	900.00
106	SERVICE	1800.00
TOTAL		14670.00

The prompting sequence is:

Schedule Title (or . for none) <ROOM INVENTORY>: ↵

Create sub-totals <Yes>: **n [includes subtotals for numerical fields, then opens *Sort by tag name* dialog box to select sorting field based on attribute tag name]**

Output to (Drawing/Printer/Screen) <Drawing>: **[inserts schedule into current drawing, prints schedule or prompts for additional information, display results on text screen]**

Digitize start point: **[pick point to place schedule]**

Number of rows per page (Show/Maximum) <Maximum>: ↵ **["Show" prompts to "Show bottom of available space:". Choosing a point sets schedule's length, then creates a second column with the remaining information]**

Layer to search <*>: **[searches for layers stored in zzsdesk.ly file]**

Performing attribute extract... **[the following record information can be ignored]**

** Bad numeric value for field AARMAREA, record 1

** Bad numeric value for field AARMAREA, record 2

** Bad numeric value for field AARMAREA, record 3

** Bad numeric value for field AARMAREA, record 4

** Bad numeric value for field AARMAREA, record 5

** Bad numeric value for field AARMAREA, record 6

6 records in extract file.

Merge with data from another drawing <No>: ↵ **["yes" opens the *Existing data file to merge* dialog box to merge information with another file]**

Save data file <No>:↵ **["yes" opens *Output data file* dialog box to save information to a text file]**

Performing sort...

Creating output........

Modify results (Move/Block/Wblock/Done) <Done>: ↵ **[allows schedule to be repositioned, created as a block within the drawing or as separate drawing file]**

In Chapter 14, interior walls will be drawn using the settings described. A variety of approaches will be explored using pull-downs, macros, and other wall routines.

WALLS

Creating Wall types and Drawing Custom Walls

Contents

The wall settings and procedures discussed in Chapter 13 provided a basic understanding of wall commands. In this chapter, additional interior walls will be drawn in the SERVICE, OFFICE-3, and ENTRY spaces in *sets* to create smaller areas. Sets may consist of drawing several walls or a single wall. The following exercises provide an overview of prompting sequences, then describe specific command-line prompts in detail. Each exercise is designed as a simple execution of the wall command to explain various methods for drawing walls.

Softdesk's walls can be drawn using faces or hatch patterns and edited using the **Wall Edit** or **Wall Hatching** commands in the Walls pull-down menu. Advanced wall features, not covered in this tutorial, include drawing a wall style, then saving it and picking existing entities to create a new wall style.

The current plan now appears with 4 1/2" interior walls and 6" exterior walls. Let's add some more interior walls. First use the Macro **ZW** to zoom into the SERVICE area shown by the rectangle at the upper left portion of the floor plan.

 Macro Command: **ZW**

(AutoCAD Command: **ZOOM, WINDOW**)

Command: **zw**

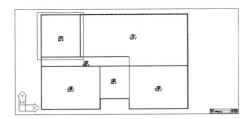

· · · · · · · · · · · · · · · · · · · ·
TURNING LAYERS OFF

Invoke the **LF** macro to open the *Layer(s) to turn off* dialog box and highlight the FL01-WALLCL layer.

 Macro Command: **LF**

(AutoCAD Command: **LAYER, OFF**)

Command: **lf**
Macro: Layer Off

 Pick OK two times to close the dialog box.

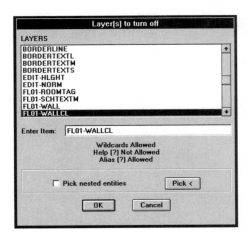

DRAWING THE FIRST SET OF INTERIOR WALLS

WALL ➤ WALL LIBRARY...

Draw walls within the SERVICE area to create the men's and women's restrooms.

Select **Wall Library...** from the Walls pull-down menu to open the *Wall Style Definitions* dialog box and highlight CENTER4 in the **Style Names** list box. The **Description** section identifies the wall as: 4" Centered wall, 8'-0" high.

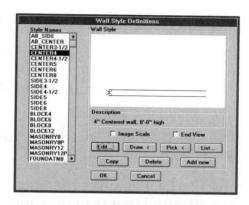

Select **Edit...** to open the *Wall Style Editor* dialog box and change the **Desc** (Description) and **Thickness** values.

Edit the values shown for **Line 1 of 2** ,which represents the top wall line.

 Dialog box:

Name:	CENTER4
Desc:	**4" Centered wall, 10'-0" high**
Offset:	2
Elevation:	0"
Thickness:	**10'**
Estimating:	(blank)
Layer	WALL
Group	(blank)

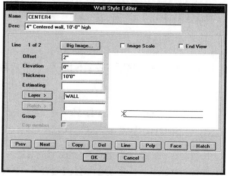

Select **Next** to edit the bottom line of the wall identified as **Line 2 of 2**. Enter 10' in the **Thickness** edit box. Notice that **Desc** (description) contains the updated information. It is important that both lines representing the wall be selected for editing. Otherwise, their extruded thickness (height) will be drawn incorrectly.

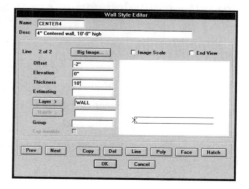

Edit the values shown for **Line 2 of 2**.

Dialog box:

Name:	CENTER4
Desc:	4" Centered wall, 10'-0" high
Offset:	-2
Elevation:	0"
Thickness:	**10'**
Estimating:	(blank)
Layer	WALL
Group	(blank)

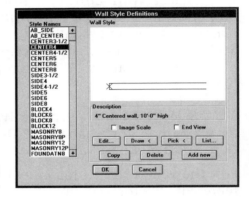

Pick OK and return to the *Wall Style Definitions* dialog box.

The CENTER4 wall style is now redefined as a 4" Centered wall, 10'-0" high.

Pick OK and the prompting sequence to draw the wall begins automatically at the command line.

USING A REFERENCE POINT FILTER TO DRAW THE FIRST WALL

Draw the first wall starting at point A, as shown in the figure, using a Softdesk point filter. Point filters can be invoked anytime during a command sequence to set base or reference points to draw a wall.

Use the .r reference point filter and draw the 4" centered 10' high wall horizontal and parallel to the corridor starting at a distance of 19'-6" from the inside left corner of the SERVICE area.

PROMPTING SUMMARY

Wall style - CENTER4

From point: **.r [reference point filter]**

>>Base point: **int** of **[point A]**

>>To reference point: **@19'6<90 [point B]**

>>To reference point: ↵

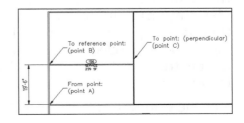

To point: **per** to [pick point C along opposite wall as shown]
To point: ↵

Note: A list of additional reference point filters can be found in Appendix B.

Enter the .r reference filter at **From point:**, then press Enter again to display both the symbols >> and prompt for **Base point:**. Invoke the intersection or endpoint osnap mode to set the interior corner as the base point, then continue with entering the distance of 19'-6" and angle of 90 degrees to find the next point.

From point: .r
>>Base point: **int** of

After the rubber-banding line moves to its new position, exit the .r reference filter prompt by pressing Enter.

>>To reference point: **@19'6<90**
>>To reference point: ↵

Next, continue the command by selecting a perpendicular point (along the inside vertical wall between SERVICE and OFFICE-3) as shown.

To point: **per** to

Press Enter to complete the command. The CENTER4 wall is drawn 4" wide offset 2" from its centerline working point as shown.

To point: ↵

An enlarged view of the CENTER4 wall is shown with a rubber-banding line ending at the working point.

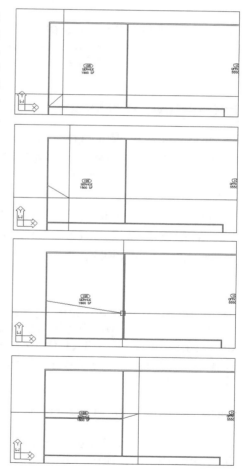

DRAWING THE SECOND SET OF WALLS

WALLS ➤ MULTIPLE WALLS ➤ ADD 1 WALL

Select **Multiple Walls** from the Walls menu to automatically draw a series of parallel walls in one operation.

Add two CENTER4 walls parallel to the interior lower left vertical wall of the SERVICE area 5' apart at a distance of 21'-6".

Walls	Door/Wind	Design
AB_CENTER {w1}		
AB_SIDE {w2}		
BLOCK8 {w3}		
FOUNDATN12 {w4}		
Wall Library...		
Draw by Example		
Query		
Swap Wall Styles		
Wall Edit	▶	
Multiple Walls		Add 1 Wall
Wall Hatching		Add 2 Walls (Corner)
Convert Polyline to Walls		Add 3 Walls
Wall Settings...		Draw Rectanglar Spac
1 CENTER4		
2 AB_CENTER		
3 AB_SIDE		
4 BLOCK8		

PROMPTING SUMMARY

Select base wall element near middle: **[pick point A]**

Select wall style... **[*Wall Style Definitions* dialog box opens]**

Center justified wall style - working to center lines.

Centerline offset distance (or eXit) <10'>: **21'6 [point B]**

Centerline offset distance (or eXit) <21'-6">: **5' [point C]**

Centerline offset distance (or eXit) <5'>: **x**

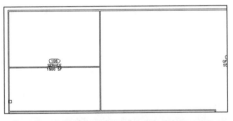

Begin the command by choosing **Add 1 Wall** from **Multiple Walls** in the Walls pull-down menu, then select the object (the interior wall line) when the pick box appears at the prompt.

Select base wall element near middle:

After selecting the base wall, the *Wall Style Definitions* dialog box automatically appears unless **Suppress Option Prompts** is set. Choose the CENTER4 wall style again, then pick OK.

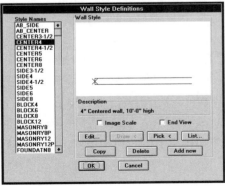

As the dialog box closes, an arrow appears confirming the centerline offset distance and direction.

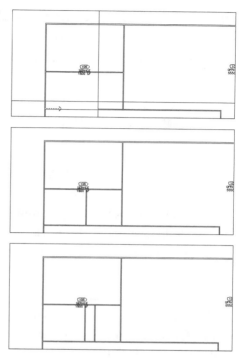

Enter a value of 21'6" at the command line, then press the return.

Centerline offset distance (or eXit) <10'>: **21'6"**

Note: Picking a point above the interior vertical wall's midpoint at the "base wall element" prompt may cause the arrow to appear along the first interior wall drawn.

Input a value of 5' at the command line, then press Enter again to draw a second wall at the specified offset distance.

Centerline offset distance (or eXit) <21'-6">: **5'**

Enter X to exit the command after the 5' offset wall appears. The two new walls in the SERVICE area are drawn with all intersections cleaned up.

Centerline offset distance (or eXit) <5'>: **x**

DRAWING THE THIRD SET OF WALLS

WALLS ➤ CONVERT POLYLINE TO WALLS

Polylines can be converted into walls by selecting the **Convert Polyline to Walls** command from the Walls pull-down menu. The command prompts to select an existing polyline or to draw a new polyline for conversion. The *Wall Style Definition* dialog box opens to select a style name; then, walls of the specified style are drawn along the polyline path. The next wall drawn will be 10"

Walls	Door/Wind	Design
AB_CENTER {w1}		
AB_SIDE {w2}		
BLOCK8 {w3}		
FOUNDATN12 {w4}		
Wall Library...		
Draw by Example		
Query		
Swap Wall Styles		
Wall Edit		▶
Multiple Walls		▶
Wall Hatching		▶
Convert Polyline to Walls		
Wall Settings...		

wide and 10'-0" high using the CENTER8 style. This wide wall will function as a plumbing wall separating the men's and women's restrooms.

Zoom closer into the lower left portion of the SERVICE area to draw the next wall.

PROMPTING SUMMARY

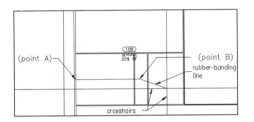

Select polyline or <Enter> to draw: ↵

Show wall path with polyline...

From point: **mid** of **[point A]**

(Arc/Undo/next point) (or Arc): **[point B]**

(Arc/Undo/next point) (Arc/Undo): ↵

Select wall style... [*Wall Style Definitions* dialog box opens]

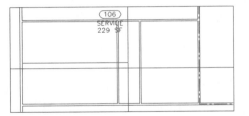

Select **Convert Polyline to Walls** from the Walls pull-down menu, accepting the default **<Enter> to draw:**, and draw a polyline starting at the midpoint of the interior wall. Press F8 to toggle orthomode on; if necessary, extend the polyline past the opposite wall as shown, then press enter.

From point: **mid** of
(Arc/Undo/next point) (or Arc): **[pick point]**

Note: Close is not an option of **Convert to Polyline to Walls**; however, choosing a last point near the start point will close the polyline.

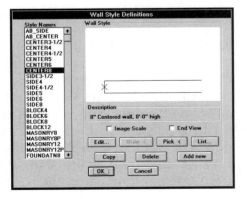

After picking points, the *Wall Style Definitions* dialog box opens for selection of a wall style. Use the CENTER8 wall described as an 8" Centered wall, 8'-0" high and modify the wall style by choosing **Edit**....

Select wall style... [*Wall Style Definitions* dialog box opens]

The *Wall Style Editor* dialog box opens to display the description labeled **Desc** as 8" Centered wall, 8'-0" high for **Line 1 of 2**.

Although other edit boxes and buttons along the side and bottom of the Wall Style Editor dialog box are not included in this tutorial, their descriptions follow:

Elevation allows you to draw components above or below the current UCS plane.

Estimating allows you to assign a *cost* to wall components which can be used by the Productivity Tools *Datalink* program to extract construction cost.

Layer > opens the *Layer Key Name Descriptions* dialog box and allows you to change the layer on which the wall components are drawn. Any existing or new layer name can also be entered in the edit box. Dialog boxes to set color and linetype appear for new layer names not previously defined.

Hatch > opens the *Select Hatch* dialog box for styles that already have hatch patterns.

Group allows you to *link* or connect different components together and determines how walls are cleaned up at intersections.

Cap member allows you to *close* components at the end of a drawn wall style. An example of the prompt **Cap walls** is discussed in Chapter 13.

Line allows you to add a new component (line) to the wall style at the working point. Entering a number (other than 0) in the Offset edit box offsets the line from the working point. A positive number relocates the line above and a negative number moves it below the working point.

Del opens the *Confirmation* dialog box to allow you to **Delete current item** from the wall style.

Poly allows you to draw a polyline as a new component. The **Offset** label changes to **Offset C/L**, allowing you to set the centerpoint of the polyline's width. The **Estimating** label changes to **Width**, allowing you to set the width of the polyline. The identification **Line 1 of 1** at the top left corner of the dialog box changes to read **Poly 1 or 1** and the bottom left corner of the dialog box displays the words "Add new poly line 1" to distinguish the component.

CHAPTER FOURTEEN

Face allows you to add a face to the wall style. The dialog box appears similar to Poly (previously described), except the identification changes to read **Face 1 of 1** and the lower left corner of the dialog box reads "Added new face 1." Faces have two points that can be the same or different. **Face** can be used to create partial-height wall styles with a top surface so they appear solid in a bird's eye view. A top face should have the same priority/group number as vertical elements. The left side of the dialog box replaces the first four edit boxes with **Offset1, Offset2, Elev1,** and **Elev2** to determine horizontal and vertical endpoints of a face. Checking **End View** helps you to visualize and confirm endpoint locations in the image box.

Modify the information in the **Name, Desc, Thickness,** and **Offset** edit boxes to change the style name, description, working point (offset distance), and wall height for **Line 1 of 2,** then pick **Next** to change **Offset** and **Thickness** for **Line 2 of 2** as indicated.

Values for **Line 1 of 2** are:

 Dialog box:

Name: **CENTER10**
Desc: **10" Centered wall, 10'-0" high**
Offset: **5"**
Elevation: **0"**
Thickness: **10'**
Estimating: (blank)
Layer   **WALL**
Group   (blank)

Values for **Line 2 of 2** are:

 Dialog box:

Name: CENTER10
Desc: 10" Centered wall, 10'-0" high
Offset: **-5**
Elevation: **0"**
Thickness: **10'**
Estimating: (blank)

Layer	**WALL**
Group	(blank)

Pick OK.

Returning to the *Wall Style Definitions* dialog box replaces the existing style name CENTER8 with CENTER10 and the **Description** 8" Centered wall, 8'-0" high with 10" Centered wall, 10'-0" high.

Pick OK to close the dialog box and return to the command line.

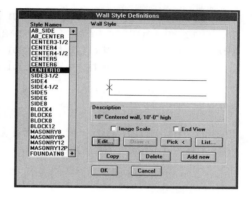

The 10-inch wide-wall is drawn with only the start point intersection cleaned. The opposite end requires cleanup using a wall editing command.

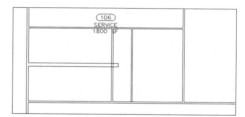

Note: The **Convert Polylines to Walls** command may be especially helpful when drawing complicated polyline paths consisting of Fit or Spline curved sections.

• •

CLEANING INTERSECTIONS

WALLS ➤ WALL EDIT ➤ CLEAN TEE, SELECT WALLS

Selecting **Clean Tee, Select Walls** from **Wall Edit** under the Walls pull-down menu will clean up wall intersections. Invoking the command can clean intersecting walls copied from one location to another when one wall segment ends on or before another wall segment.

Successful implementation of the **Clean Tee, Pick Point** command, for example, also located in the **Wall Edit** menu, requires that all the walls to be cleaned up lie within a rectangular area with sides equal to the maximum wall width defined in the *Auto-Architect General Settings* dialog box (**ArchTools>Auto-Architect Settings...>General...**) and whose center is the point picked. If these conditions are not met, use the **Clean Tee, Select Walls** command.

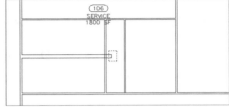

Pick two points (right to left) to create a crossing window or enter C when prompted to **Select wall objects to trim or extend:** as shown at the end of the CENTER10 wall style.

Select wall objects to trim or extend: **c**

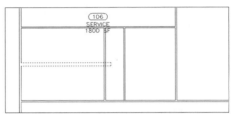

The highlighted objects shown confirm the crossing window's selection.

Other corner: 3 found
Select objects:⏎

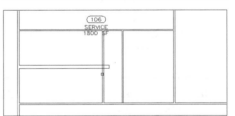

Choose the left side of the intersecting wall as the trim edge, as shown.

Select wall objects to butt to: 1 found
Select objects:⏎

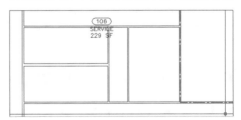

The walls are shown cleaned at the intersection.

• •

DRAWING MULTIPLE WALLS

A series of smaller offices labeled as OFFICES-2A, 2B, and 2C will be drawn in the OFFICE-2 space.

WALLS ➤ MULTIPLE WALLS ➤ ADD 2 WALLS (CORNER)

Zoom into OFFICE-2 at the lower right corner of the plan, as shown. Add a series of 10-foot wide smaller office spaces along the front of the building. Draw all walls centered 3-1/2" wide, aligning the interior horizontal wall with the front wall of the ENTRY space.

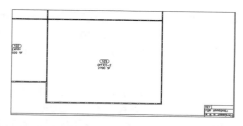

The **Add 2 Walls (Corner)** command encloses a space with two or more walls based on an initial selection of a wall line. Prompts for an offset distance allow users to draw multiple spaces.

   Select **Add 2 Walls (Corner)** from **Multiple Walls** under the Walls pull-down menu.

PROMPTING SUMMARY

Select base wall element near corner:

Select wall style... [***Wall Style Definitions*** dialog box opens]

Distance along base wall <10'-0">: **10'**

Center justified wall style - working to center lines.

Centerline offset distance (or eXit) <5'-0">: **20'**

Centerline offset distance (or eXit) <20'-0">:↵

Centerline offset distance (or eXit) <20'-0">: x

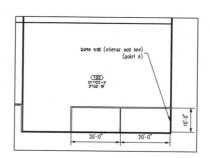

   Select the interior vertical wall line of the exterior wall along the right side corner of OFFICE-2.

If other nearby lines are detected by the command, the **Select this object <yes>:** prompt appears. Entering "no" at the prompt provides

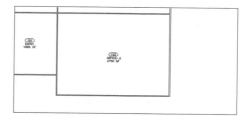

an opportunity for Softdesk to highlight another line for selection. Accepting the selection opens the *Wall Style Definitions* dialog box.

The *Wall Style Definitions* dialog box appears with the most recently used style name highlighted. Choose the CENTER3-1/2 style name displaying the **Description** 3-1/2" Centered wall, 8'-0" high. Change the thickness of the wall height from 8'-0" to 10'-0".

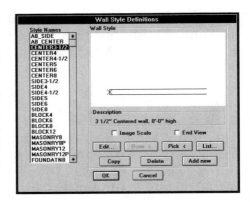

Select the **Edit...** pick box to open the *Wall Style Editor* dialog box.

Note: If a project required using both 8- and 10-foot high walls, make a **Copy** of the wall style and save it with the new style name. An example using a non-centered wall style will be discussed later.

Modify the **Desc** and **Thickness** edit boxes to reflect the new values for lines 1 and 2, then pick OK to close the dialog boxes observing the changes in the *Wall Style Definitions* dialog box for **Description** and **Thickness**.

Values for **Line 1 of 2** are:

 Dialog box:

Name:	**CENTER3-1/2**
Desc:	**3-1/2" Centered wall, 10'-0" high**
Offset:	**1-3/4"**
Elevation:	**0"**
Thickness:	**10'**
Estimating:	(blank)
Layer	**WALL**
Group	(blank)

Values for **Line 2 of 2** are:

Dialog box:

Name:	**CENTER3-1/2**
Desc:	**3-1/2" Centered wall, 10'-0" high**
Offset:	**-1-3/4"**
Elevation:	**0"**
Thickness:	**10'**
Estimating:	(blank)
Layer	**WALL**
Group	(blank)

 Pick OK.

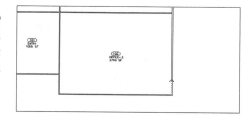

An arrow appears facing upward to confirm the direction for finding the first wall line. Enter 10' as the vertical distance from the arrow's origin point (shown at the bottom right interior corner of OFFICE-2).

Distance along base wall <10'>: **10'**

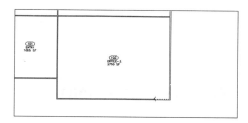

Again an arrow appears, this time confirming the offset horizontal distance from the interior vertical wall of OFFICE-2. If **Prompt for intersection** is on, the command line will request user input to clean the wall start and end points.

Enter a distance of 20' and accept the option to clean up the wall lines at both intersections.

Center justified wall style - working to center lines.
Centerline offset distance (or eXit) <5'-0">: **20'**

After the first corner wall is drawn, press enter to draw a second corner wall at the same distance, accepting the default of 20'.

Centerline offset distance (or eXit) <20'>: ↵

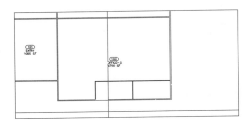

Enter X at the prompt line to exit the command, completing the second corner wall with all intersections cleaned, as shown.

Centerline offset distance (or eXit) <20'>: **x**

• • • • • • • • • • • • • • • • •

STRETCHING WALLS

WALLS ➤ WALL EDIT ➤ STRETCH WALL SEGMENTS

Stretch the new interior horizontal wall parallel to the front exterior wall of the ENTRY space.

Select **Stretch Wall Segments** under **Wall Edit** in the Walls pull-down menu to stretch the original wall to a new location.

Walls	Door/Wind	Design
AB_CENTER {w1}		
AB_SIDE {w2}		
BLOCK8 {w3}		
FOUNDATN12 {w4}		
Wall Library...		
Draw by Example		
Query		
Swap Wall Styles		
Wall Edit		
Multiple Walls		
Wall Hatching		
Convert Polyline to Walls		
Wall Settings...		
1 CENTER8		
2 CENTER4		
3 AB_CENTER		
4 AB_SIDE		

Clean Crossing Walls
Clean Tee, Pick Point
Clean Tee, Select Walls
Clean Corners
Add End Caps
Join Wall Segments
Join Wall Entities
Stretch Wall Segments
Make Wall Openings
Fillet Walls
Extend Walls to Roof
Convert Wall Lines to Faces
Restore Wall Faces to Lines
Set Face Edge Visibility

PROMPTING SUMMARY

Building Base Stretch...

Select objects with Crossing window.

First corner: Other corner:

Remove objects: ↵

Base point: **nea** to **[point A]**

New point (press Enter to drag): **per** to **[point B]**

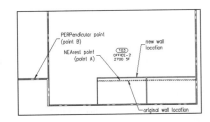

Note: **Using the Stretch Wall Segments** command for hatched or pouched walls with doors and windows inserted in them updates all the objects automatically.

Create a crossing window around the interior horizontal walls, as shown.

Select objects with Crossing window.
First corner: Other corner:
Remove objects: ↵

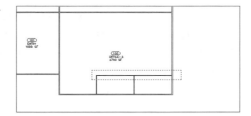

Select a point along the top interior horizontal wall and stretch it to meet the top interior horizontal wall of the ENTRY space.

Base point: **nea** to
New point (press Enter to drag): **per** to

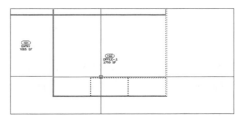

The two interior wall lines are now aligned as shown.

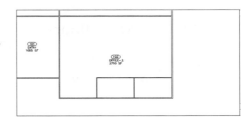

· ·
DRAWING ANOTHER WALL SET

WALLS ➤ WALL SETTINGS...

This next section describes the procedure for drawing a non-centered wall style to create a third small office in the OFFICE-2 space and changing the Preset Wall Style shortcut key for **w1** to a different wall style.

Enclose the remaining space as a third office, aligning the interior horizontal walls.

Select **Wall Settings...** from the Walls pull-down menu to open the *Wall Settings* dialog box. Assign the non-centered wall style SIDE3-1/2 to the shortcut key **w2**.

Walls	Door/Wind	Design
AB_CENTER {w1}		
AB_SIDE {w2}		
BLOCK8 {w3}		
FOUNDATN12 {w4}		
Wall Library...		
Draw by Example		
Query		
Swap Wall Styles		
Wall Edit		▶
Multiple Walls		▶
Wall Hatching		▶
Convert Polyline to Walls		
Wall Settings...		
1 CENTER8		
2 CENTER4		
3 AB_CENTER		
4 AB_SIDE		

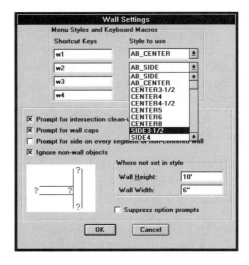

 Open the pop-up list next to the **w2** shortcut key and highlight SIDE3-1/2. After the name appears in the **Style to use** edit box, pick OK.

COPYING A WALL STYLE— DRAWING A NON-CENTERED WALL

WALLS ➤ WALL LIBRARY...

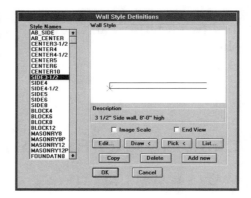

Choose **Wall Library...** from the Walls pull-down menu to open the *Wall Style Definitions* dialog box and highlight SIDE3-1/2 in the **Style Names** list box.

Pick OK.

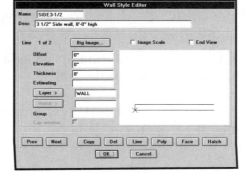

Select **Copy...** to open the *Wall Style Editor* dialog box and edit the SIDE3-1/2 wall style. Choosing this button creates a duplicate of the highlighted wall style, then displays the message "Style copied, please change style name." Change the wall style name from SIDE3-1/2 to SIDE3-1/2_10.

Modify the **Desc** and **Thickness**, as shown, to reflect the new wall values for a 10'-0" wall for **Line 1 of 2**, then pick **Next** to change **Line 2 of 2**.

Values for **Line 1 of 2** are:

 Dialog box:

Name:	**SIDE3-1/2_10**
Desc:	**3 1/2" Side wall, 10'-0" high**
Offset:	**0**
Elevation:	**0"**
Thickness:	**10'**
Estimating:	(blank)
Layer	**WALL**
Group	(blank)

Values for **Line 2 of 2** are:

 Dialog box:

Name:	**SIDE3-1/2_10**
Desc:	**3 1/2" Side wall, 10'-0" high**
Offset:	**3-1/2"**
Elevation:	**0"**
Thickness:	**10'**
Estimating:	(blank)
Layer	**WALL**
Group	(blank)

Pick OK.

Closing the *Wall Style Editor* dialog box returns the *Wall Style Definitions* dialog with the new style name appearing in the list box. Pick OK and the prompts to draw a SIDE3-1/2_10 wall style appear at the command line.

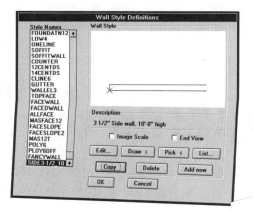

Note: Long style names may not be visible due to the width limitation of the list box.

Draw the non-centered 3-1/2" interior horizontal interior wall parallel with the adjacent smaller offices, as shown.

PROMPTING SUMMARY

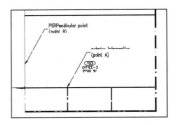

Wall style - SIDE3-1/2_10

From point: **int** of [**point A, exterior wall intersection line**]

To point: **per** to [**point B, right wall line**]

Pick side: [**pick point below wall line**]

To point: ↵

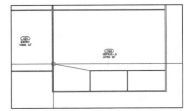

Select the first point for the wall line at the exterior intersection of the smaller office and extend it perpendicular to the vertical wall between the ENTRY and OFFICE-2 spaces, as shown.

From point: **int** of
To point: **per** to

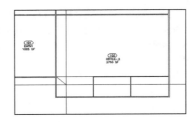

Select a point below the wall line as the pick side and the wall is drawn, with both intersections cleaned up.

Pick side:
To point: ↵

Note: Walls with matching styles or heights and layers will clean up at the intersections.

QUERY WALL FOR WALL STYLE INFORMATION

WALLS ➤ QUERY

The **Query** command can be used to identify a wall style. Select **Query** from the Walls pull-down menu.

Select one element of the wall. Repeatedly selecting objects displays the wall style at the command line.

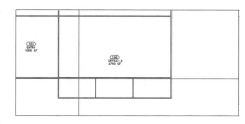

The prompting sequence is:

Select wall element (or Done): **[select a wall element]**

Wall style: SIDE3-1/2_10 - 3-1/2" Side wall, 10'-0" high

Select wall element (or Done): ↵

DRAWING A CUSTOM CURVED WALL USING POINT FILTERS

This next exercise makes extensive use of point filters to create a curved wall at a specified distance from existing wall lines. The exercise first describes how to display and apply the screen menu to set point filters, then explains the prompting sequence when invoked entirely from the command line.

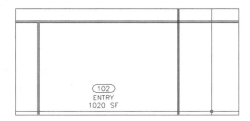

Zoom into the ENTRY area and draw a custom curved 6-inch wide wall near the rear portion of the ENTRY space.

THE (SIDE) SCREEN MENU

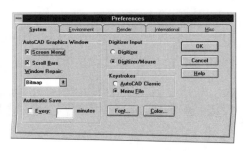

Softdesk provides wall options on both the side screen and pull-down menu. Invoking the AutoCAD **preferences** command provides access to the **AutoCAD Graphics Window Section** which offers a **Screen Menu** check box.

Softdesk Menu: FILE ➤ CONFIGURE ➤ PREFERENCES

(AutoCAD Command: **PREFERENCES**)

The screen menu initially displays the same wall commands as the Wall pull-down menu. Invoking a wall macro changes options on the screen menu offering entity-type toggles which control the type of walls drawn.

If your resolution is standard VGA resolution, type the Macro = to display the following drawing status at the screen menu:

E>0" Elevation
T>10'-0"   Wall Thickness/Height
S>1/8"   Drawing Scale
L>FL01   Floor Level
P>
6:00:00   Current time (updated by selective commands)

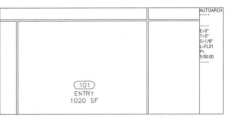

Initially one of the top lines reads =>**Line** which is a wall option toggle. Selecting this item toggles the menu to read =>**Arc**. The =>Line and =>Arc options are used with wall macros to draw straight or curved wall segments.

The additional options **X dist** and **Y dist** provide a means for entering just the "X" or "Y" direction displacement. Entering a negative or positive number produces the corresponding relative coordinate directions of 180 or 270 degrees.

Choosing CENTER4 from the Walls pull-down menu invokes the wall command. Selecting =>Line displays the =>Arc toggle. Curved walls are created when =>Arc appears on the screen menu.

The same procedures can be invoked at the command line by entering the letter A for arc.

• •

DRAWING A CURVED WALL USING POINT FILTERS

WALLS ➤ CENTER4

Draw a curved wall centered in the ENTRY space with endpoints 7' from the rear of the space and 6' from the left and right sides. Locate the center of the wall curved 5' from the rear wall as shown. Invoke the arc option at the command line.

Select the CENTER4 wall style from the bottom of the Walls pull-down menu to draw a 4" wide centered wall. If the screen menu is active, it changes to display Wall Options.

PROMPTING SUMMARY

Command:

Wall style - CENTER4

From point: **.r [enter .r reference filter]**

>>Base point: int of [point A]

>>To reference point: **@7'<0**

>>To reference point: **@6'<270**

>>To reference point: ↵

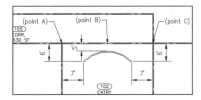

To point: a **[enter a to toggle "Arc" prompt or select from screenmenu]**

Arc (CEnter/End) <second point>: **.m [enter .m midpoint filter]**

>>From point: **mid** of **[point C]**

>>To point: **@5'<270**

Pick end point or Cancel for reference options: **[press ESC to cancel]**

Application D:\SDSK\AB\AB.EXE ERROR: Function canceled

Cancel

Unknown command "SDSK". Type ? for list of commands.

Ignore previous message...

Wall arc reference options or end point: .r [enter .r reference filter]

>>Base point: **int** of **[point C]**

>>To reference point: **@7'<180**

>>To reference point: **@6'<270**

>>To reference point: ↵

Arc (CEnter/End) <second point>: ↵

Select a base point at the interior left wall intersection of the ENTRY using the .r filter to draw a curved wall's start point at a distance of 7' to the right and 6' downward.

Type .r at the **From point:** prompt, then press enter to display the >>**Base Point:** prompt. Pick the intersection shown with the rubber-banding line.

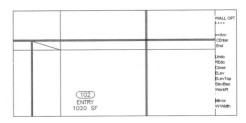

From point: **.r**
>>Base point: **int** of

After settings the base point, enter the distance and direction to set the start point of the curved wall. The wall's start point will be 7'-0" to the right and 6'-0" downward.

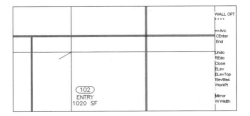

>>To reference point: **@7'<0**
>>To reference point: **@6'<270**
>>To reference point: ⏎

Enter the .m filter to locate the midpoint of the curved wall 5' below the midpoint of the interior horizontal wall in the ENTRY space as shown.

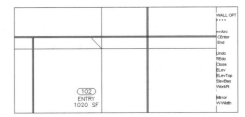

Invoking the .m filter at the command line **Arc(Center/End)<second point>:** starts a reference option to locate the arc's midpoint. Next press enter to display the >>**From point:** prompt for setting the wall's midpoint at a distance of 5' from the first point.

To point: a [**enter a to toggle "Arc" prompt or select from screen menu**]
Arc (CEnter/End) <second point>: **.m**
>>From point: **mid** of
>>To point: **@5'<270**

Note: When the command prompts to "Cancel for reference options," press ESC. These messages can be ignored.

Next, locate the curved wall's endpoint at a distance of 7' to the left and 6' downward from the top right interior corner of the ENTRY using this intersection as the start point with the .r filter.

Wall arc reference options or end point: **.r**
>>Base point: **int** of

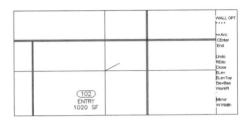

To complete the curved wall, press enter at the >>**To reference point:** prompt after inputting distances of 7' to the left and 6' downward.

>>To reference point: **@7'<180**
>>To reference point: **@6'<270**
>>To reference point: ↵
Arc (CEnter/End) <second point>: ↵

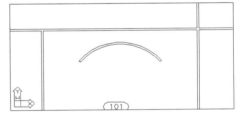

The curved wall is shown with endcaps.

All the interior walls for the SERVICE, OFFICE-2, and ENTRY spaces are now completed. If you used the side screen to create the custom wall, you may wish to remove it. Invoke PREFERENCES and uncheck **Screen Menu** in the *Preferences* dialog box, then pick OK.

Save the drawing and then continue to the next chapter to place doors in the plan.

CHAPTER FIFTEEN

DOOR SETTINGS

Overview of Door-related Settings

Contents

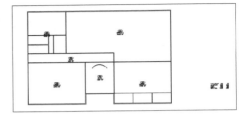

In Chapter 14, walls with varying widths were drawn in the floor plan at a thickness (height) of 10' in preparation for inserting interior and exterior doors. Commands with editable dialog boxes selected in the Door/Wind pull-down menu break lines to insert doors into walls. Understanding door settings and procedures will help when invoking these commands. This chapter provides an overview of the dialog boxes and commands that affect door insertion routines plus door styles. Select commands to view dialog box options and settings only, then pick Cancel.

In addition to the four preset wall styles described in the last chapter, Softdesk provides four preset door and window styles located at the top of the Door/Wind pull-down menu. Door and window specifications are saved to a Style Name similar to walls. The information includes door type, frame dimensions, rough and masonry opening sizes, plus energy efficiency values saved to the WINDOORI.DBF database file.

Doors can be created as 2D and/or 3D assemblies consisting of sidelight windows or other similar combinations and placed into walls at a preset distance. The *General Settings* dialog box in the ArchTools pull-down menu under **Auto-Architect Settings...** provides edit boxes to control door settings.

SETTING CONTROLS FOR DOORS

ARCHTOOLS ➤ AUTO-ARCHITECT SETTINGS... ➤ GENERAL...

Auto-Architect Settings... selected from the ArchTools pull-down menu opens the *Softdesk Auto-Architect Settings* dialog box. Choosing the **General...** pick button opens the *General Settings* dialog box. The same dialog box is available from other pull-down menu locations. Softdesk provides this feature for user convenience and accessibility.

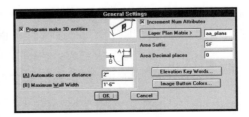

DRAWING ENTITIES IN 3D

The **Programs make 3D entities** check box discussed in Chapter 13 for walls (a portion of the dialog box is shown) will draw door and window frames, sills, glazing, muntins, and trim in both 2D and 3D.

SETTING CORNER DISTANCES

The **Automatic corner distance** edit box allows users to preset the distance that a door is inserted from the nearest wall end. The **Maximum Wall Width** edit box establishes a search distance for creating openings and for the **Wall Edit** commands to find all adjacent entities involved in an intersection condition for cleanup. Softdesk recommends that the minimum value used should not be less than the largest wall thickness in the drawing. An unnecessarily large setting, however, can result in unintentionally breaking a nearby wall (perhaps a closet).

SETTING SEQUENTIAL CALLOUT NUMBERS

Checking **Increment Num Attributes** assigns sequential numbers to any label or tag with attribute names containing "num," including door or room callouts.

DOOR/WIND PULL-DOWN MENU

The Door/Wind pull-down menu displays four preset door and window styles at the top with associated keyboard macros:

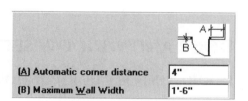

Preset Styles

Shortcut Key	Door Styles	Description
O1	DR3680	Hinged 3' x 6'-8"
O2	OH144x84	Overhead door 12' x 7'

Shortcut Key	Window Styles	Description
O3	DH2448	Double Hung 2' x 4'
O4	CA2460	Casement 2' x 5'

DOOR AND WINDOW SETTINGS

DOOR/WIND ➤ DOOR/WINDOW SETTINGS...

Door/Window Settings... under the Door/Wind pull-down menu opens the *Door and Window Settings* dialog box.

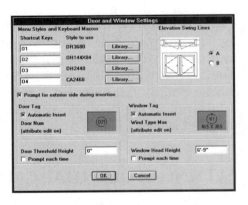

Note: This dialog box is also accessible by selecting **Auto-Architect Settings...** from the ArchTools pull-down menu and clicking on the **Doors and Windows...** pick box.

The *Door and Window Settings* dialog box displays the four shortcut keys in edit boxes along the left side of the **Menu Style and Keyboard Macros** section, similar to the *Wall Settings* dialog box. These settings are stored in the filename <drawing>.DFM. All files are stored in the \SDSKPROJ\(project)\AB\DWG directory. (For this tutorial, the project directory created in Chapter 10 is ARCHTUT.)

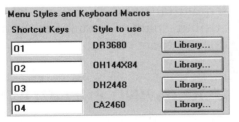

The **Menu Styles and Keyboard Macros** section contains a **Shortcut Keys** edit box and **Library...** pick box. Shortcut keys can be modified or replaced with any user-defined letters and/or numbers. Selecting the **Library...** pick box next to the name opens the *Select Window or Door Style* dialog box. Choosing the **Library...** command under the Door/Wind pull-down menu also opens the *Select Window or Door Style* dialog box.

Prompt for exterior side during insertion check box is helpful for placing doors into a wall style which does not have an obvious exterior and interior side. Such a wall may have been drawn using points on either the exterior or the interior. Door and window styles contain 3D information which is specifically for the exterior or interior; therefore, it is necessary to know which side of the wall is intended to be the exterior. For wall styles which have a definite exterior side, such as

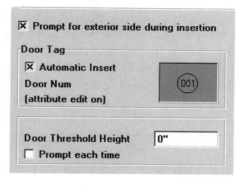

MASONRY12P (brick and block), this prompt is not needed. It is also not necessary for Quick door and windows, which have no exterior/interior differences, or for interior doors where both the casing and trim are the same and the frame depth matches the wall width.

Double-clicking on the image tile in the **Door Tag** section opens the *Symbol Manager* dialog box displaying a variety of door tags, as shown.

The **Door Threshold Height** edit box sets the initial height of the threshold for doors drawn in 3D. This value must be set before inserting the door. Checking the box labeled **Prompt each time** requests user input to set the threshold height whenever doors are inserted. Usually this value will be set to 0.

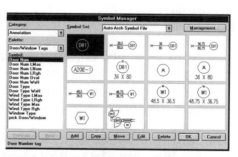

● ●

DOOR STYLE SYMBOL LIBRARY

DOOR/WIND ➤ LIBRARY...

Library... under the Door/Wind pull-down menu displays a **Filters** section with pop-up

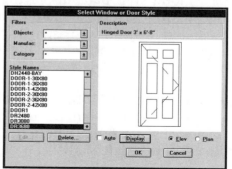

lists, a **Style Names** list box, and **Description** of the highlighted item besides various pick boxes, check boxes, and radio buttons. Softdesk provides this command as the primary source for selecting, creating, and editing styles and assemblies.

Note: **Check existing Door/Window blocks <Yes>** This prompt appears at the command line the first time the Style Manager System is loaded, usually seen when selecting Library... for the first time. If "Yes" is answered, each existing Door and Window style object is checked to see if it was created after the most recent edit of its style. If the object is older, it will be updated to match the current style data. This is intended to make sure a change in style data gets applied to objects in drawings other than the drawing which was current when the style was edited.

The **Filters** section contains pop-up lists for **Objects, Manufac** (Manufacturer), and **Category**, functioning as a tool for organizing the style library. The **Objects:** filter is used to restrict style names that appear for Assemblies, Doors, or Windows only. Selecting the asterisk (*) displays all objects.

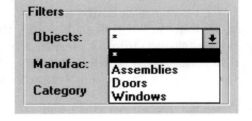

Choosing Assemblies (only) from the **Objects:** pop-up list in the **Filters** section shows a Double Casement Assembly consisting of a fixed window combined with casement windows.

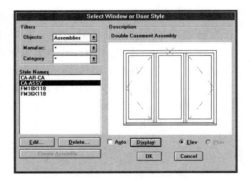

The **Manufac:** filter list is intended to be used for window style data, displaying styles associated with a particular manufacturer, if available. Currently only an asterisk (*) and dash (-) appear in this pop-up list with the dash serving as a place holder.

When objects of other manufacturers are added, the dash can be used to filter for "generic" objects; this would not be possible if the entry were left blank.

The **Category** filter displays selections for Bay Window, Commercial, Curtain Wall, Residential, and Simple.

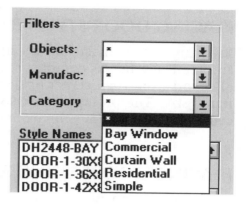

The **Style Names** list box displays all of the available styles specified in the **Filters** section. Although Softdesk provides defaults, style names are user-definable and limited to 12 characters. Choosing **Edit...**, **Delete...**, or **Create Assembly...** pick boxes opens the corresponding dialog boxes.

If the check box next to **Auto** is selected, an image automatically appears; otherwise, selecting **Display** shows the image for the highlighted style name. Image tiles can appear as plans or elevations, depending upon whether the **Elev** or **Plan** radio button is active.

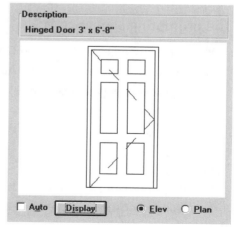

Note: Plan image is not available for Assemblies.

PLACING DOOR STYLES INTO WALLS

Invoking a door macro or selecting a style from the pull-down menu automatically breaks complex straight or curved walls to place 2D and 3D doors from their center or side with headers based on their specified frame size. The prompt **Center/Side/<<Auto - Pick side of wall near center or end>>:** offers three options for inserting doors into walls.

PLACING DOORS USING AUTO OPTION

The **Auto** option places either a center-justi-fied door at the midpoint of a wall or a side-justified door at a preset distance from an end-point. The preset distance value is reset by editing **Automatic corner distance** from the *General Settings* dialog box (**ArchTools>Auto-Architect**).

Choosing a point near the wall lines' endpoint automatically sets the opening's start point relative to its preset distance along the selected wall. Choosing a point near a wall's midpoint automatically centers the door's opening at the midpoint of the selected wall. If the prompt **Auto - pick side of wall near center or end (Center/Side):** does not appear, change the door placement method by entering the letter A as indicated by the following prompting sequence. Object snap should not be invoked when using the **Auto** option.

The prompting sequence is:

Place Door style DR3680: Hinged Door 3' x 6'-8"

Side - pick corner reference point (Auto/Center): **a**

Auto - pick side of wall near center or end (Center/Side):

Show direction for exterior <arrow>:

Select Hinge point:

Creating door...done.

Place tag...

Inserting Door Num at elevation 0.

New callout location <same>:

Note: Once set at the command line, the options for **Side, Center,** or **Auto** remain until another is chosen.

The arrow appears to set the door's exterior direction if **Prompt for exterior side during insertion** is checked in the *Door and Window Settings* dialog box.

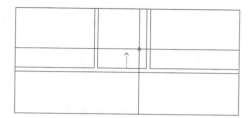

Pick an X mark at the **Select Hinge point:** prompt to set the door's hinge point.

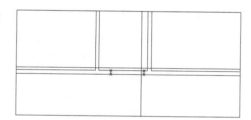

After the door unit is created and placed into the wall, the *Edit Attributes* dialog box opens for input when **Automatic Insert** in checked in the *Door and Window Settings* dialog box.

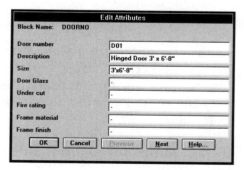

Although the tag's default placement is centered at the threshold, the prompt **New callout location<same>:** offers the opportunity to reposition the door tag. Placing the door tag completes the process.

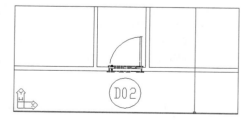

PLACING DOORS USING CENTER OPTION

The **Center** option creates an opening centered about a selected point. This option allows you to place the door or window with the center of the opening related to something other than the center of the wall line. One example of its usage would be to place a door in an exterior wall centered on the room, where the exterior wall is a different style than the interior and, therefore, is not broken at the interior walls. Here you can use the Center placement option, entering .m (for mid of two points) at the "pick side of wall" prompt. At the >>**From point** and >>**To point** prompts, designate the closest endpoints of the two interior walls where they join the exterior wall (osnaps may be used).

The prompting sequence is:

> Place Door style DR3680: Hinged Door 3' x 6'-8"
> Side - pick corner reference point (Auto/Center): **c [changes option to Center]**
> Center - pick side of wall (Auto/Side):
> Show direction for exterior <arrow>:
> Select Hinge point:
> Place tag...
> Inserting Door Num at elevation 0.
> New callout location <same>:

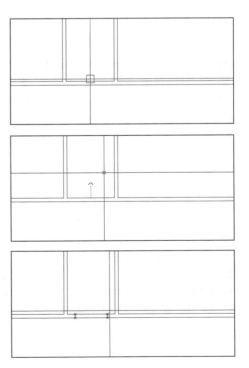

To insert a door into a wall, a door macro can be invoked; the **Center - pick side of wall (Auto/Side):** prompt appears to select a point near the wall or you can use an osnap to set an exact placement.

If the **Prompt for exterior side during insertion** is checked in the *Door and Window Settings* dialog box, an arrow appears prompting to **Show direction for exterior <arrow>:** door swing. Door and related trim are placed along the exterior or interior side of a wall, depending on the arrow's direction.

As X marks appear, selecting a point near an X mark sets the door's hinge or swing point.

If **Automatic Insert** is checked in the *Door and Window Settings* dialog box, a door tag is automatically inserted, and the *Edit Attributes* dialog box appears. Dialog boxes vary, depending on the current tag displayed in the image box of the **Door Tag** section of the *Door and Window Settings* dialog box.

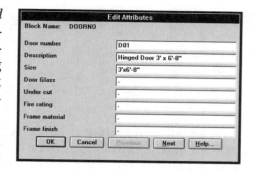

Only the first of five dialog boxes is shown here with the first eight attributes. Each time **Next** is selected, another dialog box opens to view and edit attributes associated with the tag.

Picking OK closes the dialog box and the door reappears with the callout or door tag. The **New callout location <same>:** prompts to retain the tag's original location or provides an opportunity to displace it.

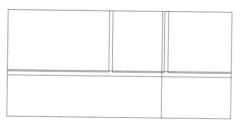

PLACING DOORS USING SIDE OPTION

The **Side** option creates an opening by prompting to select a corner reference point. This option is recommended when the desired distance from the corner is different from the default distance shown in the *General Settings* dialog box (**ArchTools>Auto-Architect Settings>General...**). Also, use Side when breaking a wall into an interior/exterior wall intersection.

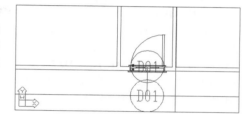

The prompting sequence is:

    Place Door style DR3680: Hinged Door 3' x 6'-8"
    Center - pick side of wall (Auto/Side): **s [prompt changes to Side]**
    Side - pick corner reference point (Auto/Center):
    Side of opening:
    Which direction for break:

Show direction for exterior <arrow>:

Select Hinge point:

Creating door...done.

Place tag...

Inserting Door Num at elevation 0.

New callout location <same>:

Invoke an osnap (e.g.,. intersection or end-point) at the **Side - pick corner reference point (Auto/Center):** prompt to set an exact location.

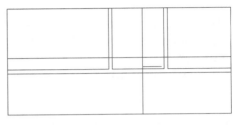

At the **Side of opening:** prompt, pick a point dynamically with a pointing device or enter a distance and direction (e.g.,. @3"<0) to set the opening's start point.

Which direction for break: prompts for a selection using your pointing device to set the opening's opposite end.

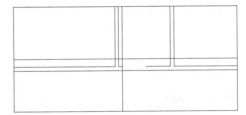

Show direction for exterior <arrow>: prompts to find the exterior wall side to set the door jamb location for doors with jambs or casings. This prompt is suppressed when **Prompt for exterior side during insertion** is unchecked in the *Door and Window Settings* dialog box.

As X marks appear, **Select Hinge point:** prompts to set the hinge side and position the door's swing. Choose a point near any X mark.

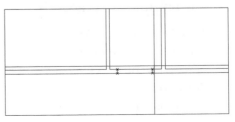

The callout or door tag appears for acceptance or editing if **Attribute Insert** is checked in the *Door and Window Settings* dialog box. Attribute dialog box prompts and default values vary for each door tag. Selecting the image box in the **Door Tag** section displays the default Softdesk callouts.

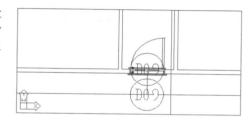

Picking OK closes the dialog box; the callout will appear at the door threshold. The **New callout location <same>:** prompt allows you to accept or reposition its location.

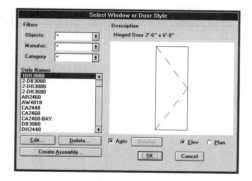

DOOR STYLES

DOOR/WIND ➤ LIBRARY... ➤ EDIT...

Door types, hand (left or right), and orientation insertions are based on the wall's angle and selected hinge point. Exterior and/or interior sills are based on the door's style. As previously mentioned, Softdesk provides a library of default styles in the *Select Window or Door Style* dialog box. Highlighting a door style and choosing **Edit...** opens the *Edit Door Style* dialog box to create a new door or modify an existing style.

The *Edit Door Style* dialog box displays detailed information about the highlighted door in a pop-up list. Picking the down arrow next to each pop-up list provides default values that can be chosen to modify the selected door style, including **Type**, **Height**, and **Width**, as described in the following sections.

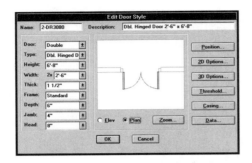 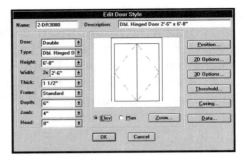

Select Window or Door Style Dialog Box: Pop-up Lists

Name: Edit box containing the name of the door style high-lighted in the **Style Names** list box in the *Select Window and Door Style* dialog box. Selecting a value from the **Type:**, **Height:**, and **Width:** pop-up lists automatically changes the name and description. Softdesk default style names include a code for their type and size, such as DP for pocket door. Although names can be modified to suit user preference, a user-specified style name is not updated automatically if changes are made to the door type or dimensions for the style.

Description: Edit box containing brief summary describing selected door style.

Door: Pop-up list with Single, Double, and Other options.

Type: Pop-up list with Hinged, Existing, 2-Way, Pocket, Bi-fold, and Flexible default options when **Door:** is set to Single. Double offers the same options with the addition of Double Egress.

Height: Pop-up list with 6'-8" and Other as options. Choosing Other opens the *Edit list* dialog box where a new value can be entered then saved to its specific pop-up list box.

Width: Pop-up list with 6', 2', 2' 6", 3', 3'-6", and Other. Choosing the **Door:** edit box displays a 2X next to the **Width:** edit box identifying the value entered referring to each leaf of the double door.

Thick:	Pop-up list with 1 1/2", 1 3/4", and Other.
Frame:	Pop-up list with Standard and Metal frame options. The primary difference between Standard and Metal frames is the way they combine together to form a mullion in assemblies. Standard frames are simply joined together, with spacing added if desired, so that their dimensions are additive. Metal frames are joined by sharing the frame between the two units, so the combined size is less than the sum of two individual units. No spacing adjustment is possible for Metal frames. Also, neither casing nor trim can be applied to Metal frames. A Standard frame is usually made of wood, but could actually be made of metal if the method of forming a mullion were to join two frames together.
Depth:	Pop-up list with 0, 4 1/2", and Other. Depth references frame depth and requires its dimensions be less than or equal to the width of the wall. This is normally a standard manufactured door frame dimension, sized for a 2 x 4 stud wall. If the wall is wider (perhaps 2 x 6 or masonry), extension jambs are applied on the interior side (in 3D) to make up the difference, as in actual practice.
Jamb:	Pop-up list with 0, 1", and Other.
Head:	Pop-up list with 0, 1", and Other. The *Edit Door Style* dialog box is shown with the **Jamb:** at 4" and **Head:** at 8". Entering a value of 0 for the jamb or a value equal to the wall width for the depth prevents them from being displayed in plan view.

Note: Jambs are generated automatically by door style. To avoid seeing jambs try one of the following:

1. Set value to 0

2. Make the width depth the same as the wall width

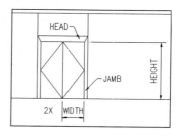

Select Window or Door Style Dialog Box: Pick Boxes

Position...
Opens the *Position of Frame in Wall* dialog box to display an image tile for placing a door's position in a wall. Choosing Other from the **Edge of Frame to Exterior:** pop-up list shows the door's recessed position in the wall. 0" is a normal flush exterior position.

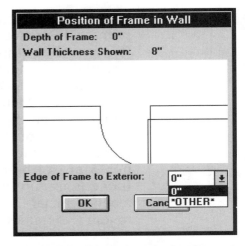

2D Options...
Displays the *2D Plan Options* dialog box with radio buttons for choices to draw the door in plan view as a **Single or Double Line** with **Swing Angles** of 45, 90, or 180 degrees. Not all swing angles are applicable to all door types.

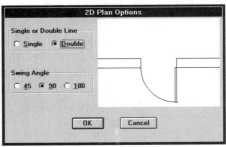

3D Options...
Displays the *3D Door Options* dialog box by choosing from pop-up lists (as shown) or double-clicking the image tile for selecting **Door Shapes** and **Knobs/Latches**. Door shapes include panel and glazing variations. Knobs/Latches include U-shaped, bars, levers, and pull styles. The image tile opens the *3D Door Shape or Door Knobs and Latches* dialog box to select from icon images. Different selections appear for different door types, as appropriate.

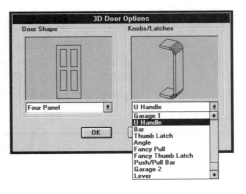

Double-clicking on the door shape image box opens the *3D Door Shapes* dialog box to view and select.

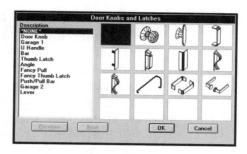

Note: *3D Door Shape* dialog box is similar to *Door Knobs and Latches* dialog box, just examined.

Threshold...   Opens the *Threshold Condition* dialog box to set an overall, exterior and interior thickness when **Include Thickness** is checked. Values for **Edge Thickness** and **Projection** can be modified with corresponding letters shown in the image tile. Choosing **Draw in Plan view** offers an option to include the exterior and/or interior threshold with the door in the plan view.

Casing...   Opens the *Casing and Trim* dialog box to include exterior and interior trim in elevations and 3D drawings. Values for **Casing Width** and **Casing Thickness** can be modified in edit boxes. **Exterior Casing** is not available if the **Position of Frame in Wall** is not 0".

Data...   Entering data in the *User Supplied Door Data* dialog box includes information available for door schedules and reports. Much of the data entered here might very well be made invalid by editing of the door style. As a safeguard against this, many of these items are cleared (blanked out or set to 0) when changes are made to the door style. This dialog should be rechecked before saving, after all other changes to the style have been made.

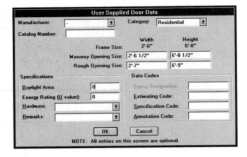

Editing Other Values

Width:, **Thick:**, **Depth:**, **Jamb:**, or **Head:** edit boxes display an option labeled as OTHER. Choose this option to open the *Edit List* dialog box and add additional values to the pop-up list for each edit box. Only dimensional values can be saved, adding nondimensional information, such as "3 1/2" wide" discards the entire entry.

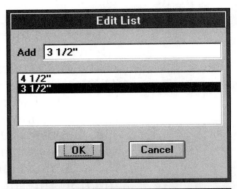

Image Tiles

The **Plan** radio button changes the image box to display a plan view of the door.

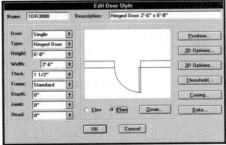

The **Elev** radio button changes the image box to display an elevation view of the door.

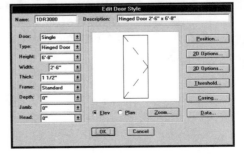

Zoom... opens the Zoomed Image dialog box to enlarge the elevation or plan image.

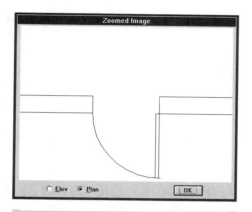

More Pick Boxes

Additional pick boxes offer opportunities to **Edit...** and **Delete...** door styles. Selecting **Edit...** opens the *Edit Door Style* dialog box with options as previously described. Choosing **Create Assembly...** provides a way to join doors and windows into complex combinations.

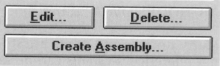

Selecting the **Delete...** pick box opens the *Delete Style* dialog box to remove a style from the WINDOORI.DBF database when using imperial units of measure and WIND-DORM.DBF, if working in metric units.

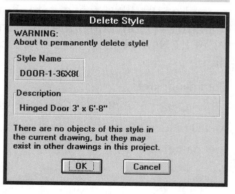

Note: This action will permanently delete the selected style from the WINDOORI.DBF database.

If an object of the selected style already exists in the current drawing, deletion of that style will not be allowed (a message will appear).

Picking **Create Assemblies...** first opens the *Swing Orientation* dialog box to select a **Hinge Point**. After choosing a radio button, the *Create Assembly* dialog box appears.

Assemblies are created using door and/or window styles that have previously been saved in the style library. Highlighting an existing style name in the **Style Name** list box of the *Select Window or Door Style* dialog box displays its image for editing. Additional window and door units can be appended to the existing style and saved to a new style name.

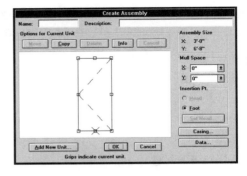

THE DOORS DRAWING FILE

AB_DOORS.DWG FILE

Many door components are stored in the AB_DOORS.DWG as an external reference file. This can be seen in any drawing once a door has been placed or the library accessed. Entering the AutoCAD **Xref** command (or selecting it from the pull-down menu under **FILE>IMPORT>EXTERNAL REFERENCE>LIST**) identifies the external reference file's path and name.

Command: **xref**

?/Bind/Detach/Path/Reload/Overlay/<Attach>: **?**

Xref(s) to list <*>: ⏎

Xref name	Path	Xref type
AB_DOORS	d:\sdsk\ab\dwg\ab_doors	Attach

Total Xref(s): 1

This drawing file becomes an external reference to provide models for creating the 2D symbol component of a door style block. Door blocks may be customized here to conform to your office standards. The layer names used in this drawing are layer *key* names which are used by Softdesk programs and *must not* be changed. When your door style block is created, these layer key names will become the layer names you have chosen in Layer Settings.

The AB_DOORS drawing also contains block definitions for door elevations as displayed in the library dialogs. They are simplified versions of the elevation components actually used in your drawings. If customization is desired, the actual components used may be found as drawing files in the \SDSK\AB\DWG directory. The 3D components are files DOOR3D*.DWG (single doors) and DDOR3D*.DWG (double doors). Elevation blocks are DOOREL*.DWG and DDOREL*.DWG. Most users will not need to bother with any of these drawing files, including AB_DOORS.DWG. If your curiosity is aroused, open the drawing and review the contents.

This brief overview of door settings should provide an understanding and background for the next chapter in which doors will be placed into walls.

CHAPTER SIXTEEN

DOORS

Placing Single and Double Doors into Walls

Contents

In this chapter we will place some doors created from the Style Library, as described in Chapter 15, and also some Quick doors. Quick doors are quicker to use, especially on older systems, because they do not access a style database. Any size can be specified on-the-fly without creating a new style for a new size. Unlike Style Library doors, Quick doors do not include jambs, cannot be made into assemblies, and have only rudimentary 3D capabilities. They may, however, be entirely adequate for some users. Others may find it efficient to use Quick doors initially, then swap them for Style Library doors at a later time.

THE DOOR SCHEDULE

The following table is a door schedule listing information about the doors to be inserted into walls for this exercise. The first series of doors will be inserted into the small office spaces in OFFICE-2. Insert single and double doors into the walls as specified in the door schedule table.

Door Schedule

Number	Width	Height	Room Name	Door Type	Location
01	3' 0"	6' 8"	OFFICE-2A	Single	between OFFICE-2A and OFFICE-2
02	3' 0"	6' 8"	OFFICE-2B	Single	between OFFICE-2B and OFFICE-2
03	3' 0"	6' 8"	OFFICE-2C	Single	between OFFICE-2c and OFFICE-2
04	6' 0"	6' 8"	ENTRY	Wall Opening	between ENTRY and CORRIDOR
05	6' 0"	6' 8"	OFFICE-3	Double	between OFFICE-3 and CORRIDOR
06	6' 0"	6' 8"	OFFICE-1	Double	between OFFICE-1 and ENTRY
07	6' 0"	6' 8"	OFFICE-2	Double	between OFFICE-2 and ENTRY
08	3' 0"	6' 8"	MEN	Single	MEN'S RESTROOM
09	3' 0'	6' 8"	WOMEN	Single	WOMEN'S ROOM
10	3' 0"	6' 8"	OFFICE-3	Single	OFFICE-3
11	3' 0"	6' 8"	SERVICE	Single	between SERVICE and PASSAGE
12	3' 0"	6' 8"	CORRIROR	Single	between CORRIDOR and PASSAGE
13	3' 0"	6' 8"	OFFICE-1	Single	between OFFICE-1 and CORRIDOR
14	3' 0"	6' 8"	CORRIDOR	Single	CORRIDOR and exterior
15	3' 0"	6' 8"	OFFICE-3	Single	OFFICE-3 and exterior
16	6' 0"	6' 8"	ENTRY	Double	ENTRY and exterior

The figure shows the doors and door numbers. Room names have been added in OFFICE-2 to identify the smaller office spaces.

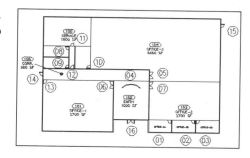

SETTING CONTROLS FOR DOORS

ARCHTOOLS ➤ AUTO-ARCHITECT SETTINGS... ➤ GENERAL...

 Select **Auto-Architect Settings...** from the ArchTools pull-down menu to open the *Softdesk Auto-Architect Settings* dialog box,

Choose **General...** to open the *General Settings* dialog box. Enter 4" in the **Automatic Corner Distance** edit box to set automatic door placement during insertion (if not already set).

Dialog box:

Automatic Corner Distance **4"**

Pick OK, returning to the Softdesk *Auto-Architect Settings* dialog box.

ARCHTOOLS ➤ AUTO-ARCHITECT SETTINGS... ➤ DOORS AND WINDOWS...

Next, pick **Doors and Windows...** to open the *Door and Window Settings* dialog box and uncheck **Prompt for exterior side during insertion**. In the **Door Tag** section, uncheck **Automatic Insert** and **Prompt each time** for **Door Threshold Height**.

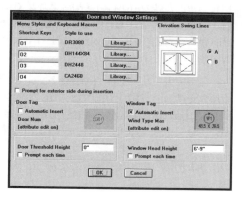

Later in this chapter we will turn **Automatic Insert** back on; and in Chapter 18 we will discuss how to add tags to doors which did not get placed automatically.

ASSIGNING A SHORTCUT KEY TO A DOOR STYLE

ARCHTOOLS ➤ AUTO-ARCHITECT SETTINGS... ➤ DOORS AND WINDOWS...LIBRARY...

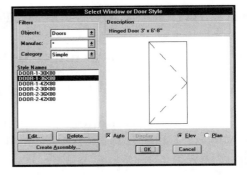

Next, using the same dialog box, assign the shortcut key **O1** to the **DR-1-36X80** door style by picking **Library...** located adjacent to the shortcut key O1 edit box. The *Select Window or Door Style* dialog box opens.

In the **Filters** section, open the pop-up list for **Objects:** and pick Doors. Repeat the procedure for **Category** and pick Simple.

Dialog box:
Objects: **Doors**
Category: **Simple**

The **Style Names** list box updates displaying new default names. Highlight DOOR-1-36X80 and the **Description** will read: Hinged Door 3' x 6'-8".

Check **Auto** to permanently display the door in the image tile.

The *Select Window or Door Style* dialog box displays the **Edit...** pick box as grayed out. Editing door styles requires choosing **Library...** from the Door/Wind pull-down menu then **Edit....**

Pick OK and return to the *Door and Window Settings* dialog box, noting that the new **Style to use** name assigned for O1 is DR-1-36X80. Pick OK to exit all dialog boxes.

PLACING THE FIRST THREE DOORS

Zoom into the lower right corner of the building to place 3'-0" wide doors into the 3 1/2" walls for each of the three small office spaces within OFFICE-2. If necessary, refer to the door schedule at the start of this chapter when you need additional door location, size, or type information.

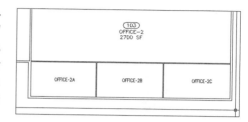

EDITING A DOOR STYLE

Zoom closer into the upper right corner of OFFICE-2A, as shown with the dashed rectangle. Before placing the first door, edit the current depth, jamb, and head settings for DOOR-1-36X80.

Note: Editing values, then exiting a dialog box automatically invokes commands.

DOOR/WIND ➤ LIBRARY... ➤ EDIT...

Choose **Library...** under the Door/Wind pull-down menu, then highlight the style name DOOR-1-36X80.

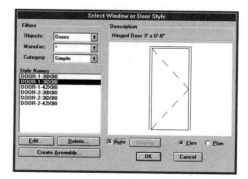

The **Filters** section should appear with **Objects:** set to Doors and **Category** set to Simple. Pick **Edit...** to open the *Edit Door Style* dialog box. Select from each of the pop-up lists along the left side of the dialog box to reflect the specifications listed. If the pop-up list does not contain the required default value, pick OTHER from the specific pop-up list to open the *Edit List* dialog box and enter the appropriate values, described as follows.

Dialog box:

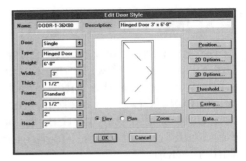

Door:	**Single**
Type:	**Hinged Door**
Height:	**6'-8"**
Width:	**3'-0"**
Thick:	**1 1/2"**
Frame:	**Standard**
Depth:	**3 1/2"**
Jamb:	**2"**
Head:	**2"**

Note: If the image tile shows a plan view, and you wish to view the door elevation, select the **Elev** radio button.

Select OTHER to enter a new value for depth in the *Edit List* dialog box, then pick OK.

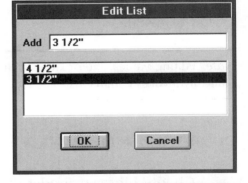

Repeat the procedure to specify widths for **Jamb** and **Head**, then pick OK. Notice that the image tile updates as each new dimension appears in its corresponding edit box.

Pick OK to close the dialog box and the *Save Window or Door Style* dialog box appears to save the modified settings to a new style name. Pick OK to replace the current settings with the original door style name DOOR-1-36X80, then pick OK again to exit from the *Select Window or Door Style* dialog box and place the selected door.

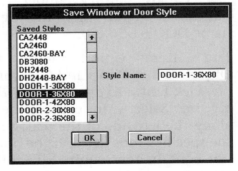

Note: If doors already exist of that style present in the drawing, the *Select Window or Door Style* dialog box is temporarily suspended and all objects of that style name are automatically updated. If any changes were made to the height, width, or shape of the style, the wall opening for each object is updated individually. If the width has changed, the opening will be changed according to how the object was placed. If it was side-justified (placed using either the Side placement option or Auto near a corner), the location of that side will remain fixed. If it was center-justified (placed with either the Center option or Auto at the midpoint of the wall), the center of the resized opening will remain at the same point. If the height, width, or shape of the style has not changed, no updating of the wall openings is required.

New styles are created by simply editing an existing style and saving to a new name.

PLACING DOOR 01

PROMPTING SUMMARY

Place Door style DOOR-1-36X80: Hinged Door 3' x 6'-8"

Center - pick side of wall (Auto/Side): **a**

OFFICE-2A

Note: Pick a point near the interior corner if the prompt reads:
Auto - pick side of wall near center or end (Center/Side):

Auto - pick side of wall near center or end (Center/Side): **[pick a point near the interior corner walls]**

Select Hinge point: **[pick X mark at bottom right]**

Creating door...

Redefining block ABWD$DOOR-1-36X80

Select the inside corner (near the end of the lower horizontal line) of OFFICE-2A at the **Auto - pick side of wall near center or end (Center/Side):** prompt.

Auto - pick side of wall near center or end (Center/Side):

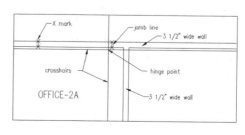

Note: If the prompt **Wall element not found, try again.** appears, select another point nearer to the line where the door is to be placed.

Select the bottom right X mark at the **Set Hinge point:** prompt.

Select Hinge point:

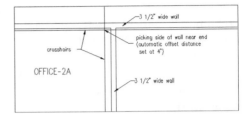

Door 01 is shown inserted 4" from the corner wall with a 2" jamb.

The figure shows the door in isometric view. It has been inserted into the drawing as both a 2D and 3D symbol.

At this point the 3D wall and door layers are displayed as well as the 2D layers. This is as it should be while working on the drawing. If 3D layers were not displayed, they would get left behind during editing operations such as moving or stretching. An easy way to turn the 3D layers off for plotting is to use the command sequence: Layer, Off, *3D*, [Enter].

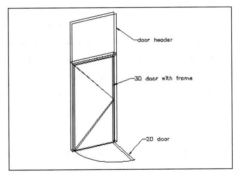

PLACING DOOR 02

Zoom into the lower right portion of OFFICE-2 to place Door 02 into the upper right corner of OFFICE-2B.

Insert Door 02 using the same door style DOOR-1-36X80. Since the style has been

assigned to the shortcut key **O1**, this macro can be invoked at the command line,

 MACRO Command: **O1**

Note: Be careful to type the letter "O" and not the number "0."

Select the inside corner of OFFICE-2B at the **Auto - pick side of wall near center or end (Center/Side): prompt.**

Select the bottom right X mark at the **Set Hinge point:** prompt.

The second door is inserted into the wall.

PLACING DOOR 03

DOOR/WIND ➤ DRAW BY EXAMPLE

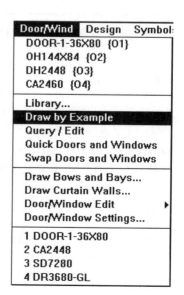

Door macros are programmable labels stored at the top of the Door/Wind pull-down menu and controlled from the *Door/Window Settings* dialog box. Place doors by choosing a style from the pull-down menu or invoking its associated shortcut key at the prompt line.

The bottom of the menu stores the most recently invoked door styles and changes as selections are made from the Library.

Softdesk also offers the **Draw by Example** command under the Door/Wind pull-down menu to place a new door, window, or assembly that matches the style of a previously inserted door.

PROMPTING SUMMARY

Check existing Door/Window blocks <Yes>: **y**

Checking style objects...

All objects are current.

Draw object by example...

Select door or window: **[pick door in OFFICE-2B]**

Place Door style DOOR-1-36X80: Hinged Door 3' x 6'-8"

Auto - pick side of wall near center or end (Center/Side): [pick point near wall corner]

Select Hinge point: **[pick X mark at bottom left]**

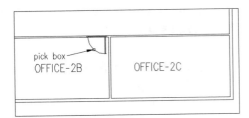

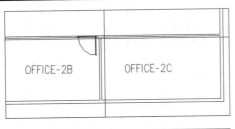

Select **Draw by Example** from the Door/Wind pull-down menu, then at the **Select door or window** prompt: pick the door previously inserted (as shown with pick box along door swing) in the OFFICE-2B. (Room names have been added to identify the smaller office spaces.)

Draw object by example...
Select door or window:

***

Note: Enter "Yes" whenever prompted to check door/window blocks.

***

Check existing Door/Window blocks <Yes>: **y**
Checking style objects...
All objects are current.

Next, the **Auto - pick side of wall near center or end (Center/Side):** prompt appears. Select the upper left interior corner of OFFICE-2C.

Auto - pick side of wall near center or end (Center/Side):

Choose the bottom left X mark when prompted to **Select Hinge point:**

Select Hinge point:

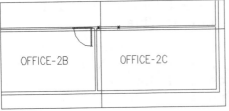

Door 03 is shown placed into the wall in OFFICE-2C.

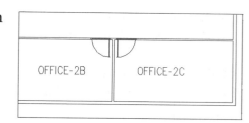

CREATING AN OPENING IN A WALL—PLACING DOOR 04

Zoom into the rear portion of the ENTRY space and create a 6' wide X 6' 8" high opening without a door frame behind the curved wall.

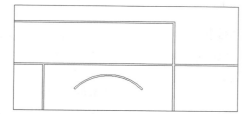

The prompting sequence is:

Break existing wall lines...
Bottom elevation of opening <0">: ⏎
Top elevation of opening <6'-10">: **6'8**
Break width <3'-4">: **6'**
Auto - pick side of wall near center or end (Center/Side): **[pick point near midpoint of lower wall line]**

Note: Although the opening does not have a frame or door, we will identify the exercise here as Door 04. To create an opening with a frame and no door (cased opening), use the **Create Assembly...** pick box in the *Select Door and Window Style* dialog box to draw the components.

WALLS ➤ WALL EDIT ➤ MAKE WALL OPENINGS

Select **Make Wall Openings** under **Wall Edit** in the Walls pull-down menu. The command inserts a rectangular opening in a wall segment by first requesting a bottom and top elevation, then a break width.

The **Auto** option prompts to pick a point, automatically creating a center-justified break at the midpoint of a wall, if the point selected

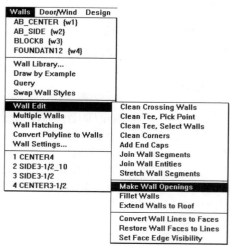

is near the wall's midpoint. Otherwise, choosing a wall intersection point creates a side-justified break at a preset distance from a corner.

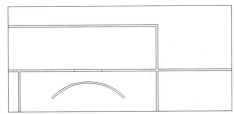

 Enter 0 for the bottom door elevation and 6' 8" for the top elevation.

Break existing wall lines...
Bottom elevation of opening <0">: ↵
Top elevation of opening <6'-10">: **6'8**

 Type 6' for the door opening or break width, then pick near the midpoint of the bottom horizontal wall line.

Break width <3'-4">: **6'**
Auto - pick side of wall near center or end (Center/Side):

The isometric view shows the opening created with the **Make Wall Openings** command. The 3D wall above the opening is drawn on layer FL01-WALL3D and jambs (drawn as a single line on each side) on FL01-JAMB based the previously set layer group components.

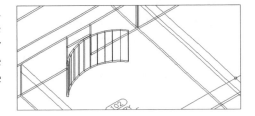

PLACING DOORS WITH DOOR TAGS

DOOR/WIND ➤ DOOR/WINDOW SETTINGS...

Inserting Door 05

Insert Door 05 centered in the wall with a door tag between OFFICE-3 and the CORRIDOR space.

Select **Door/Window Settings...** from the Door/Wind pull-down menu to open the *Door and Window Settings* dialog box. Check the box labeled **Automatic Insert** in the **Door Tag** section to include the callout with the door placement command.

Pick OK.

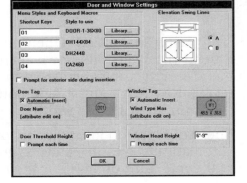

DOOR/WIND ➤ LIBRARY...

    Select **Library...** from the Door/Wind pull-down menu to open the *Select Window or Door Style* dialog box.

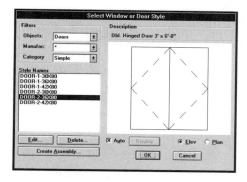

Insert Door 05 as a double-hinged door 6'-0" wide X 6'-8" high. Pick the down arrows in the **Filters** section and choose Doors for **Objects:** and Simple for **Category.** Highlight DOOR-2-36X80 in the **Style Names** list box, then pick the **Edit...** box to open the *Edit Door Style* dialog box.

Dialog box:

Objects: **Doors**
Category: **Simple**

Edit the values as shown. If necessary, select OTHER to enter new sizes for **Depth, Jamb,** and **Head** edit boxes, then pick OK.

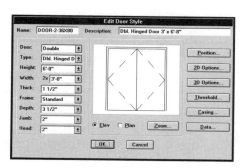

Dialog box:

Door:	**Double**
Type:	**Dbl.Hinged Door**
Height:	**6'-8"**
Width:	**2x 3'-0"**
Thick:	**1 1/2"**
Frame:	**Standard**
Depth:	**3 1/2"**
Jamb:	2
Head:	2

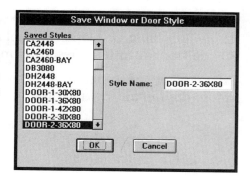

The *Save Window or Door Style* dialog box appears, requesting that the revised door style be saved to a new name. Pick OK to replace the new settings while saving them to the same Door Style name.

Pick OK again, and the prompts are automatically invoked at the command line.

PROMPTING SUMMARY

Accessing Door/Window Library...

Place Door style DOOR-2-36X80: Dbl. Hinged Door 3' x 6'-8"

Auto - pick side of wall near center or end (Center/Side): **[pick point near midpoint of wall]**

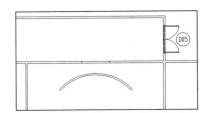

Select Hinge point: **[pick X mark at lower right]**

Creating door......done.

Place tag...

Initial load. Please wait...

Inserting Door Num at elevation 0.

New callout location <same>: **[relocate door tag to right side of door]**

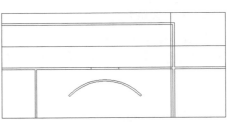

Select a point near the middle of the vertical wall at the **Auto - pick side of wall near center or end (Center/Side):** prompt.

Auto - pick side of wall near center or end (Center/Side):

Note: Picking the interior side would place the door centered on the interior CORRIDOR space.

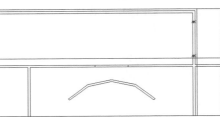

Select the bottom right X mark when the **Select Hinge point:** prompt appears.

Select Hinge point:

After the door is inserted into the wall, the *Edit Attributes* dialog box opens, displaying values for the **Door number**, **Description**, and **Size**.

Change **Door number** from D01 to D05, then accept the remaining defaults.

 Dialog box:

Door number   **D05**

Note: Picking **Next** displays additional dialog boxes specifying information about the door. Information which can be obtained from the style data for the door is entered automatically. Other information will vary from one door to the next and must be entered manually. Information entered manually will be remembered and carried over to the next door tag, except when new information is available from style data for the next door. The information stored in these tags can later be used to create a door schedule.

   Pick OK.

The door tag is placed, prompting for a **New callout location <same>:** or defaulting to retain its position.

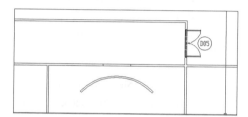

   Select a new location, picking a point along the right side of the door.

Place tag...
Inserting Door Num at elevation 0.
New callout location <same>:

PLACING DOOR 06 AND DOOR 07

DOOR/WIND ➤ 1 DOOR-2-36X80

or

DOOR/WIND ➤ DRAW BY EXAMPLE

Insert Door 06 between the ENTRY and OFFICE-1 and Door 07 between the ENTRY and OFFICE-2, as shown. These doors can be placed in the wall by selecting **DOOR-2-36X80** or by choosing **Draw by Example** from the Door/Wind pull-down menu.

Note: Pressing the spacebar will also repeat the last command and invoke the previous door insertion routine.

The prompting sequence that follows was evoked by selecting 1 DOOR-2-36X80 from the pull-down menu, then pressing the spacebar to repeat the last command.

The prompting sequence for Door 06 is:

Reading data -- Please wait...
Place Door style DOOR-2-36X80: Dbl. Hinged Door 3' x 6'-8"
Auto - pick side of wall near center or end (Center/Side): **[pick point near vertical wall intersection]**

Select Hinge point: **[pick X mark on left side of wall]**
Creating door......
Redefining block ABWD$DOOR-2-36X80
done.
Place tag...
Inserting Door Num at elevation 0.
New callout location <same>: **[position tag as shown]**

The prompting sequence for Door 07 is:

Command: SDSK
Reading data -- Please wait...
Place Door style DOOR-2-36X80: Dbl. Hinged Door 3' x 6'-8"
Auto - pick side of wall near center or end (Center/Side): **[pick point near vertical wall intersection]**

Select Hinge point: **[pick X mark on right side of wall]**
Place tag...
Inserting Door Num at elevation 0.
New callout location <same>: **[position tag as shown]**

Door 06 and Door 07 are shown inserted into the wall with their corresponding callouts (door tags). Notice that the door numbers are automatically incremented based on the previous value-set for Door 05 in the *Edit Attributes* dialog box.

Select hinge points and callout locations to match the figure shown.

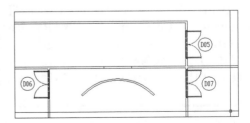

PLACING QUICK DOORS (08, 09, 10, 11, AND 12)

DOOR/WIND ➤ QUICK DOORS AND WINDOWS

Zoom into the SERVICE and PASSAGE spaces to place single-hinged 3'-0" x 6'-8" doors using the **Quick Doors and Windows** command.

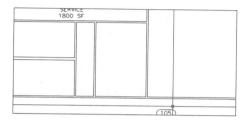

Doors 08, 09, 10, 11, and 12 will be placed by invoking **Quick Doors and Windows**, then placing them into various walls with a single call of the command.

Note: If necessary, invoke the Macro **MO** (AutoCAD Command **MOVE**) to reposition the room tag away from the walls.

PROMPTING SUMMARY

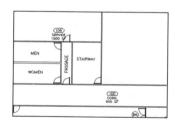

Previous: Single Door, Hinged, 90 deg (Width = 3', Height = 6'-8")

Place Previous object or Select from library (Previous/Select) <Previous>: s[*Quick Doors and Windows* **dialog box opens to select values**]

(Inserting Door 08)

Auto - pick side of wall near center or end (Center/Side): **[pick point at top right inside corner near vertical wall of MEN's room]**

Select Hinge point: **[pick top left X mark]**

(Inserting Door 09)

Auto - pick side of wall near center or end (Center/Side): **[pick point at bottom right corner near vertical wall of WOMEN'S room]**

Select Hinge point: **[pick bottom left X mark]**

(Inserting Door 10)

Auto - pick side of wall near center or end (Center/Side): **[pick point at lower left corner of OFFICE-3]**

Select Hinge point: **[pick bottom left X mark]**

(Inserting Door 11)

Auto - pick side of wall near center or end (Center/Side): **[pick point at middle of lower wall line in vertical PASSAGE space]**

Select Hinge point: **[pick top right X mark]**

(Inserting Door 12)

Auto - pick side of wall near center or end (Center/Side): **[pick point at middle of upper wall in vertical Passage space]**

Select Hinge point: **[pick top right X mark]**

Auto - pick side of wall near center or end (Center/Side): ⏎

Select **Quick Doors and Windows** from the Door/Wind pull-down menu and prompts will appear at the command line. To open the *Quick Doors and Windows* dialog box type **S** or **Select** at the prompt **Place previous object or Select from library (Previous/Select)<Previous>:** for setting values.

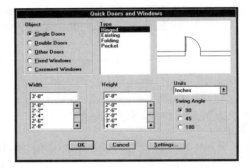

Previous: Single Door, Hinged, 90 deg (Width = 3', Height = 6'-8")
Place Previous object or Select from library (Previous/Select) <Previous>: **s**

Enter the values as shown for the various sections.

    Dialog box:

Object:	**Single Doors**
Type:	**Hinged**
Width:	**3'-0"**
Height:	**6'-8"**
Units:	**Inches**
Angle:	**90**

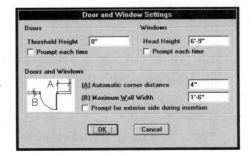

Next, select **Settings...** to open the *Door and Window Settings* dialog box to set **Threshold Height** to 0 and **Automatic corner distance** to 4".

Dialog box:

Threshold Height: **0**
Automatic corner distance: **4"**

Note: Part of the dialog box appears similar to the *General Settings* dialog box. These settings are all duplicates of settings previously seen prior to placing Style doors. They have been included in this dialog as a convenience when using Quick doors and windows. Any changes made here will apply both to Quick doors and windows and to Style doors and windows.

Pick OK twice to close all dialog boxes and return to the prompts at the command line.

Place Door 08 into the upper right corner of the men's restroom as shown. (If necessary, refer to the Prompting Summary for room names.)

Use the **Auto** option to place each door in position.

Auto - pick side of wall near center or end (Center/Side):

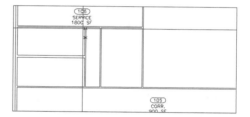

Set the hinge point at the top left, swinging the door against the horizontal wall by selecting the appropriate X mark.

Select Hinge point:

Insert Door 09 into the lower right corner of the bottom space (women's restroom) and set the swing against the horizontal wall using the Auto option.

Auto - pick side of wall near center or end (Center/Side):
Select Hinge point:

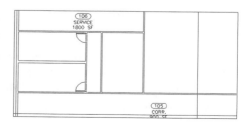

Place Door 10 into the bottom left corner of the OFFICE-3 space.

Auto - pick side of wall near center or end (Center/Side): Select Hinge point:

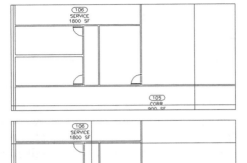

Insert Door 11 at the top portion of the vertical (Passage) space using the center option. Selecting a point near the middle of the lower wall automatically positions the door in this location.

Auto - pick side of wall near center or end (Center/Side):

Select the top right X mark as the hinge point.

Select Hinge point:

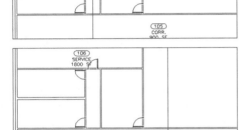

Repeat this procedure to insert Door 12 at the opposite end of the passage. Choose a point near the middle of the upper wall line for door placement.

Auto - pick side of wall near center or end (Center/Side): Select Hinge point:

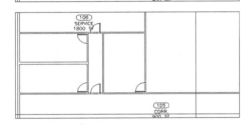

PLACING ANOTHER QUICK DOOR

Zoom into the left portion of the CORRIDOR to insert the next door near the end of the lower interior wall, as shown.

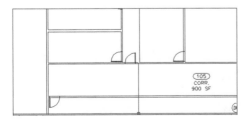

Select **Quick Doors and Windows** from the Door/Wind pull-down menu to place Door 13 in the upper left corner of OFFICE-1. Door 13 is the same as the previously inserted doors.

Accepting the default **<Previous>** restricts prompts to the command line and does not open the dialog box.

The prompting sequence is:

Previous: Single Door, Hinged, 90 deg (Width = 3'-0", Height =6'-8")
Place Previous object or Select from library (Previous/Select) <Previous>: **p**
Auto - pick side of wall near center or end (Center/Side)**: [pick point near end of lower left horizontal wall line]**
Select Hinge point: **[pick lower left X mark]**
Auto - pick side of wall near center or end (Center/Side): ⏎

PLACING EXTERIOR DOORS (14 AND 15) USING PROMPT FOR EXTERIOR SIDE DURING INSERTION

Place the last three doors as exterior glass doors with the setting **Prompt for exterior side during insertion** on. Insert Door 14 at the left portion of the CORRIDOR space and Door 15 at the top right corner of OFFICE-3 as commercial glass doors.

PLACING DOOR 14

DOOR/WIND ➤ DOOR AND WINDOW SETTINGS...

 Select **Door/Window Settings...** from the Door/Wind pull-down menu to open the *Door and Window Settings* dialog box. Check the box next to **Prompt for exterior side during insertion** providing the option for setting the door's location in the exterior wall.

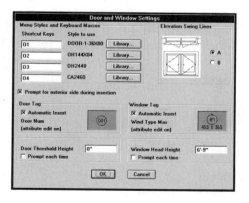

Usually, the Softdesk program knows the exterior side of walls based on the working point (the wall's insertion point) determined in the *Wall Style Editor* dialog box. This setting prompts for offset side to place a door off center from a wall's thickness.

 Pick OK.

DOOR/WIND ➤ LIBRARY...

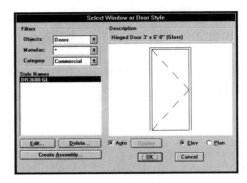

Next, select **Library...** from the Door/ Wind pull-down menu. When the dialog box opens, choose Doors from **Objects:** and Commercial from the **Category** pop-up list to display the default **Style Name** DR3680-GL.

Dialog box:

Objects: **Doors**
Category: **Simple**

PROMPTING SUMMARY

Accessing Door/Window Library... [**Select *Window or Door Style* dialog box opens**]

Place Door style DR3680-GL: Hinged Door 3' x 6'-8" (Glass)

Auto - pick side of wall near center or end (Center/Side): [**pick midpoint of interior vertical wall line**]

Show direction for exterior <arrow>:

Select Hinge point: [**pick top left X mark**]

Creating door.....done.

Place tag...

Inserting Door Num at elevation 0.

New callout location <same>: [**reposition tag**]

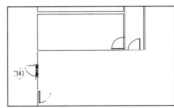

Choose **Edit...** to verify or set the following values.

 Dialog box:

Door:	**Single**
Type:	**Hinged Door**
Height:	**6'-8"**
Width:	**3'-0"**
Thick:	**1 3/4"**
Frame:	**Metal**
Depth:	**4 1/2"**
Jamb:	**2"**
Head:	**2"**

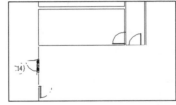

Pick OK twice to close the dialog boxes.

 Select the midpoint of the interior corridor wall to place Door 14.

Auto - pick side of wall near center or end (Center/Side):

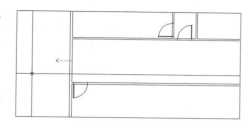

 Drag the arrow to the left, then pick again as shown.

Show direction for exterior <arrow>:

 Select the top left X mark for the hinge point.

Select Hinge point:

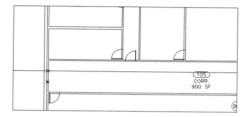

 The *Edit Attributes* dialog box automatically opens after the hinge point is selected. Replace the incremental door number with the value D14.

Edit Attributes	
Block Name: DOORNO	
Door number	D14
Description	Hinged Door 3' x 6'-8" (Glass)
Size	3'-0"x6'-8"
Door Glass	-
Under cut	-
Fire rating	-
Frame material	-
Frame finish	-
OK Cancel Previous Next Help...	

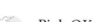 Dialog box:

Door number: **D14**

 Pick OK.

Reposition the callout (room tag) as shown.

Place tag...
Inserting Door Num at elevation 0.
New callout location <same>:

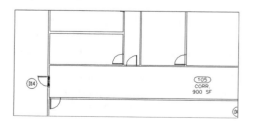

PLACING DOOR 15

Repeat this procedure by picking **DR3680-GL** from the Door/Wind pull-down menu. Insert Door 15 at a distance of 4' from the upper right interior corner of OFFICE-3.

Door/Wind	Design	Symbol
DOOR-1-36X80 {01}		
OH144X84 {02}		
DH2448 {03}		
CA2460 {04}		
Library...		
Draw by Example		
Query / Edit		
Quick Doors and Windows		
Swap Doors and Windows		
Draw Bows and Bays...		
Draw Curtain Walls...		
Door/Window Edit ▶		
Door/Window Settings...		
1 DR3680-GL		
2 DOOR-2-36X80		
3 DOOR-1-36X80		
4 CA2448		

PROMPTING SUMMARY

Reading data -- Please wait... .

Place Door style DR3680-GL: Hinged Door 3' x 6'-8" (Glass)

Auto - pick side of wall near center or end (Center/Side): **s**

Side - pick corner reference point (Auto/Center): int of **[top right interior corner of OFFICE-3]**

Side of opening: **@4'<270**

Which direction for break: **[pick point downward]**

Show direction for exterior <arrow>: **[pick point to the right]**

Select Hinge point: **[top right X mark]**

Place tag...

Initial load. Please wait...

Inserting Door Num at elevation 0.

New callout location <same>: **[reposition callout]**

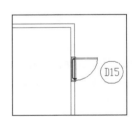

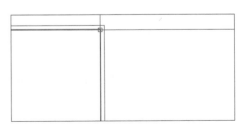

Select the top right inside corner of OFFICE-3 as the corner reference point, then enter a distance of 4' downward.

Using the **Side** option, enter distance and direction, to place the door along the right interior corner wall of OFFICE-3

Auto - pick side of wall near center or end (Center/Side): **s**
Side - pick corner reference point (Auto/Center): **int** of
Side of opening: **@4'<270**

Pick a point toward the bottom of the screen at the **Which direction for break:** prompt.

Which direction for break:

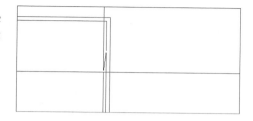

Drag the arrow toward the right, then pick when prompted to **Show direction for exterior <arrow>:**. Select the top right X mark at **Select Hinge Point:**.

Show direction for exterior <arrow>:
Select Hinge point:

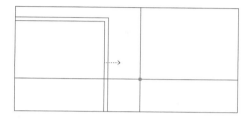

Accept the default Door number D15 when the *Edit Attributes* dialog box opens, then pick OK.

Since the last door number was changed to door 14, automatic insert is reset.

The dialog box values should appear as shown:

Door number   D15
Description   Hinged Door 3' x 6'-8" (Glass)
Size   3'-0" x 6'-8"

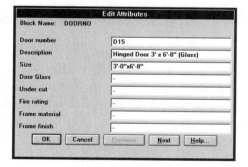

Reposition the callout as shown for Door 15.

Place tag...
Initial load. Please wait...
Inserting Door Num at elevation 0.
New callout location <same>:

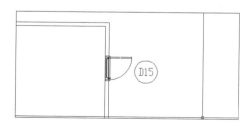

. . . .

PLACING A DOUBLE DOOR—DOOR 16

DOOR/WIND ➤ LIBRARY...

Place Door 16 (the last door) as a double door at the front of the ENTRY space. Select **Library...** from the Door/Wind pull-down menu to open the *Select Window or Door Style* dialog box.

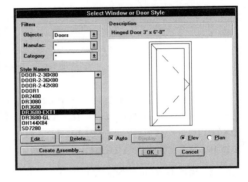

Dialog box:

Objects: **Doors**
Category: *

Select Doors from the **Objects:** pop-up list and asterisks for all other edit boxes in the **Filters** section.

Highlight default door style **DR3680-EXT1** in the **Style Name** list box.

Choose **Edit...** to open the *Edit Door Style d*ialog box.

Pick the **Door:** pop-up list and select Double, then change the values as shown. Replace the existing name 2-DR3680 in the **Name:** edit box with **2-DR3680EXT2**.

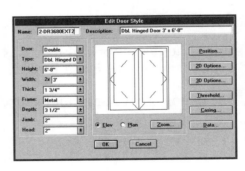

 Dialog box:

Name:	**2-DR3680EXT2**
Description:	**Dbl Hinged Door 3' x 6'-8"**
Door:	**Double**
Type:	**Dbl. Hinged Door**
Height:	**6'-8"**
Width:	**2x 3'**
Thick:	**1 3/4"**
Frame:	**Metal**
Depth:	**3 1/2"**
Jamb:	**2"**
Head:	**2"**

Pick OK and the *Save Window or Door Style* dialog box opens to confirm the new door name.

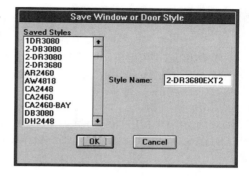

Pick OK to save the new door style.

The *Select Window or Door Style* dialog box returns, displaying the updated information.

Pick OK.

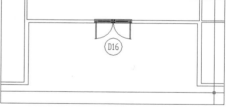

Insert the exterior door using the **Auto** option, picking a point near the middle of the exterior wall. Drag the arrow downward to show direction for exterior, select the bottom hinge point, then place the tag. Accept the default door number 16 and reposition the callout below the door swing.

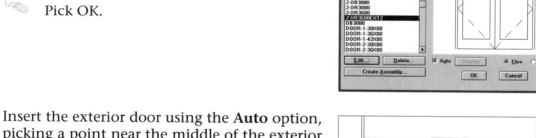

PROMPTING SUMMARY:

Accessing Door/Window Library...

Place Door style 2-DR3680EXT2: Dbl. Hinged Door 3' x 6'-8"

Side - pick corner reference point (Auto/Center): **a**

Auto - pick side of wall near center or end (Center/Side): **[pick midpoint of exterior wall]**

Show direction for exterior <arrow>: **[pick point below exterior wall]**

Select Hinge point: **[pick bottom X mark]**

Creating door......done.

Place tag...

Inserting Door Num at elevation 0.

New callout location <same>: **[relocate tag]**

Insertion of all the doors is complete. Save the drawing, then proceed to the next chapter and place windows into the walls.

CHAPTER SEVENTEEN

WINDOW SETTINGS

Overview of Window-related Settings

Contents

Before inserting windows into the walls, Chapter 17 will explore some commands and settings controlling this procedure. As discussed in previous chapters, Softdesk uses Door and Window style libraries to place doors and windows in plan, elevation, and 3D. Chapter 15 provides an overview of the preset default door and window styles. Window information is saved to a style name in the database files: WINDOORM.DBF for metric and WINDOORI.DBF for imperial drawings. This data includes type, such as sliding or casement; frame dimensions; rough or masonry openings; and energy efficiency values. Doors can be combined with windows as vertical or horizontal adjacent units and inserted into walls as both 2D and 3D assemblies.

The door and window insertion commands are available under the Door/Wind pull-down menu. Since window settings and procedures are the same as doors, the controls discussed in Chapter 15 still apply. The window command emulates doors by requesting its position in the wall and hinge point, if applicable. This chapter includes a brief overview of window settings with dialog box references specific to windows.

SETTING CONTROLS FOR WINDOWS

DOOR/WIND ➤ DOOR/WINDOW SETTINGS...

Selecting **Door/Window Settings...** from the Door/Wind pull-down menu opens the *Door and Window Settings* dialog box.

Some settings reviewed in this dialog box, as discussed in Chapter 15, are used equally for doors and windows. **Menu Styles and Keyboard Macros** plus **Door Tag** were previously discussed in Chapter 15.

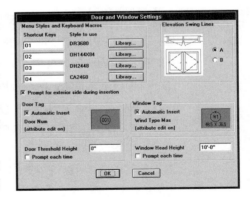

The right side of the dialog box is used to set window controls for swing, height, and tag insertion.

SETTING ELEVATION SWING LINES

The **Elevation Swing Lines** section controls which way the dashed lines indicating swing direction are drawn. Choice **A** has the two lines converge on the hinge side, the standard convention in the United States. Choice **B** has the two lines converge on the strike side, the convention in many other countries.

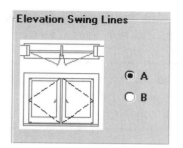

SETTING WINDOW HEAD HEIGHT

The **Window Head Height** edit box sets the height of the window header for 3D windows. Editing the value does not affect existing window head heights.

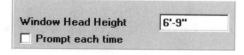

Checking **Prompt each time** displays the following prompt to set the header head height for each window insertion.

Place Window style DH2448: Double-hung 2' x 4'
Head height <8'-0">:

SETTING WINDOW TAG INSERTION AND TYPE

Checking **Automatic Insert** in the **Window Tag** section places window tags or callouts into the plan for specific window styles as they are inserted into walls.

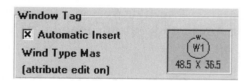

Note: Tags are inserted for all window types except curtain walls and Quick windows.

Picking the window tag image button opens the *Symbol Manager* dialog box to choose an alternate tag for insertion with a window. The figure shows the **Palette:**, **Category:**, and **Symbol Set:** picks for a window with Masonry Opening width and height. Setting pop-up lists for Door/Window Tags, Annotation, and Auto-Arch Symbol File displays the specified

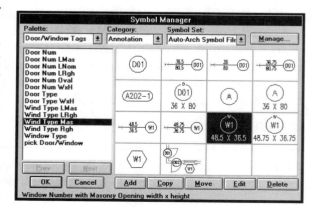

tags. The same dialog box is also available under **Annotation** in the Symbols pull-down menu as discussed later.

Note: Window tags, unlike door tags, do not automatically number incrementally during window placement because they are usually identified by a window type rather than a sequential number.

AUTOMATIC INCREMENT OF WINDOW TAG ID MARKS

Window tags can be customized by the experienced user to number sequentially during placement if the tag name for ID Mark matches the tag name for Door number. The procedure involves opening the block WINDNOCM (located in the \SDSK\AA\DWG\LNG directory) and editing the ID Mark attribute definition WINDNOCM used for the tag name as discussed next.

The ID Mark for WINDNOCM can, of course, be edited after the window tag is placed using the AutoCAD DDATTE command. The figure shows the window tag with all attribute names and locations made visible.

```
          AAWIANNOT2
AAWIANNOT
       AAWIMASONRY
AAWIDESC       AAWIDEPTH
AAWIGLASS      AAWIJAMBWID
               AAWIHEADTH
               AAWICASEW
AAWIFMATL      AAWICASIW
AAWIFFIN       AAWIHEAD
AAWIROOM       AAWIJAMB
AAWICOST       AAWISILL
AAWISWG_CODE   AAWIMANUF
               AAWICATEGORY
AAWIROUGH      AAWIMODEL
AAWITYPE       AAWIESTI
               AAWISPEC

AAWIFIN        AAWIDAYLI
AAWIHARDWARE   AAWIUVAL
AAWIFTYPE      AAWIREMARKS
```

CUSTOMIZING THE WINDOW TAG FOR SEQUENTIAL NUMBERING

To customize the window tag for sequential numbering, open the window tag block (drawing) and invoke the AutoCAD DDEDIT command to open the *Edit Attribute Definition* dialog box. Select the tag name AAWIANNOT associated with the prompt ID Mark and change the name to AAWIANNUM.

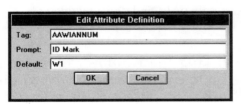

Exit and save the drawing.

Note: If the window tag has already been inserted into the drawing, remember to invoke the AutoCAD DDINSERT command to redefine the WINDNOCM block name.

INSERTING TAGS DIRECTLY FROM THE PULL-DOWN MENU

Selecting **Annotation...** from the Symbols pull-down menu also opens the *Symbol Manager* dialog box. Choosing defaults from **Palette:**, **Category:**, and **Symbol Set:** pop-up lists display various image buttons. Picking a button or highlighting the defining text name in the list box, then choosing OK inserts a window tag into the drawing with prompts as shown.

Inserting Wind Type Mas at elevation 0.
Insertion point:

Symbols	ArchTools
Annotation...	
Appliance...	
Ceiling...	
Door...	
Electric...	
Equipment...	
Furniture...	
Kitchen Cabinet...	
Plumbing...	
Site...	
Softdesk...	
Window...	
Symbol Manager...	
Symbol Settings...	

Note: The *Symbols Manager* dialog box is discussed in Chapter 21 in more detail.

WINDOW STYLES

DOOR/WIND ➤ LIBRARY...

Window styles are stored in the *Select Window or Door Style* dialog box located under **Library...** in the Door/Wind pull-down menu.

Highlighting a window **Style Name** in the list box displays the selection in the image tile when **Auto** is checked or **Display** is chosen.

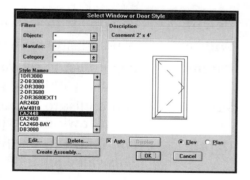

DOOR/WIND ➤ LIBRARY... ➤ EDIT...

Picking **Edit...** opens the *Edit Window Style* dialog box with pop-up list boxes, radio buttons, and pick boxes similar to the *Edit Door Style* dialog box discussed in Chapter 15.

Select Window or Door Style Dialog Box: Pop-Up Lists

Name:	Edit box containing the name of the window style highlighted in the **Style Names** list box.
Description:	Edit box containing brief summary of selected window style. Changes to **Type:**, **Height:**, and **Width:** edit boxes automatically update the description for default style names only.
Type:	Pop-up list containing window styles, including Fixed Metal, Arch Top, Awning, Casement, Double Hang, Hopper, Slider, Fixed, Arch Top, Chord, Gothic, Circle, Quarter Round, Circular, and Triangle. The Fixed Metal type is unique when included in an assembly. Normally the minimum mullion spacing for frames is twice the jamb value for an individual unit because the center mullion is twice as wide. Metal frames, however, have single-width center mullions. Another difference in Fixed Metal widows is that the bottom member of the frame is the same size and shape as the side, rather than the sloping sill of other window types.
Height:	Pop-up list to set window height.
Width:	Pop-up list to set window width.
Radius:	Pop-up list to set values for Arch Top, Chord, Gothic, and Circular window types only.
Sub-ht:	Pop-up list to set values for Arch Top, Chord, Gothic, and Circular window types only.
Depth:	Pop-up list to set the depth or y-axis of the window jamb. This value must be less than or equal to the wall in which the window is inserted.
Jamb:	Pop-up list to set window jamb size. Jambs can be effectively eliminated by setting their value to 0".
Head:	Pop-up list to set window head size. The Head dimension specifies the top of the window frame.

Note: A head dimension that is different from the jamb dimension can only be entered if a rectangular window or door is being drawn.

Select Window or Door Style Dialog Box: Pick Boxes

Position...   Opens the *Position of Frame in Wall* dialog box to display an image tile for placing the window's location in the wall. Picking *OTHER* from the **Edge of Frame to Exterior:** pop-up list offers a choice to alter the window position.

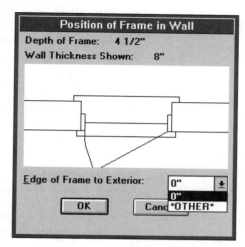

Glazing...   Displays the *Glazing Options* dialog box to draw glazing as single or double lines. Radio buttons also offer options to insert glazing as Normal (standard) or Special (spandrel or nonstandard) glass. The **Glazing Position in Frame** section can be set to centered, flush interior or exterior by selecting defaults from a pop-up list; it does not apply to double-hung windows, which are always centered.

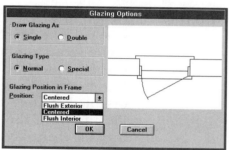

Note: The Special glazing type is simply an alternate glazing layer which may be used to represent spandrel glass or any other type of glazing as desired.

Sash...   The prompts displayed in the *Sash* dialog box are unique to each window style. This figure shows the *Sash* dialog box for double-hung. Choosing **Glazing Includes Sash** offers the option to include a sash with the frame.

This setting is normally on and can be turned off only for nonoperable windows.

Note: For a double-hung window, the height of the top sash is normally half of the total sash height. This value is automatically adjusted whenever the window height is changed to maintain this relationship. The top sash may be changed (to create perhaps a "cottage" style window), but keep in mind that any future change in overall height will again set the top sash value to half the total sash height. The total sash height is shown for reference; it is the frame height minus the head and sill thickness.

Picking *OTHER* from the pop-up list opens the *Edit List* dialog box and allows entry of custom window dimensions.

Muntins... Depending on the window selected, the *Muntin Bars* dialog box displays prompts specific to the window type. In some cases, the prompts may be greyed or disabled if they do not apply. Picking from the **Pattern:** pop-up list displays choices to include a rectangle or diamond

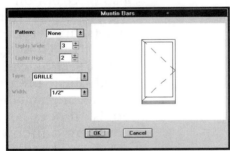

grille pattern within the glazed area. Choosing a pattern ungreys the edit boxes and allows for selection. Edit values for **Lights Wide:** and **Lights High:** by entering a new number or picking plus (+) or minus (-). Although the entry for **Type:** appears in the window schedule as a description, only **Width:** affects the muntin bar's design.

Sill... The *Sill Condition* dialog box contains options to change **Overall Thickness:** or height of the sill. The sill can be drawn as a **Projected Sill:** or **Flush Sill:**. with dimension set by values

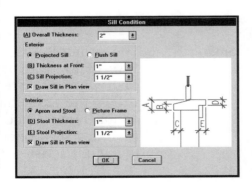

entered in the **Thickness at Front:** and **Sill Projection:** edit boxes. Checking **Draw Sill in Plan view** displays the sill when specified.

Note: The sill is the bottom member of the window frame and is not intended to represent something like a precast concrete sill below the window.

Casing...
Opens the *Casing and Trim* dialog box to include exterior and interior trim in elevations and 3D drawings. When check marks appear for **Apply Exterior Casing** and **Apply Interior Casing**, the image tile in the *Edit Window Style* dialog box is updated accordingly.

Note: When specifying a window frame size with a depth less than the wall width, the area between the frame and trim is filled in automatically with an *extension jamb*. This happens for 3D only and not for 2D, per the normal drafting convention.

Note: Casing is not available for windows or doors which are not flush with the exterior. Neither Casing nor Trim is available for Metal frame windows or doors.

Trim and Casing Width also control the sill extension along the wall beyond the width of the opening. This applies to both the 3D and 2D sill.

Data...
Entering data in the *User Supplied Window Data* dialog box includes the information available for window schedules or reports.

More Pick Boxes

DOOR/WIND ➤ LIBRARY ➤ DELETE...

Choosing **Delete...** displays the *Delete Style* dialog box warning which indicates that the style is about to be permanently deleted. If any objects of the style exist in the current drawing, deletion is not allowed.

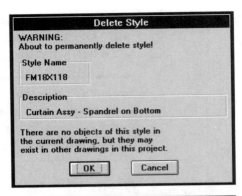

DOOR/WIND ➤ LIBRARY ➤ CREATE ASSEMBLY...

Selecting **Assembly...** initially opens the *Swing Orientation* dialog box to set the window's pivot point, then displays the *Create Assembly* dialog box.

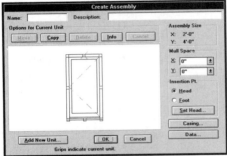

CREATING A WINDOW ASSEMBLY

If desired, the following descriptions can be implemented as an exercise; however, the intent is to explain how an assembly can be created. The components include modifying a window style and using it with an existing door style, assembled to create a 3' x 6'-8" door with transom above.

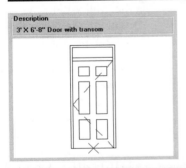

DOOR/WIND ➤ LIBRARY...

To create a new fixed window style for the transom, for example, choose **Library...** from the Door/Wind pull-down menu, then highlight FX2460.

   Pick Edit...

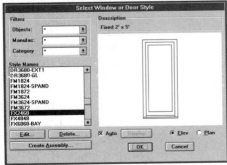

Change the sill **Width** to 3'-2" (to fit over a 3'-0" door with 1" jambs). The **Height** can be 12".

Next, change the **Sills...** and **Sash...** dimensions by choosing their pick buttons.

DOOR/WIND ➤ LIBRARY ➤ EDIT... ➤ SILLS...

Change the sills to a **Flush Sill** and **Picture Frame**.

 Pick OK.

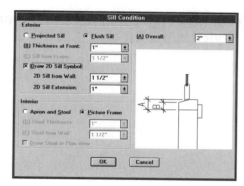

DOOR/WIND ➤ LIBRARY ➤ EDIT... ➤ SASH...

Uncheck the box **Glazing includes Sash** to remove the sash.

 Pick OK.

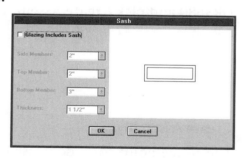

Returning to the *Edit Window Style* dialog box, the image tile displays the new window style.

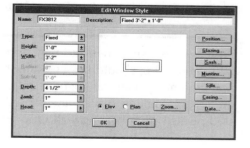 Pick OK to save the new style.

Use the new default name "FX3812" to save the style in the *Save Window or Door Style* dialog box.

Pick OK.

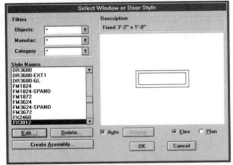

The new style name FX3812 appears in the **Style Names** list box.

Now select the 3' door to use. Highlight DR3680 and pick **Create Assembly...**

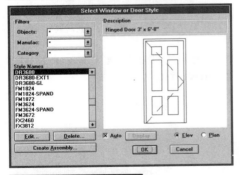

Create Assembly...

The hinge point for a door used in an assembly must be chosen at this time. Select **Hinge Point** 1 from the *Swing Orientation* dialog box.

Note: An advisory message may appear, saying that mullion spacing should be set while there is only one unit present. Spacing cannot be changed once two units are joined. Mullion space may be used either to create stud pockets for a bearing wall or to add stiffeners to a

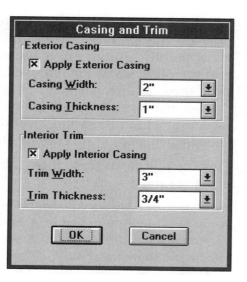

large assembly. For this assembly, the frames will be simply joined together with no additional space.

   Pick OK.

The image in the *Create Assembly* dialog box shows the door with *grips* located at each corner and midpoint, at the edge of the frame. These grips indicate the points where the unit can join a similar point on another unit. The unit which the grips surround is the *current* unit.

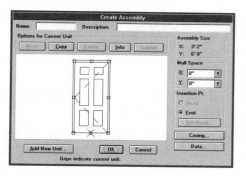

The image also shows an X at the bottom center, which indicates the insertion point of the assembly. The insertion point is always centered in the X direction. All assemblies containing doors have an insertion point at the bottom or *foot*. Assemblies of windows (without any doors) normally have the insertion point aligned with the top of one of the windows; this point is placed at the specified *head* height when inserted. This point may be set to align with a corner or midpoint of any window unit. This would be done by picking **Set Head**. Window assemblies may also be given an insertion point at the foot. This might be appropriate for a storefront type of window.

Casing...

Values for casing are automatically the same as the first unit in the assembly. Other units may be added which have different values. They may be set here as desired for the assembly— the casing and trim values of the individual units are then ignored.

   Pick OK or Cancel without changing any values.

Add New Unit...

Now pick **Add New Unit...** Select FX3812 from the *Select Window or Door Style for Assembly* dialog which appears in the **Style Names** list box.

 Pick OK.

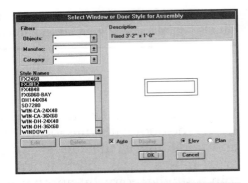

This unit now appears in the assembly, but not where we want it.

A prompt at the bottom of the dialog box appears with the statement "Grips indicate current unit."

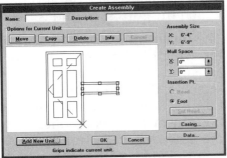

In the **Options for Current Unit** section, pick **Move** (or use the **M** macro to activate the Move button). Another prompt at the bottom of the dialog then says "Select base point."

Select the grip at the bottom center of the window and the prompt changes to "Select placement point." This grip now becomes a *hot* grip and the other seven are removed, but there are now three additional grips at the top of the door. These grips indicate every point on the assembly which is a valid location for placing the selected grip of the current unit.

Pick the middle of these three (above the door) and the image is updated.

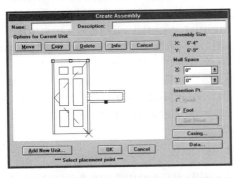

Note: Don't try to pick and drag the bottom window grip to the top door middle grip. Simply pick the other middle grip above the door.

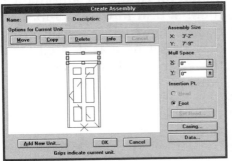

Copy

Picking **Copy** (or using the **C** macro) makes another window above the original, in similar fashion to the previous Move. The newest unit is now the current unit.

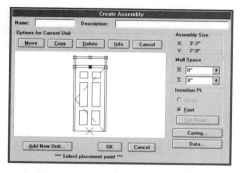

Delete

This extra window may not really be necessary, so picking **Delete** will delete it. It is removed and the previous window is again current.

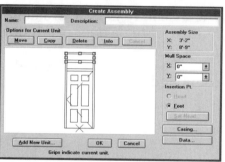

Note: Since the window still contains the grips, it is assigned as the item to delete.

Cancel and Info

The **Cancel** button may be used to cancel a **Move** or **Copy** after a base point has already been selected.

The **Info** button may be picked to see relevant data about the current unit, as well as the quantity of that unit in the assembly. A different unit may be designated as the current unit by simply picking anywhere within the desired unit image.

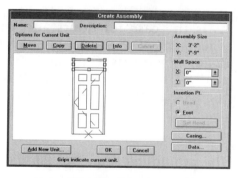

Enter a description and save assembly using the **Description** and **Name** edit boxes.

 Pick OK.

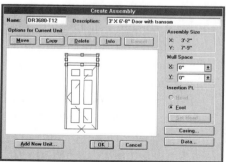

The *Save Window or Door Assembly Style* dialog box opens with the new name DR3680-T12.

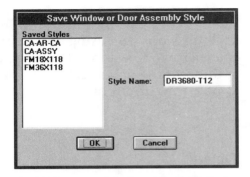

Pick OK.

The assembly is now available for placement just like a single door or window.

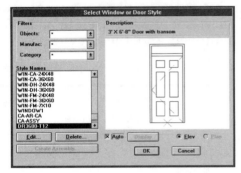

Pick OK and prompts are invoked at the command line.

As is the case for doors and windows, after placement of the assembly, the *Edit Attributes* dialog box opens. Choose the desired tag type at the **Use Door callout or Window callout for assembly (Door/Window) <Window>:** prompt.

The prompting sequence is:

Accessing Door/Window Library...

Place Assembly style DR3680-T12: 3' X 6'-8" Door with transom

Auto - pick side of wall near center or end (Center/Side):

Show direction for exterior <arrow>:

Creating assembly..............done.

Use Door callout or Window callout for assembly (Door/Window) <Window>: **d**

Inserting Door Num at elevation 0.

New callout location <same>:

Packing assembly data file...done.

The assembly just created was made of units with standard frames. If fixed metal frames were used, the process is almost the same, except that Mullion Spacing is not available, Casing is not available, and units are joined by sharing a common frame element instead of joining two frames together. Fixed metal frame units may not be joined by standard frame units. Likewise, standard frame units may not be joined by metal frame units. When using **Add New Unit**, only units of the proper frame type (matching the first unit of the assembly) are displayed.

PLACING A BOW WINDOW

DOOR/WIND ➤ DRAW BOWS AND BAYS...

Selecting **Draw Bows and Bays...** from the Door/Wind pull-down menu opens the *Bow and Bay Window* dialog box.

Although bow or bay windows will not be inserted into the plan used for this exercise, the command procedures are similar to other window and door insertions.

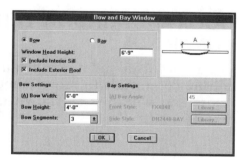

The dialog box shows a **Bow Height:** 4'-0" high and **Bow Width:** of 6'-0" high with three **Bow Segments. The Window Head Height:** is set to 6'-9". Check marks offer options to **Include Interior Sill** and **Include Exterior Roof** boxes.

PROMPTING SUMMARY

Inserting Bow Window...

Auto - pick side of wall near center or end (Center/Side): [**pick a point in center of interior wall**]

Show direction for exterior <arrow>: [**pick a point to left of plan**]

Inserting Wind Type Mas at elevation 0.

New callout location <same>: [**reposition window tag**]

Bow window insertion procedures are similar to those for casement windows, requiring selection of a point near the wall and arrow orientation, as shown.

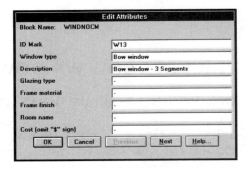

After the window is inserted, the *Edit Attributes* dialog box opens. Entering the ID Mark number, then picking OK completes the procedure to draw the window.

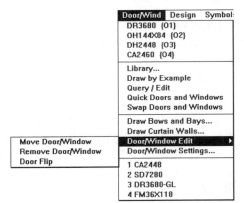

DOOR AND WINDOW EDITING COMMANDS

The Door/Wind pull-down menu offers other editing commands to move, remove, and flip doors and windows as shown under **Door/ Window Edit.**

DOOR/WIND ➤ DOOR/WINDOW EDIT ➤ MOVE DOOR/WINDOW

Moving a door or window prompts for crossing window points to select the object to be repositioned. Drag the object by pressing enter, then pick its new location.

The prompting sequence is:

Command:
Base Stretch...
Select objects with Crossing window.
First corner: Other corner:
Remove objects:↵
Base point: **[pick a point]**
New point (press Enter to drag):↵

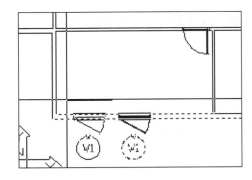

DOOR/WIND ➤ DOOR/WINDOW EDIT ➤ REMOVE DOOR/WINDOW

Removing a door or window prompts to select the object, then deletes the object. The command may turn additional layers on. If so, it then prompts to restore the original layering status.

The prompting sequence is:

Pick door, window, or assembly to remove:
Accessing layers: FL01-WALLCL
Restore previous layer display <Yes>:
Restoring layers.

DOOR/WIND ➤ DOOR/WINDOW EDIT ➤ FLIP DOOR

Flipping a door swing requires selecting the object then positioning the cursor to relocate the door's new swing, hinged horizontally or vertically adjacent to the opposite side of the door jamb.

The prompting sequence is:

Pick door symbol (or Exit) <Exit>:
Move cursor to show position. (Any key or pick = done)
Pick door symbol (or Exit) <Exit>:

SWAPPING DOORS AND WINDOWS

DOOR/WIND ➤ SWAP DOORS AND WINDOWS

The **Swap Doors and Windows** command, selected from the Door/Wind pull-down menu, provides a valuable feature for replacing single or multiple doors and/or windows. It is especially useful when quick doors or windows are inserted during the early phase of a project, then converted or swapped with more detailed symbols for the construction document phase. Schematic or detailed doors or windows can be exchanged with other windows and/or doors. This command will be discussed in more detail in chapter 18.

Proceed to Chapter 18 to insert windows into the walls located in OFFICE-1, OFFICE-2, and OFFICE-3.

CHAPTER EIGHTEEN

WINDOWS

Placing Casement and Curtain Wall Windows into Walls

Contents

In the exercises for this chapter windows will only be placed into the exterior walls. Begin by inserting casement windows in the small offices at the front of the building, then proceed to the rear of the building; finally, conclude with a storefront type of window in OFFICE-1.

THE WINDOW SCHEDULE

The following table is a window schedule listing information about the windows to be inserted into walls for this exercise.

WINDOW SCHEDULE

Window	*Type*	*Window Width*	*Window Height*	*Window Head Height*	*Room Name*	*Window Type*
1	W1	3'-0"	5'-0"	7'-0"	OFFICE-2A	Casement
2	W1	3'-0"	5'-0"	7'-0"	OFFICE-2B	Casement
3	W1	3'-0"	5'-0"	7'-0"	OFFICE-2C	Casement
4 - 8		6'-0"	5'-6"	3'-0"	OFFICE-3	Casement
9		7'-0"	10'-0"	10'-0"	OFFICE-1	Fixed Metal
10		8 each 7'-0"	10'-0"	10'-0"	OFFICE-1	Curtain wall

The figure shows casement windows (numbers 1-3) along the right front side, quick windows (numbers 4-8) along the rear, and curtain wall windows (numbers 9-10) along the left front side of the building.

EDITING WINDOW SETTINGS

DOOR/WIND ➤ DOOR/WINDOW SETTINGS...

Choose **Door/Window Settings...** from the Door/Wind pull-down menu to open the *Door and Window Settings* dialog box and verify **Prompt for exterior side during insertion** is checked. Insert windows with window tags (callouts) by checking **Automatic Insert** in the

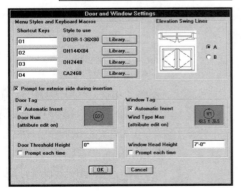

Window Tag section. Set the **Window Head Height** to 7'-0" by editing the value in this edit box and uncheck **Prompt each time**.

Replace shortcut key O2 for the overhead door style OH144X84 with a casement window style.

ASSIGNING A WINDOW STYLE TO THE PULL-DOWN MENU

 Reassign the shortcut key O2 to a window style by choosing the adjacent **Library...** pick box and opening the *Select Window or Door Style* dialog box.

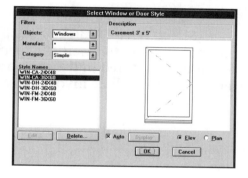

In the **Filter** section, first open the pop-up list for **Objects:** and pick Windows; then, select Simple from **Category**.

The **Style Names** list box displays several default names. Highlight WIN-CA-36X60 and **Description** appears as Casement 3' × 5'.

 Dialog box:

Object:	**Windows**
Category	**Simple**
Style Name:	**WIN-CA-36X60**
Description:	Casement 3' × 5'

Note: Notice that the **Edit...** box is greyed and does not allow modification of the window style. Editing features are available when **Library...** is selected directly from the Door/Wind pull-down menu.

Pick OK to close the dialog box and return to the *Door and Window Settings* dialog box. Notice that shortcut key O2 now has WIN-CA-36X60 as the **Style to use**.

Pick OK.

Shortcut Keys	Style to use	
O1	DOOR-1-36X80	Library...
O2	WIN-CA-36X60	Library...
O3	DH2448	Library...
O4	CA2460	Library...

PLACING WINDOW 1 FROM THE PULL-DOWN MENU

Zoom into the lower right corner of the building to insert a single 4'-0" high x 4'-0" wide window into each of the three small office spaces labeled as OFFICE-2A, OFFICE-2B, and OFFICE-2C.

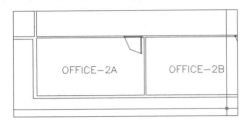

DOOR/WIND ➤ WIN-CA-36X60 {O2}

Select **WIN-CA-36X60 {O2}** from the Door/Wind pull-down menu to insert the specified window. (Notice that it is now stored in the top portion of the pull-down menu. Later it will be invoked as a macro.)

PROMPTING SUMMARY

Command: SDSK

Reading data -- Please wait...

Place Window style WIN-CA-36X60: Casement 3' x 5'

Auto - pick side of wall near center or end (Center/Side): **[pick point near interior center of wall line in OFFICE-2A]**

Show direction for exterior <arrow>: **[drag arrow, then pick point below plan]**

Select Hinge point: **[pick bottom left X mark]**

Creating window......done.

Place tag...

Inserting Wind Type Mas at elevation 0.

New callout location <same>: **[reposition window tag]**

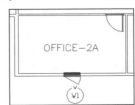

👆 Pick a point adjacent to the interior wall line close to the wall's midpoint or center at the **Auto - pick side of wall near center or end (Center/Side):** prompt.

Place Window style WIN-CA-36X60: Casement 3' x 5' Auto - pick side of wall near center or end (Center/Side):

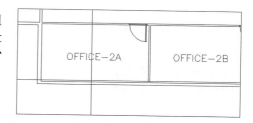

.Note: Choosing a point too distant from the wall or zooming closely into the wall may display the prompt, **Wall element not found, try again.**

Drag the arrow toward the exterior of the building by placing the crosshairs toward the bottom of the floor plan, then press the pick button when prompted to **Show direction for exterior <arrow>:**,

Show direction for exterior <arrow>:

👆 Pick the bottom left X mark when prompted to **Select Hinge point:**

Select Hinge point:

👆 The *Edit Attributes* dialog box opens to display information about the **ID Mark, Window type,** and **Description.** Selecting **Next...** provides review as well as editing of the default prompts and values assigned to this specific window tag.

Accept the default values W1, Casement, and Casement 3' x 5'. Enter any additional information to the remaining prompts in the dialog box if desired.

Dialog Box:

ID Mark	W1
Window Type	Casement
Description	Casement 3' × 5'

 Pick OK to close the dialog box.

Drag and reposition the callout below the window as shown when prompted for **New callout location<same>:**.

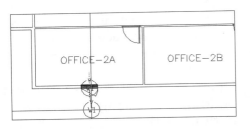

Place tag...
Inserting Wind Type Mas at elevation 0.
New callout location <same>:

Notice that the procedure for inserting windows is the same as for doors, based on controls set in the *Door and Windows Settings* dialog box.

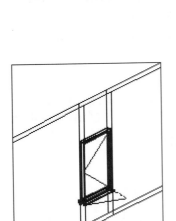

The figure shows the 3D window in isometric view drawn using the compound layer group set in Chapter 10. The 3D window header, similar to a door header, is the area located above the window and is drawn on layer FL01-WALL3D. The 3D window and frame, similar to a door and frame, are drawn on FL01-OPENING. The window footer located below the window is drawn on FL01-WALL3D. The window block actually contains several nested blocks all of which are drawn on root layer names such as 3DWSWING, 3DWINDOW, GLAZE, WSWINGARC, and 3DTRIM.

Some objects, for example 3DDJAMB, HEADER, and FL01-HEADER, use the linetype INVISIBLE to allow layers to remain on while editing the drawing. These linetypes can be controlled automatically through the use of Plan Types for plotting purposes without affecting their appearance in the drawing.

INVOKING WINDOW COMMANDS AS SHORTCUT KEYS OR MACROS—PLACING WINDOW 2

Zoom out to display all three office spaces in OFFICE-2. Insert windows matching OFFICE-2A into OFFICE-2B and OFFICE-2C by typing its assigned Macro O2.

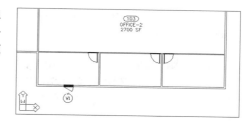

PROMPTING SUMMARY

Command: O2

Reading data -- Please wait...

Place Window style WIN-CA-36X60: Casement 3' x 5'

Auto - pick side of wall near center or end (Center/Side): **[pick point at center of interior wall line]**

Show direction for exterior <arrow>: **[drag arrow, then pick point below exterior wall line]**

Select Hinge point: **[pick point at bottom left X mark]**

Place tag...

Inserting Wind Type Mas at elevation 0.

New callout location <same>: [pick point to relocate window tag]

MACRO COMMAND: O2

Enter O2 at the command line, then pick a point near the center of the interior wall line of OFFICE-2B to set the window placement.

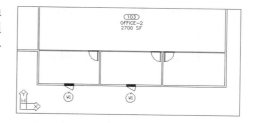

Command: **O2**

Place Window style WIN-CA-36X60: Casement 3' x 5'

Auto - pick side of wall near center or end (Center/Side):

Next, select a point toward the exterior wall line to orient the exterior face of the window. Determine the window's swing or hinge point by picking the bottom left X mark.

Show direction for exterior <arrow>:

Select Hinge point:

Finally, the *Edit Attributes* dialog box opens to display the window tag information. Accept the default **ID Mark** W1, then pick OK to close the dialog box. Pick to reposition the window tag below the window.

Place tag...

Inserting Wind Type Mas at elevation 0.

New callout location <same>:

REPEATING THE LAST COMMAND—PLACING WINDOW 3

 Press **Enter** (return key) or the spacebar to repeat the last command (Macro O2) inserting window style WIN-CA-36X60 in OFFICE-2C.

The windows should now be inserted into each office space as shown in the prompting summary below.

PROMPTING SUMMARY

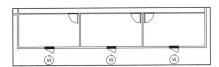

 Command: O2

Reading data -- Please wait...

Place Window style WIN-CA-36X60: Casement 3' x 5'

Auto - pick side of wall near center or end (Center/Side): **[pick a point at center of wall]**

Show direction for exterior <arrow>: **[drag arrow, then pick a point at building exterior]**

Select Hinge point: **[pick bottom left X mark]**

Place tag...

Inserting Wind Type Mas at elevation 0.

New callout location <same>: **[reposition window tag]**

OVERVIEW FOR PLACING QUICK DOORS AND WINDOWS

Zoom into the upper portion of the plan and insert five schematic windows into the rear wall of OFFICE-3.

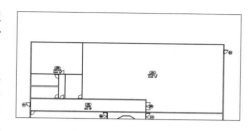

After inserting quick windows using **Quick Doors and Windows**, invoking the **Swap Doors and Windows** command replaces the schematic representation with a more detailed 3D window style.

Note: Schematic window styles are intended to be used in the preliminary drawing phase of a project. The **Quick Doors and Windows** command offers a range of both door and window types.

The figure to the right shows a schematic window in isometric view.

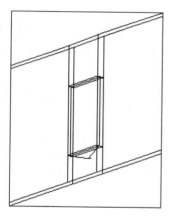

QUICK DOORS AND WINDOWS— INSERTING WINDOWS 4 THROUGH 11

DOOR/WIND ➤ QUICK DOORS AND WINDOWS

Select the **Quick Doors and Windows** command from the Door/Wind pull-down menu, then type **S** to open the *Quick Doors and Windows* dialog box. Typing **S** or **Select** displays the prompt **Place Previous object or Select from library (Previous/Select) <Previous>:**

Place Previous object or Select from library (Previous/Select) <Previous>: **s**

Pick Casement Windows from the **Object** section and Single from the **Type** section to update the image box with the selected window style. Values can be entered directly in their edit boxes or chosen by highlighting a size from a list box in the **Width** and **Height** sections. Select from the **Units** pop-up list and choose inches. Other available units of measure include feet, millimeters, centimeters, decimeters, and meters. The **Swing Angle** section is ungreyed for single- and double-hinged doors only, offering choices for 90, 45, and 180.

   Dialog box:

Object	**Casement Windows**
Type	**Single**
Width	**3'-0"**
Height	**5'-0"**
Units:	**Inches**

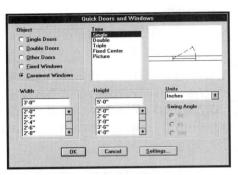

Next, select the **Settings...** pick box to open the *Door and Window Settings* dialog box.

DOOR/WIND ➤ QUICK DOORS AND WINDOWS ➤ SETTINGS...

Set window values as follows and verify that no X mark appears for **Prompt each time** in the **Windows** section.

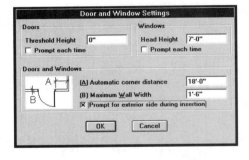

   Dialog box:

Threshold Height	**0"**
Head Height	**7'-0"**
Automatic corner distance	**18'-0"**
Maximum Wall Width	**1'-6"**

Place a check mark in **Prompt for interior side during insertion**.

Removing this check mark displays the AutoCAD Message dialog box shown in the accompanying figure.

   Pick OK to close all dialog boxes.

PROMPTING SUMMARY

Command: SDSK

Previous: Casement Window, Single (Width = 3'-0", Height = 5'-0")

Place Previous object or Select from library (Previous/Select) <Previous>: **s [open dialog box to edit settings]**

(Inserting window 4)

Auto - pick side of wall near center or end (Center/Side): **s [change to Side option]**

Side - pick corner reference point (Auto/Center): **[insert window at specific distance from corner]**

Side of opening: **@12'8<0**

Which direction for break: **[pick point to right side of plan]**

Show direction for exterior <arrow>: **[pick point above plan]**

Select Hinge point: **[pick top left X mark]**

(Inserting window 5)

Side - pick corner reference point (Auto/Center): **a [change to Auto option]**

Auto - pick side of wall near center or end (Center/Side): **[pick point near wall line]**

Show direction for exterior <arrow>: **[pick point above plan]**

Select Hinge point: **[pick top left X mark]**

(Inserting window 6)

Auto - pick side of wall near center or end (Center/Side): **[pick point near wall line]**

Show direction for exterior <arrow>: **[pick point near wall line]**

Select Hinge point: **[pick top left X mark]**

(inserting window 7)

Auto - pick side of wall near center or end (Center/Side): **[pick point near wall line]**

Show direction for exterior <arrow>: **[pick point near wall line]**

Select Hinge point: **[pick top left X mark]**

(inserting window 8)

Auto - pick side of wall near center or end (Center/Side): **[pick point near wall line]**

Show direction for exterior <arrow>: **[pick point near wall line]**

Select Hinge point: **[pick top left X mark]**

Auto - pick side of wall near center or end (Center/Side):⏎

PLACING WINDOWS 4 THROUGH 11 USING QUICK DOORS AND WINDOWS

Insert the first schematic casement window, Window 4, at a distance of 12' 8" to the right of the interior left corner of OFFICE-3 when prompted for **Side of opening:**

 Command line:

Auto - pick side of wall near center or end (Center/Side): **s**
Side - pick corner reference point (Auto/Center):
Side of opening: **@12'8<0**

Pick a point to the right of the plan when the **Which direction for break:** prompt appears.

Which direction for break:

Drag the arrow upward, then select a point above the plan when prompted to **Show direction for exterior <arrow>:**

Show direction for exterior <arrow>:

Pick the top left X mark at **Select Hinge point.**

Select Hinge point:

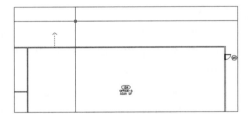

Change to the **Auto** option, then continue with the quick window insertion command to place Windows 5 through 8.

At the prompt **Side- pick corner reference point(Auto/Center)**, enter **a**, then pick a point near the right side of the window close to the exterior wall line.

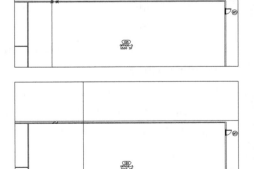

Side - pick corner reference point (Auto/Center): **a**
Auto - pick side of wall near center or end (Center/Side):

Select a point above the plan when requested to **Show direction for exterior <arrow>:**

Show direction for exterior <arrow>:

Choose the top left X mark at **Select Hinge point.**

Select Hinge point:

Each window will be inserted a distance of 18' 0" as previously set by the **Automatic corner distance** value entered in the *Door and Window Settings* dialog box.

After Window 5 is inserted, continue repeating the procedure for Windows 6 through 8 by selecting a point to the right of the previous window to set its location, orienting the arrow and picking the top left hinge point.

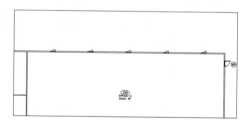

Press Enter to complete the command and Window 8 is inserted.

Auto - pick side of wall near center or end (Center/Side):↵

Note: If you make mistakes during the execution of this command, invoke the command again using the <Previous> option. Place the next window starting at the right side of the last quick.

SWAPPING WINDOW STYLES—WINDOWS 4 THROUGH 11

DOOR/WIND>SWAP DOORS AND WINDOWS

Selecting **Swap Doors and Windows** from the Door/Wind pull-down menu and picking any of the previously installed windows in OFFICE-3 searches the drawing for all blocks of the same name and offers choices to include them in the selection set for swapping. The command line confirms the number of units (doors or windows) found, as well as the block name chosen.

Replace all the schematic windows with a 4'-0" wide x 4'-0" high commercial type of fixed metal window.

The prompting sequence is:

Door/Window object swap...

Check existing Door/Window blocks <Yes>⏎

Checking style objects...

All objects are current.

Select door, window, or assembly to be replaced:

  Found 5 WINDQC -- Width: 3'-0", Height: 5'-0", Wall thickness: 6"

Remove/Choose/Manual/Single/Done <Done>:⏎

  Found 5 WINDQC -- Width: 3'-0", Height: 5'-0", Wall thickness: 6"

Accessing library...

Swapping...

Accessing layers: FL01-WALLCL

Restore previous layer display <Yes>:⏎

Restoring layers...

Creating window............done..

Pick **Swap Doors and Windows** from the Door/Wind pull-down menu to display the **Select door, window, or assembly to be replaced:** prompt as well as information about the schematic windows. The five windows found are highlighted to confirm their selection.

Select door, window, or assembly to be replaced:

Found 5 WINDQC -- Width: 3'-0", Height: 5'-0", Wall thickness: 6"

The next prompt, **Remove/Choose/Manual/Single/Done <Done>:**, appears with options that include removing a window from the selection set or manually selecting a specific unit. **Choose** deselects all the windows, allowing you to re-enter another option. **Manual** allows you to pick specific units and **Single** selects the original unit picked. Accept the default **<done>** to accept the current selection of five WINDQC windows and the *Select Window or Door Style* dialog box opens.

Remove/Choose/Manual/Single/Done <Done>:⏎

Open the pop-up list in the **Filters** section for **Objects:** and pick Windows, then select Commercial from **Category**.

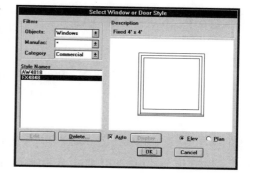

 After the **Style Name** list box updates choose FX4848, then pick OK.

 Dialog box:

Objects:	**Windows**
Category	**Commercial**
Style name:	**FX4848**

As the wall centerline layer (FL01-WALLCL) is turned on, the windows are replaced. Accept the final prompt to restore the previous layers.

Restore previous layer display <Yes>:⏎
Restoring layers...

- -

CREATING A NEW WINDOW STYLE—PLACING WINDOW 9

Zoom into OFFICE-1 to insert a 10'-0" high x 7'-0" wide fixed metal window at the left exterior wall of the Entry (lower right side of OFFICE-1).

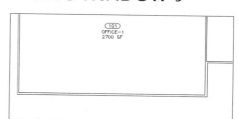

DOOR/WIND ➤ DOOR/WINDOW SETTINGS...

 Select **Door/Window Settings...** from the Door/Wind pull-down menu. Change **Window Head Height** from 7'-0" to 10'-0".

 Dialog box:

Window Head Height:	**10'-0"**

 Pick OK.

PROMPTING SUMMARY

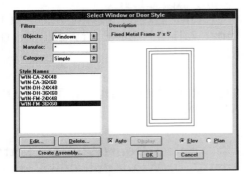

Command: SDSK

Accessing Door/Window Library...

Place Window style WIN-FM-7X10: Fixed Metal Frame 7'-0" x 10'-0"

Auto - pick side of wall near center or end (Center/Side): **c [change to Center option]**

Center - pick side of wall (Auto/Side): **[pick point near center of exterior wall line]**

Show direction for exterior <arrow>: **[pick point to right of plan]**

Creating window......

Redefining block ABWD$WIN-FM-7X10

done.

Place tag...

Inserting Wind Type Mas at elevation 0.

New callout location <same>:**[edit value in dialog box, pick OK, then reposition window tag]**

DOOR/WIND ➤ LIBRARY...

Select **Library...** from the Door/Wind pull-down menu to open the *Select Window or Door Style* dialog box. Pick the down arrows in the **Filters** section and choose Windows for **Objects:** and Simple for **Category.**

Highlight WIN-FM-36X60 in the **Style Names** list box, then pick **Edit...** to open the *Edit Window Style* dialog box.

 Dialog box:

Objects:	**Windows**
Category	**Simple**
Style Name:	**WIN-FM-36X60**

Edit the values as shown, then pick OK.

Dialog box:

Type:	Fixed Metal Frame
Description:	Fixed Metal Frame 7'-0" x 10'-0"
Height:	**10'-0"**
Width:	**7'-0"**
Depth:	4 1/2"
Jamb:	2"
Head:	2"

The **Description:** Fixed Metal Frame 10'-0" x 7'-0" and its associated image tile are updated automatically when the **Height:** and **Width:** edit boxes are modified.

Note: Although the **Name:** edit box does not automatically update, a new name can be entered at this time in the edit box or entered in the next dialog box that appears.

 Pick OK.

Modifying an existing default window style name in the *Edit Window Style* dialog box causes the *Save Window or Door Style* dialog box to open. Modifications to an existing style are saved by overriding the name or by entering a new style name.

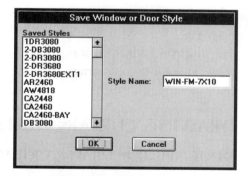

 Change the style name to WIN-FM-7X10 signifying a fixed metal frame window 7'-0" wide x 10'-0" high, then pick OK.

Note: Style names are limited to 12 characters.

The *Select Window or Door Style* dialog box returns displaying the updated information.

 Pick OK.

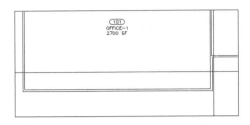

 Select a point near the center of the exterior wall line to locate the window, then press Enter after the arrow is oriented to the right.

Auto - pick side of wall near center or end
  (Center/Side): **c**
Center - pick side of wall (Auto/Side):
Show direction for exterior <arrow>:

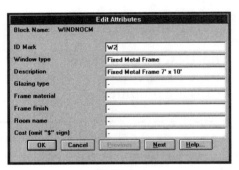

The *Edit Attributes* dialog box opens displaying information about the window.

Enter **W2** in the **ID Mark** edit box, then pick OK.

Dialog box:

ID Mark   **W2**

Reposition the window tag to the right of the window as shown.

Place tag...
Inserting Wind Type Mas at elevation 0.
New callout location <same>:

DRAWING CURTAIN WALLS—PLACING WINDOW 10

DOOR/WIND ➤ DRAW CURTAIN WALLS...

Draw a full-height curtain wall along the front of OFFICE-1, centered within the entire wall length.

Select **Draw Curtain Walls...** from the Door/Wind pull-down menu to open the *Curtain Walls* dialog box.

Pick **Library...** adjacent to **(A)Main Style** in the **Parameters** section and the *Select Window or Door Style* dialog box opens.

PROMPTING SUMMARY

Creating Curtain Wall...

Head placement method -- Height: 10'

Center - pick side of wall (Auto/Side): [**pick near midpoint of wall line**]

Show direction for exterior <arrow>: [**orient downward and pick a point**]

Creating window......

Redefining block ABWD$WIN-FM-7X10

done.

Highlight the new style name WIN-FM-7X10 previously created for the exterior side of the ENTRY area, then pick OK.

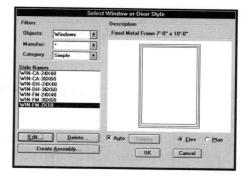

Note: The message "Note: ignoring End assembly insertion height" may appear temporarily. This is because a different style on the ends is called for and there is a mismatch between the insertion height of the end style and the main style just selected. This should be resolved either by selecting an end style which has an insertion height matching that of the main style or by not using a different style on the ends. The end style, if used, is normally identical to the main style except for the width (usually narrower), a common practice for curtain walls.

Turn off **Use Different Style on Ends** for this exercise.

The *Curtain Walls* dialog box reappears with the updated window name adjacent to **(A)Main Style:**.

Enter 8 in the **Total Number of Units:** edit box, then remove check marks for **Use Different Style on Ends** and **Include Interior Sill**. The **Combined Length** automatically updates to reflect a new dimension of 54'-10".

Dialog box:

Total Number of Units: **8**

    Pick OK.

    Select a point at the center of the exterior front wall of OFFICE-1, orient the arrow downward, then pick.

Center - pick side of wall (Auto/Side):
Show direction for exterior <arrow>:

The plan shows the curtain wall window inserted into the wall.

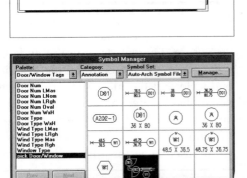

PLACING TAGS WITH DOORS AND WINDOWS

Notice that some windows were placed with tags inserted automatically; others do not yet have tags.

The preferred method of adding tags is to use **pick Door/Window** from **Annotation** under the Symbols menu. This method obtains information from the picked door or window, the same as placing a tag automatically when inserting doors and windows. A link is also created between the door or window and the tag. With this link, when a door or window is removed, the tag is automatically removed as well, even if the tag layer is turned off. The same choice of tag is used as for automatic tag insertion.

To change the tag choice, select **Door/Window Settings...** under the Door/Wind menu. Check **Automatic Insert** to enable the tag image button. Then pick the image button to display the *Symbol Manager* dialog box. Select the desired tag (do NOT choose **pick Door/Window** at this time). Pick OK to exit the *Symbol Manager* dialog box, then turn **Automatic Insert** back off and close the *Door and Window Settings* dialog box.

The figure shows an isometric view of the completed curtain wall window and fixed metal window.

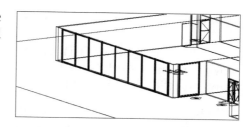

EDITING A WINDOW STYLE

Editing Windows 1,2, and 3

Return to the three small office spaces by zooming or panning into the lower right corner of the plan to edit windows 1, 2, and 3.

Query/Edit under the Door/Wind pull-down menu searches the entire drawing to redefine windows that have the same style names. This command only applies to windows with a style identity. Bow or bay windows, discussed in Chapter 17 for example, do not have style names and must be removed then redrawn.

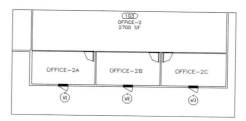

PROMPTING SUMMARY

Door/Window object query...

Select door or window: **[pick window 1, 2 or 3]**

Loading Window Style Editor. Please wait...

Updating objects...

Creating window......

Redefining block ABWD_WIN-CA-36X60_2792

Updating wall openings.. (Level FL01)...

Restoring layers...

Updating window style WIN-CA-36X60 in assemblies...

Update done.

All existing objects of style WIN-CA-36X60 have been updated.

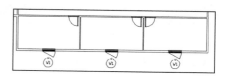

DOOR/WIND ➤ QUERY/EDIT

Select **Query/Edit** from the Door/Wind pull-down menu to edit the style parameters for the windows in OFFICE-2A, OFFICE-2B, and OFFICE-2C.

Replace the three- 3' x 5' casement windows with 4' x 5' casement windows, specifying a 4 1/2" **Depth:**, 2" **Jamb:**, and **2" Head**.

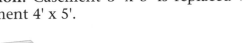

Pick one of the three casement windows and the *Query/Edit Window Object* dialog box opens.

Choose *OTHER* from the **Width:**, **Jamb:**, and **Head:** pop-up list to open their *Edit List* dialog boxes. Enter new values for each, then pick OK and return to the *Query/Edit Window Object* dialog box.

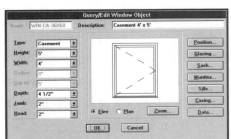

The image box and **Width:** edit box update to display the new information. The **Description:** Casement 3' x 5' is replaced with Casement 4' x 5'.

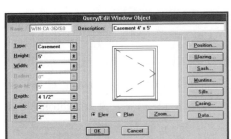

Dialog box:

Type: Casement
Height: 5''
Width: **4'**
Depth: 4 1/2
Jamb: **2"**
Head: **2"**

Note: Again, it is important to note that the **Name:** edit box, however, is greyed and remains unchanged. The name WIN-CA-36X60 does not accurately reflect the new window's description. Selecting WIN-CA-36X60 from the pull-down menu or invoking it with the O2 macro inserts a 4'-0" wide window. When inserting the edited window style, the prompt **Place Window style WIN-CA-36X60: Casement 4'-0" x 5'-0"** appears, confirming the revised description.

 Pick OK (retaining the original name).

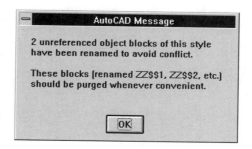

AutoCAD Message

2 unreferenced object blocks of this style have been renamed to avoid conflict.

These blocks (renamed ZZ$$1, ZZ$$2, etc.) should be purged whenever convenient.

OK

Note: The AutoCAD Message box may appear to warn that two additional window styles of the same name exist in the drawing. These windows have been updated and renamed to avoid conflict.

This completes the placement of all the windows in the exterior walls. A variety of commands have been used to demonstrate various methods for inserting new windows and replacing existing windows. Proceed to the next chapter and create a roof for the building.

ROOFS

*Overview of Roof-related Commands and
Drawing a Hip Roof*

Contents

This chapter begins with a brief review of the **Roofs** menu which offers commands to draw simple and complex roofs in 2D, 3D, or both. Then, a 3D hip roof with an overhang is drawn above the exterior walls to enclose the first floor plan. Complicated roofs may require drawing several roofs of various types, such as hip, gable, and flat, then erasing portions that are not needed. Exercises include commands that help you to view the exterior building's front as well as overall design with interior objects hidden.

REVIEWING HIP, GABLE, AND SHED ROOF COMMANDS AND SETTINGS

DESIGN ➤ ROOFS

For a quick introduction of the Roof commands pick the Design pull-down menu and choose **Roofs**.

If you select **Draw Roofs...** from the Roofs menu, a simple hip, gable, or shed roof can be created from selected corner and perpendicular points. Additional commands, selected under **Roof Generator** and **Roof Edit** will be discussed later.

The command opens the *Draw Roof* dialog box to choose radio buttons for setting the **Drawing Type**, **Fascia Type**, and **Soffit Type** as shown.

Selecting from the pop-up menu in the **Roof Type:** section displays images for gable, shed, and hip roofs.

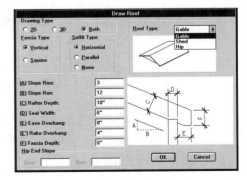

Note: The dialog box also contains edit boxes, using the image tile to assist in setting parameters such as **Slope Rise**, **Slope Run,** and **Rafter Depth**. These values are used to calculate the correct roof 3D position by compensating for structural elements.

Pick Cancel to close the *Draw Roof* dialog box.

Using the **Draw Roof...** command prompts to select a start or **Corner point:** (A), **Corner point parallel to ridge:**(B), **Corner point perpendicular to ridge:** (C), and top of wall elevation. An example of the prompting sequence, pick points, and resulting roof design is shown.

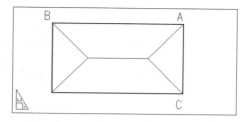

The prompting sequence is:

Draw Hip Roof...

Corner point: **int** of **[point A]**

Corner point parallel to ridge: **int** to **[point B]**

Corner point perpendicular to ridge: **int** to **[point C]**

Top of wall elevation <8'-0">: ↵

After points are selected, Softdesk attempts to find existing walls at the first point pick; if it does, the result is shown as the default for the **Top of wall elevation <default>:**.

SELECTING POINTS USING TRANSPARENT COMMANDS

VIEW ➤ ZOOM ➤ WINDOW

VIEW ➤ ZOOM ➤ PREVIOUS

Choosing the exact corner roof point for large buildings can be very difficult. Selecting the window and previous options of the AutoCAD transparent zoom command can simplify selection.

The Softdesk View pull-down menu automatically invokes transparent zooms by picking **Zoom**, then choosing **Window** or **Previous**.

View	Tools	Walls	Door/Wind	Desi

Zoom		In	zi
Pan		Out	zo
View		Previous	zp
Section		**Window**	**zw**
Redraw		Dynamic	zd
Presentation		Left	zf
AutoVision		Center	zc
CAD Overlay		All	za
Viewports		Limits	zl
Model Space	ms	Extents	ze
Paper Space	ps	.9 Extents	
Color...		Vmax	zm
Linetype		Vmin	
Layer Controls		Scale(X)	
Layer Groups		Scale(XP)	
Layer Tools		Plot Scale	

Note: AutoCAD's transparent commands are invoked by preceding the command with an apostrophe. Invoke the transparent zoom command, then enter the "w" for window (or just pick two points) and "p" for previous.

 AutoCAD Command: 'ZOOM

DRAWING A ROOF USING ROOF GENERATOR

The Roof Generator command draws a 2D, 3D, or 2D and 3D roof including fascia and soffit. The command automatically finds ridges and valleys, given a slope and overhang along each edge of the building perimeter. When selected from the cascading menu, the **Roof Generator** command will draw a complex roof with a uniform or consistent slope. However, complex roofs often have various pitches. The recommended procedures, in these situations, require three basic steps:

1. Choose the **Add Slope Tags** command to automatically place tags at the center of each perimeter segment using an existing polyline or by drawing a new one.

2. Select **Edit Roof Tags**, then pick a specific roof tag or tags to adjust the roof slope and overhang.

3. Select the **Generate Roof** command to set additional values, determine the drawing type (2D, 3D, or both), then draw the final roof slopes.

DRAWING THE ROOF—ADDING SLOPE TAGS

DESIGN ➤ ROOFS ➤ ROOF GENERATOR ➤ ADD SLOPE TAGS

Let's draw a hip roof with a 4/12 slope by picking **Design**, then **Roofs**, then **Roof Generator**, then **Add Slope Tags**. Selecting **Add Slope Tags** prompts to select an existing polyline or draw a new polyline around the building.

Select perimeter polyline or enter to draw:

PROMPTING SUMMARY

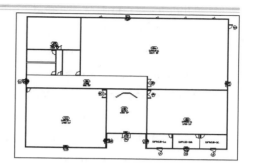

Select perimeter polyline or enter to draw:⏎

Trace building perimeter with polyline...

From point: **'zoom [transparent zoom into entrance area]**

>>Center/Dynamic/Left/Previous/Vmax/Window/<Scale(X/XP)>: **w**

>>First corner: >>Other corner:

From point: **int** of [**bottom right exterior corner of entrance area**]

Arc/Undo/next point (or Arc): **int** of [**top right exterior corner of entrance area**]

Arc/Undo/next point (Arc/Undo): **int** of [**top left exterior corner of entrance area**]

Arc/Undo/next point (Arc/Undo/Close) <Close>: **int** of [**bottom left exterior corner of entrance area**]

Arc/Undo/next point (Arc/Undo/Close) <Close>: **'zoom [transparent zoom]**

>>Center/Dynamic/Left/Previous/Vmax/Window/<Scale(X/XP)>: **p [previous view]**

Resuming .PLINE command.

Arc/Undo/next point (Arc/Undo/Close) <Close>: **'zoom**

>>Center/Dynamic/Left/Previous/Vmax/Window/<Scale(X/XP)>: **w**

>>First corner: >>Other corner:

Resuming .PLINE command.

Arc/Undo/next point (Arc/Undo/Close) <Close>: **int** of [**bottom left exterior corner of building**]

Arc/Undo/next point (Arc/Undo/Close) <Close>: **'zoom**

>>Center/Dynamic/Left/Previous/Vmax/Window/<Scale(X/XP)>: **p**

Resuming .PLINE command.

Arc/Undo/next point (Arc/Undo/Close) <Close>: **'zoom**

>>Center/Dynamic/Left/Previous/Vmax/Window/<Scale(X/XP)>: **w**

>>First corner: >>Other corner:

Resuming .PLINE command.

Arc/Undo/next point (Arc/Undo/Close) <Close>: **int** of [**top left exterior corner of building**]

Arc/Undo/next point (Arc/Undo/Close) <Close>: **'zoom**

>>Center/Dynamic/Left/Previous/Vmax/Window/<Scale(X/XP)>: **p**

Resuming .PLINE command.

Arc/Undo/next point (Arc/Undo/Close) <Close>: **'zoom**

>>Center/Dynamic/Left/Previous/Vmax/Window/<Scale(X/XP)>: **w**

>>First corner: >>Other corner:

Resuming .PLINE command.

Arc/Undo/next point (Arc/Undo/Close) <Close>: **int** of [**top right exterior corner of building**]

Arc/Undo/next point (Arc/Undo/Close) <Close>: **'zoom**

>>Center/Dynamic/Left/Previous/Vmax/Window/<Scale(X/XP)>: **p**

Resuming .PLINE command.

Arc/Undo/next point (Arc/Undo/Close) <Close>: **'zoom**

>>Center/Dynamic/Left/Previous/Vmax/Window/<Scale(X/XP)>: **w**

>>First corner: >>Other corner:

Resuming .PLINE command.

Arc/Undo/next point (Arc/Undo/Close) <Close>: **int** of [**bottom right exterior corner of building**]

Arc/Undo/next point (Arc/Undo/Close) <Close>: **'zoom**

>>Center/Dynamic/Left/Previous/Vmax/Window/<Scale(X/XP)>: **p**

Resuming .PLINE command.

Arc/Undo/next point (Arc/Undo/Close) <Close>: **c**

Accept the **enter to draw** option by pressing Enter and trace the exterior building perimeter walls using the transparent zoom command to accurately pick corners.

Select perimeter polyline or enter to draw:↵
Trace building perimeter with polyline...

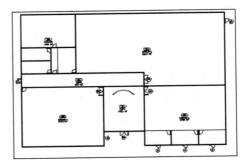

Zoom into the front of the building near the entrance and select the first point at the exterior right bottom corner, then proceed counterclockwise to the bottom left exterior corner using an object snap mode. (The rubber-banding line identifies the start point.)

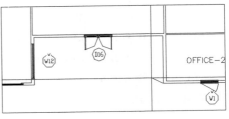

Select corner points by entering the intersection or endpoint object snap mode from the keyboard, cursor menu, or pull-down menu.

From point: 'zoom [zoom invoked transparently]
>>Center/Dynamic/Left/Previous/Vmax/Window/<Scale(X/XP)>: **w**
>>First corner: >>Other corner: [**see figure below**]
From point: int of [**start point, shown by rubber-banding line is bottom right exterior
                    corner of entry area**]
Arc/Undo/next point (or Arc): **int** of [**top right exterior corner**]
Arc/Undo/next point (Arc/Undo): **int** of [**top left exterior corner**]
Arc/Undo/next point (Arc/Undo/Close) <Close>: **int** of [**bottom left exterior corner**]

Zoom into the lower left corner of the plan to select the polyline's next point.

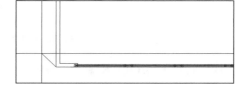

Arc/Undo/next point (Arc/Undo/Close) <Close>: **'zoom**
[**zooming transparently to next location at bottom left
exterior corner of the plan**]
>>Center/Dynamic/Left/Previous/Vmax/Window/<Scale(X/XP)>: **p [previous option of
                                                       zoom command]**

Resuming .PLINE command.
Arc/Undo/next point (Arc/Undo/Close) <Close>: **'zoom**

Continue invoking the transparent zoom commands until all exterior corners are selected. At the bottom right corner of the building, close the polyline by entering C.

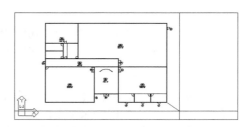

Resuming .PLINE command.
Arc/Undo/next point (Arc/Undo/Close) <Close>: **c**

The *Roof Slope Tags* dialog box opens after the perimeter tracing procedure is completed to set the **Tag insertion mode, Common Slope:,** and **Common Overhang:.**

Choose **Automatic** for the tag insertion mode, then enter the values for slope and overhang as shown.

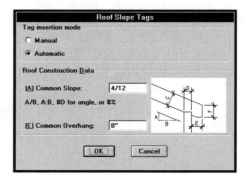

Dialog box:

Common Slope: **4/12**
Common Overhang: **8"**

 Pick OK.

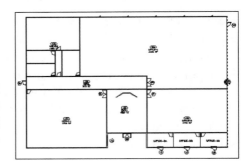

The roof slope tags automatically insert one at a time for each exterior wall length. The figure shows the first of eight tags placed along the right side center portion of the exterior building wall.

DRAWING THE ROOF—EDITING ROOF TAGS

DESIGN ➤ ROOFS ➤ ROOF GENERATOR ➤ EDIT SLOPE TAGS

Slope Tags

After all the roof tags are inserted, select **Edit Slope Tags** from **Roof Generator** under **Roofs** in the Design pull-down menu to edit slopes along the front of the building.

 Select the roof slope tag located near the curtain wall along the front of the building in OFFICE-1 and the *Edit Slope Tag* dialog box opens.

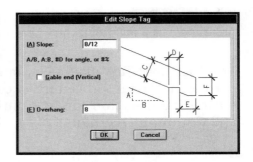

Change the slope to 8/12, then enter a value of 8 in the **Overhang:** edit box to change the roof slope along the front of the building. **Gable end (Vertical)** should remain unchecked so that the roofs are drawn sloped. Select the roof slope tag at the opposite front face of the building (near OFFICE-2B) and set the same values.

 Dialog box:

Slope: **8/12**
Overhang: **8**

PROMPTING SUMMARY

Select slope tag <done>: **[pick roof tag along front of building in OFFICE-1]**

Select slope tag <done>: **[pick roof tag along front of building in OFFICE-2B]**

Select slope tag <done>:⏎

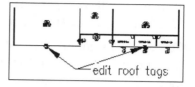

DRAWING THE ROOF—CREATING THE ROOF SURFACES

DESIGN ➤ ROOFS ➤ ROOF GENERATOR ➤ GENERATE ROOFS

To draw the 3D roof surfaces, select **Generate Roofs**, and at the **Select perimeter polyline or enter to draw:** prompt, pick the existing polyline created with the **Add Slope Tags** command. The *Roof Generator* dialog box will open to set controls for the roof's design.

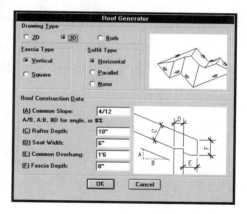

Note: Although several lines overlap along the exterior wall line, a single pick should find the polyline.

The image tile includes letters which correspond with specific edit boxes.

 Dialog box:

Drawing Type:	**3D**
Fascia Type:	**Vertical**
Soffit Type:	**Horizontal**
(A) Common Slope:	**4/12**
(B) Rafter Depth:	**10"**
(C) Seat Width:	**6"**
(D) Common Overhang:	**1'6"**
(E) Fascia Depth:	**8"**

Pick OK and the 3D roof is generated as prompts appear at the command line. Enter 10' when requested for **Top of wall height** and "No" at **Select cutting areas to project.**

Top of wall height <8'-0">: **10'**
Select cutting areas to project <No>:⏎

If a dormer, skylight, or interior court were defined within the roof, choosing a cutting area to project automatically creates the desired opening within the selected area. The resulting roof design will be shown later in elevation and isometric views.

PROMPTING SUMMARY

Select perimeter polyline or enter to draw: **[pick existing polyline]**

Top of wall height <8'-0">: **10'**

Select cutting areas to project <No>:⏎

Reading roof information from rooftags...

Processing...

7

Finding intersections...

7-7

Merging co-planars...

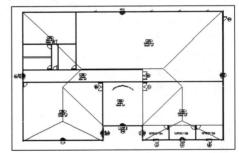

ROOF SLOPE TAGS

An enlarged view of a roof slope tag is shown with the attribute value 4/12 defining the roof slope or pitch for the specified wall segment.

The *Roof Slope Tags* dialog box offers settings to adjust roof slope values. The **Tag insertion mode** section of the *Roof Slope Tags* dialog box contains radio buttons to control the method of setting slope tags.

Choosing the radio button for **Manual** insertion prompts for slope and overhang at each perimeter roof line segment at the command line.

Slope <4/12>:

Overhang (or ?) <1'-6">:

Selecting **Automatic** inserts tags without prompting, based on slope and the overhang settings entered in the **Roof Construction Data** section.

The **Roof Construction Data** section contains edit boxes to set **Common Slope:** and **Common Overhang:**. Common slopes can be set using Rise over Run, Rise to Run, angular measures, or percentage of slope formats as described in the following table.

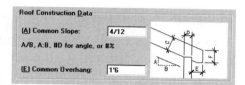

Roof Slope Formats

Format	Example	Description
A/B	4/12	Vertical Rise over Horiontal Run
A:B	4:12	Vertical Rise to Horizontal Run
#d	45d	# Represents angular measure of roof slope. (Include "d" or "D" after the number)
#%	3%	Percentage of roof slope (Include the % sign after the number)

ROOF EDITING COMMAND OVERVIEW

DESIGN ➤ ROOFS ➤ ROOF EDIT

Selecting **Roof Edit** from the **Roofs** menu under the Design pull-down menu displays commands to cut hip roofs into existing gable roofs, join two gable roofs, fill roof voids, extend, trim, and hide faces.

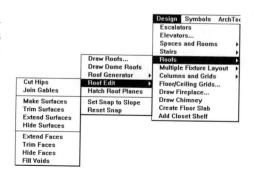

Depending on the roof design, procedures to draw a roof may require drawing multiple roofs of various types, editing slope tags, then invoking the **Generate Roof** command to remove or add slope lines and hide surfaces.

The Four Roof Commands in Upper Portion of Roof Edit Menu

Cut Hips joints a hip roof with an exiting gable roof.

Join Gables extends or trims one of two 4-pointed face(s) of a roof into an adjacent face.

Make Surfaces is used to fill a void in a completed roof.

Trim Surfaces helps to trim a roof polymesh at the implied *intersection line* formed with a second polymesh.

Extend Surfaces extends a roof polymesh to an existing adjacent roof polymesh.

Hide Surfaces changes edge visibility of a polymesh.

Cut Hips
Join Gables
Make Surfaces
Trim Surfaces
Extend Surfaces
Hide Surfaces
Extend Faces
Trim Faces
Hide Faces
Fill Voids

The Four Roof Commands in Lower Portion of Roof Edit Menu

Extend Faces, **Trim Faces**, **Hide Faces**, and **Fill Voids** shown at the lower portion of the **Roof Edit** menu differ from those in the upper portion in that they operate on simple-faced rather than roof polymesh entities.

VIEWING THE ROOF

VIEW ➤ VIEW ➤ VIEW PRESETS...

Select **View Presets...** from the **View** menu under the View pull-down menu to look at the new hip roof in elevation and isometric views.

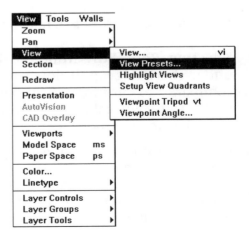

View Presets... opens the *Preset and Currently Defined Views* dialog box to display a **Views** list box.

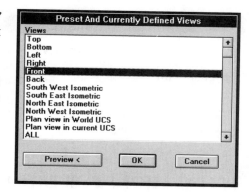

    Choose Front from the list box, then pick **Preview<** or OK to view the front of the building.

The front of the building is shown with the hip roof in elevation view.

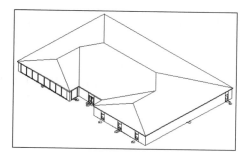

    Select **View Presets...** and highlight South East Isometric, then pick OK to view the building in isometric view.

HIDING LINES

Enter the Macro **HI** to display the entire building with interior objects hidden.

Macro Command: HI

(AutoCAD command: **HIDE**)

Command: **hi**
Macro: Hide

RESTORING THE CURRENT UCS PLAN VIEW

Restore the current UCS plan view by invoking the Macro **PN**.

Macro Command: **PN**

(AutoCAD Command: **PLAN**)

Command: **pn**
Macro: Plan
<Current UCS>/Ucs/World:⏎
Regenerating drawing.

PREPARATIONS FOR EXTRACTING A 2D ELEVATION

Door and window blocks as well as line entities can be extracted from a floor plan to automatically create a 2D elevation or section. The results can be placed in either the current drawing or a new drawing. After generating the elevation, extracted entities usually require editing to enhance as well as complete the result. Prior to creating the elevation, let's freeze some tag layers and convert wall lines to faces.

Zoom out to display the entire plan as shown and provide space below the plan to draw a 2D elevation of the building's front facade.

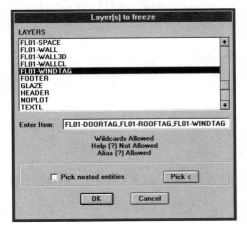

FREEZING LAYERS

Invoke the Macro **LZ** to display the *Layer(s) to Freeze* dialog box and scroll through the layers list box, then pick FL01-DOORTAG and the name appears in the **Enter Item:** edit box. Repeat the procedure to locate FL01-ROOFTAG and FL01-WINDTAG, then pick OK. The dialog box closes and continues to reopen for additional selections. Pick OK to exit from the dialog box by not entering a layer name in the **Edit Item:** edit box.

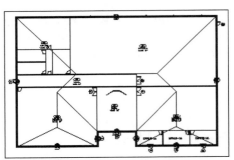

 Macro Command: **LZ**

Command: **lz**
Macro: Layer Freeze

CONVERTING AND RESTORING WALL LINES TO FACES

WALLS ➤ WALL EDIT ➤ CONVERT WALL LINES TO FACES

Prior to extracting a two-dimensional elevation from the plan, Softdesk suggests, but does not require, converting the wall lines to 3D faces. This eliminates the vertical lines above doors and windows formed by the header lines to improve the appearance of renderings.

The **Convert Wall Lines to Faces** command, located in the Walls pull-down menu under **Wall Edit**, opens the *Facewall - Convert* dialog box.

The *Facewall - Convert* dialog box contains three major sections. The **Conversion Drawing Options** section offers options to perform the conversion in the current drawing or in a new drawing.

Checking boxes in the **Include_Headers Footers** section determines if new or existing layer names are applied during conversion.

The **3D Face Creation** section sets controls to **Replace Lines, Keeping Lines, Designate Layer** name, and **Use Same Layers**. When **Hide Top Edge** and **Hide Bottom Edge** are toggled, the 3D face lines are hidden.

The **Convert to Faces** command in the Wall Edit menu restores all extended walls from faces created by the **Convert Wall Lines to Faces** command.

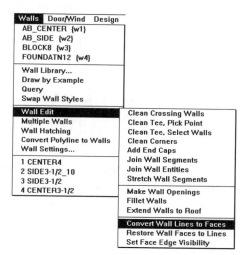

Dialog box (toggle radio buttons for):

Proceed in Current Drawing
Use Layer Names from Default File
Replace Lines
Use Same Layers

The prompting sequence is:

FACEWALL - Convert extruded wall lines to 3DFaces...
Select a wall line: **[pick any interior wall line]**
Add/Remove/Choose/Manual/Single/Done <Done>:⏎
Finding headers and footers...
Replacing lines with 3DFaces...Done.

EXTRACTING THE 2D ELEVATION

ARCHTOOLS ➤ EXTRACT 2D ELEVATION

Select **Extract 2D Elevation** from the ArchTools pull-down menu to draw a two-dimensional elevation from the 3D lines, polylines, faces, and door/window units.

> **bols** | **ArchTools** | ⬍
> Draw Symbol by Example
> Query Symbol
> Block Swap
> Adjust Symbol
> Symbol 2D<->3D
>
> Place Wall Dimensions
> Framing Notation...
> Calculate Wall Area
> Draw Shadows
>
> **Extract 2D Elevation**
> Extract 2D Section
> Schedules ▶
> Annotation ▶
>
> Energy
>
> Auto-Architect Settings...

PROMPTING SUMMARY

Creating Elevation...

Select objects to be in the elevation...

Select objects: **w [window facade at OFFICE-1]**

First corner: Other corner: 19 found

Select objects: **w [window facade at ENTRY (the number of objects found may vary depending on the selection method)]**

First corner: Other corner: 13 found

Select objects: **w [window facade at OFFICE-2A, 2B and 2C]**

First corner: Other corner: 39 found

Select objects: 1 found **[pick a roof line]**

Select objects: 1 found **[pick a roof line]**

Select objects: 1 found **[pick a roof line]**

Select objects: 1 found **[pick a roof line]**

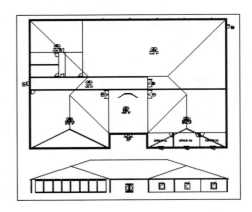

Select objects: 1 found **[pick a roof line]**

Select objects:↵

Viewing angle or look from (Right/Left/Front/Back) <Front>:↵

Pick base point near elevation: **int** of **[lower left exterior corner of building]**

Wblock elevation to another file <No>:↵

Processing elements...

Translating points...

Insertion point: [pick location for elevation]

Using a selection set consisting of three crossing windows (or a crossing polygon), pick points enclosing the facade portions of the building as shown. Include exterior walls containing the entire curtain wall area in OFFICE-1, the entry doors, and the exterior casement window areas of three smaller office spaces in the selection set, then pick all the roof lines as shown.

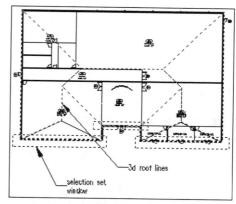

Select objects to be in the elevation...
Select objects:

Press enter to view the elevation from the front of the building.

Viewing angle or look from (Right/Left/Front/Back) <Front>:↵

Select a base point near the lower left exterior corner of the building plan.

Pick base point near elevation:

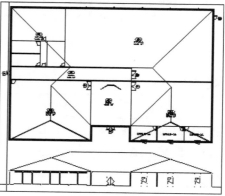

Insert the elevation into the current drawing by accepting the default.

Wblock elevation to another file <No>:↵

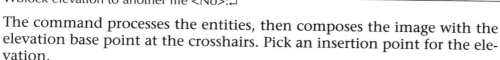

The command processes the entities, then composes the image with the elevation base point at the crosshairs. Pick an insertion point for the elevation.

Insertion point:

Although the command extracts 2D and 3D blocks to create the elevation as line entities, editing is required. Elevational symbols such as trees, cars, and people can be selected from the **Palette** pop-up list in the *Symbol Manager*

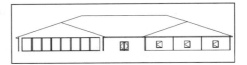

dialog box. Choose any command in the Symbols pull-down menu and pick Auto-Architect Symbol File for the **Symbol Set** and Site for the **Category** .

Note: Notice that the extruded lines that normally appear above and below door and/or window headers and footers were removed. Final appearance of the extraction may differ depending on the objects selected.

ROOF LAYERS

ARCHTOOLS ➤ AUTO-ARCHITECT SETTINGS... ➤ LAYERS

The roof layers are stored in the *Layer Settings* dialog box. Selecting **Auto-Architect Settings...** from the ArchTools pull-down menu and choosing **Layers...** will show you the roof layer descriptions and names. The table identifies the layers created to draw the 3D roof. We will be adding additional levels to the building and moving the 3D roof surfaces in Chapter 21.

ROOF LAYERS

Layer Name	Linetype	Color	Description
FL01-ROOFSOF	Continuous	20	3D roof fascia and soffit
FL01-ROOFTAG	Continuous	1	Roof slope information
FL01-3DROOF	Continuous	7	3D Roof faces

Save the drawing, then proceed to Chapter 20 where annotations and tags will be inserted into the drawing along with plumbing fixtures in the men's and women's restrooms, in Chapter 21.

CHAPTER TWENTY

ANNOTATIONS

Adding Leadered Notes and Reference Tags

Contents

Annotations are available from the ArchTools ,Tools, and Symbols pull-down menus. ArchTools commands offer special architectural notation features. The Tools pull-down menu offers commands that create or edit objects in a drawing. The **Annotation** menu under Tools includes symbols and text with leader lines as well as various reference markers. Annotations under the Symbols pull-down menu consist primarily of labels or tags and will be discussed in Chapter 21. This chapter provides a brief overview using some simple exercises from annotations in the ArchTools and Tools pull-down menus.

ANNOTATIONS

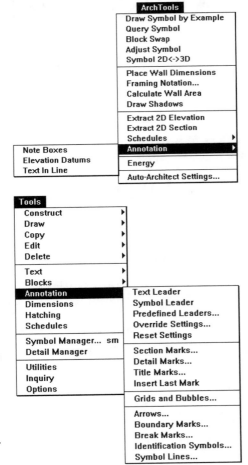

The ArchTools menu is unique to the Auto-Architect module and provides commands to draw **Note Boxes**, **Elevation Datums**, and **Text In Line**. **Note Boxes** draw rectangular shapes with shadow edges on two sides. The **Elevation Datum** symbol is used to define a floor level or elevation. The symbol is drawn as a partially filled circle with a line extending from a quad point and related text. The **Text In Line** command creates short line segments separated with text. The command can be used to define a property line with the text "PL" placed between line segments.

The Tools menu is part of Softdesk's Core application. These commands draw notations and reference labels consisting of text leaders and markers as listed in the pull-down menu.

ARCHTOOLS ➤ ANNOTATION

The ArchTools pull-down menu draws the annotation commands shown.

TOOLS ➤ ANNOTATION

The Tools pull-down menu draws the annotation commands shown.

ANNOTATION SETTINGS

FILE ➤ PROJECT SETTINGS... ➤ ANNOTATION...

The Project Settings... command is located under the File pull-down menu. This opens the *Project Settings* dialog box to set the controls for projects. Selecting the **Annotation....** pick box opens the *Annotation Settings* dialog box.

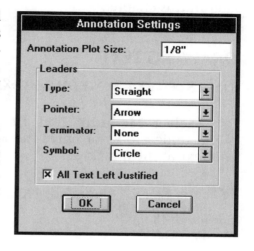

The *Annotation Settings* dialog box contains an edit box to globally set the **Annotation Plot Size,** adjusting the size in plotted units of parametrically generated symbols such as leaders, break marks, and so forth. The text height of all tag symbols is also affected by this value.

The **Leaders** sections offer options to draw leaders lines as described:

Type:
When the **Text Leader** or **Symbol Leader** commands are chosen, selecting straight or arc from the pop-up list sets the type of leader drawn.

Pointer:
Sets the type of pointer for the **Text Leader** or **Symbol Leader** commands. Point types include Arrow, Dot, Tick, Tilde, Tilde/Arrow, Loop, Bar, and None.

Terminator:
Pick None, Bar, or Tail from the pop-up list as the leader type drawn adjacent to text for the **Text Leader** command.

Symbol:
Choosing Circle, Square, Hex, or Diamond from the pop-up list inserts the symbol with the **Symbol Leader** command.

Toggling the check box sets **All Text Left Justified** for the **Text Leader** command when drawing leadered text right to left or left to right. When this setting is off, multiple lines of text are left-justified when the leader is drawn from left to right (head to tail), but right-justified when the leader is drawn from right to left. The example shown is drawn using the **Text Leader** command discussed later in this chapter.

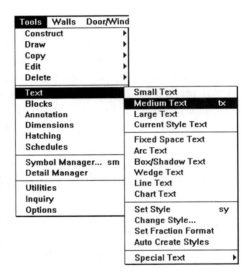

• • • • • • • • • • •

DRAWING TEXT

TOOLS ➤ TEXT ➤ MEDIUM TEXT

  Select **Medium Text** from the **Text** menu under Tools or enter the Macro **TX** to add text to the drawing.

Macro Command: **TX**

Command: **TX**
Macro: DText

Pick a point at the upper left corner of the note box, then enter the heading GENERAL NOTES followed by two notes as listed in the prompting summary. Pressing enter without typing text at the **Text:** prompt exits the command.

PROMPTING SUMMARY

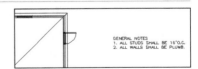

Command: **tx**

Macro: Text

Justify/Style/<Start point>: **[pick a point at top left corner of note box]**

Height <0'-9">:↵

Rotation angle <0.00>:↵

Text: **GENERAL NOTES**

Text: 1. **ALL STUDS SHALL BE 16" O.C.**

Text: 2. **ALL WALLS SHALL BE PLUMB.**

Text:↵

DRAWING A NOTE BOX

ARCHTOOLS ➤ ANNOTATION ➤ NOTE BOXES

Zoom into the upper portion of the floor plan to draw a note box.

Select **Note Boxes** under **Annotation** in the ArchTools pull-down menu and the command prompts to select two points. Select points, from the lower left to the upper right, to draw a shadow box with wide edges along the bottom and right side.

PROMPTING SUMMARY

Graphic Rectangle for Boxed Notes...

First Corner: **[pick lower left point]**

Other Corner: **[pick upper point right]**

Note: Each edge width is 2/5 the annotation plot size times the drawing scale and can be adjusted in the Annotation Settings dialog box.

DRAWING LEADERED TEXT

TOOLS ➤ ANNOTATION ➤ TEXT LEADER

Select **Text Leader** from the **Annotation** menu under the Tools pull-down menu to draw leadered text. As previously discussed earlier, leader types are set in the *Annotation Settings* dialog box.

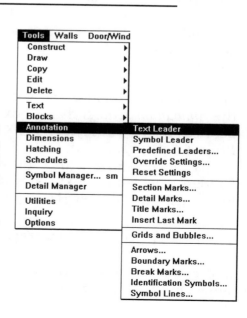

Note: Leader lines automatically append short-line horizontal segments to the end of the last leader line drawn.

PROMPTING SUMMARY

Arrow point: **[pick start point near roof line]**

To point: **[pick second point (short segment added automatically)]**

To point:↵

Text: **EDGE OF ROOF LINE**

Text:↵

Arrow point:↵

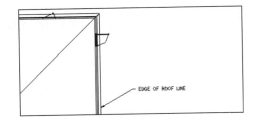

DRAWING TITLE MARKS

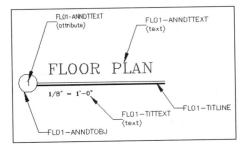

Mark symbols consist of a circle, lines, text, and an attribute on layers as shown. Root layer names are defined in the ZZSDESK.LY file stored in the \SDSKPROJ\ARCHTUT (project)\directory. Selecting File, then **Project Settings...**, then **Layers...** would open the *Layer Settings* dialog box and allow editing of the root layer names. The layers are located in the Annotation section. FL01 represents the layer group component for Level discussed in Chapter 10.

The attribute and circle are separate objects that can be adjusted from the *Annotation Settings* dialog box. The height of the title and scale are defined in the text style TITTEXTL and can be modified by selecting **Project Settings...** in the File pull-down menu. Picking **Text Styles...** opens the *Text Style Settings* dialog box displaying information about Softdesk's predefined text styles stored in the ZZSTYLE.DAT file located in the \SDSKPROJ\ ARCHTUT (project)\ directory.

TOOLS ➤ ANNOTATION ➤ TITLE MARKS... ➤ MARKA1

Add a title mark symbol below the floor plan near the entrance as shown in the figure at the bottom of page 377.

Select **Title Marks...** from the Tools pull-down menu, under **Annotation** to open the **Title Marks** icon box. Choose the **MarkA1** icon, then pick OK.

Select a start point to place the symbol when prompted for **Bubble point:**, then pick a second point toward the right. Toggle ortho-mode on by pressing the F8 function key. The *Edit Attributes* dialog box opens next to enter a value for the mark number, then pick OK and the command line returns to enter a title and scale.

PROMPTING SUMMARY

Bubble point: [**pick point toward left of entrance area**]

To point: [**press F8 to toggle orthomode on, then pick point toward the right side of plan and** *Edit Attributes* **dialog box opens.**]

Title: **FLOOR PLAN**

Scale <1/8" = 1'-0">:↵

Bubble point:↵

Accept the default value in the **Number** edit box, then pick OK.

Type FLOOR PLAN as the **Title:** prompt appears and press enter to accept the default value for the drawing scale.

 Command line:

Title: **FLOOR PLAN**
Scale <1/8" = 1'-0">:↵

Finally, to exit the command press Enter at the **Bubble point:** prompt.

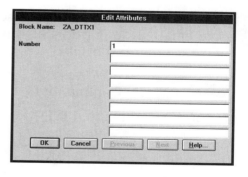

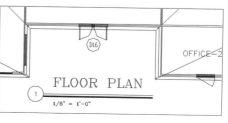

TEXT OVERVIEW

Softdesk prototype drawings SDSK_I and SDSK_M contain three default text sizes defined with the Romans.shx font. Each style of text will be drawn on a different layer so the plotted pen width can be controlled by the layer color. Small text is drawn 6" high on layer TEXTS, medium text is set to 9" high on layer TEXTM, and large text is 24" high created on the TEXTL layer. Invoking the text command sets the specific layer name current. Review Chapter 8 for additional information on text layers, special fonts, and text styles.

Entering the Softdesk List Layer macro **LL** and selecting the text "**GENERAL NOTES**" in the Note Box displays the text screen and describes layer information for the text.

 Macro Command: **LL**

(AutoCAD Command: **LIST**)

Command: **LL**
Macro: List Layer
Layer ---> FL01-TEXTM
Next object <done>:↵

Typing the List macro **LI** and selecting "**GENERAL NOTES**" offers a more detailed description of the text, including the layer name, text style, font file, and height.

 Macro Command: **LI**

(AutoCAD Command: **LIST**)

Command: **LI**
Macro: List
Select objects: 1 found
Select objects:↵
 TEXT Layer: FL01-TEXTM
 Space: Model space
 Handle = 509A
 Style = TEXTM Font file = romans.shx

start point, X=206'-7 1/4" Y=130'-4 1/16" Z= 0'-0"

height 0'-9"

text GENERAL NOTES

rotation angle 0.00

width scale factor 1.000000

obliquing angle 0.00

generation normal

This short review should help you find and apply the appropriate annotations for your needs. Save the drawing, then continue to Chapter 21 to learn the procedures for drawing symbols.

CHAPTER TWENTY-ONE

SYMBOLS

Drawing 2D and 3D Plumbing Fixtures

Contents

The Symbol Manager primarily contains symbols such as Appliances, Furniture, and Equipment which represent real objects. The Annotation symbols menu includes tags used to label rooms, doors, or walls. This chapter explores objects created with the **Plumbing...** command. Symbols such as toilet stalls, counters with lavatories, and urinals will be drawn by selecting **Plumbing...** from the Symbols pull-down menu. The Symbols pull-down menu, however, can be changed to display only the more frequently used objects.

SYMBOLS OVERVIEW

Softdesk's architectural symbols are controlled with the **Symbol Manager...** and **Symbol Settings...** commands. **Symbol Manager...** , selected from the Symbol pull-down menu, opens the *Symbol Manager* dialog box for choices to **Add**, **Copy**, **Move**, **Edit**, and **Delete** symbols. The **Symbol Settings...** command can be selected from either the File, Symbols, or ArchTools pull-down menus as indicated here:

ARCHTOOLS ➤ AUTO-ARCHITECT SETTINGS... ➤ SYMBOLS...

FILE>PROJECT SETTINGS... ➤ (AUTO-ARCHITECT) EDIT... ➤ SYMBOLS...

SYMBOLS ➤ SYMBOL SETTINGS...

Picking the command opens the *Symbol Settings* dialog box listing **Symbol Menu Items** for Categories and Palettes that can be drawn in 2D and/or 3D (when available). Checking **Insert 3D Symbols** toggles 2D/3D symbol insertion on and off. Selecting **Symbol 2D<->3D** from the ArchTool menu swaps two-dimensional symbols with three-dimensional symbols.

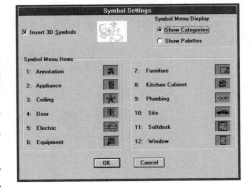

Radio buttons in the **Symbol Menu Display** section offer options to **Show Palettes** or **Show Categories** for **Symbol Menu Items**. These toggles change the commands offered in the Symbols pull-down menu.

When **Show Palettes** is enabled, the Symbols pull-down menu appears with the same commands shown in the *Symbol Settings* dialog box.

Picking **Show Palettes** replaces the 12 descriptions for the **Special Menu Items**. For example, item 1 is listed as Annotation when **Show Categories** is selected and Room Tags when **Show Palettes** is chosen.

Normally the Categories option should be used for general work. An interior designer, for example, might only work with furniture symbols; therefore, it would not be more productive to have the Symbol pull-down menu listing "Furniture" rather than "Site" commands.

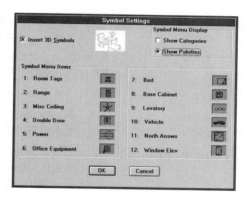

When **Show Categories** is enabled, the Symbols pull-down menu appears with the same commands shown .

Picking an image tile in the **Special Menu Items** Section, when **Show Palette** is enabled, opens the *Symbol Manager* dialog box.

The following table identifies the **Palettes** available for each **Category** when **Auto-Arch Symbol File** is selected from the **Symbol Set:** pop-up list.

Auto-Arch Symbol File

Category	*Palette*
Annotation	Bar scale, Door/Window Tags, Finish Tags, Misc Annotation and Object Tags
Appliance	Dishwasher, Misc Appliance, Refrigerator, and Range
Ceiling	Misc Ceiling
Door	Double Door, Double Door M (metric), Single Door, Single Door M (metric)
Electric	Communication, Exit Sign, Fluorescent, Incandescent, Misc. Electric, Power, Switch, and Track Light
Equipment	Misc Equipment and Office Equipment
Furniture	Bed, Bookcase, Chair, Credenza, Desk, File, Lamp, Misc. Furniture, Panel, and Plants
Kitchen Cabinet	12in High Wall, 15in High Wall, 18in High Wall, 24in High Wall, 30in High Wall, Base Cabinet, Base with drawer, Cabinet Doors, Cabinet Handles, and Corner Cabinet
Plumbing	Bath, Bath Elevation, Drains, Fountain, Grab Bar, Lavatory, Lavatory Elevation, Misc. Plumbing, Plumbing Accessory, and Shower
Site	Boats, Misc. Site, Parking, People, Scale Figure, Signs, Sports, Tree, Tree Elevation, and Utilities

The next table identifies the **Palettes** available for each **Category** when **Annotation Symbols** is selected from the **Symbol Set:** pop-up list.

Annotation

Category	*Palette*
Softdesk	Arrows, Circles, Dim Pointer, Hexagons, Miscellaneous, North Arrows and Squares

SETTING CONTROLS FOR 3D SYMBOLS

SYMBOLS ➤ SYMBOL SETTINGS...

Select **Symbol Settings...** from the Symbols pull-down menu to open the *Symbol Settings* dialog box and verify that **Insert 3D Symbols is checked.**

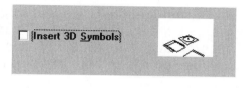

The image box changes the 2D furniture icon to 3D.

Pick OK.

Note: If Insert 3D symbols is not checked and 2D symbols have been inserted, 2D blocks will continue to be inserted. Erasing the symbols and checking Insert 3D symbols will not insert the new symbols in 3D because the 2D blocks exist in the drawing. To change all existing and newly inserted symbols from 2D to 3D select **Symbol 2D<->3D** from the ArchTools pull-down menu and choose a 2D symbol.

The prompting sequence is:

Convert symbols from 2D to 3D or vice versa...
Select blocks to be converted (RETURN for all)...
Select objects: 1 found **[select all 2D symbols to change to 3D]**
Select objects:↵
Convert to (3d/2d) <3d>:↵
Redefining Symbols...
Insert all future symbols in 3d <Yes>:↵ **[all existing and new symbols will now be inserted in 3D]**

Zoom into the SERVICE space at the top left corner of the building and draw the plumbing fixtures as specified in the exercises.

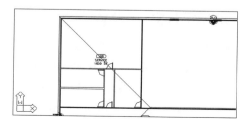

DRAWING MULTIPLE TOILET STALLS

In this exercise, plumbing fixtures will be drawn in the lower space designated as the men's restroom and the upper space, assigned as the women's restroom. A wheel chair (handicap) stall, multiple ambulatory stalls, standard stalls, and countertop with lavatories include some of the symbols that will be drawn. Procedures include opening dialog boxes to select objects and set controls, then selecting points and orientations to draw them.

Select **Plumbing...** from the Symbols pull-down menu to open the *Symbol Manager* dialog box and draw multiple toilet stalls in the two smaller rooms.

In the following exercises, four stalls will be drawn in the upper space (women's restroom) and two stalls with two urinals in the lower space (men's restroom). Draw a counter with two lavatories in both spaces.

Toilet Stalls for the Women's Restroom

Choose the **Symbol Set:** for Auto-Arch Symbol File, then select Plumbing as the **Category** and Toilet from the **Palette** pop-up list.

The icon menu is:

Symbol Set:	Auto-Arch Symbol File
Category:	Plumbing
Palette:	Toilet
Image button	multi-stall

Double-click on the multi-stall image button to open the *Multiple Stalls* dialog box.

PROMPTING SUMMARY

Starting point on back wall: int of **[lower left interior intersection]**

Direction along back wall: <Ortho on> **[pick point to right]**

Inserting WC Tank 1 at Floor elevation=0".

Inserting Grab Bar 36 at GRABBAR elevation=3'-0".

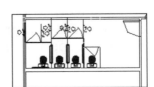

Inserting Grab Bar 40 at GRABBAR elevation=3'-0".

Select wheelchair stall door hinge point: **[pick left X mark]**

Inserting WC Tank 1 at Floor elevation=0".

Inserting Grab Bar 42 at GRABBAR elevation=3'-0".

Inserting Grab Bar 42 at GRABBAR elevation=3'-0".

Select alternate stall door hinge point: **[pick left X mark]**

Inserting WC Tank 1 at Floor elevation=0".

Inserting Grab Bar 42 at GRABBAR elevation=3'-0".

Inserting Grab Bar 42 at GRABBAR elevation=3'-0".

Inserting WC Tank 1 at Floor elevation=0".

Select standard stall hinge point: **[pick bottom left X mark]**

Multi-stall draws a row of toilets specified by values entered in edit boxes for **Quantity**, **Width**, **Length**, and **Door Width**.

Specify a row consisting of one Wheel chair, two Ambulatory, and one Standard toilet stalls in the women's restroom.

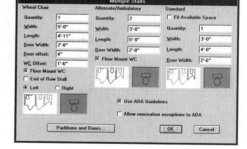

 Dialog box:

Wheel Chair		Alternate/Ambulatory		Standard	
Quantity:	**1**	Qualtity:	**2**	Quantity:	**1**
Width:	**5'-0"**	Width:	**3'-0"**	Width:	**3'-0"**
Length:	**4'-11"**	Length:	**5'-9"**	Length:	**4'-0"**
Door Width:	**2'-8"**	Door Width:	**2'-8"**	Door Width:	**2'-6"**
Door Offset:	**4"**				
WC Offset:	**1'-6"**				

Toggle **Use ADA Guidelines** so that Softdesk checks compliance of stall dimensions while the command is processing. **Allow renovation exceptions to ADA** , which controls whether standard ADA guidelines or ADA renovation exceptions are used to check the stall setting dimensions, should remain unchecked.

Check **Floor Mount WC** (water closet) to install floor-mounted toilets and **Left** to set the stall orientation. Picking the radio button for **Right** and the check box for **End of Row Stall** displays selected toilet stall configurations in the image box. This setting changes automatically whenever a different toilet is selected. Softdesk looks for the words "floor" or "wall" in the symbol's extended description. This toggle can be thought of as an override to be applied if required, which would allow using a "wall" mount symbol but calling it floor-mounted for purposes of the stall length calculation.

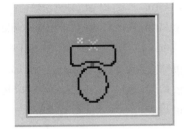

Picking an image button opens the *Symbol Manager* dialog box to select a new symbol.

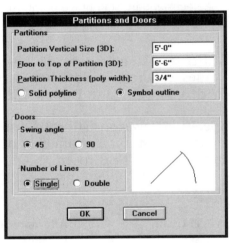

 Pick **Partitions and Doors...** to open the *Partitions and Doors* dialog box. Stall height is set with **Partition Vertical Size (3D):. Floor to Top of Partition (3D):** determines the distance between the bottom of the partition and the floor. **Partition Thickness (poly width):** controls the partition's width. The **Partitions** section offers radio buttons to draw the partition as a **Solid polyline** or **Symbol outline**.

Toggle the **Symbol outline** radio button, then set values in the **Partitions** section as follows:

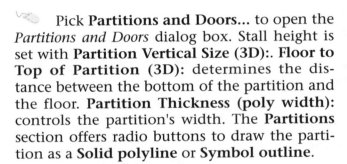 Dialog box:

Partition Vertical Size (3D):	**5'-0"**
Floor to Top of Partition (3D):	**6'-6"**
Partition Thickness (poly width):	**3/4"**
Swing angle	45
Number of lines	Single

Select the **45** radio button to set the **Swing angle** and **Single** as the **Number of Lines** drawn for the partition doors.

Pick OK twice to exit dialog boxes, then respond to the prompts at the command line for the start point and direction.

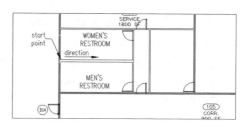

Start at the lower left interior corner of the upper room (labeled as the women's restroom), then pick a point toward the right as shown. (Toggle orthomode on with the F8 function key.)

Starting point on back wall: **int** of
Direction along back wall: <Ortho on>

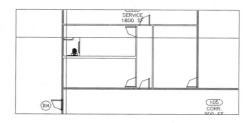

Pick left X mark as the door hinge point for the wheelchair and alternate stalls and the bottom left X mark for the standard stall.

Select wheelchair stall door hinge point:
Select alternate stall door hinge point:
Select standard stall door hinge point:

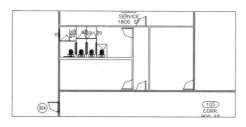

The completed wheel chair, ambulatory, and standard stalls are shown.

Symbols Pull-down Menu for Multi-Stall

Once invoked from the *Symbol Manager* dialog box, current commands are saved for additional selection at the bottom portion of the pull-down menu. Notice that the plumbing fixtures can be selected from **Plumbing...** or the lower portion of the pull-down menu depending on the last object drawn.

Symbols	ArchTools
Annotation...	
Appliance...	
Ceiling...	
Door...	
Electric...	
Equipment...	
Furniture...	
Kitchen Cabinet...	
Plumbing...	
Site...	
Softdesk...	
Window...	
Symbol Manager...	
Symbol Settings...	
1 multi-stall	
2 Grab Bar 42	
3 Grab Bar 40	
4 WC Tank 1	

Toilet Stalls for the Men's Restroom

Next, draw a row of stalls in the men's restroom consisting of one wheel chair and one ambulatory compartment with the similar specifications as the women's restroom.

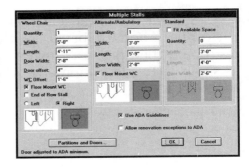

 Dialog box:

Wheel Chair		Alternate/Ambulatory		Standard	
Quantity:	1	Qualtity:	1	Quantity:	0
Width:	5'-0"	Width:	3'-0"	Width:	[greyed out]
Length:	4'-11"	Length:	5'-9"	Length:	[greyed out]
Door Width:	2'-8"	Door Width:	2'-8"	Door Width:	[greyed out]
Door Offset:	4"				
WC Offset:	1'-6"				

Pick the radio button for **Right** in the wheel chair section. All other check boxes are the same as previously selected.

Begin at the upper left corner of the men's restroom and proceed toward the right along the back wall.

PROMPTING SUMMARY

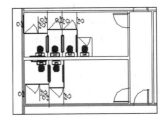

Starting point on back wall: **[pick top left corner of restroom]**

Direction along back wall: <Ortho on> **[pick point to right]**

Inserting WC Tank 1 at Floor elevation=0".

Inserting Grab Bar 36 at GRABBAR elevation=3'-0".

Inserting Grab Bar 40 at GRABBAR elevation=3'-0".

Select wheelchair stall door hinge point: **[pick left X mark]**

Inserting WC Tank 1 at Floor elevation=0".

Inserting Grab Bar 42 at GRABBAR elevation=3'-0".

Inserting Grab Bar 42 at GRABBAR elevation=3'-0".

Select alternate stall door hinge point: **[pick left X mark]**

DRAWING A COUNTER WITH LAVATORIES

SYMBOLS ➤ PLUMBING...

Insert a countertop with back splashes and two lavatories in both restrooms as shown in figure on page 394.

 Select **Plumbing...** from the Symbols pull-down menu to open the *Symbol Manager* dialog box.

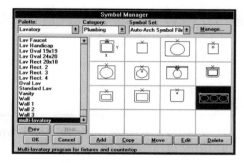

Choose Plumbing as the **Category:** and Auto-Arch Symbol File as the **Symbol Set:**.

Pick Lavatory from the **Palette:** pop-up list, scroll to the bottom of the list, and highlight **multi-lavatory**.

 Icon screen:

Symbol Set:	**Auto-Arch Symbol File**
Category:	**Plumbing**
Palette:	**Lavatory**
(list box)	**multi-lavatory**

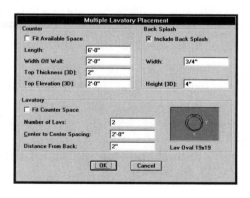

Pick OK and the *Multiple Lavatory Placement* dialog box opens for selection.

Draw a counter 6'-0" wide with two oval 19" x 19" lavatories in both restrooms, starting at the right rear wall of each room.

Note: Enter 2 in the **Number of Lavs** edit box before setting the counter **Length** to avoid an error message.

Dialog box:

Counter

Length:	**6'-0"**
Width Off Wall:	**2'-0"**
Top Thickness(3D):	**2"**

Top Elevation (3D):	**2'-0"**
Fit Available Space	**unchecked**
Back Splash	
Include Back Splash	**checked**
Width:	**3/4"**
Height (3D):	**4"**
Lavatory	
Fit Counter Space	**unchecked**
Number of Lavs:	**2**
Center to Center Spacing:	**2'-0"**
Distance From Back	**2"**

Pick OK.

Note: Notice that the prompt, "This symbol not available in 3D," appears during insertion.

PROMPTING SUMMARY

Start of counter on back wall: int of **[intersection at rear of wall of restoom]**

Direction along wall: <Ortho on> **[pick point toward the left]**

Inserting Lav Oval 19x19 at elevation 0.

This symbol not available in 3D.

Inserting Lav Oval 19x19 at elevation 0.

This symbol not available in 3D.

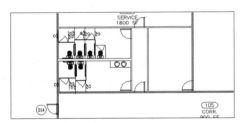

Select the start point for the counter at the top right corner of the men's restroom.

Start of counter on back wall: **int** of

Press F8 to set orthomode on, then pick a point toward the left.

Direction along wall: <Ortho on>

Repeat the command by pressing the spacebar and draw the same countertop in the women's restroom.

DRAWING URINALS WITH SCREENS

SYMBOLS ➤ PLUMBING...

 Change the **Palette:** to Urinal, highlight the multi-urinal image button, and draw two urinals in the men's restroom.

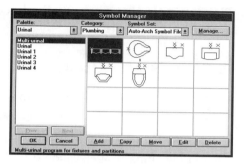

 Icon screen:

Symbol Set:	**Auto-Arch Symbol File**
Category:	**Plumbing**
Palette:	**Urinal**
(list box)	**multi-urinal**

 Double-click on the multi-urinal image button to open the *Multiple Urinal Placement* dialog box.

The dialog box opens to display an image button with a urinal icon. If the current image button name is not shown as Urinal 2, double-click the icon box to reopen the *Symbol Manager* dialog box and click on it.

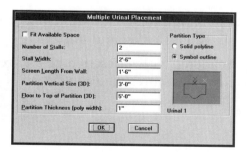

 Pick OK to close the dialog box and return to the *Multiple Urinal Placement* dialog box.

The new Urinal 2 should now appear. Verify the edit box settings, then pick OK.

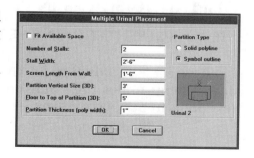

 Dialog box:

Number of Stalls:	**2**
Stall Width:	**2'-6"**
Screen Length From Wall:	**1'-6"**
Partition Vertical Size (3D):	**3'-0"**
Floor to Top of Partition:	**5'-0"**
Partition Thickness (poly width):	**1"**

Fit Available Space should be unchecked and set **Partition Type** to **Symbol outline.**

   Pick OK.

Place urinals along rear wall adjacent to the ambulatory stall by selecting a point and direction.

PROMPTING SUMMARY

Starting point on back wall: **nea** to **[pick point along wall line near stall]**

Direction along wall: <Ortho on> **[pick point toward right]**

Inserting Urinal 1 at elevation 0.

Inserting Urinal 1 at elevation 0.

The completed restrooms are shown with stalls, lavatories, and urinals.

Leadered notes describe reference start points for the countertop and urinal.

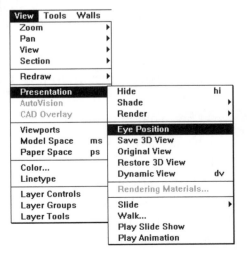

DISPLAYING SPACES IN PERSPECTIVE VIEW

VIEW ➤ PRESENTATION ➤ EYE POSITION

   Select **Eye Position** in the View pull-down menu under **Presentation** to view the restrooms in perspective view.

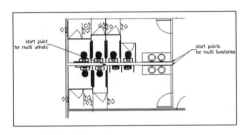

Choose a target point at the left side of the 10-inch wide plumbing wall and an eye point toward the opposite (right) side of the same wall to view the rooms from the entry side. Change the lens length from 30mm to 15mm to view the perspective when the **Lens length in millimeters <30>:** prompt appears.

The prompting sequence is:

Command: sdsk
Eye level is 5'-6", target height is 5'-6", lens mm is 30.
Pick target point in plan (Eye/Target/Lens): **l [type l to change lens length]**
Lens length in millimeters <30>: **15 [setting lens length to 15 millimeters]**
Eye level is 5'-6", target height is 5'-6", lens mm is 15.
Pick target point in plan (Eye/Target/Lens): **[pick point in the center of plumbing wall along left side]**
Pick eye point in plan: **[pick point at opposite end of plumbing wall]**
Select objects to view during interactive stepping...
Select objects:⏎

Picking an object at the **Select objects to view during interactive stepping... Select objects:** prompts opens the *Step Options* dialog box for additional detailed viewing choices.

• •

CHANGING BACK TO PLAN VIEW

Invoke the Macro **PN** to restore the plan view.

 Macro Command: **PN**

(AutoCAD command: **PLAN**

Command: **pn**
Macro: Plan
<Current UCS>/Ucs/World:⏎
Regenerating drawing.

All of the objects have now been drawn for the first floor plan. The final chapter describes how to move and copy the objects created for the first floor to levels two and three. Save the drawing and proceed to Chapter 22.

CHAPTER TWENTY-TWO

LAYER GROUPS

Copying and Moving Levels to Create a Three-story Building

Contents

This final chapter describes the procedure to draw a three-story building using objects created from the first floor. Layers for wall, door, and window objects on level 1 will first be copied to levels 2 and 3. Then layers for the roof will be moved from level 1 to level 3. In Chapter 10, floor level names were created for each UCS level height using the format mask consisting of level and root layer group names. The purpose of the mask will now be realized as layer names and their UCS levels are manipulated to copy and move layers as a group.

After all levels are drawn, plan, elevation, and isometric views are saved in modelspace, then restored in paperspace viewports. The completed drawing appears with the views placed in the predefined titleblock created earlier.

REVIEWING THE DEFINE LEVEL COMMAND

CORE TOOLBAR: DEFINE LEVEL

or

PULL-DOWN MENU: VIEW ➤ LAYER GROUPS ➤ DEFINE LEVEL

Define Level was invoked by picking the command from either the Core toolbar or the View pull-down menu. Invoking it prompts for a level name, height, and description to set elevations relative to the UCS in a drawing. Level information was saved to the \ZZLEVELS.DBF file in the current project \SDSKPROJ\ARCH-TUT (project) directory.

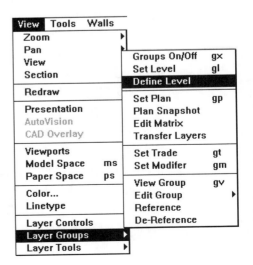

In Chapter 10, level names FL01, FL02, and FL03 were defined as shown in the Layer Groups table. A format mask must be invoked at the start of a project.

LAYER GROUPS

Level Name	Description	UCS (level)
FL01	First Floor	0
FL02	Second Floor	10" above previous level
FL03	Third Floor	10" above previous level

The prompting sequence invoked with the Define Level command is:

Command: sdsk

Level name: **FL01**

Height of level above current UCS <0">: **0**

Description: **First Floor**

Level name (or . for none) <FL02>: **FL02**

Height of level above previous level <10'>: **10'**

Description (or . for none) <First Floor>: **Second Floor**

Level name (or . for none) <FL03>: **FL03**

Height of level above previous level <10'>: **10'**

Description (or . for none) <Second Floor>: **Third Floor**

Level name (or . for none) <FL04>: **.** (period)

Restore layers now? <Yes>: **n**

Group settings are ON.

Level: FL01 Description: First Floor (Elev. 0")

● ●

SETTING LAYERS IN THE CURRENT DRAWING

Invoke the Macro **LD** to open the *Layer Control* dialog box and display all the layers in the current drawing.

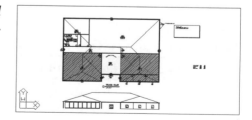

 Macro Command: **LD**

AutoCAD Command: **Ddlmodes**

Command: **ld**

Macro: Layer Dialogue

Choose **Select All**, then **On**, **Thaw**, and **Unlock**. Pick **Clear All**, then highlight layer 0 and set it **Current**.

Pick OK.

The drawing should appear similar to the figure shown.

Press enter to invoke **LD** again.

Macro Command: **LD**

(AutoCAD Command: **Ddlmodes**)

Choose **Select All** to highlight all layer names. Pick **Lock**, then **Clear all**. Next, selectively highlight all layers that represent wall, door, window, and plumbing fixture objects in plan view (include layer 0) and choose **Unlock**. Exclude layer names containing "ELEV" and layers ending with "E" that were created for objects drawn in the elevation. Review the layer names listed in the table and verify their **On**, **Thaw**, and **Unlock** status.

Pick OK.

Note: Root layers appearing without a level name are nested in blocks, such as doors and windows, then created using the specified format mask (Level and Root). For example, doors drawn on layer FL01-OPENING contain an arc representing the door swing on layer 3DDSWING. Objects created with the layer name FL01-OPENING and drawn on the UCS level 0, can be copied or moved to the level name FL02-OPENING on UCS level 10'.

Layer Names to turn ON, THAW and UNLOCK

Layer Name	Layer Name	Layer Name	Layer Name
0	DJAMB	FL01-PLUMBING	WIND
3DCASE	DOOR	FL01-STALL	WINDSILL
3DDHDW	DSILL	FL01-STALLDR	WJAMB
3DDOOR	DSWING3D	FL01-STALLDR3D	WMETSILL

Layer Name	Layer Name	Layer Name	Layer Name
3DDSWING	DSWINGP	FL01-TOILACC	WSWINGARC
3DGLAZE	FL01-CNTR	FL01-WALL	
3DGLAZE2	FL01-HEADER	FL01-WALL3D	
3DTRIM	FL01-JAMB	GLAZE	
3DWINDOW	FL01-JAMB3D	HEADER	
3DWSWING	FL01-OPENING	STALL	

Note: Careful planning of which layer names are to be included with the layer component group would have simplified the selection process. For example, excluding the Hatch layer from Level in the Groups section of the *Layer Settings* dialog box, discussed in Chapter 10 would not make it eligible for a layer component group. However, these exercises are designed to help you explore and resolve some of the real problems that usually occur during the CAD drafing process.

• •

VIEW AND EDIT THE CURRENT LAYER STATUS

Note: Objects on locked layers cannot be edited, but will continue to appear in the drawing. To conceal the visibility of locked layers and avoid confusion, it might be helpful to also turn them off.

Make all locked layers invisible by setting a filter then turning them off. Enter the Macro **LD** and use the **Filters** section to turn off all locked layers.

 Macro Command: **LD**

When the *Layer Control* dialog box opens, pick **Set...** in the **Filters** section to display the *Set Layer Filters* dialog box. Set a filter to view only locked layers by picking Locked from the **Lock/Unlock:** pop-up list.

Set Layer Filters

O**n/Off:**	Both
Fr**eeze/Thaw:**	Both
Lock/Un**lock:**	Locked
Current Vport:	Both
New Vports:	Both
Layer Names:	*
Colors:	*
Ltypes:	*
Reset	
OK	Cancel	Help...

Pick OK and return to the *Layer Control* dialog box.

Next, confirm that **On** is checked in the pick box in the **Filters** section . The list of all the locked layers appears in the **Layer Name** list box. If necessary, verify that layers listed in the table are not locked.

Choose **Select All**, then pick **Off** to prevent all locked layers from being visible in the drawing.

Pick OK to exit the dialog box.

The drawing should now display only those objects representing walls, doors, windows, and plumbing fixtures in plan view. All other objects not visible (off) are also locked.

If the drawing shows a layer that should be locked, reinvoke the Macro **LD**, and uncheck **On** in the **Filters** section to display the full list of layers. Scroll through the layer list, highlight the appropriate layer(s), then pick **Off** and **Lock**. Exit the dialog box and peruse the drawing again.

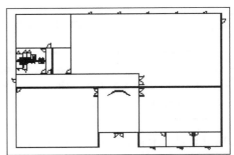

CREATING TILED VIEWPORTS

Enter the Macro **VP** to create two tiled vertical viewports.

 Macro Command: **VP**

(AutoCAD Command: **Viewports** or **Vports**)

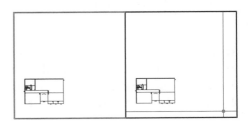

The prompting sequence is:

Command: **vp**
Macro: Vports
Save/Restore/Delete/Join/Single/?/2/<3>/4: **2**
Horizontal/<Vertical>: **v**
Regenerating drawing.

Pick the right viewport to make it active and the viewport border will appear heavier. Use **View Presets...** to restore a predefined isometric view.

VIEWING THE FIRST FLOOR LEVEL IN PLAN AND ISOMETRIC VIEW

VIEW ➤ VIEW ➤ VIEW PRESETS...

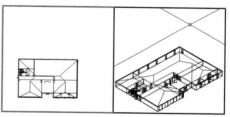

Select the **View** menu under the View pull-down menu, then pick **View Presets...** to open the *Preset And Currently Defined Views* dialog box. Choose South West Isometric from the **Views** list box to show the drawing of the first floor in both plan and isometric view.

Creating tiled viewports is very helpful in visualizing objects that are moved or copied from one layer group to another. **Edit Group** commands, located under the **View** menu, offer options to **Move**, **Copy**, or **Delete** objects in selected layer groups. A second and third story (floor level) will be created by copying first-floor level objects at UCS level 0 to the UCS levels previously defined using the format mask. Once copied, the roof is then moved from the first level to the third level.

COPYING LEVEL FL01 TO FL02

VIEW ➤ LAYER GROUPS ➤ EDIT GROUP ➤ COPY

Selecting the **Copy** command from the **Edit Group** menu (as shown on next page) will duplicate objects using the layer names that were created for the first floor at UCS level 0 to UCS level 10'.

Pick the left viewport to make it active, then select **Copy** from the **Edit Group** menu under **Layer Groups** in the View pull-down menu. The first four prompts apply to the source—what is being copied. The remaining procedures reference the target layer group and level. Enter a period (.) or press enter as the prompt appears at the command line for **Trade name:** and the *Plan name (or ?)* dialog box opens.

Trade name: ⏎

Note: Invoke the **Edit Group** commands with the left viewport active (appearing with heavier border) to avoid any potential conflicts with the UCS.

If this component were included in the format mask, it might serve to specify disciplines such as "architectural" or "mechanical". The layer name FL01-WALL-ARCH represents an example of the Group Format Mask with the components {L}{R}{T}

PROMPTING SUMMARY

Command: sdsk

Trade name: ⏎

Modifier: ⏎

Scanning layer⏎s) FL01-*,*|FL01-**

Set target layer group and level...

Modifier: ⏎

Copying layer FL01-WALL to layer FL02-WALL.

Copying layer FL01-JAMB to layer FL02-JAMB.

Copying layer FL01-WALL3D to layer FL02-WALL3D.

Copying layer FL01-JAMB3D to layer FL02-JAMB3D.

Copying layer FL01-OPENING to layer FL02-OPENING.

Copying layer FL01-HEADER to layer FL02-HEADER.

Copying layer FL01-STALLDR3D to layer FL02-STALLDR3D.

Copying layer FL01-STALLDR to layer FL02-STALLDR.

Copying layer FL01-STALL to layer FL02-STALL.

Copying layer FL01-PLUMBING to layer FL02-PLUMBING.

Copying layer FL01-TOILACC to layer FL02-TOILACC.

Copying layer FL01-CNTR to layer FL02-CNTR.

Group settings are ON.

Level: FL01 Description: (Elev. 0")

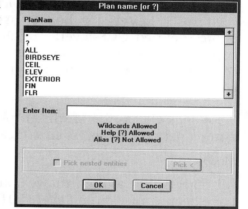

Highlight the period in the **PlanNam** list box or leave the **Enter Item:** edit box blank, then pick OK.

Next, the *Level name (or ?) (or . for none)* dialog box opens to specify a level name.

Highlight the component level name FL01. The Levels current UCS is used to copy layers to other UCS levels.

Pick OK and the **Modifier:** prompt appears at the command line. Type a period (.) or press Enter as the prompt appears and the *Plan name (or ?)* dialog box reopens.

Modifier: ↵

If this component were included in the format mask, it might serve to specify a work phase for "Existing" or "New," or a project phase such as "PhaseI." The layer name FL01-NEW-WALL represents an example of the Group Format Mask with the components {L}{M}{R}.

As the *Level name (or ?) (or . for none)* dialog box reappears, the command line displays the prompt **Set target layer group and level...**

Set target layer group and level...

Note: Double-clicking a name in the **Levels** list box automatically selects and closes the dialog box.

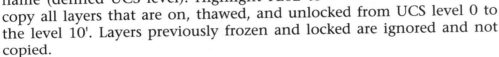

The *Level name (or ?) (or . for none)* dialog box contains a **Levels** list box to assign a layer name (defined UCS level). Highlight FL02 to copy all layers that are on, thawed, and unlocked from UCS level 0 to the level 10'. Layers previously frozen and locked are ignored and not copied.

Pick OK; as the **Modifier:** prompt reappears at the command line, enter a period (.) or press enter again.

Modifier: ↵

All objects that are on, thawed, and unlocked have been copied from Level FL01 (First Floor) to FL02 (Second Floor).

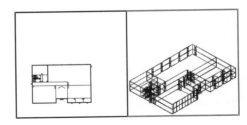

Invoke the Macro **LD**, uncheck **On** in the **Filters** section, then peruse the layer dialog box for the new FL02 layer names.

   Macro Command: **LD**

Prior to creating the third floor, we will delete the three exterior doors on the second floor.

• • • • • • • • • • • • • •

SETTING A LEVEL

VIEW ➤ LAYER GROUPS ➤ SET LEVEL

Select **Set Level** under the **Layer Group** menu in the View pulldown menu to open the *Level name (or ?) (or . for none)* dialog box.

Choose FL02 to set the current UCS to 10', then pick OK.

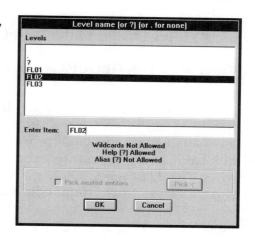

The prompting sequence is:

Command: sdsk
Restore layers now? <Yes>: **y**
Restoring layer(s) FL02-*,*IFL02-**
Group settings are ON.
Level: FL02 Description: Second Floor (Elev. 10'-0")

Set Level specifies the current level, making it the current UCS . Choosing the command freezes all those layers—except the level name being set—that contain the "Level" layer group component. In this case, setting the level to FL02 freezes the FL01 layers. We will use **Set Level** to remove objects from the current level.

* *

EDITING OBJECTS ON LEVEL FL02

DOOR/WIND ➤ DOOR/WINDOW EDIT ➤ REMOVE DOOR/WINDOW

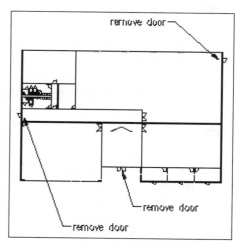

Select **Remove Door/Window** under **Door/Window Edit** in the Door/Wind pull-down menu. Remove each exterior door on level FL02 located at the top right corner, entrance, and left center portion of the building. Repeat the command until all doors are deleted from level FL02. (Zoom into the floor plan to select doors if necessary.)

The prompting sequence is:

Pick door, window, or assembly to remove:

Since objects on the FL01 layers are frozen by the **Set Level** command, those objects will not be edited.

• •
COPYING LEVEL FL02 TO FL03

VIEW ➤ LAYER GROUPS ➤ EDIT GROUP ➤ COPY

 Select the **Copy** command from the **Edit Group** menu to create the third floor at UCS level 20'. Repeat the same procedure by pressing enter at **Trade name:**, then picking OK when the *Plan name (or ?)* dialog box opens (with a empty **Enter Item:** edit box).

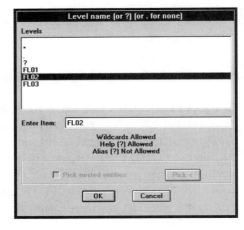

 Trade name: ↵

When the *Level name (or ?) (or . for none)* dialog box appears, choose FL02 (as the level to copy), then pick OK. As the command line returns again, press Enter at the **Modifier:** prompt.

 Modifier: ↵

 Finally, choose FL03 as the target layer group and level when the *Level name (or ?) (or . for none)* dialog box appears. Pick OK, then press Enter when prompted for **Modifier:**.

 Modifier: ↵

All layers with level name FL02 on UCS level 10' are copied to FL03 on UCS level 20' (10' above the previous level).

The prompting sequence is:

    Command: sdsk
    Trade name: ↵
    Modifier: ↵
    Scanning layer(s) FL02-*,*IFL02-**

Set target layer group and level...

Modifier: ↵

Copying layer FL02-WALL to layer FL03-WALL.

Copying layer FL02-JAMB to layer FL03-JAMB.

Copying layer FL02-WALL3D to layer FL03-WALL3D.

Copying layer FL02-JAMB3D to layer FL03-JAMB3D.

Copying layer FL02-OPENING to layer FL03-OPENING.

Copying layer FL02-HEADER to layer FL03-HEADER.

Copying layer FL02-STALLDR3D to layer FL03-STALLDR3D.

Copying layer FL02-STALLDR to layer FL03-STALLDR.

Copying layer FL02-STALL to layer FL03-STALL.

Copying layer FL02-PLUMBING to layer FL03-PLUMBING.

Copying layer FL02-TOILACC to layer FL03-TOILACC.

Copying layer FL02-CNTR to layer FL03-CNTR.

Group settings are ON.

Level: FL02 Description: Second Floor (Elev. 10'-0")

The building now has three floor levels. The final procedure to complete the three-story building requires moving the roof objects from level FL01 to FL03.

MOVING ROOF OBJECTS FROM LEVEL FL01 TO FL03

   Type **LD** to open the *Layer Control* dialog box and uncheck **On** in the **Filters** section to show all the layers in the drawing. Next, pick **Select All**, then choose **Lock**, then **Clear All**. Finally, highlight layers 0, FL01-3DROOF, and FL01-ROOFSOF, pick **Unlock**, then **Thaw**(and **On**, if necessary) to view and allow editing of the roof object. Pick OK to close the dialog box.

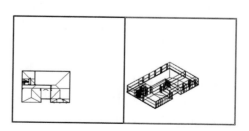

Macro Command: **LD**

Command: **ld**

Macro: Layer Dialogue

VIEW ➤ LAYER GROUP ➤ EDIT GROUP ➤ MOVE

Select **Move** from the **Edit Group** menu to raise the roof of the building from level FL01 to FL03. Repeat the procedures invoked earlier by pressing enter at the **Trade name:** prompt and picking OK when the *Plan name (or ?)* dialog box appears.

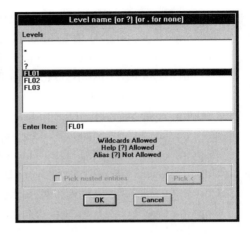

Select FL01 in the *Level name (or ?) (or . for none)* dialog box, then pick OK.

Press Enter at the **Modifier:** prompt and the *Level name (or ?) (or . for none)* dialog box reappears.

Choose FL03 as the target layer group and level for the roof objects, then pick OK. Press Enter at the **Modify:** prompt.

The prompting sequence is:

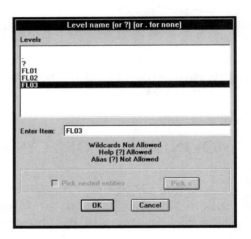

    Command: sdsk
    Trade name: ↵
    Modifier: ↵
    Scanning layer(s) FL01-*,*|FL01-**
    Set target layer group and level...
    Modifier: ↵
    Moving layer FL01-3DROOF to layer
    FL03-3DROOF.
    Moving layer FL01-ROOFSOF to layer FL03-ROOFSOF.
    Group settings are ON.
    Level: FL02 Description: Second Floor (Elev. 10'-0")

Note: After the roof objects are moved from FL01 level name, corresponding FL03 layers are created. For example, moving layers does not delete the layer, but instead makes a new FL03-3DROOF layer from the FL01-3DROOF layer for the 3D roof surfaces.

VIEWING THE FIRST FLOOR LAYERS

Enter the Macro **LD** and set a filter for FL01 by picking **Set...** to open the *Set Layer Filter* dialog box and typing FL01* in the **Layer Names** edit box.

Pick OK, returning to the *Layer Control* dialog box, then choose **Select All**. After all the layers are highlighted, deselect FL01-ELEVATION, then pick **Thaw** and **Unlock**.

Pick OK again and the building should appear without the elevation, annotations, and title marks.

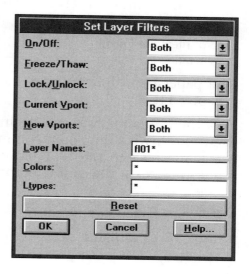

VIEWING THE BUILDING IN ISOMETRIC VIEW WITH HIDE ON

Enter the Macro **HI** in the isometric viewport to view the three-story building with interior lines hidden.

 Macro Command: **HI**

(AutoCAD command: **HIDE**)

Command: **hi**
Macro: Hide

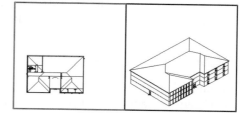

SETTING UP A PAPERSPACE DRAWING

Enter the Macro **TI** to toggle paperspace and change the drawing environment to tilemode 0.

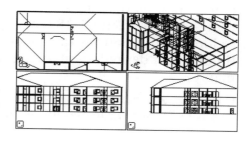

Macro Command: **TI**

(AutoCAD Command: **TILEMODE**)

Command: **ti**
Macro: Tilemode Toggle
Regenerating drawing.

The paperspace drawing appears with the preset viewports created in Chapter 11.

Pick the top left viewport containing the plan view and invoke the Zoom command. Set the viewport's scale to 1/16" = 1'-0" by entering the value 1/182xp at the command prompt .

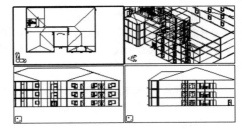

 Macro Command: **Z**

(AutoCAD Command: **ZOOM**)

Command: **z**
All/Center/Dynamic/Extents/Left/Previous/Vmax/Window/<Scale(X/XP)>: **1/182xp**

Pick the viewport to the right and use the Zoom command to reduce the scale (perhaps 1/2 or .5x) so that it fits the viewport.

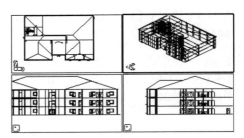

 Macro Command: **Z**

Command: **z**
All/Center/Dynamic/Extents/Left/Previous/Vmax/Window/<Scale(X/XP)>: **.5x**

Select the bottom left viewport and enter a plotted drawing scale of 1/16"=1' 0" by using the scale factor 1/182xp. Repeat the procedure for the bottom right viewport. (Adjust the image if desired by invoking the Pan command.)

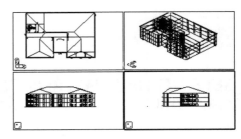

Command: **z**
All/Center/Dynamic/Extents/Left/Previous/Vmax/Window/<Scale(X/XP)>: **1/182xp**

THE THREE-STORY BUILDING—FINAL DRAWING IN PAPERSPACE

VIEW ➤ PAPERSPACE

Select Paperspace from the View pull-down menu or enter the Macro **PS** at the command line to exit from the modelspace viewport.

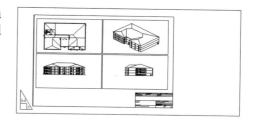

 Macro Command: **PS**

(AutoCAD Command: **Pspace**)

The viewport borders are on the layer DEF-POINTS which does not plot.

Final preparations before plotting might include:

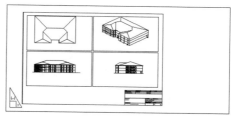

1. Removing hidden lines from the isometric viewport.

2. Turning on and thawing the notation layers to include the text leader, note box and title marker in the plan viewport.

3. Thawing the elevation layers and adding an additional viewport along the lower left portion of the titleblock.

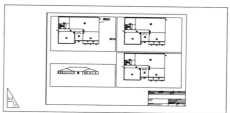

4. Creating another drawing showing a floor and reflected ceiling plans for each of the floor levels in separate viewports similar to the examples shown.

This completes the tutorial to draw a three-story building. These exercises should provide you with a thorough background and understanding of the commands and features to more effectively and productively use the Softdesk software.

APPENDIX A

MACRO COMMAND LIST

The following table lists keyboard command aliases that provide a quick means of invoking Softdesk commands. Softdesk macros are invoked in some chapters to initialize commands. Typing **HE** at the command will display this help file listing macro names and descriptions.

Macros List

Macro	Description	Acad Equivalent
3M	3D Mesh	3DMESH
3P	3D Polyline	3DPOLY
AC	Arc	ARC
AD	Attribute Define	ATTDEF
AE	Area	AREA
AR	Array	ARRAY
BA	Break @	BREAK @
BF	Break First	BREAK F
BL	Block	BLOCK
BR	Break	BREAK
BX	Box	BOX
C3	3 Point Circle	CIRCLE 3P

415

(continued)

Macros List (*Continued*)

Macro	Description	Acad Equivalent
CC	Continuous Copy	COPY - Asks angle & distance, repeats
CE	Change Entity	DDMODIFY
CF	Chamfer	CHAMFER
CH	Change	CHANGE
CI	Circle	CIRCLE
CL	Change Layer (Pro-Tools)	CHANGE, Layer (multiple selection sets)
CM	Copy Multiple	COPY, Multiple
CO	Copy	COPY
CN	Cone	CONE (3D Entity)
CP	Change Property	DDCHPROP
CY	Cylinder	CYLINDER (3D Entity)
D	Draw by Example (Pro-Tools)	By entity, creates new entities
DAL	Aligned dimension	DIM, Align
DBA	Baseline dimension	DIMBASE or DIMBASELINE
DCO	Continue dimensioning	DIMCONTINUE
DDI	Diameter dimension	DIMDIA or DIMDIAMETER
DAN	Angular dimension	DIMANG or DIMANGULAR
DHO	Horizontal dimension	DIM, Horizontal
DI	Distance	DIST
DIV	Divide	DIVIDE
DLE	Dimension Leader	DIM, Leader or LEADER
DCE	Center marks	DIM, Center or DIMCENTER
DO	Doughnut	DONUT or DOUGHNUT
DOB	Oblique dimension	DIM, Oblique or DIMEDIT, Oblique
DOR	Ordinate dimension	DIM, Ordinate or DIMORDINATE
DRA	Radius dimension	DIM, Radius or DIMRADIUS
DRO	Rotate dimension	DIM, Rotated or DIMLINEAR, Rotated
DS	Day stamp (Pro-Tools)	
DV	Dview	DVIEW
DVE	Vertical dimension	DIM, Vertical or DIMLINEAR

Macros List (*Continued*)

Macro	Description	Acad Equivalent
EA	Attribute edit (Pro-Tools)	DDATTE
EB	Edit block (Pro-Tools)	
EL	Erase last	ERASE, Last
ELP	Ellipse	ELLIPSE
EM	Edit multi-line	MLEDIT
EP	Edit polyline	PEDIT
ER	Erase	ERASE
ES	Edit spline	PEDIT, Spline
ESU	Edge surface	EDGESURF
ET	Edit text	DDEDIT
EXP	Explode	EXPLODE
EXT	Extend	EXTEND
F0	Fillet radius 0	FILLET, Radius= 0
FA	3Dface	3DFACE
FI	Fillet	FILLET
FR	Fillet radius	FILLET, Radius
GL	Group level	
GM	Group modifier	
GP	Group plan type	
GR	Grid	GRID
GT	Group trade	
GU	Glue	
GV	Group view	
GX	Group toggle On/Off	
HA	Boundary hatch	BHATCH
HD	Dynamic hatch (dialog box)	
HE	Help catalogue	HELP
HI	Hide	HIDE
IN	Insert	INSERT
IP	Isoplane toggle	ISOPLANE

(*continued*)

Macros List (*Continued*)

Macro	Description	Acad Equivalent
L1	Layer isolate	
L3	Line with locked Z	
LA	Layer	LAYER
LC	Layer Properties	
LD	Layer dialogue	DDLMODES
LF	Layer off	
LG	Lenghten	LENGHTEN
L	Line	LINE
LK	Layer Lock	
LL	List Layer	LIST
LO	Layer on	
LOA	Layer on all	
LQ	Layer query	
LS	Layer set	
LSP	Load lisp	APPLOAD
LI	List	LIST
LSU	Ruled surface	RULESURF
LT	Layer thaw	
LU	Layer unlock	
LVP	VP Layer	VPLAYER
LZ	Layer freeze	
MB	Make block (Pro-Tools)	
ME	Measure	MEASURE
MI	Mirror	MIRROR
ML	Multi-line	MLINE
MN	Menu	MENU
MO	Move	MOVE
MS	Modelspace	MSPACE
MV	Modelview	MVIEW
OF	Offset	OFFSET

Macros List (*Continued*)

Macro	Description	Acad Equivalent
OP	Oops	OOPS
OS	Osnap	DDOSNAP
PA	Pan	PAN
PE	Polyline edit	PEDIT
PG	Polygon	POLYGON
PL	Polyline	PLINE
PN	Plan	PLAN
PO	Point	POINT
PR	Print/plot	PLOT
PS	Paperspace	PSPACE
QC	Quick copy (Pro-Tools)	
QM	Quick move(Pro-Tools)	
QU	Quit	QUIT, Yes
RB	Redefine block (Pro-Tools)	
RC	Rectangle	RECTANG
RE	redrawall	REDRAWALL
RG	Regenall	REGENALL
RL	Ray line	RAY
RO	Rotate	ROTATE
ROC	Rotate copy	
RQ	Rotate quick (Building Base)	
RS	Reset settings	
RSU	Revolution surface	REVSURF
SA	Save	SAVE
SC	Scale	SCALE
SD	Change Softdesk product	
SE	Select	SELECT
SK	Sketch	SKETCH
SM	Symbol Manager	
SN	Snap	SNAP

(continued)

Macros List (*Continued*)

Macro	Description	Acad Equivalent
SO	Solid	SOLID
SP	Spell	SPELL
SPH	Sphere	SPHERE (3D Entity)
SR	Snap Rotate	SNAP, Rotate
SS	Build selection set	
ST	Stretch	STRETCH
STS	Stretch select	
SY	Set style	STYLE
TS	Text small	DTEXT
TI	Tilemode toggle	TILEMODE (on/off)
TL	Text large	DTEXT
TM	Text medium	DTEXT
TO	Torus	TORUS (3D Entity)
TQ	Text Quality	TEXTQLTY (system variable)
TR	Trim	TRIM
TT	Text title	DTEXT
TX	Text	DTEXT
TXF	Text x-fine	STYLE
UB	Undo back	UNDO, Back
UC	UCS	DDUCS
UM	Undo mark	UNDO, Mark
UP	UCS previous	UCS, Previous
UV	UCS view	UCS, View
UW	UCS world	UCS, World
VI	View	VIEW
VP	Vports	VPORTS or VIEWPORTS
VR	View restore	VIEW, Restore
VS	Vslide	VSLIDE
VT	Vpoint	VPOINT
WB	Wblock	WBLOCK

Macros List (*Continued*)

Macro	Description	Acad Equivalent
WC	Window copy	
WD	Wedge	WEDGE
WE	Window erase	ERASE
WH	Window change	
WM	Window move	
WP	Window chprop	
WR	Window rotate	
WS	Window scale	
XL	Infinite line	XLINE
XP	Explode	EXPLODE
XSU	Extruded surface	
XT	Extend	EXTEND
YC	Layer copy	
YE	Layer erase	
YH	Layer change	
YM	Layer move	
YP	Layer chprop	
YR	Layer rotate	
YS	Layer scale	
ZA	Zoom all	ZOOM, All
ZC	Zoom center	ZOOM, Center
ZD	Zoom dynamic	ZOOM, Dynamic
ZE	Zoom entents	ZOOM, Extents
ZF	Zoom left	ZOOM, Left
ZI	Zoom in	
ZM	Zoom view max	ZOOM, Vmax
ZO	Zoom out	
ZL	Zoom limits	ZOOM, Limits
ZP	Zoom previous	ZOOM, Previous
ZW	Zoom window	ZOOM, Window

APPENDIX B

POINT FILTERS

Contents

In Chapter 14 point filters were used to draw walls using a base point different from the wall's starting point. Softdesk point filters are similar to AutoCAD's point filters and use a period (.) accompanied by a single character (letter) to initialize the filter. Point filters can be selected from the cursor menu, also known as the POP 0 menu.

This appendix includes a chart of all the point filters and provides some examples of their use.

Miscellaneous Filters

Filter	Type	Description
.?	HELP	Returns a list of filters compatible with current prompt.
.sl	SLOPE	When selected from the cursor menu, calculates a slope or associated values based on the entry of values for two of the following factors: rise, run, slope length, and slope angle. Prompting sequence: Calculate Slope... Supply values for any 2 prompts... Enter Rise: **4** Enter Run: **12** (Note: If values are not supplied for both of the first two prompts, the third prompts are: Enter slope length: Enter Angle:) Rise = 4" Run = 1'-0" Length = 1'-0 21/32" Slope angle = 18.43 Slope grade = 33.333% Slope ratio rise/run = 1/3 Use slope value (RIse/RUn/Length/Angle/Grade/ RAtio) <Rise>: 4.0

Point Filters

Filter	Type	Description
.d	DISTANCE	Locates a point determined from a base point, angle, and distance
.f	FRACTION	Locates a point at a fractional distance between two points

Filter	Type	Description
.i	INTERSECTION	Locates a point at the implied intersection of two non-parallel lines (need not actually intersect)
.m	MID OF	Locates midpoint of two selected points
.r	RELATIVE	Locates a point based on a reference point
.t	TRACKING (Press F5 function key)	Displays information about entities when the crosshairs are positioned over the entity. Returns entity information to command line related to command in progress.
.zm	Z MATCH	Returns a point based on the x and y coordinates of a selected point and the z coordinate of another point. When selected from the cursor menu, prompts to:

>>Select XY base point: int of

>>Select Z point to match (or RETURN for current): ↵

(2460.63 1480.8 0.0)

POINT FILTER EXERCISES

CURSOR MENU (Hold shift key + right mouse button)

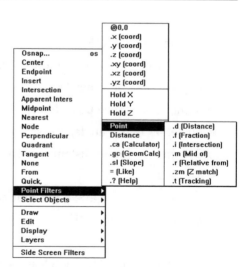

WALLS ➤ WALL SETTINGS...

Select **Wall Settings...** from the Walls pull-down menu to open the *Wall Settings* dialog box and check all prompts as shown prior to experimenting with the following exercises.

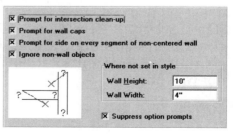

.d—DISTANCE POINT FILTER

The **.d** point filter provides a method for obtaining an exact point relative to a known, selectable point based on angle and distance. The crosshairs change their snap angle to the specified point filter angle at the >>**Angle** prompt, requesting a distance value at the >>**Distance** prompt.

Exercise: The example shows a U-shaped space drawn using 6-inch-wide walls. Draw a 45-degree wall 5'-0" long within the space. Using the .d point filter, draw the wall starting from a near (or mid) point along the horizontal interior wall line.

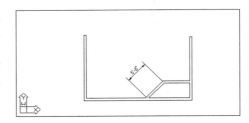

The prompting sequence is:

Command: w1

Wall style - AB_CENTER

Width: 4" Height: 10' (wall prompts suppressed)

From point: nea of [point A]

To point: **.d [distance point filter]**

>>Angle: **45 [enter angle, crosshairs snap to specified angle]**

>>Distance: **5' [enter distance, shown as point B; wall line temporarily disappears]**

>>Angle:⏎

Clean intersection <No>: **y [prompt cleans up intersection at point A]**

To point: **per** to **[point B]**

To point:⏎

Clean intersection <No>: **y [clean up intersection at point B]**

Step 1: Select AB_CENTER from the Walls pull-down menu and draw a wall with the start point (Point A) at any location along the interior wall line.

To point: **.d**

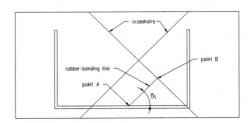

Step 2: Draw the first wall length at a distance of 5' in a direction of 45 degrees.

>>Angle: **45**
>>Distance: **5'**
>>Angle:⏎

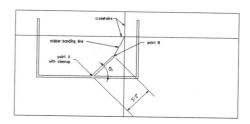

Step 3: Enclose the space by drawing the next wall line perpendicular to the right vertical wall line.

To point: **per** to

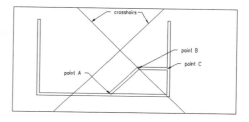

.f—FRACTION POINT FILTER

The **.f** point filter provides a method for obtaining an exact point relative to a known, selectable point based on the percentage of distance between two points. First and second points appear with >>**From point:** and >>**To point:** prompts to establish the total distance to be divided into equal segments.

Exercise: The example shows an L-shaped 4-inch-wide wall with the horizontal wall line divided into four equal segments. Select AB_CENTER from the Walls pull-down menu and draw a vertical wall with the start point at 1/4 the distance of the full interior horizontal length.

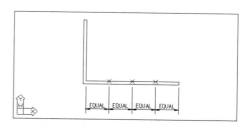

The prompting sequence is:

Command: W1

Wall style - AB_CENTER

Width: 4" Height: 10' (wall prompts suppressed)

From point: **.f [fractional point filter]**

>>From point: **end** of **[point A]**

>>To point: **end** of **[point B]**

>>Numerator <1>: **1 [enter value]**

>>Denominator <2>: **4 [enter value, the value 4 divides the line into 4 equal segments]**

To point: **@5'<90 [point C]**

Clean intersection <No>: **y [clean up intersection]**

To point: **per** to **[point D]**

To point:

Clean intersection <No>: **y [clean up intersection]**

Step 1: Select AB_CENTER from the Walls pull-down menu and begin by picking a start point (point A) at the left interior intersection, then second point (point B) at the opposite end.

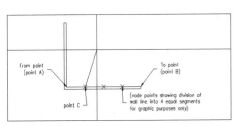

From point: **.f**
>>From point: **end** of
>>To point: **end** of

Step 2: After selecting endpoints, prompts appear that divide the line into equal segments by requesting a fractional distance. To set a fractional distance of 1/4, enter the numerator value of 1 and denominator value of 4.

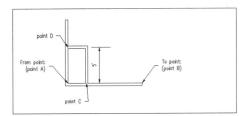

>>Numerator <1>: **1**
>>Denominator <2>: **4**

Step 3: Next, enter the length and direction of the first wall segment drawn at the specified quarter-point distance.

To point: **@5'<90**

Step 4: Enter the length and direction of the next wall to enclose the space. Prompts to clean up intersections appear when the setting is toggled on.

Clean intersection <No>: **y**
To point: **per** to

. . . .

.i—INTERSECTION FILTER POINT

The **.i** point filter provides a method for obtaining an implied point relative to two selectable points. The >>**Select first intersecting entity:** and

>>**Select second intersecting entity:** prompts appear to determine the implied distance between the two points.

Exercise: The example shows an irregular shaped space as shown with aligning horizontal and vertical walls. To align a new horizontal wall with an existing horizontal wall, the .i filter locates an implied intersection to set a start point. Select AB_SIDE from the Walls pull-down menu; using the .i point filter, draw a 4' 0" long horizontal wall.

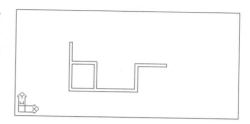

The prompting sequence is:

Wall style - AB_SIDE

Width: 6" Height: 8'-0" (wall prompts suppressed)

From point: **.i [intersection point filter]**

>>Select first intersecting entity: **[select point A, interior (right) vertical wall line at left wall]**

>>Select second intersecting entity: **[select point B interior (top) horizontal wall line of top right wall)**

To point: **@4'<0 [starting wall line at point C (apparent intersection of points A and B) enter value for wall length and angle]**

Pick side: [pick point downward]

Clean intersection <No>: y **[clean up intersection at point A]**

To point: **per** to [**interior horizontal wall line, point D]**

Pick side: **[pick point to the left]**

To point:⏎

Clean intersection <No>: y **[clean up intersection at point D]**

Step 1: Select the first point, interior vertical wall line.

>>Select first intersecting entity:

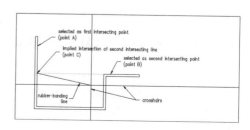

Step 2: Select a second point, interior horizontal wall line and a rubber-banding line appears at the apparent intersection.

>>Select second intersecting entity:

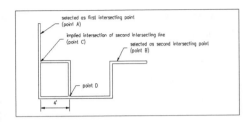

Step 3: Enter a distance and direction, pick a side to set wall width, then clean up the start point.

To point: **@4'<0**
Pick side:
Clean intersection <No>: **y**

Step 4: Close space by selecting a point parallel to the lower horizontal wall line (point D).

.?—HELP FILTER

The .? filter returns a list of filters that are compatible with the current prompt and can be invoked for most Softdesk commands. Select AB_CENTER from the Walls pull-down menu. Pick the first point prior to selecting the first point and invoke the .? filter.

The prompting sequence is:

Command: w1

Wall style - AB_CENTER

Width: 4" Height: 10' (wall prompts suppressed)

From point: **.?** **[enter period (.) with question mark to list available point filters]**

(.D dist/angle) (.R relative) (.I intersection) (.F fraction)

(.M midof) (.ZM match Z) (.T tracking) (.H hold fraction) (.GC GeomCal)

From point: **[enter desired point filter]**

.t—TRACKING POINT FILTER

The **.t** filter displays information such as layer names, linetypes, colors, and block names about an entity as the crosshairs pass over the entity. Select AB_CENTER from the Walls pull-down menu and pick two points to draw a single wall. Press enter to draw another wall, enter the **.t** filter, and place the osnap box near the midpoint of the previously drawn wall line entities. An X mark appears identifying osnap locations.

The prompting sequence is:

Command: w1

Wall style - AB_CENTER

Width: 4" Height: 10' (wall prompts suppressed)

From point: **.t**

Track point <Dsnaps On> **[node point identifies entity tracked, status line reports entity information as (_midp)]**

To point:

MIDPOINT AND RELATIVE FILTERS

These filters were used in Chapter 14 to draw a custom curved wall in the ENTRY space.

.m—MIDPOINT POINT FILTER

The **.m** point filter provides a method for obtaining a midpoint relative to two selectable points.

The prompting sequence is:

Command: w1

Wall style - AB_CENTER

Width: 4" Height: 10' (wall prompts suppressed)

From point: **.m [midpoint filter]**

>>From point: **int** of **[point A]**

>>To point: **per** to **[point B]**

To point: **@4'<0 [starts at point C, enter distance and direction]**

Cap wall <Yes>: **y [add end cap at start of wall]**

To point:⏎

Cap wall <Yes>: **y [add end cap at end of wall]**

Step 1: Select AB_CENTER from the Walls pull-down menu and draw two parallel horizontal walls.

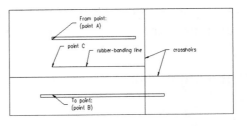

Step 2: Add a third parallel horizontal wall 4'-0" long midway between the two walls by invoking the .m filter.

From point: **.m**
>>From point: **int** of
>>To point: **per** to
To point: **@4'<0**

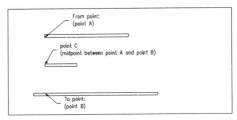

.r—RELATIVE FROM POINT FILTER

The **.r** point filter provides a method for obtaining a point relative to another (base) point.

The prompting sequence is:

Command: W1

Wall style - AB_CENTER

Width: 4" Height: 10' (wall prompts suppressed)

From point: **.r [relative from filter]**

>>Base point: **int** of **[point A]**

>>To reference point: **@5'<0 [point B, enter distance from base point A]**

>>To reference point: ↵

To point: **@8'<90 [enter distance and direction for next point]**

Clean intersection <No>: **y [no end cap at start of wall]**

To point:↵

Cap wall <Yes>: **y [add end cap at end of wall]**

Step 1: Select AB_CENTER from the Walls pull-down menu and draw walls for a U-shaped space.

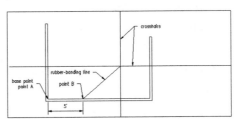

Step 2: Add a new vertical wall 8'-0" long at a distance of 5'-0" away from the interior left corner.

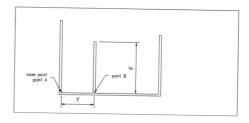

From point: **.r**
>>Base point: **int** of
>>To reference point: **@5'<0**
>>To reference point:↵
To point: **@8'<90**

DISTANCE MENU

Select the cursor menu by holding the Shift key and pressing the right mouse button to open the cursor menu. Highlight **Point Filters**, then **Distance** to display the distance menu.

This allows input of linear measurement in units other than the current drawing. After input, the values are converted into the current drawing units, translating according to the filter selected.

The prompting sequence is:

Command: **L [invoking the Macro Line]**

Macro: Line

From point: **[pick a point]**

To point: **.d [distance point filter]**

>>Angle: **0 [angle]**

>>Distance: **.in [distance filter for inch]**

>>Enter value in inches: **68 [enter a value]**

>>Angle:↵

To point (or Undo):↵

Distance/Length Filters

Filter	Description
.in	Return a value entered in inches
.ft	Return a value entered in feet
.mm	Return a value entered in millimeters

(*continued*)

Distance/Length Filters (*Continued*)

Filter	Description
.cm	Return a value entered in centimeters
.dm	Return a value entered in decimeters
.me	Return a value entered in meters

Productivity Filters

Filter	Type	Description
.=	LIKE (PRO TOOLS)	Takes value from selected entity as input for type of value expected for a prompt. If type of value is ambiguous, the filter allows selection of values available for return.
.ca	CALCULATOR (PRO TOOLS)	Pops up a dialog box scientific calculator.

.ca—CALCULATOR FILTER

To display a calculator, select **.ca** from the cursor menu (hold Shift key and press right mouse button) under Point Filters.

The *Calculator* dialog box appears for input. Choosing a number, then picking the + button sets the calculator in add mode. Pick an operand (number) then an operator (function such as +, - or /) to perform calculations.

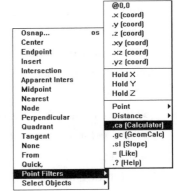

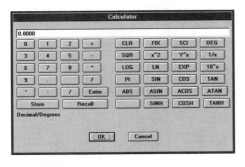

Example of button selection:

Calculation	Button Selection Sequence	Result
9+3–4=	9 Enter 3 + 4 –	8

SOFTDESK S7 SUPER PRODUCTIVITY CD

For AutoCAD® Release 13 Windows® 3.1 & Release 13 Windows NT™
* Also for ACAD Release 12/13 DOS, and 12 Windows

Quick Install Guide

This document provides information on installing Softdesk 7.2 products from the Softdesk S7 Super Productivity CD. Additional installation information can be found by running the readdos.bat file located in the root directory of this CD. Full documentation of all Softdesk products is also provided in an electronic format which can be viewed using the Adobe™ Acrobat™ Reader included on this CD. Documents on installing and running the Adobe™ Acrobat™ Reader as well as other products included on this CD can be found in various readme documents located through-out the CD as detailed below.

System Requirements:

System Requirements are the same as those noted in the Installation Guide provided as an electronic document on this CD with the following exceptions.

- Microsoft DOS 6.0 (or later). For information on installing using Microsoft DOS 5.0 (or earlier) consult the readme.bat file in the \supercd\products directory on the CD-ROM drive.
- AutoCAD 13c2b (or later) DOS, Windows or NT installed configured and working or...

  AutoCAD 12c3 DOS or AutoCAD 12c4 WIN installed configured and working.

Prerequisites:

- Working knowledge of Windows and AutoCAD environments and configuration

Installing and running the Adobe™ Acrobat™ Reader for Windows:

1. You must run this installation from inside Windows.
2. From the Windows Program Manager or File Manager, run Acroread.exe in the \supercd\docs\acroread directory on the CD-ROM drive.
3. Follow the instructions on the screen.
4. After installation is complete, run the Acrobat™ Reader in the Adobe™ Acrobat™ program group.
5. Using the file Browser, access the \supercd\docs directory on the CD-ROM drive. Select a portable document file (pdf) in one of the docs subdirectories, then select OK.

Note that the Adobe™ Acrobat™ Reader for Windows does not support NT. If you are using NT, you may use the Adobe™ Acrobat™ Reader for DOS inside a DOS Shell. For more information on installing the Adobe™ Acrobat™ Reader for Windows, consult the readme.bat file in the \supercd\products directory on the CD-ROM drive. For more information on using Adobe™ Acrobat™ Reader for Windows, consult the portable document file located in the help directory under the directory where Adobe™ Acrobat™ is installed.

Installing Adobe™ Acrobat™ Reader for DOS:

1. You must run this installation from the DOS command line. Do not install from a DOS shell within Windows.
2. Access the \supercd\docs\read_10 directory on the CD-ROM drive.
3. Run Install.exe
4. Follow the instructions on the screen.
5. After installation is complete, run the Acrobat™ Reader by changing directory to the directory where you installed Acrobat™ and run Acrobat.exe.
6. Using the file Browser, change directory to the \supercd\docs directory on the CD-ROM drive. Select a portable document file (pdf) in one of the docs subdirectories then select Open.

For more information on installing the Adobe™ Acrobat™ Reader for DOS, consult the readme.txt file in the \supercd\docs\read_10 directory on the CD-ROM drive. For more information on using Adobe™ Acrobat™ Reader for DOS, consult the portable document files located in the directory where Adobe™ Acrobat™ is installed.

Installing Softdesk Core and Productivity Tools:

1. You must run this installation from the DOS command line. Do not install from a DOS shell within Windows.
2. Access the \supercd\products directory on the CD-ROM drive.
3. Run the Load.bat batch file using the following syntax:

    Load [A] [B]

    A = Drive letter of CD-ROM.

    B = Drive letter for temporary installation files (this must be a local drive).

For example, to install from CD-ROM drive E: using local drive C: type the following:

Load E C

The installation files are copied from the CD-ROM drive to the local drive, then deleted after the installation is completed.

4. A list of installable modules is displayed on the screen. Enter the number that corresponds to the module you wish to install. You will be prompted for the location where the products will be installed.

For more information on installing Softdesk Core and Productivity Tools, consult the readme.bat file in the \supercd\products directory on the CD-ROM drive. Also refer to the sections titled Installing Softdesk Core and Installing Softdesk Modules in the Softdesk Installation Guide. This guide is provided in the Adobe™ Acrobat™ portable document file, instal_e.pdf, found in the \supercd\docs\install directory on this CD.

Configuring Softdesk Core and Productivity Tools for AutoCAD for Windows:

Information on configuring Softdesk Core and Productivity Tools for AutoCAD for Windows can be found in the section titled Configuring Softdesk Modules for Windows in chapter 3, Windows Installation, of the Softdesk Installation guide. This guide is provided in the Adobe™ Acrobat™ portable document file instal_e.pdf found in the \supercd\ docs\install directory on this CD. Printing of the Windows Installation chapter is highly recommended before configuring Softdesk for use with AutoCAD for Windows.

Configuring Softdesk Core and Productivity Tools for AutoCAD for DOS:

Information on configuring Softdesk Core and Productivity Tools for AutoCAD for DOS can be found in the section titled Technical Information in chapter 2, DOS Installation, of the Softdesk Installation guide.

This guide is provided in the Adobe™ Acrobat™ portable document file, instal_e.pdf, found in the \supercd\docs\install directory on this CD. Printing of the DOS Installation chapter is highly recommended before configuring Softdesk for use with AutoCAD for DOS.

Installing CAD Overlay Classic for AutoCAD for Windows:

CAD Overlay Classic is available for AutoCAD for Windows and NT only. When using CAD Overlay Classic for Windows, you must configure for the Rasterex video driver supplied with AutoCAD 13 for Windows. Other video drivers are not supported.

1. You must run this installation from inside Windows.
2. Softdesk Core and Productivity Tools for AutoCAD for Windows must be installed previous to installing CAD Overlay Classic.
3. From the Windows Program Manager or File Manager, run setup.exe in the \supercd\products\classic directory on the CD-ROM drive.
4. Follow the instructions on the screen.
5. The installation program will create a new Windows program group titled CAD Overlay Classic. CAD Overlay Classic must be run by selecting the CAD Overlay Classic Icon from within this program group. If you wish to run Softdesk Core and Productivity Tools in conjunction with CAD Overlay Classic, you must select the CAD Overlay Classic Icon in the CAD Overlay Classic program group

Using Softdesk Core, Productivity Tools and CAD Overlay Classic:

Information on using Softdesk Core, Productivity Tools and CAD Overlay Classic can be found in the electronic documents provided with this CD and can be viewed using the Acrobat™ Reader also provided on this CD. These documents can be found in the \supercd\docs subdirectories on this CD. If you wish to run Softdesk Core and Productivity Tools in conjunction with CAD Overlay Classic, you must select the CAD Overlay Classic Icon in the CAD Overlay Classic program group.

Trouble Shooting (Dial 1-800-SOFTDESK for 14 days of free support.)

Application	Symptom	Solution
Load.bat	Text scrolls across the screen immediately after running with the following errors: • Bad command or file name • Extended error 65 • Invalid drive specification	• Microsoft DOS 6.0 or greater is recommended. See the \supercd\products\readme.bat file for MS-DOS 5.0 (or earlier) information. • DOS directory has to be included in DOS search path as specified in path= statement in Autoexec.bat
Load.bat	Text scrolls across the screen after selecting module to install with the following errors: • Cannot SUBST a network drive • Extended error 65 • Invalid drive specification	• Load.bat can not be run in a DOS Shell from within Windows • An existing network drive map can not be used as the Temporary File drive during installation.
AutoCAD/ Softdesk (all versions)	• Error: SDSK unknown command • Softdesk does not initialize • Softdesk does not run	• Current dwg is unnamed. Create a new dwg or open an existing dwg. • Softdesk directories are not specified in AutoCAD support path. Add directories to support path. • Verify program root path in SDSK.dfm in Softdesk root directory. (Ex. SDSK=c:\sdsk) • AutoCAD support path is being truncated. Problem with AutoCAD installation. Reinstall AutoCAD after deleting original installation or upgrade to latest version of AutoCAD. • AutoCAD does not recognize the support path. Edit AutoCAD preferences. Highlight the support path then select OK.
AutoCAD/ Softdesk (Windows)	Win32s Error while initializing or running Softdesk products	• Problem with Softdesk Core. Reinstall Softdesk Core. Do not overwrite existing SDSK.DFM file. • Problem with AutoCAD installation. Reinstall AutoCAD after deleting original installation.
AutoCAD/ Softdesk (Windows 3.1x only)	• Error: SDSK unknown command • Softdesk does not initialize • Softdesk does not run	Not enough System Resources Free (Program Manager/Help/About Program Manager) • Shut down all Windows applications except for Program Manager and AutoCAD • Free up more base RAM • Upgrade to Windows NT
Softdesk Initialization	Softdesk Core Toolbar is not visible at left side of screen	• Move the AutoCAD toolbars, Draw & Modify, from the left side of the AutoCAD window to another location in the window.
Softdesk Initialization	Menus displays "Integrate with AutoCAD" after Softdesk Initializes	• Recompile Core menu: Type menu; Change 'List of File Types' to *.mnu; Select CR.mnu.
Softdesk Initialization	Softdesk Toolbars contain smiley faces	• Add Softdesk support directories to AutoCAD support path. (ACAD=c:\sdsk;c:\sdsk\pat;\sdsk\bmp;c:\acad...) Recompile Core menu: Type menu;. Change 'List of File Types' to *.mnu; Select CR.mnu.
AutoCAD 13/ Softdesk (Windows 3.1x only)	Software runs too slowly	• Upgrade to Windows NT

SOFTDESK
Technical Application Software Worldwide

SOFTDESK, INC.
Customer Software License

-READ THIS BEFORE USE-

Please read this License carefully.

You are purchasing a license to use SOFTDESK Software. The Software is owned by and remains the property of SOFTDESK and/or its licensors, is protected by international copyrights, and is transferred to the original purchaser and any subsequent owner of the Software media for their use only upon the license terms set forth below. Opening the packaging and/or using SOFTDESK Software indicates your acceptance of these terms. If you do not agree to all of the terms and conditions, or if after use you are dissatisfied with your SOFTDESK Software, return the Software, manuals, and any partial or whole copies within thirty (30) days of purchase to the party from whom you received it for a full refund.

Grant of License. SOFTDESK, INC. ("SOFTDESK") hereby grants the original purchaser ("Licensee") the limited rights to possess and use the accompanying SOFTDESK Software ("Software"), consisting of machine-readable computer code and documentation, upon the terms and conditions specifically set out in this License.

YOUR AGREEMENT

• Licensee agrees that the Software will be used solely for Licensee's internal purposes, and that at any one time, the Software will be installed on a single computer only. If the Software is installed on a networked system, or on a computer connected to a file server or other system that physically allows shared access to the Software, Licensee agrees to provide technical or procedural methods to prevent used of the Software by more than one user at one time. Additional Software copies (and license rights) must be purchased for multiple users.

• Licensee is granted a perpetual, royalty-free license to copy and distribute the block symbols or other graphic representations ("SOFTDESK SYMBOLS") included within the Software, in both hard-copy format or upon computer-readable media, PROVIDED:

    - such distribution arises exclusively from the inclusion of SOFTDESK SYMBOLS within Licensee's proprietary drawings, plans or other workproduct ("Licensee Workproduct") developed in the ordinary course of Licensee's business;

    - SOFTDESK SYMBOLS are not incorporated within a software application or file which is or is part of a software application;

    - no Software code is distributed; and

    - Licensee provides clear notice as to the inclusion within Licensee Workproduct of proprietary, copyrighted material owned by SOFTDESK, INC.

• One machine-readable copy of the Software may be made for BACK-UP PURPOSES ONLY, and the copy shall display all proprietary notices, and be labeled externally to show that the back-up copy is the property of SOFTDESK, and that its use is subject to this License. Documentation in whole or in part may not be copied.

- Use of the Software by any department, agency or other entity of the U.S. Federal Government is limited by the terms of the attached "Rider for U.S. Government Entity Users," which is incorporated by reference.

- Licensee may transfer its rights under this License, PROVIDED that the party to whom such rights are transferred agrees to the terms and conditions of this License, and written notice is proved to SOFTDESK. Upon such transfer, Licensee must transfer or destroy all copies of the Software.

- Except as expressly provided in this License, Licensee may not use, copy (except for the backup copy), disseminate, modify, translate, decompile, reverse engineer, disassemble, create derivative works based on, distribute, sub-license, sell, rent, lease, lend, give or in any other way transfer, by any means or in any medium, including telecommunications, the Software or accompanying documentation. Licensee will use its best efforts and take all reasonable steps to protect the Software from unauthorized use, copying or dissemination, and will maintain all proprietary notices intact.

TERM. This License is effective as of the time Licensee receives the Software, and shall continue in effect until Licensee ceases all use of the Software and either destroys, or returns to SOFTDESK, all copies thereof, or until automatically terminated upon the failure of Licensee to comply with any of the terms of this License.

LIMITED WARRANTY. SOFTDESK warrants the Software media to be free of defects in workmanship for a period of ninety (90) days from purchase. During this period SOFTDESK will replace at no cost any such media returned to SOFTDESK, postage prepaid. This service is SOFTDESK's sole liability under this warranty.

DISCLAIMER. LICENSE FEES FOR THE SOFTWARE DO NOT INCLUDE ANY CONSIDERATION FOR ASSUMPTION OF RISK BY SOFTDESK, AND SOFTDESK DISCLAIMS ANY AND ALL LIABILITY FOR INCIDENTAL OR CONSEQUENTIAL DAMAGES ARISING OUT OF THE USE OR OPERATION OR INABILITY TO USE THE SOFTWARE, OR ARISING FROM THE NEGLIGENCE OF SOFTDESK OR ITS EMPLOYEES, OFFICERS, DIRECTORS, CONSULTANTS OR DEALERS, EVEN IF ANY OF THESE PARTIES HAVE BEEN ADVISED OF THE POSSIBILITY OF SUCH DAMAGES. FURTHERMORE, LICENSEE INDEMNIFIES AND AGREES TO HOLD SOFTDESK HARMLESS FROM SUCH CLAIMS. THE ENTIRE RISK AS TO THE RESULTS AND PERFORMANCE OF THE SOFTWARE IS ASSUMED BY THE LICENSEE. THE WARRANTIES EXPRESSED IN THIS LICENSE ARE THE ONLY WARRANTIES MADE BY SOFTDESK, AND ARE IN LIEU OF ALL OTHER WARRANTIES, EXPRESS OR IMPLIED, INCLUDING BUT NOT LIMITED TO IMPLIED WARRANTIES OF MERCHANTABILITY AND OF FITNESS FOR A PARTICULAR PURPOSE.

THIS WARRANTY PROVIDES LICENSEE SPECIFIED LEGAL RIGHTS, AND LICENSEE MAY ALSO HAVE OTHER RIGHTS WHICH VARY FROM JURISDICTION TO JURISDICTION. SOME JURISDICTIONS DO NOT ALLOW THE EXCLUSION OR LIMITATION OF WARRANTIES, SO THE ABOVE LIMITATIONS OR EXCLUSIONS MAY NOT APPLY.

GENERAL. This License is the complete and exclusive statement of the Parties' agreement. Should any provision of this License be held to be invalid by any court of competent jurisdiction, that provision will be enforced to the maximum extent permissible, and the remainder of the License shall nonetheless remain in full force and effect. This License shall be controlled by the laws of the State of New Hampshire and the United States of America, as applicable.

RIDER FOR U.S. GOVERNMENTAL ENTITY USERS

This is a rider to the SOFTDESK, INC. Customer Software License, ("License"), and shall take precedence over the License where a conflict occurs.

1. The Software was: developed at private expense, no portion was developed with government funds; is a trade secret of SOFTDESK and its licensor for all purposes of the Freedom of Information Act; is "commercial computer software" subject to limited utilization as provided in any contract between the vendor and the government entity; and in all respects is proprietary data belonging solely to SOFTDESK and its licensor.

2. For units of the DOD, the Software is sold only with "Restricted Rights" as that term is defined in the DOD Supplement to DFAR 252.227-7013 (b)(3)(ii), and use, duplication or disclosure is subject to restrictions set forth in subparagraph (c)(1)(ii) of the Rights in Technical Data and Computer Software clause at 252.227-7013. Manufacturer: SOFTDESK, Inc., 7 Liberty Hill Road, Henniker, NH 03242 USA

3. If the Software was acquired under a GSA Schedule, the Government has agreed to refrain from changing or removing any insignia or lettering from the Software or Documentation or from producing copies of manuals or disks (except for backup purposes) and: (1) Title to and ownership of the Software and Documentation and any reproductions thereof shall remain with SOFTDESK and its licensor; (2) use of the Software shall be limited to the facility for which it is acquired; and (3) if the use of the Software is discontinued at the original installation and the Government wishes to use it at another location, it may do so by giving prior written notice to SOFTDESK, specifying the new location site and class of computer.

4. Governmental personnel using the Software, other than a DOD contract or GSA Schedule, are hereby on notice that use of the Software is subject to restrictions that are the same or similar to those specified above.

rev 393

Index